CASE CLOSED

VOLUME 31

Gosho Aoyama

Case Briefing:

Subject: Jimmy Kudo, a.k.a. Conan Edogawa
Occupation: High School Student/Detective
Special Skills: Analytical thinking and deductive reasoning, Soccer
Equipment: Bow Tie Voice Transmitter, Super Sneakers,
                      Homing Glasses, Stretchy Suspenders

The subject is hot on the trail of a pair of suspicious men in black when he is attacked from behind and administered a strange substance which physically transforms him into a first grader. When the subject confides in the eccentric inventor Dr. Agasa, they decide to keep the subject's true identity a secret for the safety of everyone around him. Assuming the new identity of first-grader Conan Edogawa, the subject continues to assist the police force on their most baffling cases. The only problem is that most crime-solving professionals won't take a little kid's advice!

Table of Contents

CONFIDEN

CASE CLOSED
Volume 31
Shonen Sunday Edition

Story and Art by GOSHO AOYAMA

© 1994 Gosho AOYAMA/Shogakukan
All rights reserved.
Original Japanese edition "MEITANTEI CONAN" published by SHOGAKUKAN Inc.

Translation
Tetsuichiro Miyaki

Touch-up & Lettering
Freeman Wong

Cover & Graphic Design
Andrea Rice

Editor
Shaenon K. Garrity

Printed in the U.S.A.

Published by VIZ Media, LLC
P.O. Box 77010
San Francisco, CA 94107

10 9 8 7 6 5 4 3 2
First printing, September 2009
Second printing, April 2014

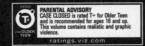

PARENTAL ADVISORY
CASE CLOSED is rated T+ for Older Teen
and is recommended for ages 16 and up.
This volume contains realistic and graphic
violence.
ratings.viz.com

FILE 1: THE HIDDEN WORD

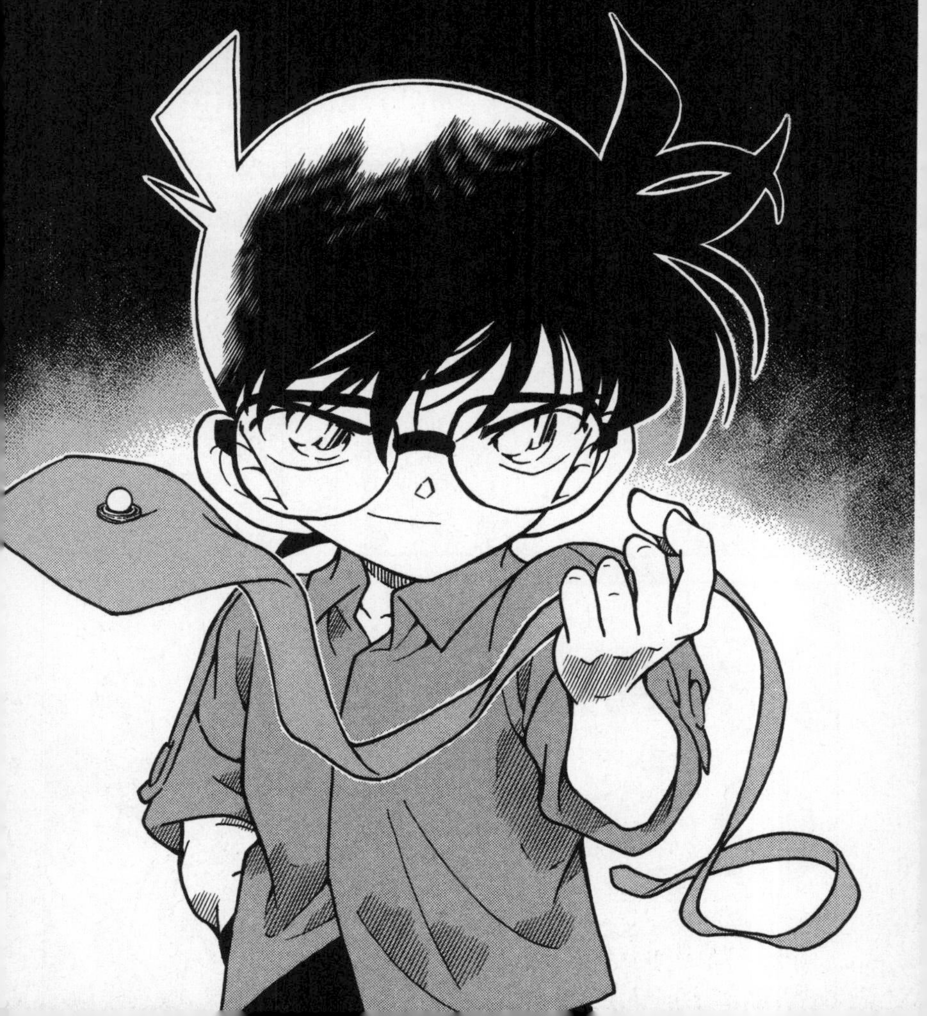

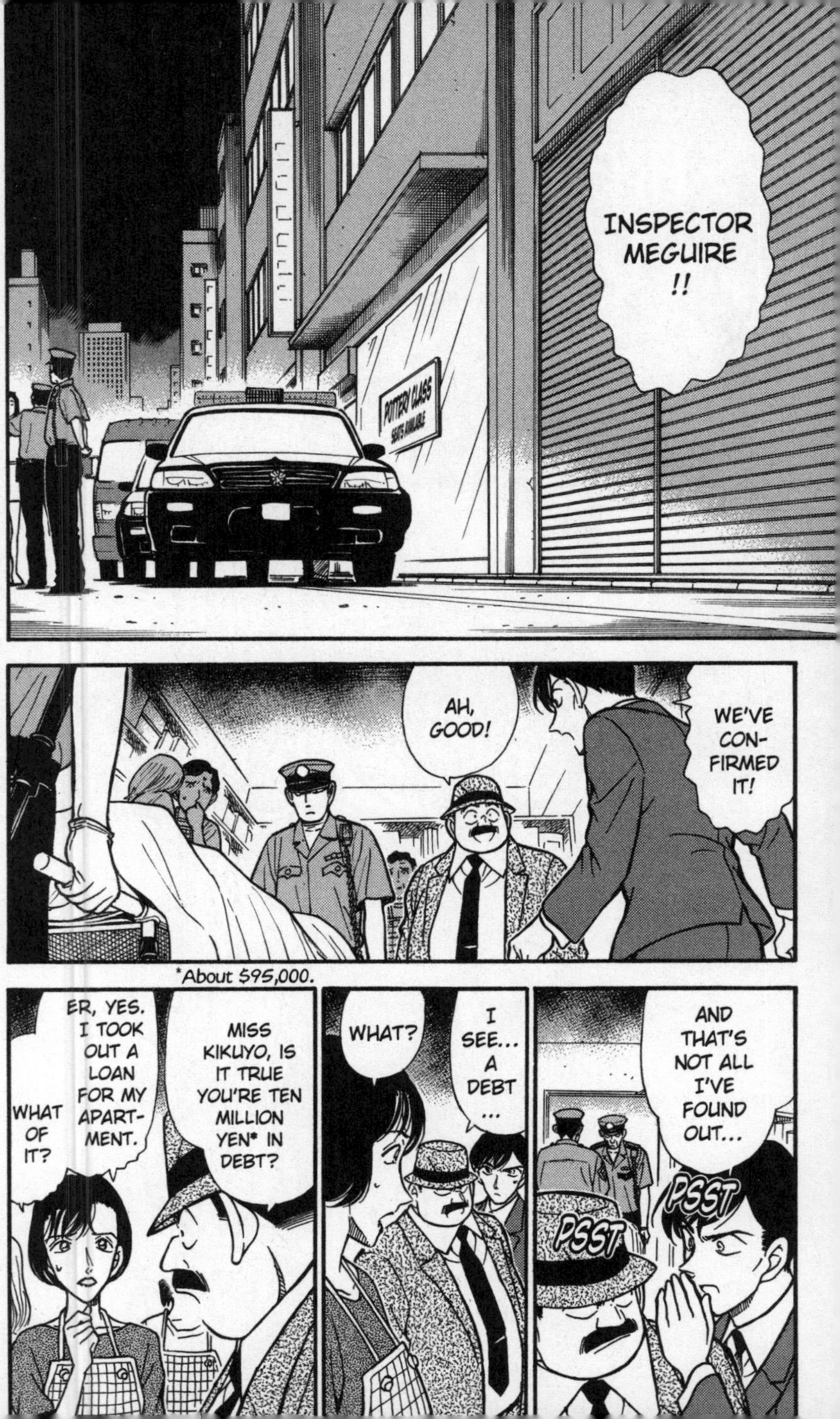
INSPECTOR MEGUIRE !!
POTTERY CLASS
WE'VE CONFIRMED IT!
AH, GOOD!
AND THAT'S NOT ALL I'VE FOUND OUT...
PSST
PSST
I SEE... A DEBT ...
WHAT?
MISS KIKUYO, IS IT TRUE YOU'RE TEN MILLION YEN* IN DEBT?
ER, YES. I TOOK OUT A LOAN FOR MY APARTMENT.
WHAT OF IT?

*About $95,000.

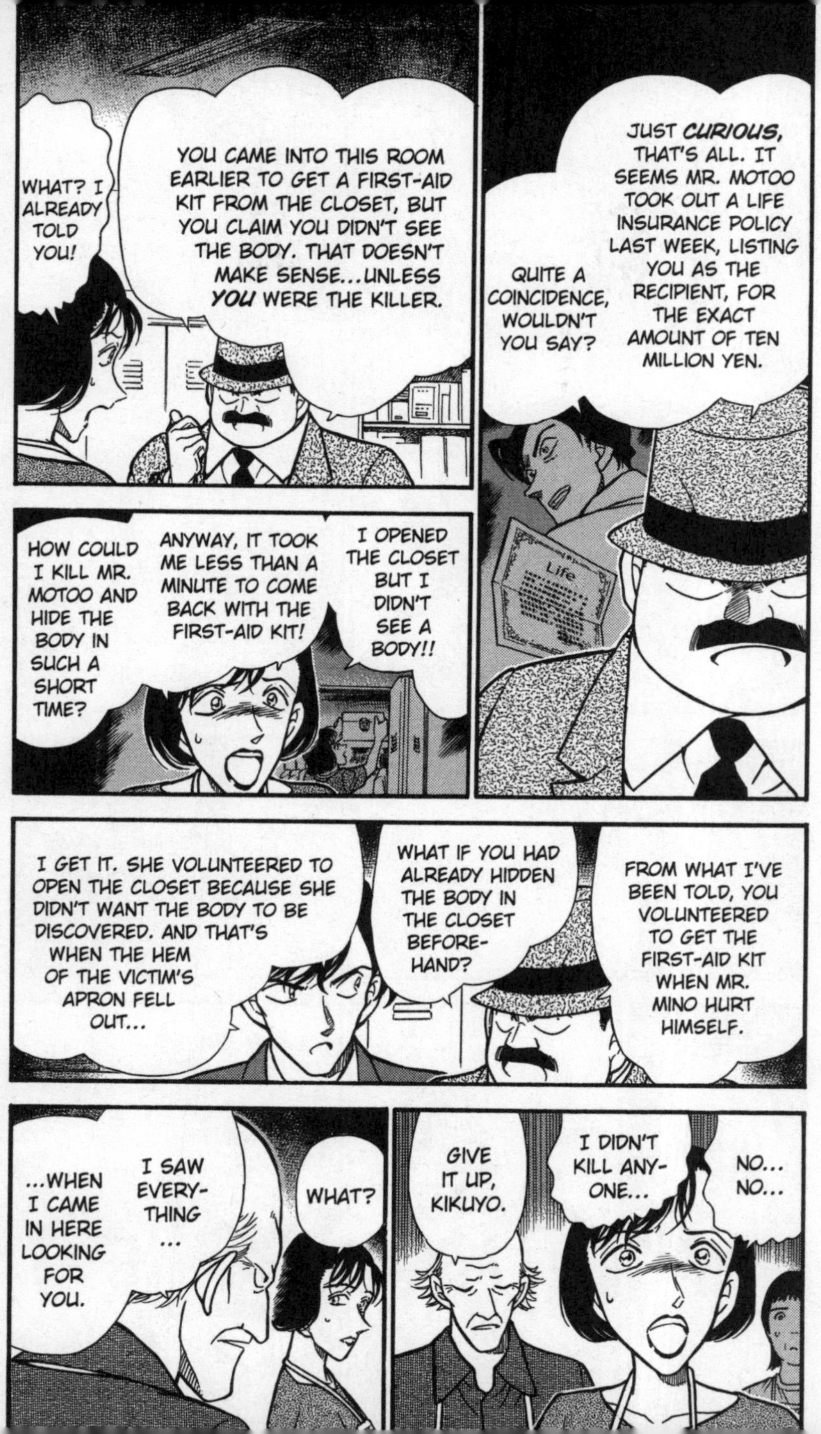
JUST *CURIOUS,* THAT'S ALL. IT SEEMS MR. MOTOO TOOK OUT A LIFE INSURANCE POLICY LAST WEEK, LISTING YOU AS THE RECIPIENT, FOR THE EXACT AMOUNT OF TEN MILLION YEN.
QUITE A COINCIDENCE, WOULDN'T YOU SAY?
Life
YOU CAME INTO THIS ROOM EARLIER TO GET A FIRST-AID KIT FROM THE CLOSET, BUT YOU CLAIM YOU DIDN'T SEE THE BODY. THAT DOESN'T MAKE SENSE...UNLESS *YOU* WERE THE KILLER.
WHAT? I ALREADY TOLD YOU!
I OPENED THE CLOSET BUT I DIDN'T SEE A BODY!!
ANYWAY, IT TOOK ME LESS THAN A MINUTE TO COME BACK WITH THE FIRST-AID KIT!
HOW COULD I KILL MR. MOTOO AND HIDE THE BODY IN SUCH A SHORT TIME?
FROM WHAT I'VE BEEN TOLD, YOU VOLUNTEERED TO GET THE FIRST-AID KIT WHEN MR. MINO HURT HIMSELF.
WHAT IF YOU HAD ALREADY HIDDEN THE BODY IN THE CLOSET BEFORE-HAND?
I GET IT. SHE VOLUNTEERED TO OPEN THE CLOSET BECAUSE SHE DIDN'T WANT THE BODY TO BE DISCOVERED. AND THAT'S WHEN THE HEM OF THE VICTIM'S APRON FELL OUT...
NO... NO...
I DIDN'T KILL ANY-ONE...
GIVE IT UP, KIKUYO.
WHAT?
I SAW EVERY-THING...
...WHEN I CAME IN HERE LOOKING FOR YOU.

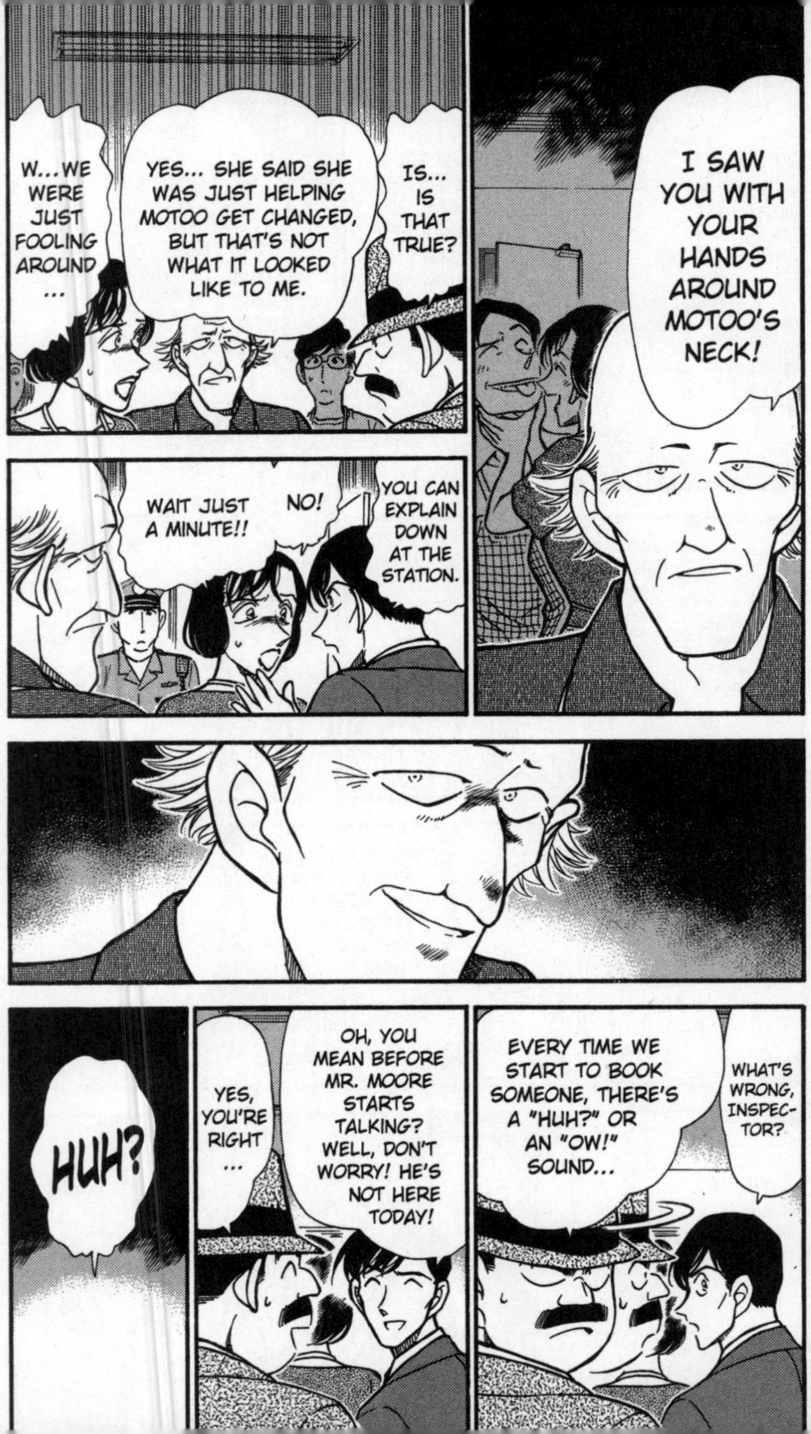
I SAW YOU WITH YOUR HANDS AROUND MOTOO'S NECK!
IS... IS THAT TRUE?
YES... SHE SAID SHE WAS JUST HELPING MOTOO GET CHANGED, BUT THAT'S NOT WHAT IT LOOKED LIKE TO ME.
W...WE WERE JUST FOOLING AROUND...
YOU CAN EXPLAIN DOWN AT THE STATION.
NO!
WAIT JUST A MINUTE!!
WHAT'S WRONG, INSPECTOR?
EVERY TIME WE START TO BOOK SOMEONE, THERE'S A "HUH?" OR AN "OW!" SOUND...
OH, YOU MEAN BEFORE MR. MOORE STARTS TALKING? WELL, DON'T WORRY! HE'S NOT HERE TODAY!
YES, YOU'RE RIGHT...
HUH?

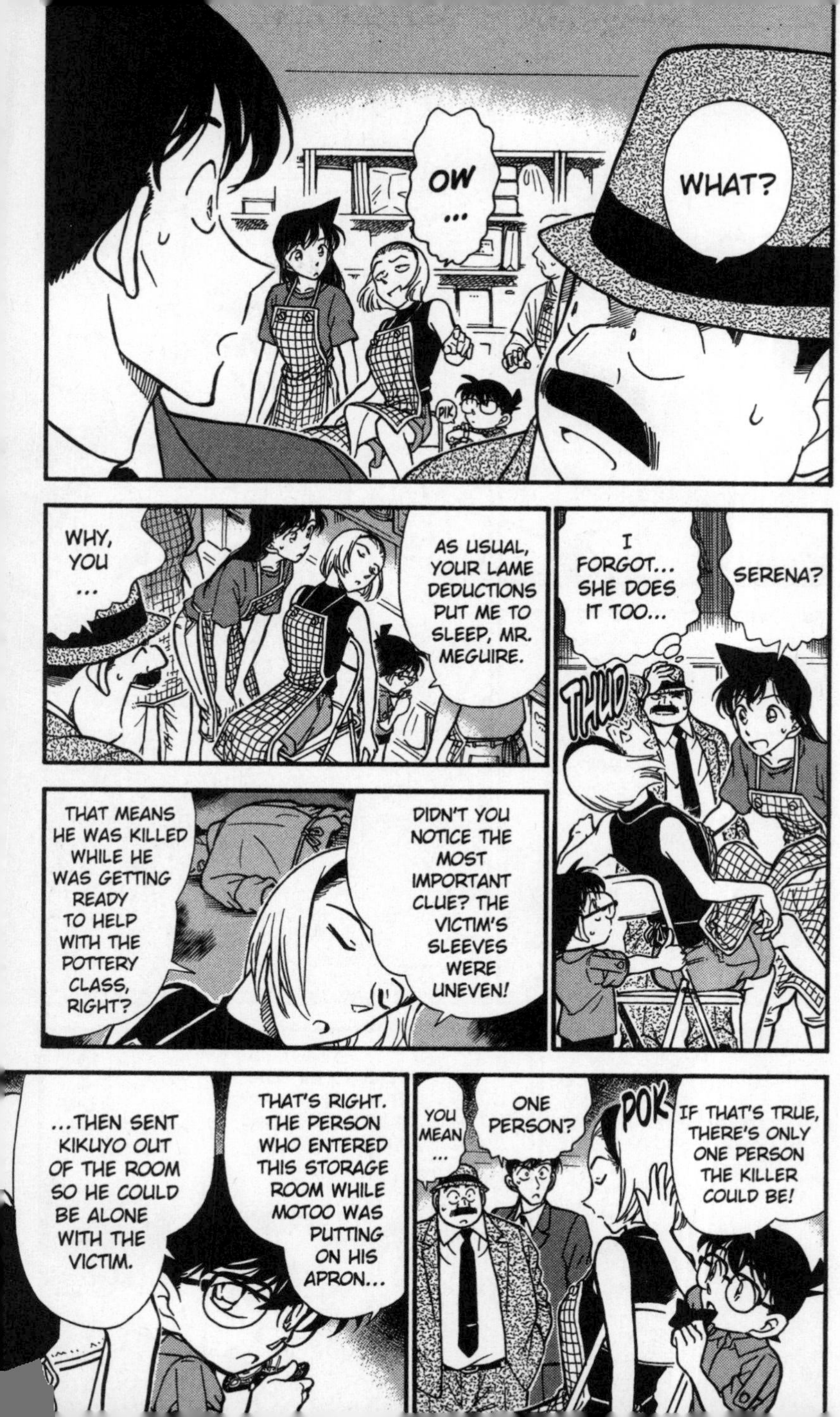
WHAT?
OW ...
PIK
SERENA?
I FORGOT... SHE DOES IT TOO...
THUD
AS USUAL, YOUR LAME DEDUCTIONS PUT ME TO SLEEP, MR. MEGUIRE.
WHY, YOU ...
DIDN'T YOU NOTICE THE MOST IMPORTANT CLUE? THE VICTIM'S SLEEVES WERE UNEVEN!
THAT MEANS HE WAS KILLED WHILE HE WAS GETTING READY TO HELP WITH THE POTTERY CLASS, RIGHT?
IF THAT'S TRUE, THERE'S ONLY ONE PERSON THE KILLER COULD BE!
POK
ONE PERSON?
YOU MEAN ...
THAT'S RIGHT. THE PERSON WHO ENTERED THIS STORAGE ROOM WHILE MOTOO WAS PUTTING ON HIS APRON...
...THEN SENT KIKUYO OUT OF THE ROOM SO HE COULD BE ALONE WITH THE VICTIM.

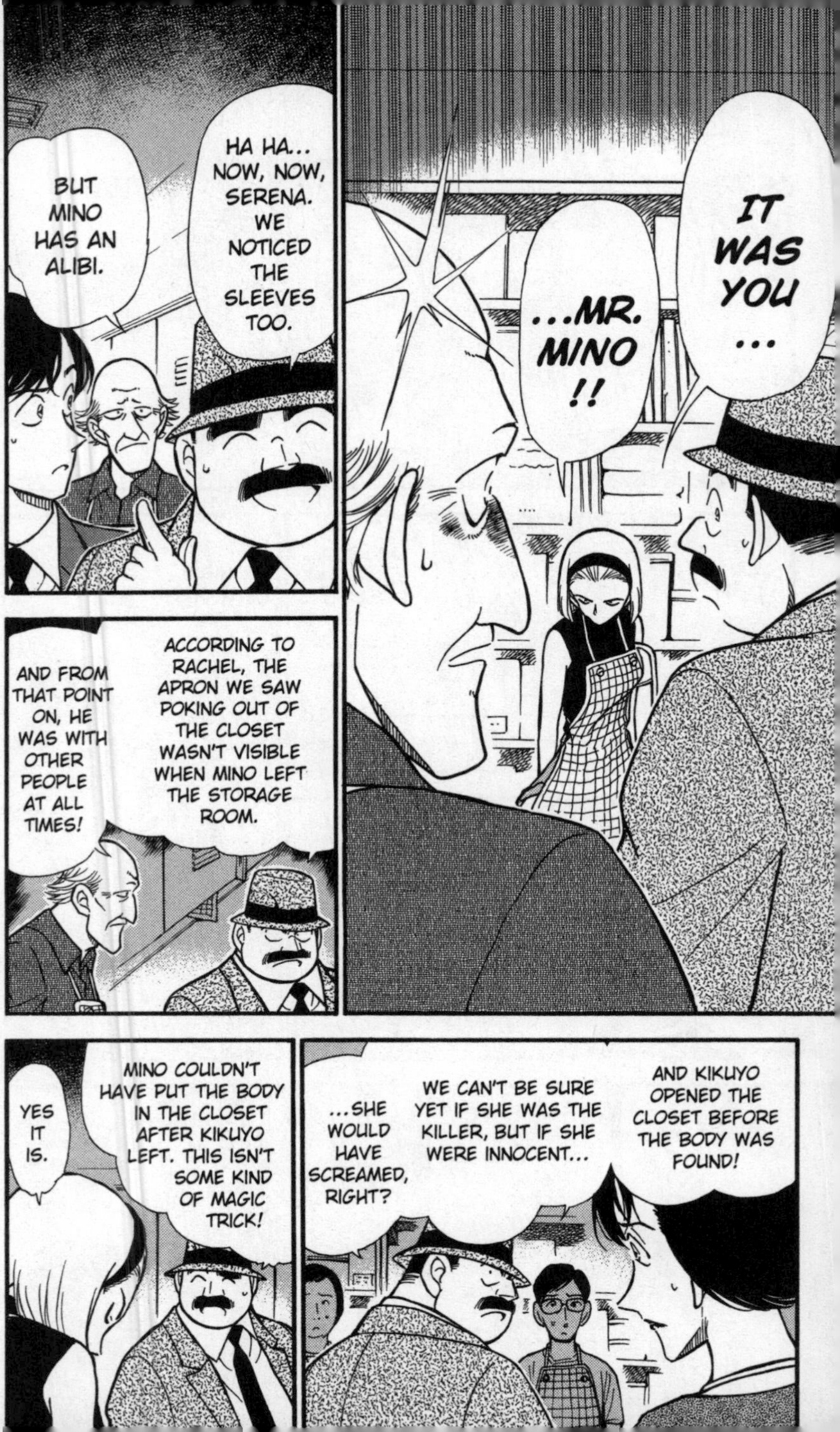
IT WAS YOU...
...MR. MINO!!
HA HA... NOW, NOW, SERENA. WE NOTICED THE SLEEVES TOO.
BUT MINO HAS AN ALIBI.
ACCORDING TO RACHEL, THE APRON WE SAW POKING OUT OF THE CLOSET WASN'T VISIBLE WHEN MINO LEFT THE STORAGE ROOM.
AND FROM THAT POINT ON, HE WAS WITH OTHER PEOPLE AT ALL TIMES!
AND KIKUYO OPENED THE CLOSET BEFORE THE BODY WAS FOUND!
WE CAN'T BE SURE YET IF SHE WAS THE KILLER, BUT IF SHE WERE INNOCENT...
...SHE WOULD HAVE SCREAMED, RIGHT?
MINO COULDN'T HAVE PUT THE BODY IN THE CLOSET AFTER KIKUYO LEFT. THIS ISN'T SOME KIND OF MAGIC TRICK!
YES IT IS.

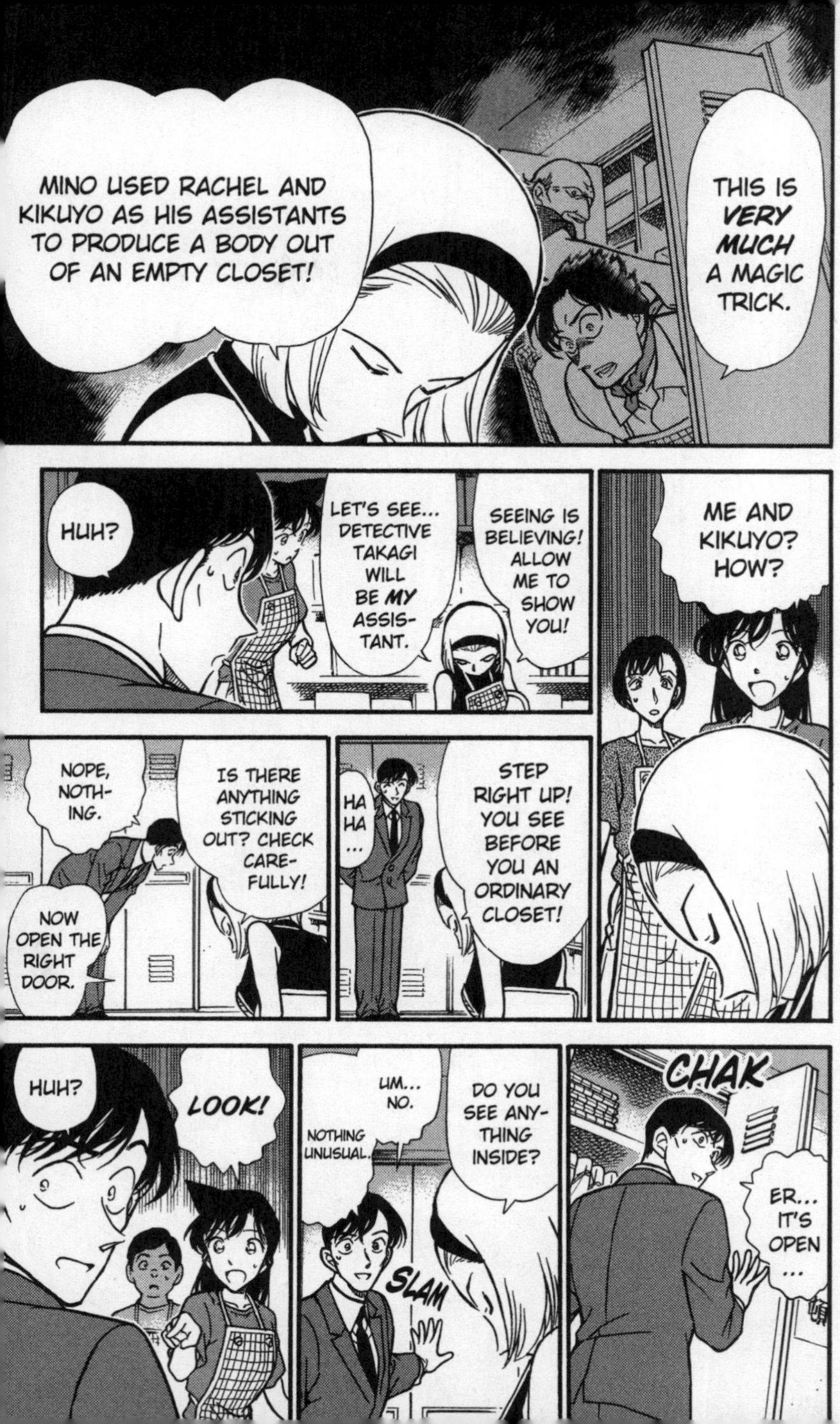
THIS IS VERY MUCH A MAGIC TRICK.
MINO USED RACHEL AND KIKUYO AS HIS ASSISTANTS TO PRODUCE A BODY OUT OF AN EMPTY CLOSET!
ME AND KIKUYO? HOW?
SEEING IS BELIEVING! ALLOW ME TO SHOW YOU!
LET'S SEE... DETECTIVE TAKAGI WILL BE MY ASSISTANT.
HUH?
STEP RIGHT UP! YOU SEE BEFORE YOU AN ORDINARY CLOSET!
HA HA ...
IS THERE ANYTHING STICKING OUT? CHECK CAREFULLY!
NOPE, NOTHING.
NOW OPEN THE RIGHT DOOR.
CHAK
ER... IT'S OPEN ...
DO YOU SEE ANYTHING INSIDE?
UM... NO.
NOTHING UNUSUAL.
SLAM
LOOK!
HUH?

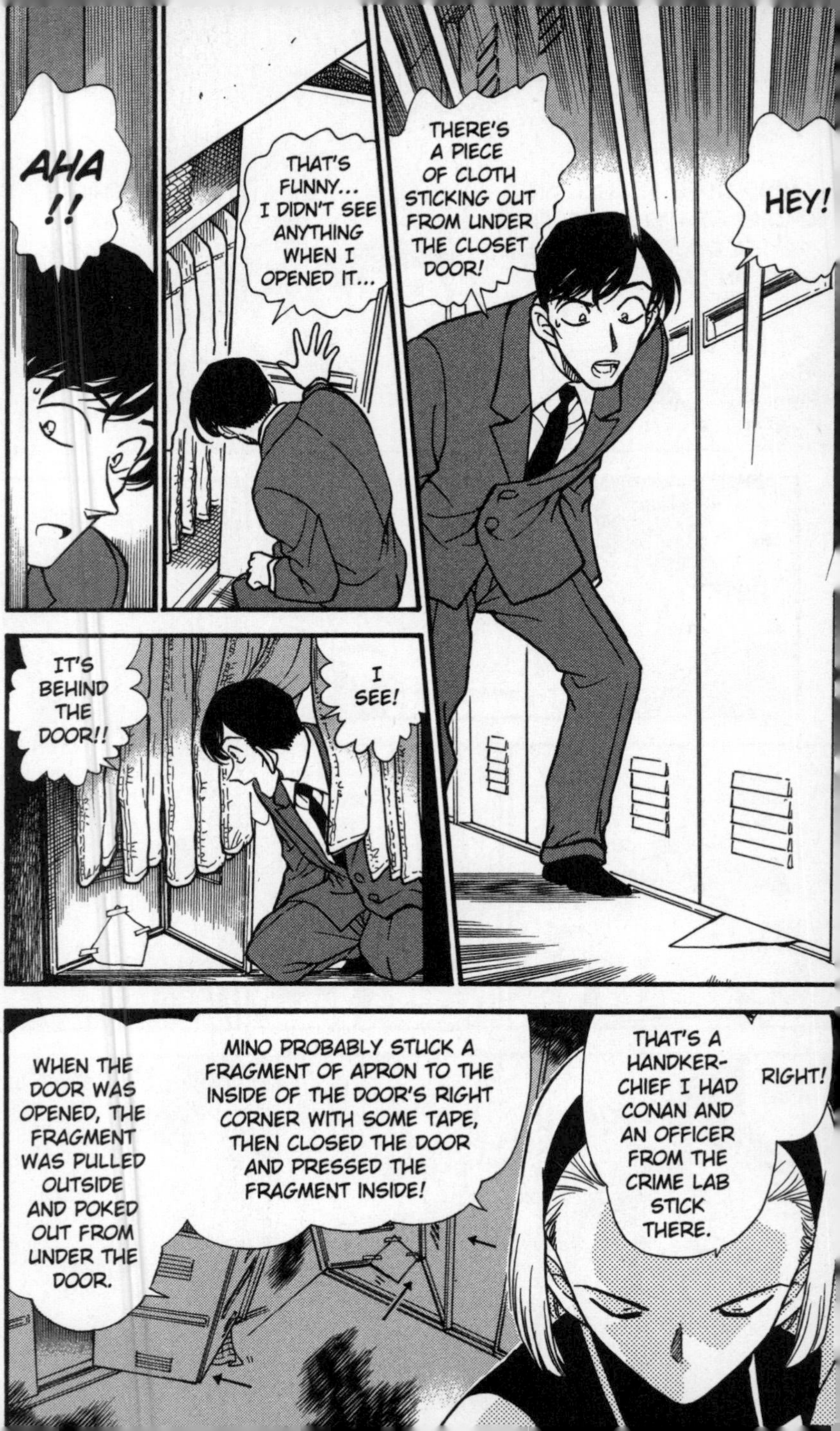
HEY!
THERE'S A PIECE OF CLOTH STICKING OUT FROM UNDER THE CLOSET DOOR!
THAT'S FUNNY... I DIDN'T SEE ANYTHING WHEN I OPENED IT...
AHA!!
I SEE!
IT'S BEHIND THE DOOR!!
RIGHT!
THAT'S A HANDKERCHIEF I HAD CONAN AND AN OFFICER FROM THE CRIME LAB STICK THERE.
MINO PROBABLY STUCK A FRAGMENT OF APRON TO THE INSIDE OF THE DOOR'S RIGHT CORNER WITH SOME TAPE, THEN CLOSED THE DOOR AND PRESSED THE FRAGMENT INSIDE!
WHEN THE DOOR WAS OPENED, THE FRAGMENT WAS PULLED OUTSIDE AND POKED OUT FROM UNDER THE DOOR.

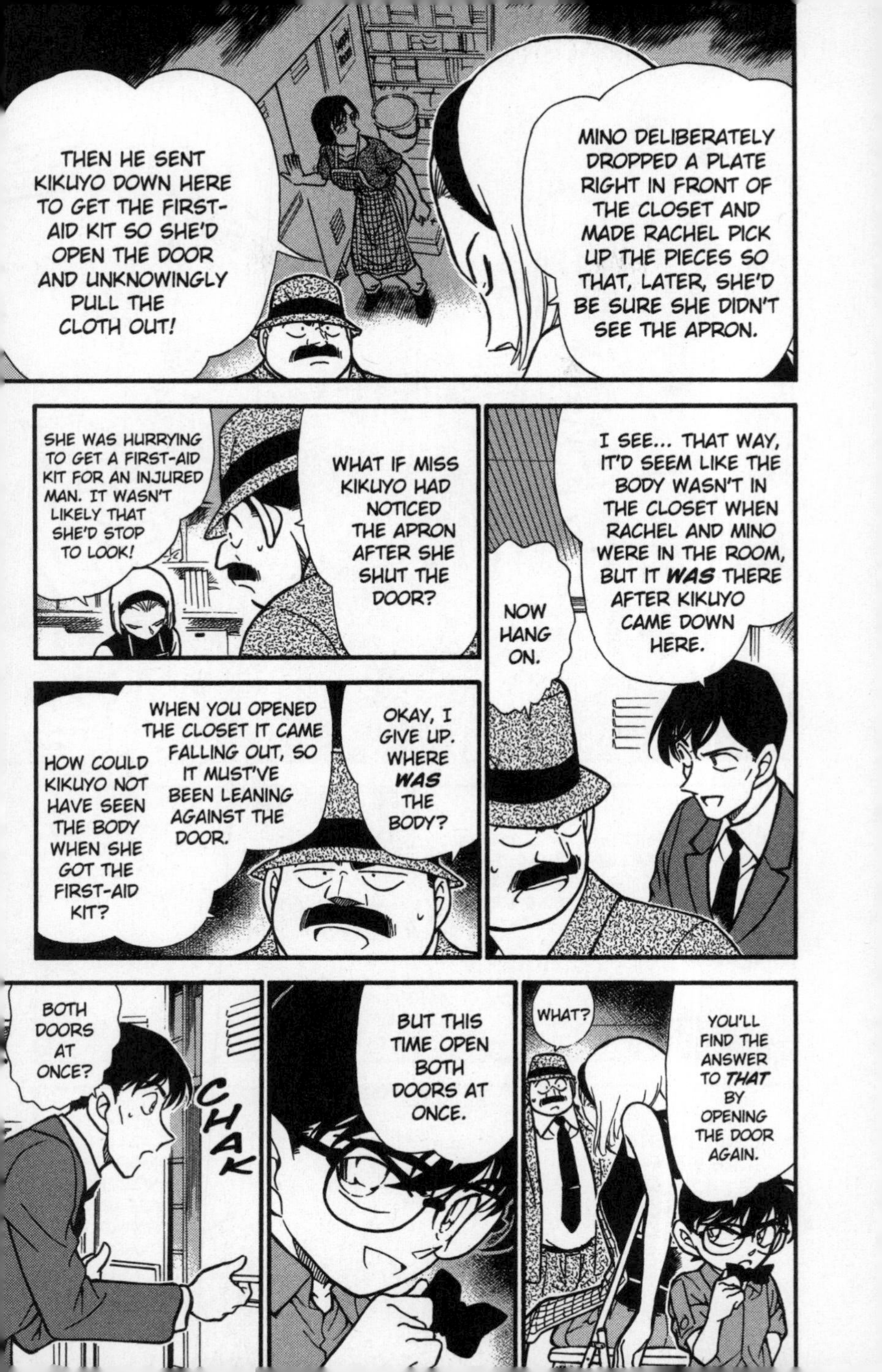
MINO DELIBERATELY DROPPED A PLATE RIGHT IN FRONT OF THE CLOSET AND MADE RACHEL PICK UP THE PIECES SO THAT, LATER, SHE'D BE SURE SHE DIDN'T SEE THE APRON.
THEN HE SENT KIKUYO DOWN HERE TO GET THE FIRST-AID KIT SO SHE'D OPEN THE DOOR AND UNKNOWINGLY PULL THE CLOTH OUT!
I SEE... THAT WAY, IT'D SEEM LIKE THE BODY WASN'T IN THE CLOSET WHEN RACHEL AND MINO WERE IN THE ROOM, BUT IT *WAS* THERE AFTER KIKUYO CAME DOWN HERE.
NOW HANG ON.
WHAT IF MISS KIKUYO HAD NOTICED THE APRON AFTER SHE SHUT THE DOOR?
SHE WAS HURRYING TO GET A FIRST-AID KIT FOR AN INJURED MAN. IT WASN'T LIKELY THAT SHE'D STOP TO LOOK!
OKAY, I GIVE UP. WHERE *WAS* THE BODY?
WHEN YOU OPENED THE CLOSET IT CAME FALLING OUT, SO IT MUST'VE BEEN LEANING AGAINST THE DOOR.
HOW COULD KIKUYO NOT HAVE SEEN THE BODY WHEN SHE GOT THE FIRST-AID KIT?
YOU'LL FIND THE ANSWER TO *THAT* BY OPENING THE DOOR AGAIN.
WHAT?
BUT THIS TIME OPEN BOTH DOORS AT ONCE.
BOTH DOORS AT ONCE?
CHAK

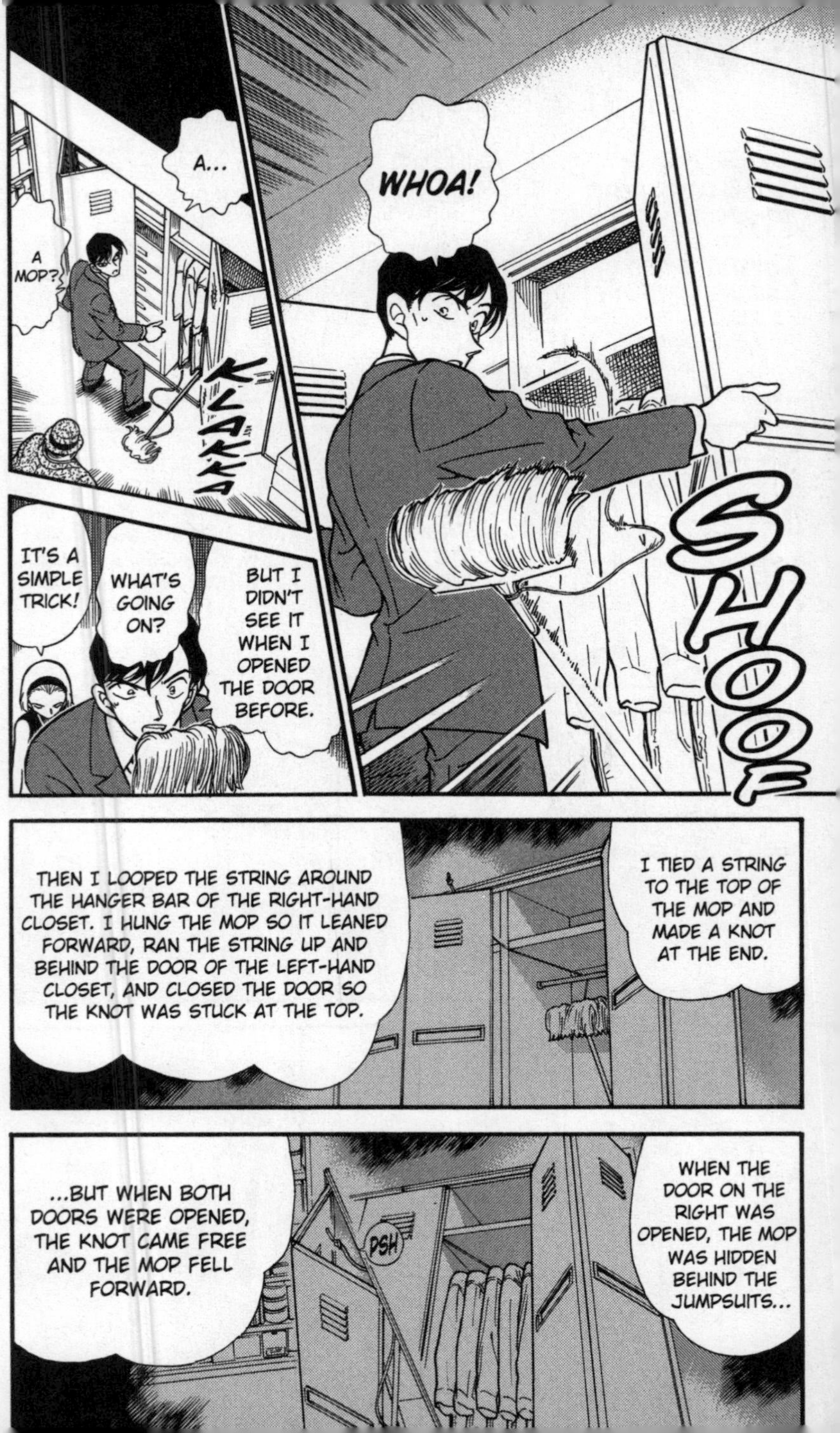
WHOA!
SHOOF
A...
A MOP?
KLAKKA
BUT I DIDN'T SEE IT WHEN I OPENED THE DOOR BEFORE.
WHAT'S GOING ON?
IT'S A SIMPLE TRICK!
I TIED A STRING TO THE TOP OF THE MOP AND MADE A KNOT AT THE END.
THEN I LOOPED THE STRING AROUND THE HANGER BAR OF THE RIGHT-HAND CLOSET. I HUNG THE MOP SO IT LEANED FORWARD, RAN THE STRING UP AND BEHIND THE DOOR OF THE LEFT-HAND CLOSET, AND CLOSED THE DOOR SO THE KNOT WAS STUCK AT THE TOP.
WHEN THE DOOR ON THE RIGHT WAS OPENED, THE MOP WAS HIDDEN BEHIND THE JUMPSUITS...
...BUT WHEN BOTH DOORS WERE OPENED, THE KNOT CAME FREE AND THE MOP FELL FORWARD.
PSH

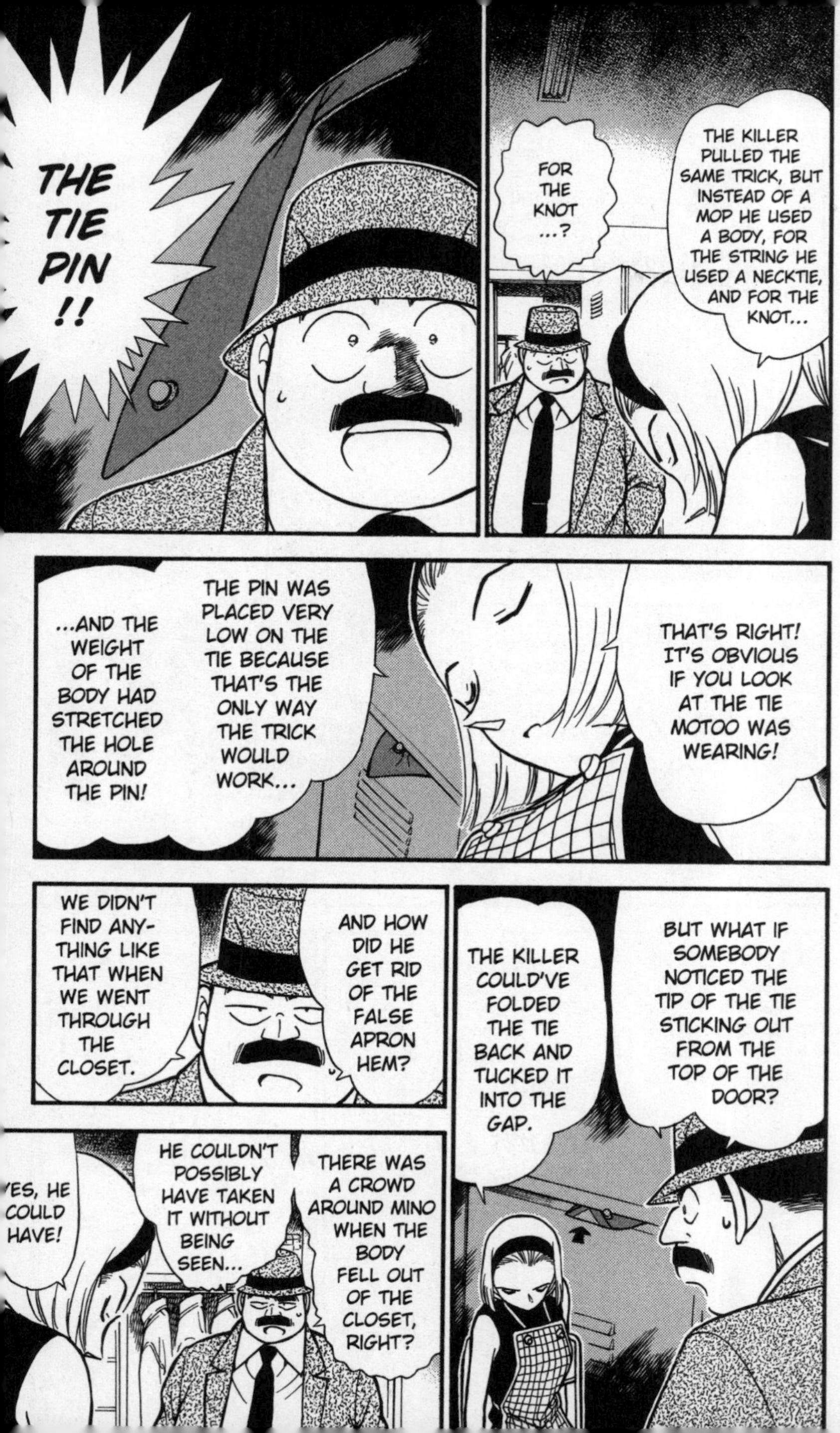
THE KILLER PULLED THE SAME TRICK, BUT INSTEAD OF A MOP HE USED A BODY, FOR THE STRING HE USED A NECKTIE, AND FOR THE KNOT...
FOR THE KNOT ...?
THE TIE PIN !!
THAT'S RIGHT! IT'S OBVIOUS IF YOU LOOK AT THE TIE MOTOO WAS WEARING!
THE PIN WAS PLACED VERY LOW ON THE TIE BECAUSE THAT'S THE ONLY WAY THE TRICK WOULD WORK...
...AND THE WEIGHT OF THE BODY HAD STRETCHED THE HOLE AROUND THE PIN!
BUT WHAT IF SOMEBODY NOTICED THE TIP OF THE TIE STICKING OUT FROM THE TOP OF THE DOOR?
THE KILLER COULD'VE FOLDED THE TIE BACK AND TUCKED IT INTO THE GAP.
AND HOW DID HE GET RID OF THE FALSE APRON HEM?
WE DIDN'T FIND ANY-THING LIKE THAT WHEN WE WENT THROUGH THE CLOSET.
HE COULDN'T POSSIBLY HAVE TAKEN IT WITHOUT BEING SEEN...
'ES, HE COULD HAVE!
THERE WAS A CROWD AROUND MINO WHEN THE BODY FELL OUT OF THE CLOSET, RIGHT?

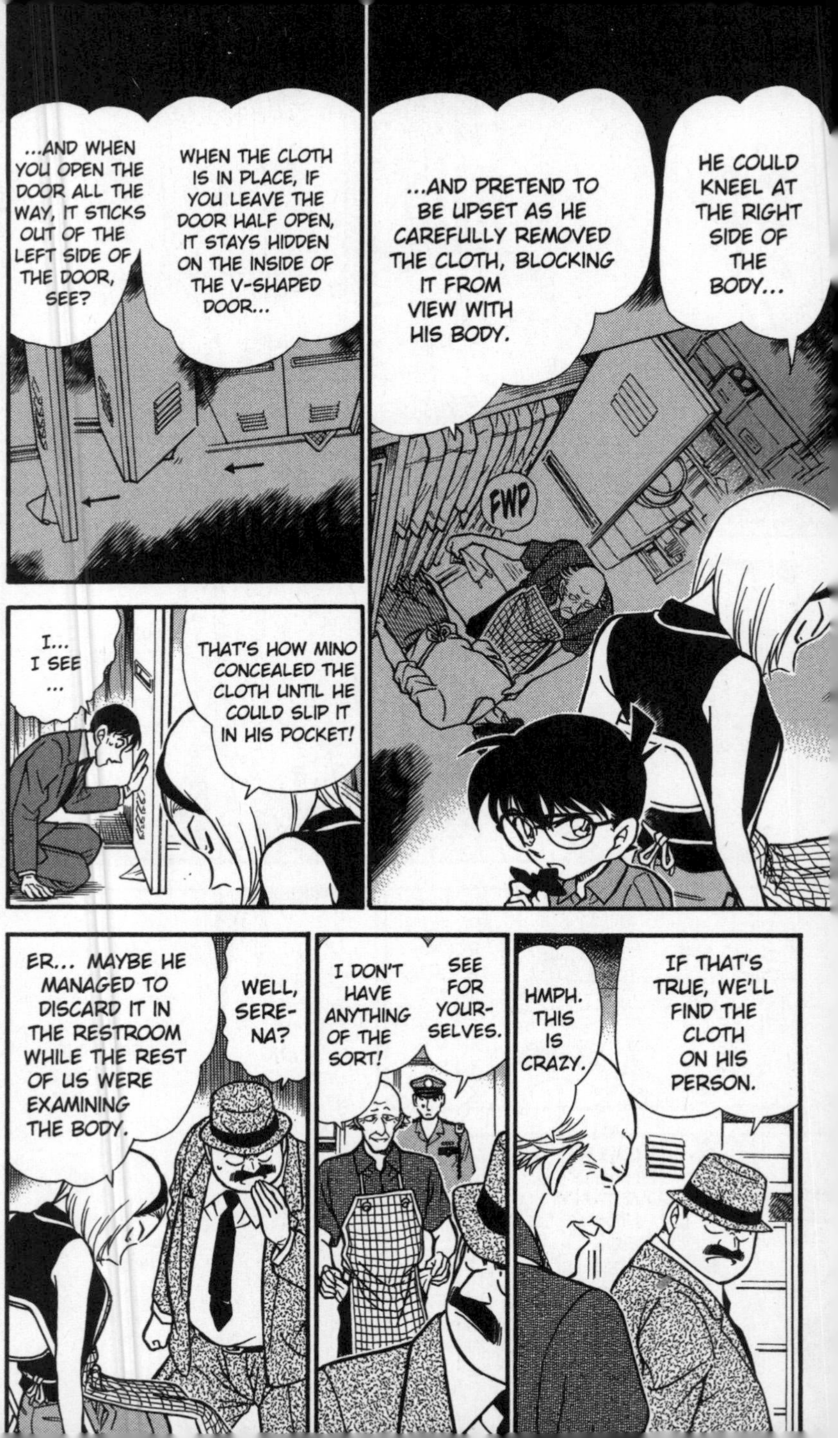
HE COULD KNEEL AT THE RIGHT SIDE OF THE BODY...
...AND PRETEND TO BE UPSET AS HE CAREFULLY REMOVED THE CLOTH, BLOCKING IT FROM VIEW WITH HIS BODY.
FWP
WHEN THE CLOTH IS IN PLACE, IF YOU LEAVE THE DOOR HALF OPEN, IT STAYS HIDDEN ON THE INSIDE OF THE V-SHAPED DOOR...
...AND WHEN YOU OPEN THE DOOR ALL THE WAY, IT STICKS OUT OF THE LEFT SIDE OF THE DOOR, SEE?
THAT'S HOW MINO CONCEALED THE CLOTH UNTIL HE COULD SLIP IT IN HIS POCKET!
I... I SEE ...
IF THAT'S TRUE, WE'LL FIND THE CLOTH ON HIS PERSON.
HMPH. THIS IS CRAZY.
SEE FOR YOURSELVES.
I DON'T HAVE ANYTHING OF THE SORT!
WELL, SERENA?
ER... MAYBE HE MANAGED TO DISCARD IT IN THE RESTROOM WHILE THE REST OF US WERE EXAMINING THE BODY.

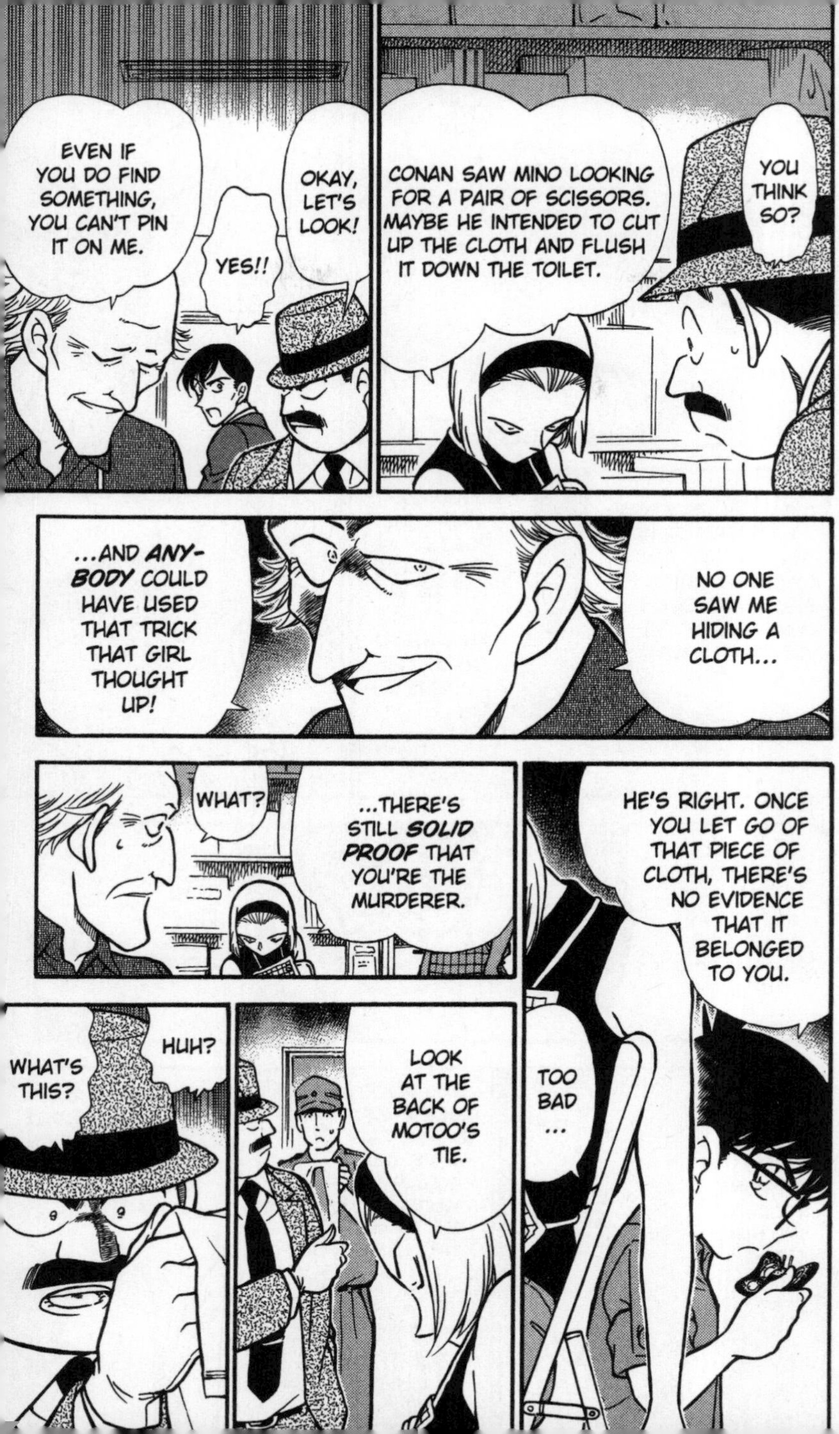
CONAN SAW MINO LOOKING FOR A PAIR OF SCISSORS. MAYBE HE INTENDED TO CUT UP THE CLOTH AND FLUSH IT DOWN THE TOILET.
YOU THINK SO?
OKAY, LET'S LOOK!
YES!!
EVEN IF YOU DO FIND SOMETHING, YOU CAN'T PIN IT ON ME.
NO ONE SAW ME HIDING A CLOTH...
...AND *ANYBODY* COULD HAVE USED THAT TRICK THAT GIRL THOUGHT UP!
HE'S RIGHT. ONCE YOU LET GO OF THAT PIECE OF CLOTH, THERE'S NO EVIDENCE THAT IT BELONGED TO YOU.
TOO BAD...
...THERE'S STILL *SOLID PROOF* THAT YOU'RE THE MURDERER.
WHAT?
LOOK AT THE BACK OF MOTOO'S TIE.
HUH?
WHAT'S THIS?

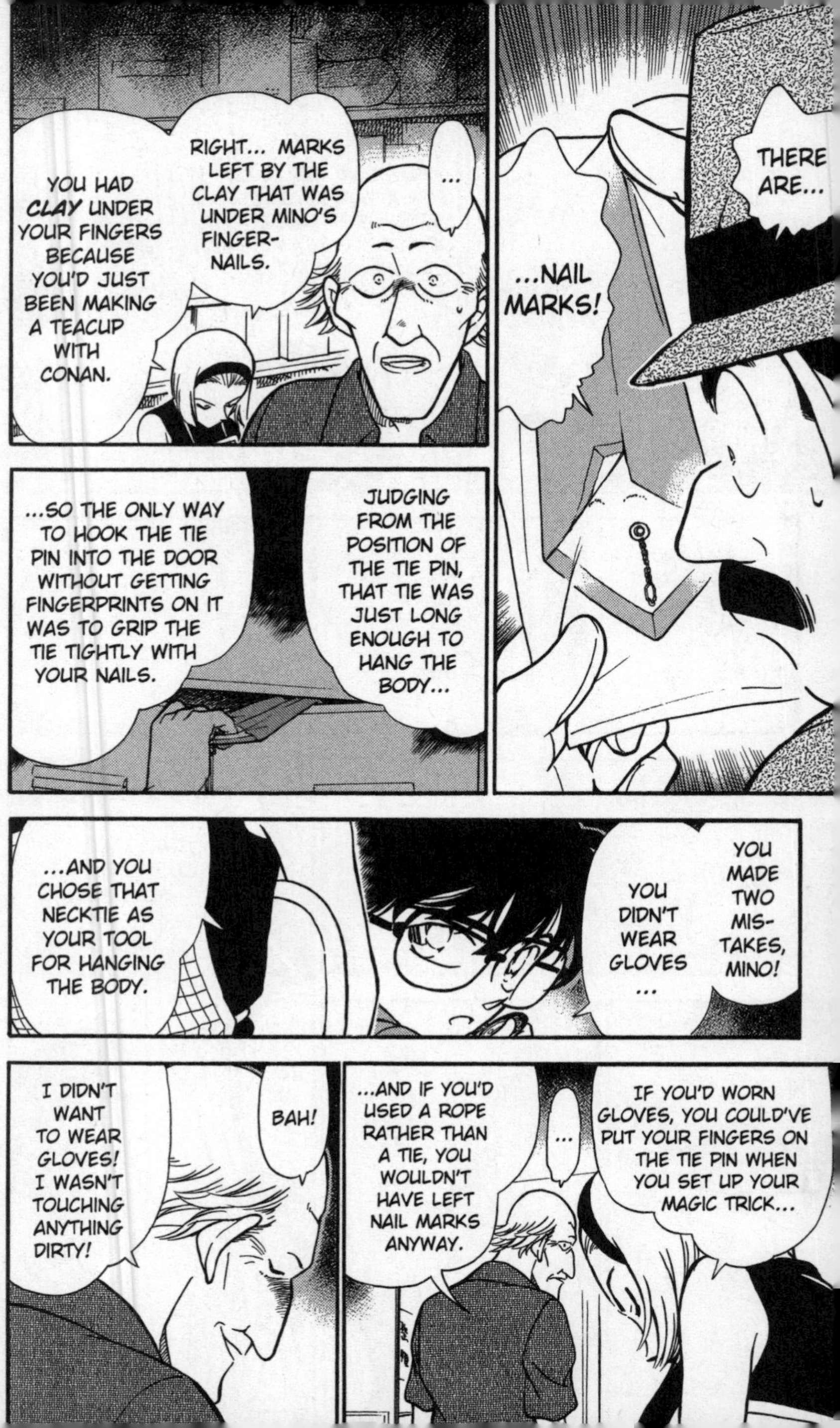
THERE ARE...
...NAIL MARKS!
...
RIGHT... MARKS LEFT BY THE CLAY THAT WAS UNDER MINO'S FINGER-NAILS.
YOU HAD CLAY UNDER YOUR FINGERS BECAUSE YOU'D JUST BEEN MAKING A TEACUP WITH CONAN.
JUDGING FROM THE POSITION OF THE TIE PIN, THAT TIE WAS JUST LONG ENOUGH TO HANG THE BODY...
...SO THE ONLY WAY TO HOOK THE TIE PIN INTO THE DOOR WITHOUT GETTING FINGERPRINTS ON IT WAS TO GRIP THE TIE TIGHTLY WITH YOUR NAILS.
YOU MADE TWO MIS-TAKES, MINO!
YOU DIDN'T WEAR GLOVES...
...AND YOU CHOSE THAT NECKTIE AS YOUR TOOL FOR HANGING THE BODY.
IF YOU'D WORN GLOVES, YOU COULD'VE PUT YOUR FINGERS ON THE TIE PIN WHEN YOU SET UP YOUR MAGIC TRICK...
...
...AND IF YOU'D USED A ROPE RATHER THAN A TIE, YOU WOULDN'T HAVE LEFT NAIL MARKS ANYWAY.
BAH!
I DIDN'T WANT TO WEAR GLOVES! I WASN'T TOUCHING ANYTHING DIRTY!

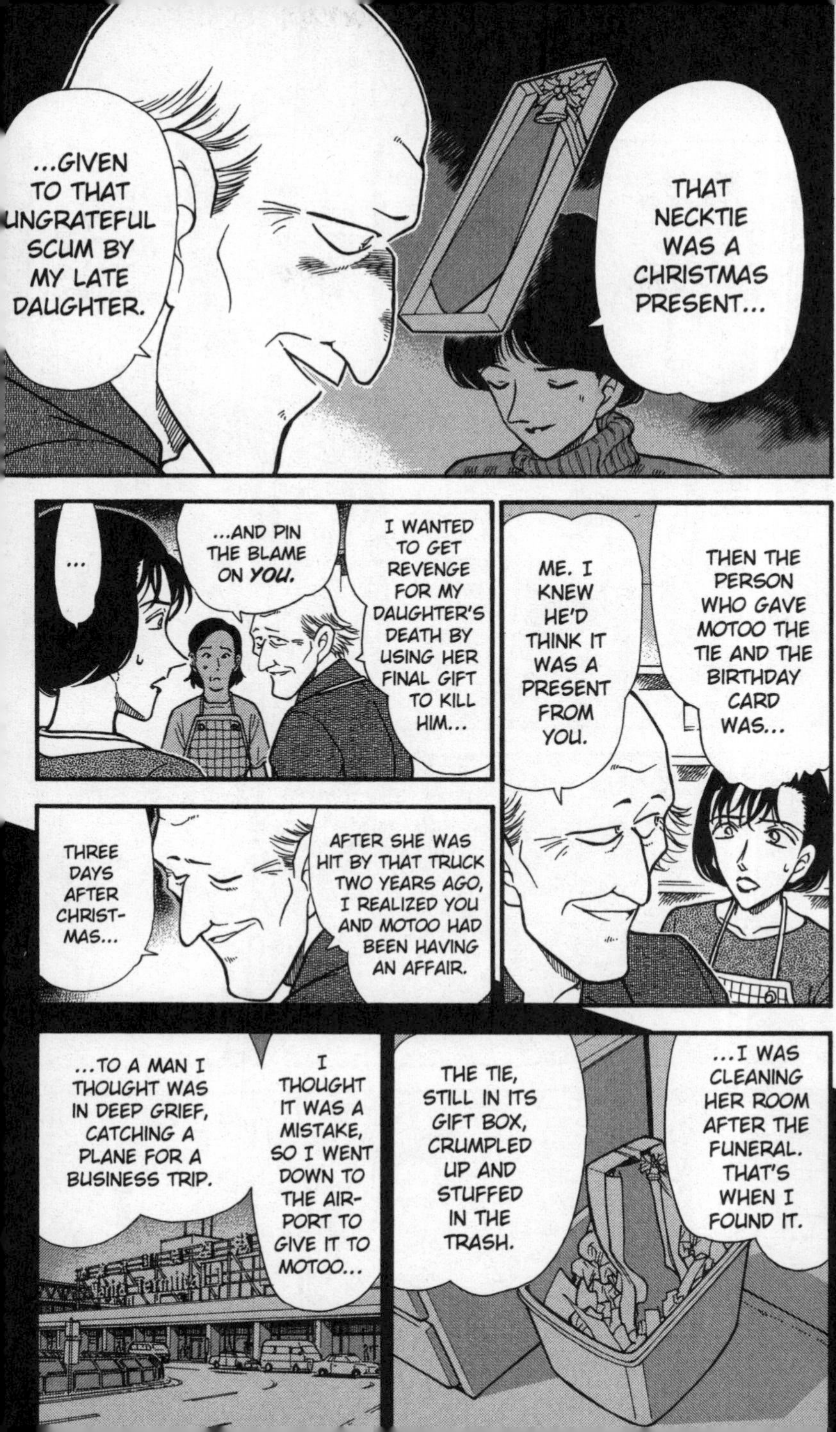

THAT NECKTIE WAS A CHRISTMAS PRESENT...
...GIVEN TO THAT UNGRATEFUL SCUM BY MY LATE DAUGHTER.
THEN THE PERSON WHO GAVE MOTOO THE TIE AND THE BIRTHDAY CARD WAS...
ME. I KNEW HE'D THINK IT WAS A PRESENT FROM YOU.
I WANTED TO GET REVENGE FOR MY DAUGHTER'S DEATH BY USING HER FINAL GIFT TO KILL HIM...
...AND PIN THE BLAME ON *YOU.*
...
AFTER SHE WAS HIT BY THAT TRUCK TWO YEARS AGO, I REALIZED YOU AND MOTOO HAD BEEN HAVING AN AFFAIR.
THREE DAYS AFTER CHRIST-MAS...
...I WAS CLEANING HER ROOM AFTER THE FUNERAL. THAT'S WHEN I FOUND IT.
THE TIE, STILL IN ITS GIFT BOX, CRUMPLED UP AND STUFFED IN THE TRASH.
I THOUGHT IT WAS A MISTAKE, SO I WENT DOWN TO THE AIR-PORT TO GIVE IT TO MOTOO...
...TO A MAN I THOUGHT WAS IN DEEP GRIEF, CATCHING A PLANE FOR A BUSINESS TRIP.

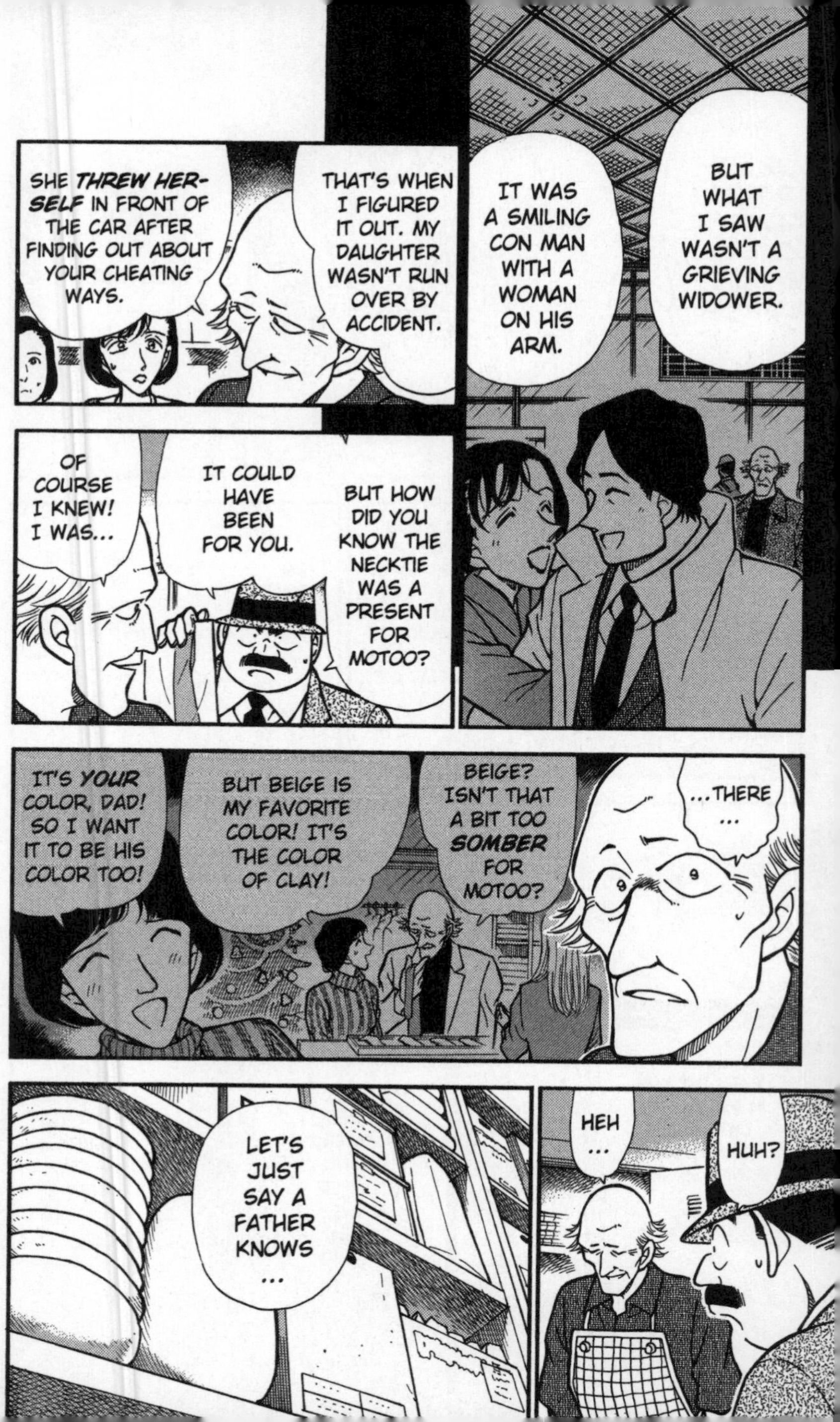
BUT WHAT I SAW WASN'T A GRIEVING WIDOWER.
IT WAS A SMILING CON MAN WITH A WOMAN ON HIS ARM.
THAT'S WHEN I FIGURED IT OUT. MY DAUGHTER WASN'T RUN OVER BY ACCIDENT.
SHE *THREW HER-SELF* IN FRONT OF THE CAR AFTER FINDING OUT ABOUT YOUR CHEATING WAYS.
BUT HOW DID YOU KNOW THE NECKTIE WAS A PRESENT FOR MOTOO?
IT COULD HAVE BEEN FOR YOU.
OF COURSE I KNEW! I WAS...
...THERE ...
BEIGE? ISN'T THAT A BIT TOO *SOMBER* FOR MOTOO?
BUT BEIGE IS MY FAVORITE COLOR! IT'S THE COLOR OF CLAY!
IT'S *YOUR* COLOR, DAD! SO I WANT IT TO BE HIS COLOR TOO!
HUH?
HEH ...
LET'S JUST SAY A FATHER KNOWS ...

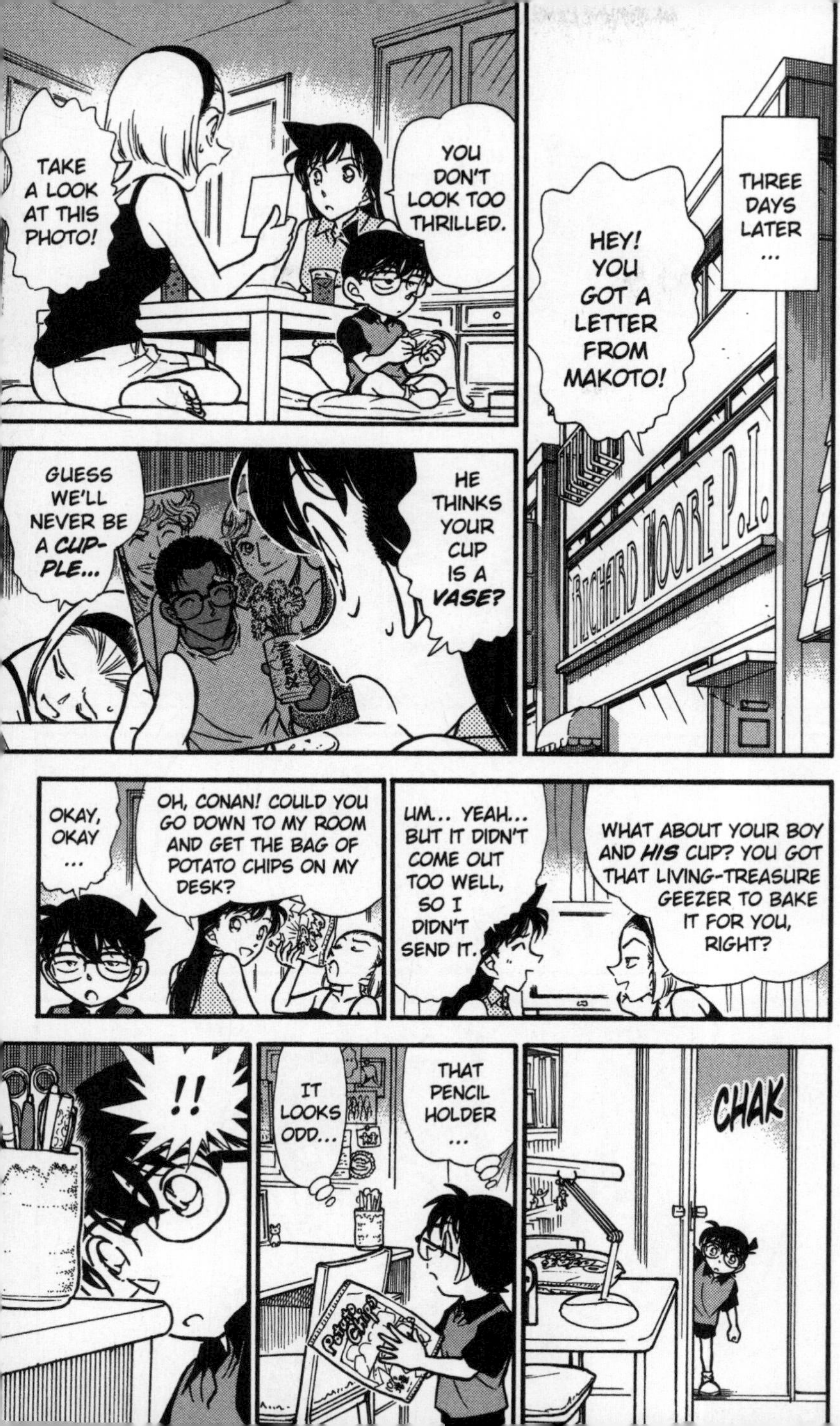
THREE DAYS LATER ...
HEY! YOU GOT A LETTER FROM MAKOTO!
RICHARD MOORE P.I.
YOU DON'T LOOK TOO THRILLED.
TAKE A LOOK AT THIS PHOTO!
HE THINKS YOUR CUP IS A *VASE?*
GUESS WE'LL NEVER BE A *CUP-PLE...*
WHAT ABOUT YOUR BOY AND *HIS* CUP? YOU GOT THAT LIVING-TREASURE GEEZER TO BAKE IT FOR YOU, RIGHT?
UM... YEAH... BUT IT DIDN'T COME OUT TOO WELL, SO I DIDN'T SEND IT.
OH, CONAN! COULD YOU GO DOWN TO MY ROOM AND GET THE BAG OF POTATO CHIPS ON MY DESK?
OKAY, OKAY ...
CHAK
THAT PENCIL HOLDER ...
IT LOOKS ODD...
Potato Chips
!!

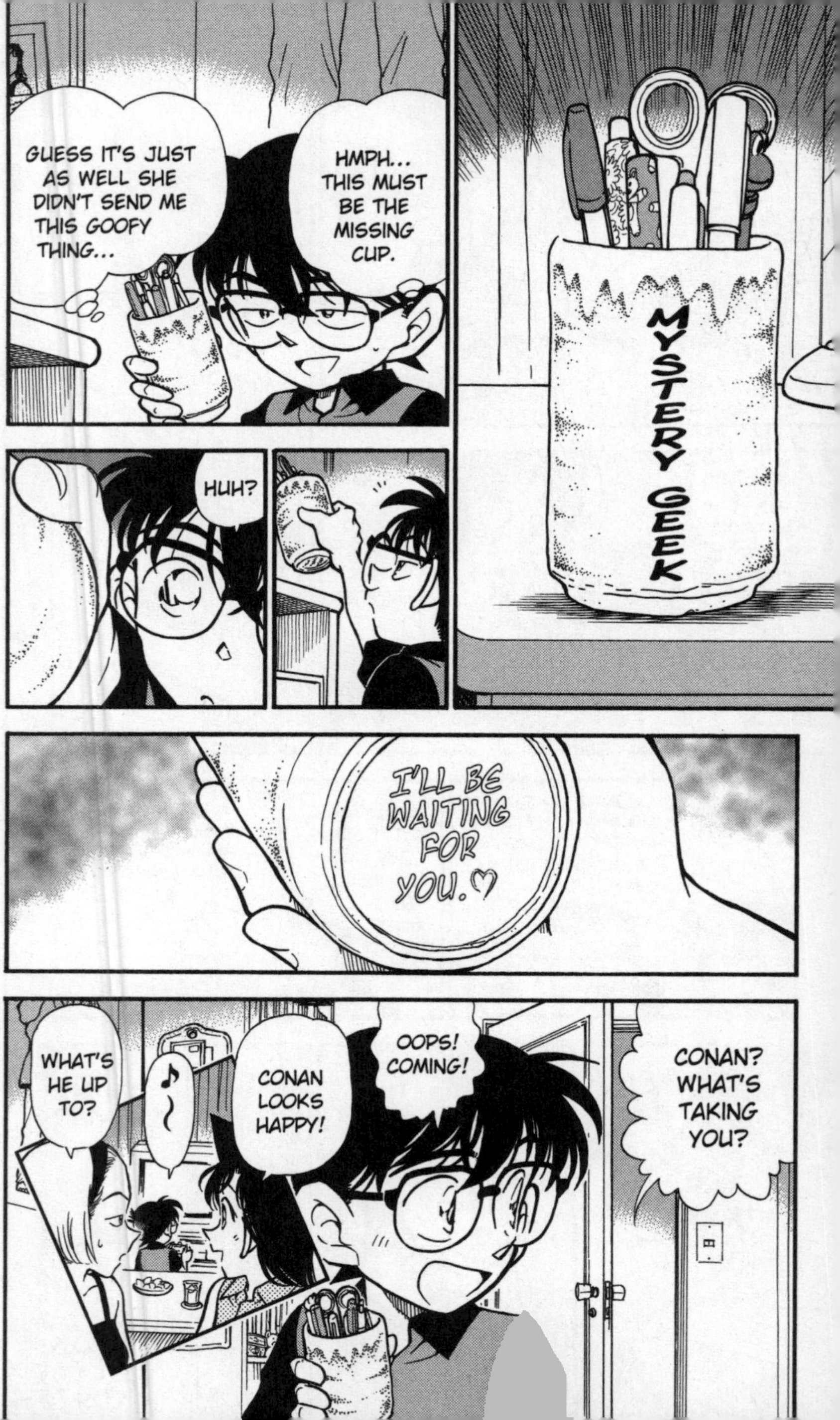
MYSTERY GEEK
HMPH... THIS MUST BE THE MISSING CUP.
GUESS IT'S JUST AS WELL SHE DIDN'T SEND ME THIS GOOFY THING...
HUH?
I'LL BE WAITING FOR YOU.♡
CONAN? WHAT'S TAKING YOU?
OOPS! COMING!
CONAN LOOKS HAPPY!
♪ ~
WHAT'S HE UP TO?

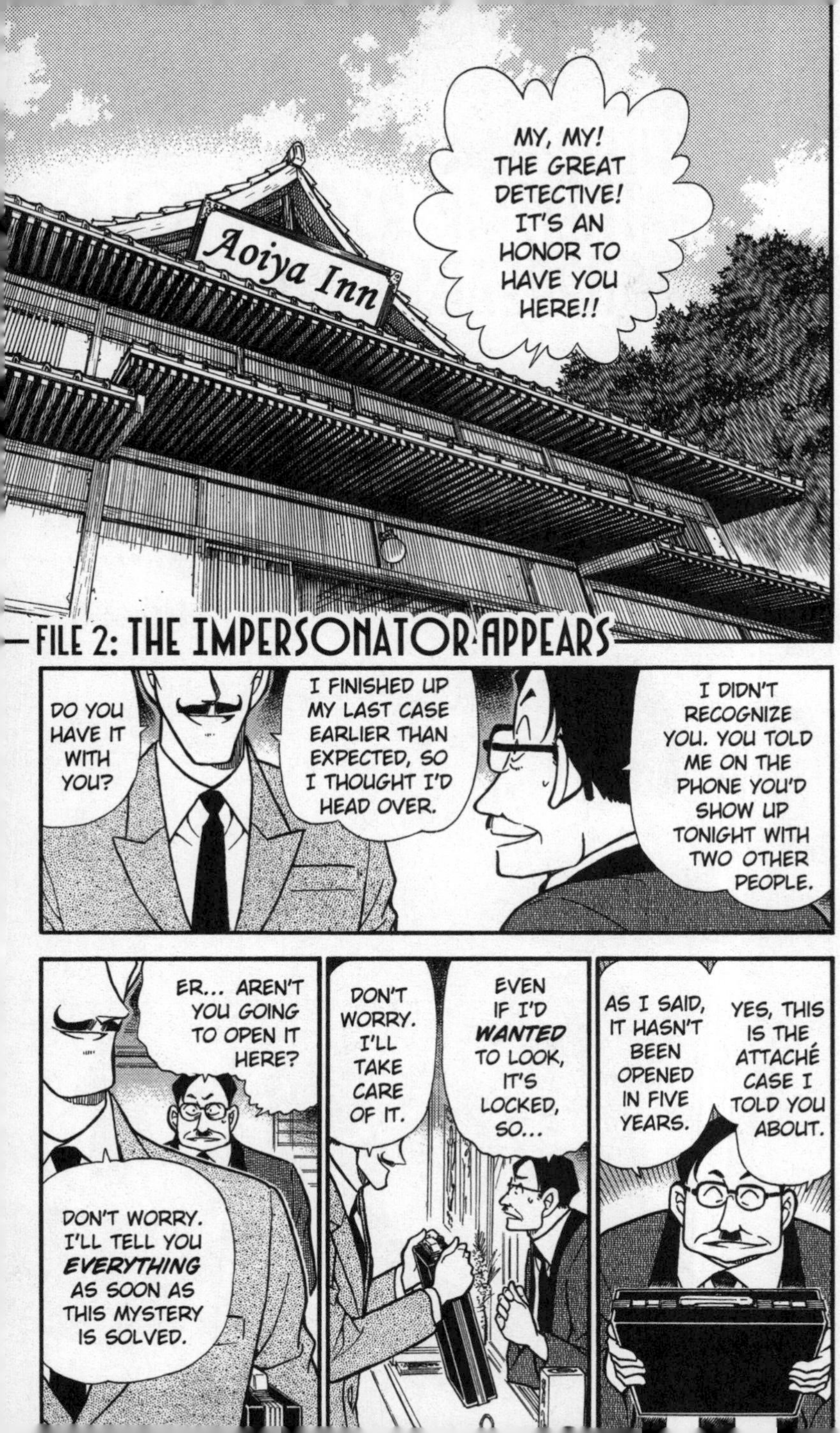
Aoiya Inn
MY, MY! THE GREAT DETECTIVE! IT'S AN HONOR TO HAVE YOU HERE!!
FILE 2: THE IMPERSONATOR APPEARS
I DIDN'T RECOGNIZE YOU. YOU TOLD ME ON THE PHONE YOU'D SHOW UP TONIGHT WITH TWO OTHER PEOPLE.
I FINISHED UP MY LAST CASE EARLIER THAN EXPECTED, SO I THOUGHT I'D HEAD OVER.
DO YOU HAVE IT WITH YOU?
YES, THIS IS THE ATTACHÉ CASE I TOLD YOU ABOUT.
AS I SAID, IT HASN'T BEEN OPENED IN FIVE YEARS.
EVEN IF I'D *WANTED* TO LOOK, IT'S LOCKED, SO...
DON'T WORRY. I'LL TAKE CARE OF IT.
ER... AREN'T YOU GOING TO OPEN IT HERE?
DON'T WORRY. I'LL TELL YOU *EVERYTHING* AS SOON AS THIS MYSTERY IS SOLVED.

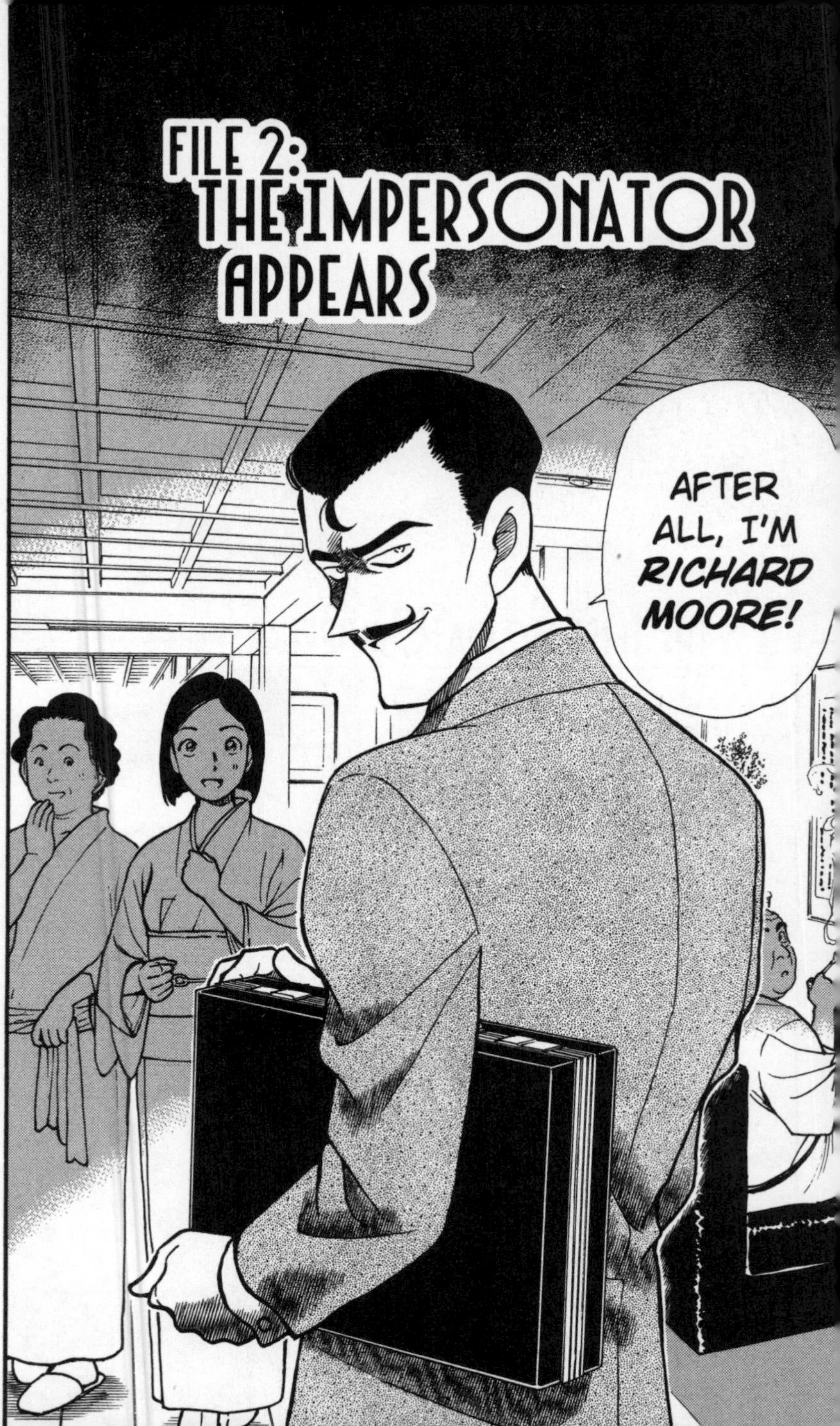
FILE 2: THE IMPERSONATOR APPEARS
AFTER ALL, I'M RICHARD MOORE!

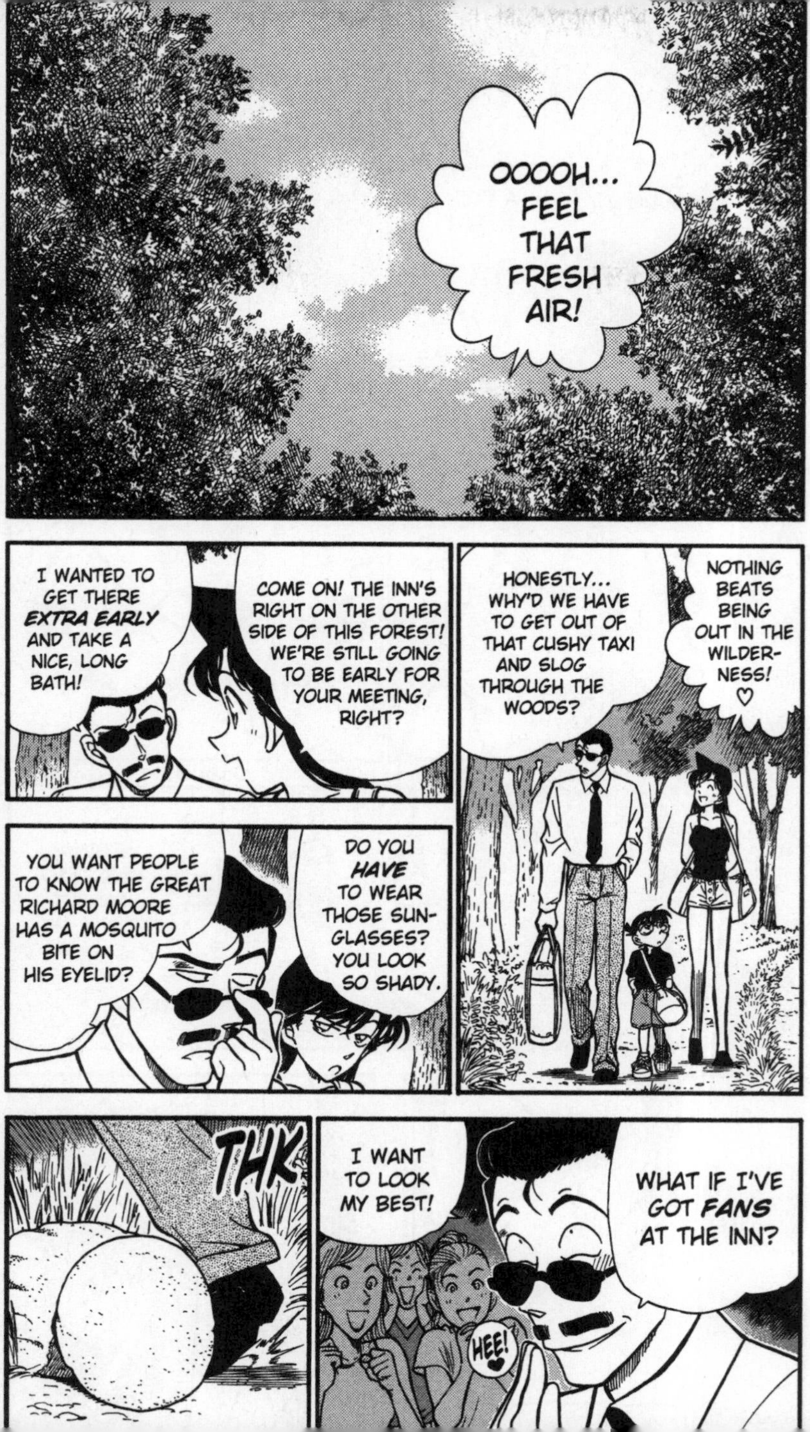
OOOOH... FEEL THAT FRESH AIR!
NOTHING BEATS BEING OUT IN THE WILDERNESS! ♡
HONESTLY... WHY'D WE HAVE TO GET OUT OF THAT CUSHY TAXI AND SLOG THROUGH THE WOODS?
COME ON! THE INN'S RIGHT ON THE OTHER SIDE OF THIS FOREST! WE'RE STILL GOING TO BE EARLY FOR YOUR MEETING, RIGHT?
I WANTED TO GET THERE ***EXTRA EARLY*** AND TAKE A NICE, LONG BATH!
DO YOU ***HAVE*** TO WEAR THOSE SUNGLASSES? YOU LOOK SO SHADY.
YOU WANT PEOPLE TO KNOW THE GREAT RICHARD MOORE HAS A MOSQUITO BITE ON HIS EYELID?
WHAT IF I'VE GOT ***FANS*** AT THE INN?
I WANT TO LOOK MY BEST!
HEE! ♥
THK

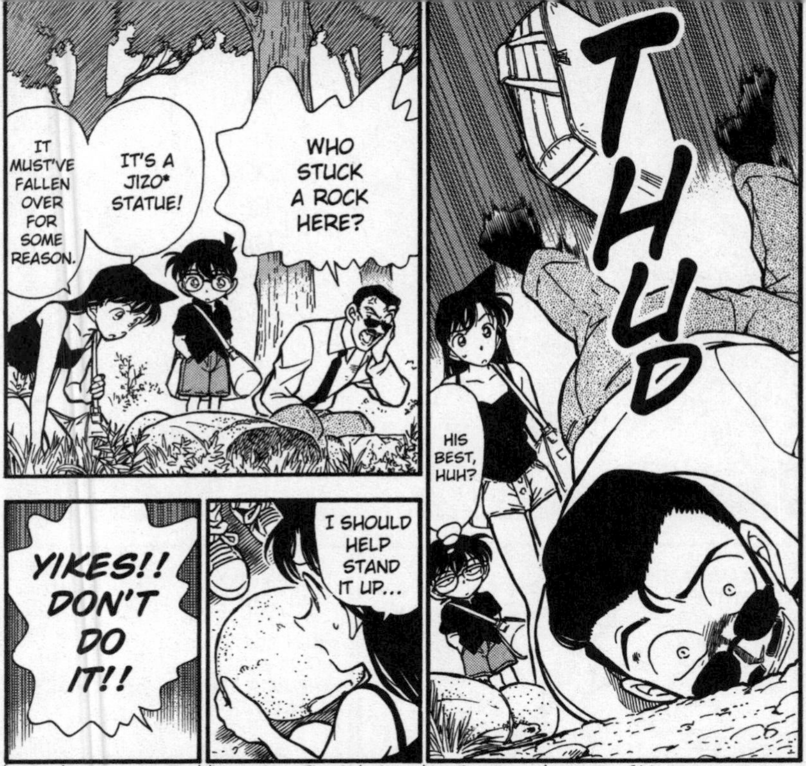
THUD
HIS BEST, HUH?
WHO STUCK A ROCK HERE?
IT'S A JIZO* STATUE!
IT MUST'VE FALLEN OVER FOR SOME REASON.
I SHOULD HELP STAND IT UP...
YIKES!! DON'T DO IT!!

*A *bodhisattva,* or Buddhist saint. Jizo is beloved in Japan, and statues of him are common.

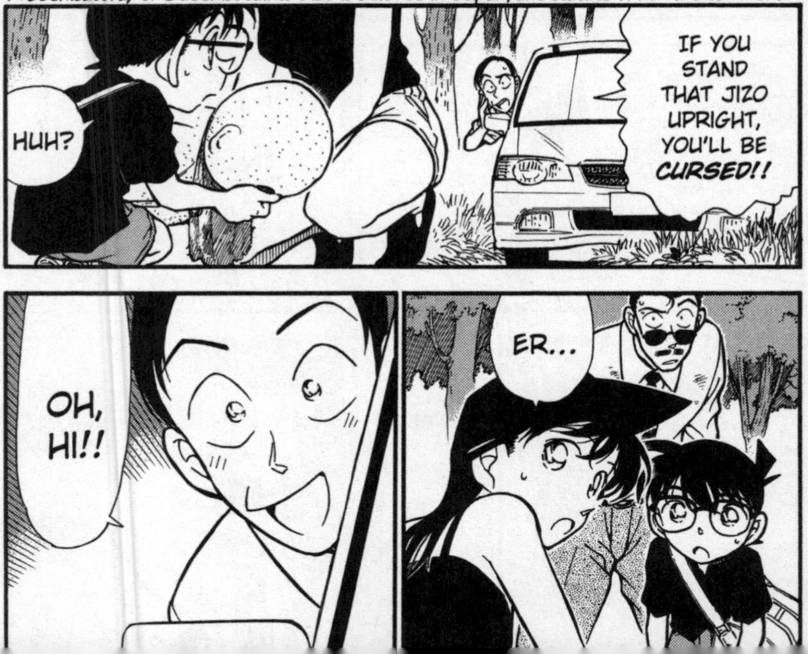
IF YOU STAND THAT JIZO UPRIGHT, YOU'LL BE CURSED!!
HUH?
ER...
OH, HI!!

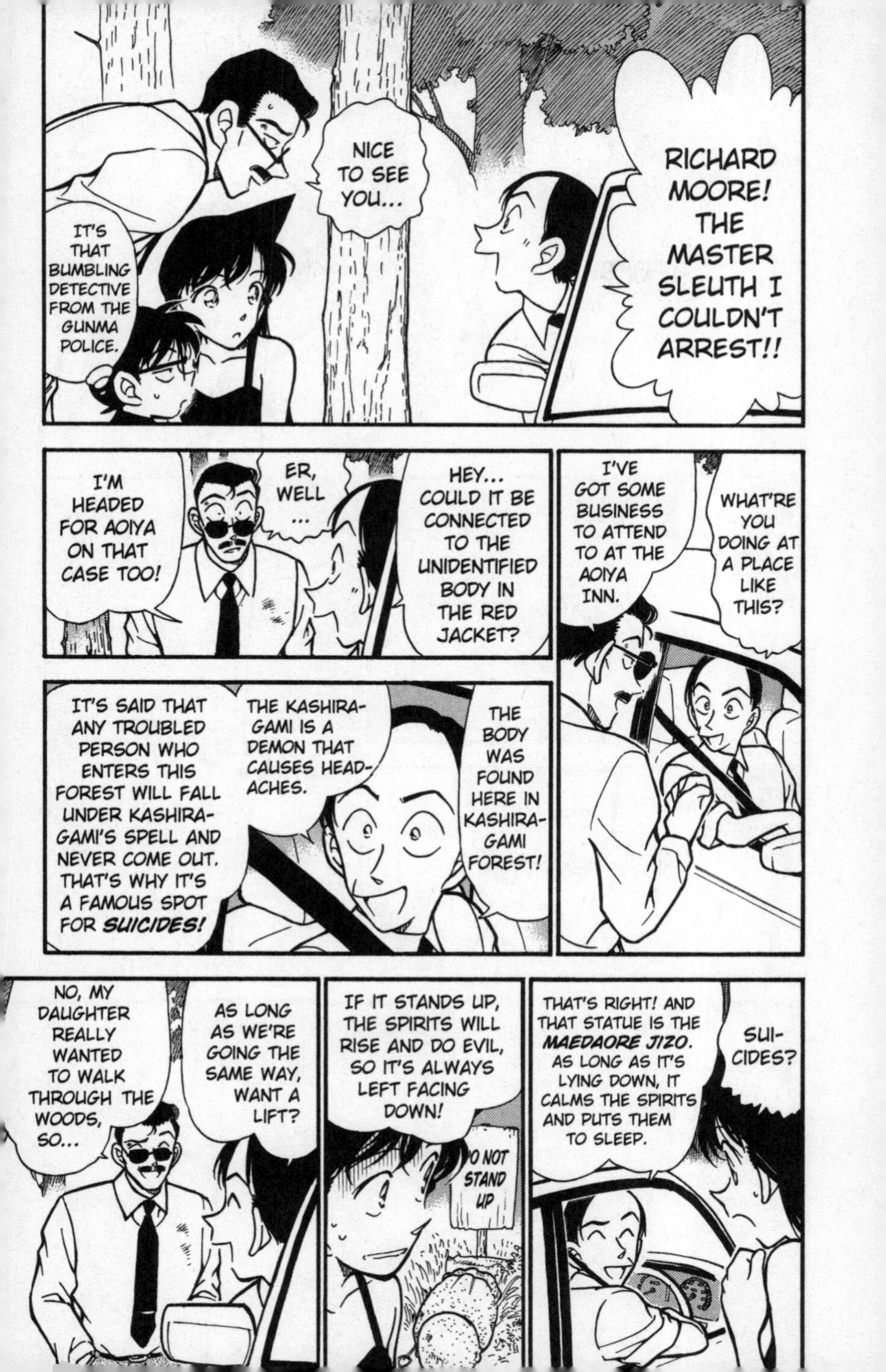
RICHARD MOORE! THE MASTER SLEUTH I COULDN'T ARREST!!
NICE TO SEE YOU...
IT'S THAT BUMBLING DETECTIVE FROM THE GUNMA POLICE.
WHAT'RE YOU DOING AT A PLACE LIKE THIS?
I'VE GOT SOME BUSINESS TO ATTEND TO AT THE AOIYA INN.
HEY... COULD IT BE CONNECTED TO THE UNIDENTIFIED BODY IN THE RED JACKET?
ER, WELL ...
I'M HEADED FOR AOIYA ON THAT CASE TOO!
THE BODY WAS FOUND HERE IN KASHIRA-GAMI FOREST!
THE KASHIRA-GAMI IS A DEMON THAT CAUSES HEAD-ACHES.
IT'S SAID THAT ANY TROUBLED PERSON WHO ENTERS THIS FOREST WILL FALL UNDER KASHIRA-GAMI'S SPELL AND NEVER COME OUT. THAT'S WHY IT'S A FAMOUS SPOT FOR ***SUICIDES!***
SUI-CIDES?
THAT'S RIGHT! AND THAT STATUE IS THE ***MAEDAORE JIZO***. AS LONG AS IT'S LYING DOWN, IT CALMS THE SPIRITS AND PUTS THEM TO SLEEP.
IF IT STANDS UP, THE SPIRITS WILL RISE AND DO EVIL, SO IT'S ALWAYS LEFT FACING DOWN!
O NOT STAND UP
AS LONG AS WE'RE GOING THE SAME WAY, WANT A LIFT?
NO, MY DAUGHTER REALLY WANTED TO WALK THROUGH THE WOODS, SO...

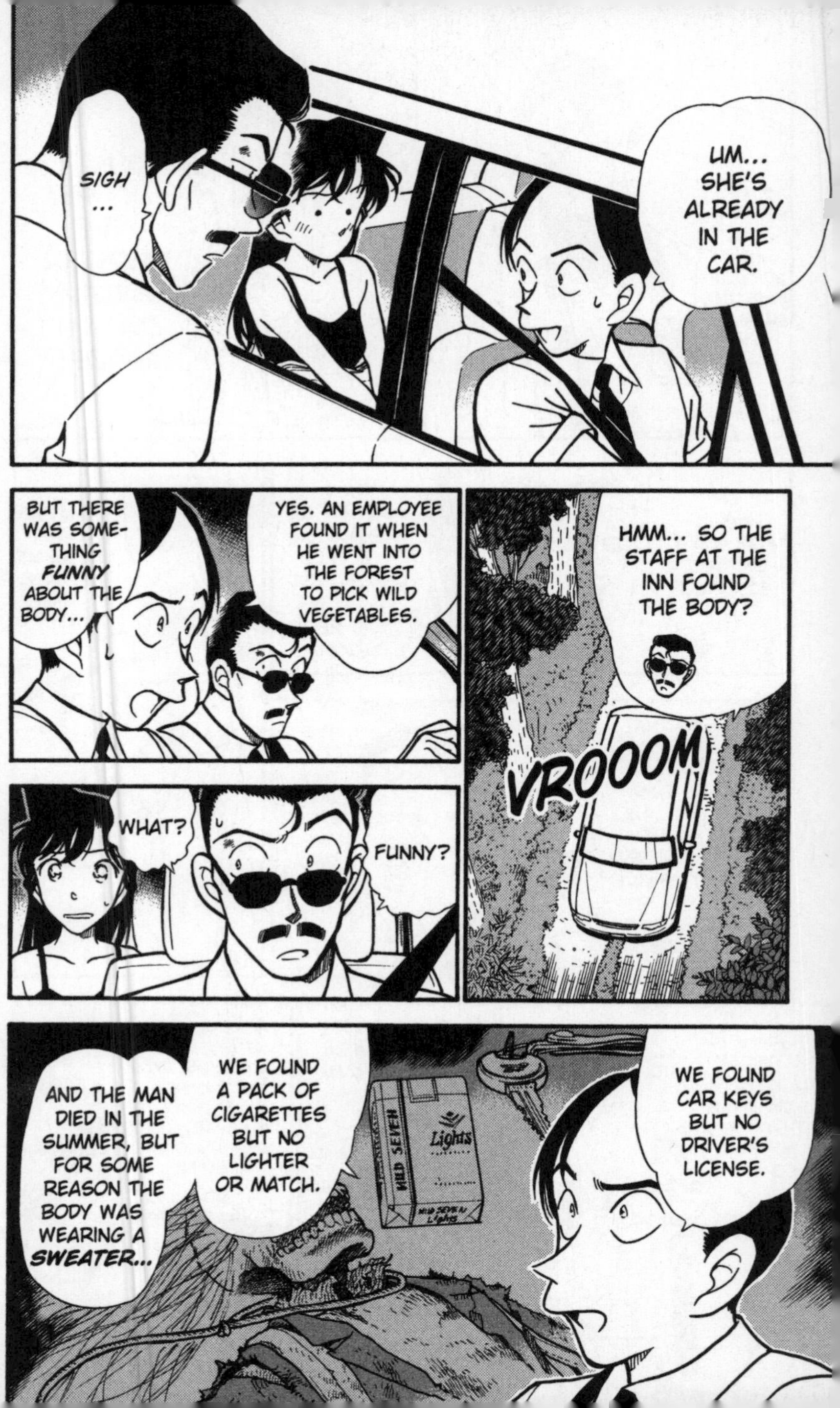
UM... SHE'S ALREADY IN THE CAR.
SIGH ...
HMM... SO THE STAFF AT THE INN FOUND THE BODY?
VROOOM
YES. AN EMPLOYEE FOUND IT WHEN HE WENT INTO THE FOREST TO PICK WILD VEGETABLES.
BUT THERE WAS SOME-THING *FUNNY* ABOUT THE BODY...
FUNNY?
WHAT?
WE FOUND CAR KEYS BUT NO DRIVER'S LICENSE.
WE FOUND A PACK OF CIGARETTES BUT NO LIGHTER OR MATCH.
AND THE MAN DIED IN THE SUMMER, BUT FOR SOME REASON THE BODY WAS WEARING A ***SWEATER...***

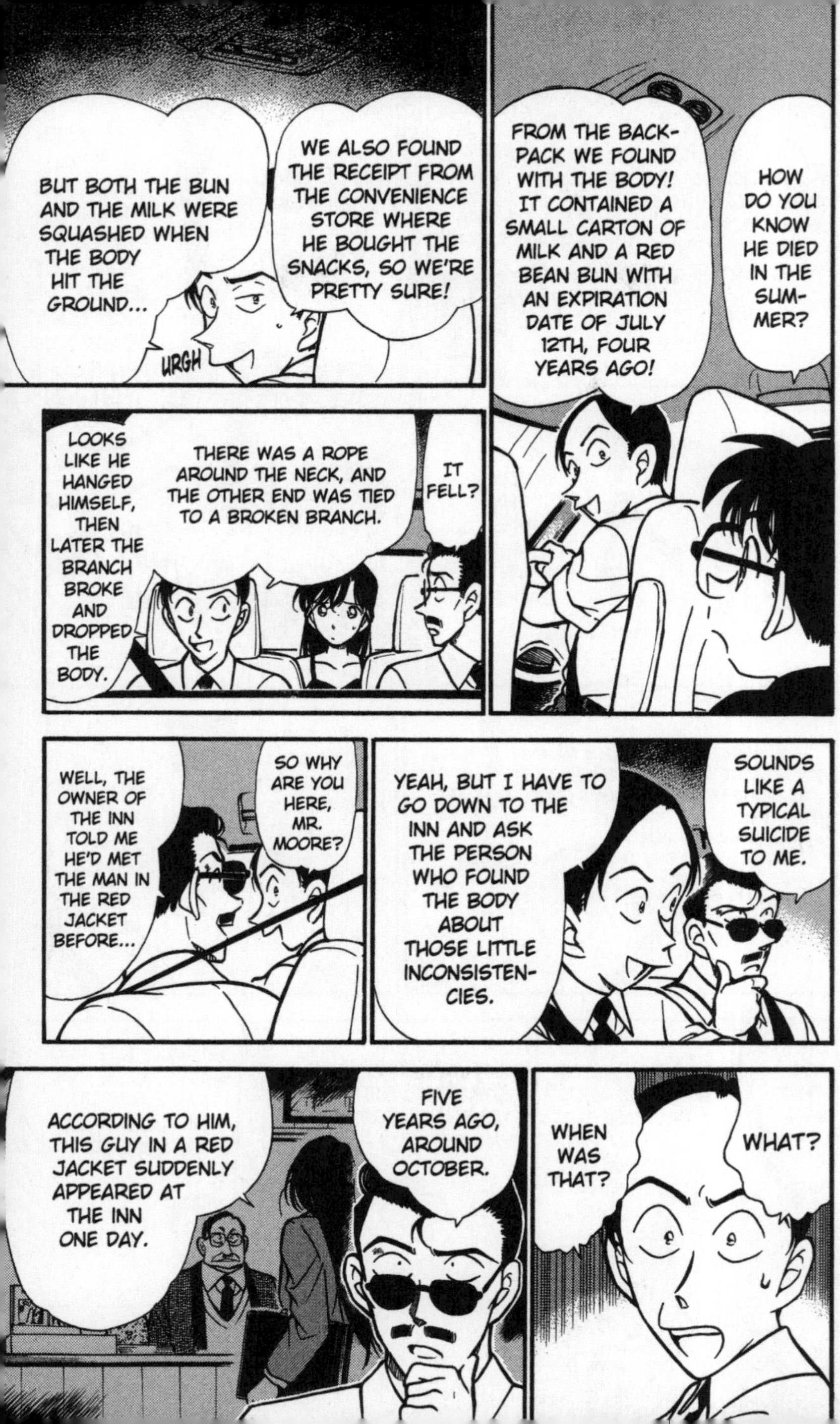
HOW DO YOU KNOW HE DIED IN THE SUMMER?
FROM THE BACKPACK WE FOUND WITH THE BODY! IT CONTAINED A SMALL CARTON OF MILK AND A RED BEAN BUN WITH AN EXPIRATION DATE OF JULY 12TH, FOUR YEARS AGO!
WE ALSO FOUND THE RECEIPT FROM THE CONVENIENCE STORE WHERE HE BOUGHT THE SNACKS, SO WE'RE PRETTY SURE!
BUT BOTH THE BUN AND THE MILK WERE SQUASHED WHEN THE BODY HIT THE GROUND...
URGH
IT FELL?
THERE WAS A ROPE AROUND THE NECK, AND THE OTHER END WAS TIED TO A BROKEN BRANCH.
LOOKS LIKE HE HANGED HIMSELF, THEN LATER THE BRANCH BROKE AND DROPPED THE BODY.
SOUNDS LIKE A TYPICAL SUICIDE TO ME.
YEAH, BUT I HAVE TO GO DOWN TO THE INN AND ASK THE PERSON WHO FOUND THE BODY ABOUT THOSE LITTLE INCONSISTENCIES.
SO WHY ARE YOU HERE, MR. MOORE?
WELL, THE OWNER OF THE INN TOLD ME HE'D MET THE MAN IN THE RED JACKET BEFORE...
WHAT?
WHEN WAS THAT?
FIVE YEARS AGO, AROUND OCTOBER.
ACCORDING TO HIM, THIS GUY IN A RED JACKET SUDDENLY APPEARED AT THE INN ONE DAY.

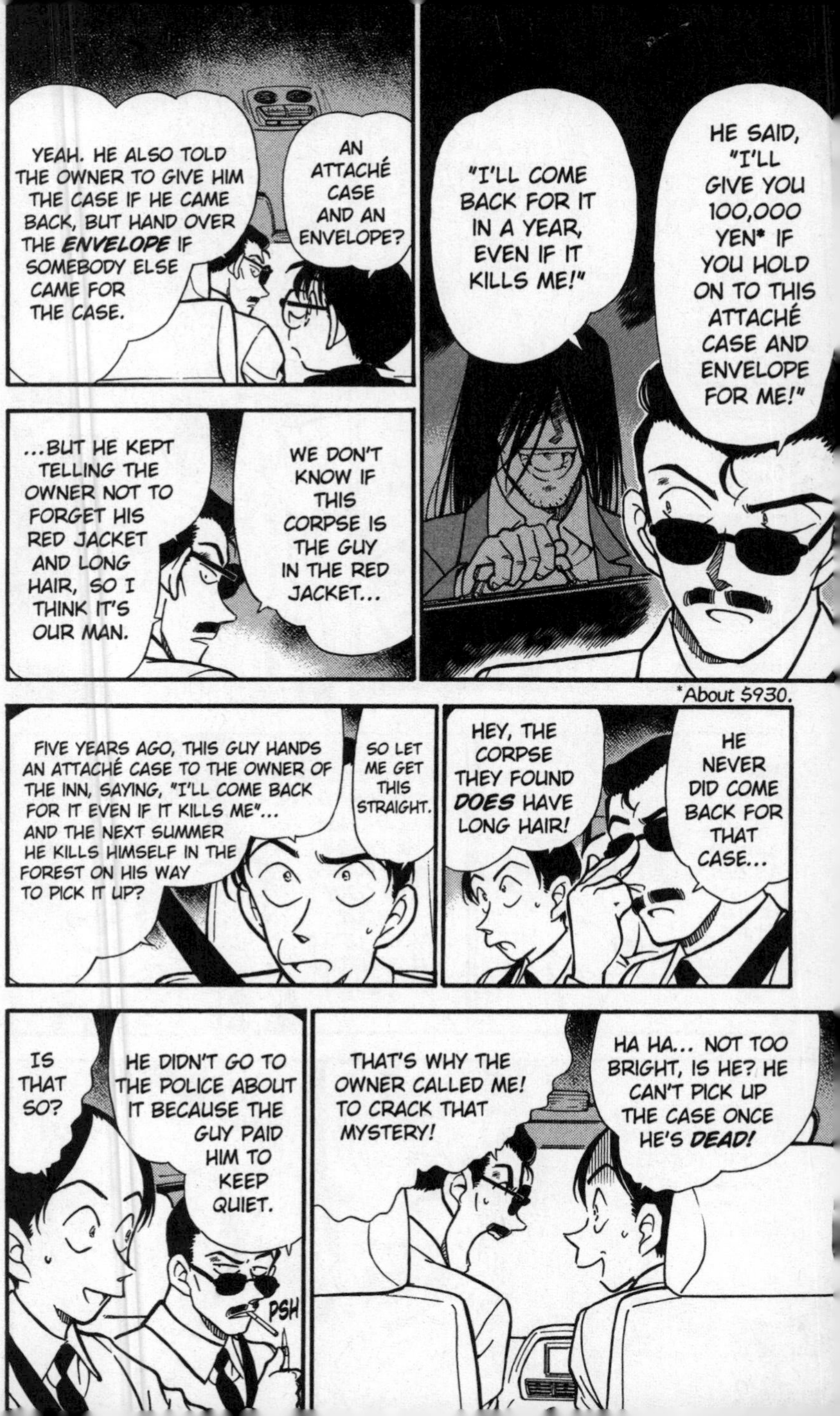
HE SAID, "I'LL GIVE YOU 100,000 YEN* IF YOU HOLD ON TO THIS ATTACHÉ CASE AND ENVELOPE FOR ME!"
"I'LL COME BACK FOR IT IN A YEAR, EVEN IF IT KILLS ME!"
AN ATTACHÉ CASE AND AN ENVELOPE?
YEAH. HE ALSO TOLD THE OWNER TO GIVE HIM THE CASE IF HE CAME BACK, BUT HAND OVER THE ***ENVELOPE*** IF SOMEBODY ELSE CAME FOR THE CASE.
WE DON'T KNOW IF THIS CORPSE IS THE GUY IN THE RED JACKET...
...BUT HE KEPT TELLING THE OWNER NOT TO FORGET HIS RED JACKET AND LONG HAIR, SO I THINK IT'S OUR MAN.
HE NEVER DID COME BACK FOR THAT CASE...
HEY, THE CORPSE THEY FOUND ***DOES*** HAVE LONG HAIR!
SO LET ME GET THIS STRAIGHT.
FIVE YEARS AGO, THIS GUY HANDS AN ATTACHÉ CASE TO THE OWNER OF THE INN, SAYING, "I'LL COME BACK FOR IT EVEN IF IT KILLS ME"... AND THE NEXT SUMMER HE KILLS HIMSELF IN THE FOREST ON HIS WAY TO PICK IT UP?
HA HA... NOT TOO BRIGHT, IS HE? HE CAN'T PICK UP THE CASE ONCE HE'S ***DEAD!***
THAT'S WHY THE OWNER CALLED ME! TO CRACK THAT MYSTERY!
HE DIDN'T GO TO THE POLICE ABOUT IT BECAUSE THE GUY PAID HIM TO KEEP QUIET.
IS THAT SO?
PSH

*About $930.

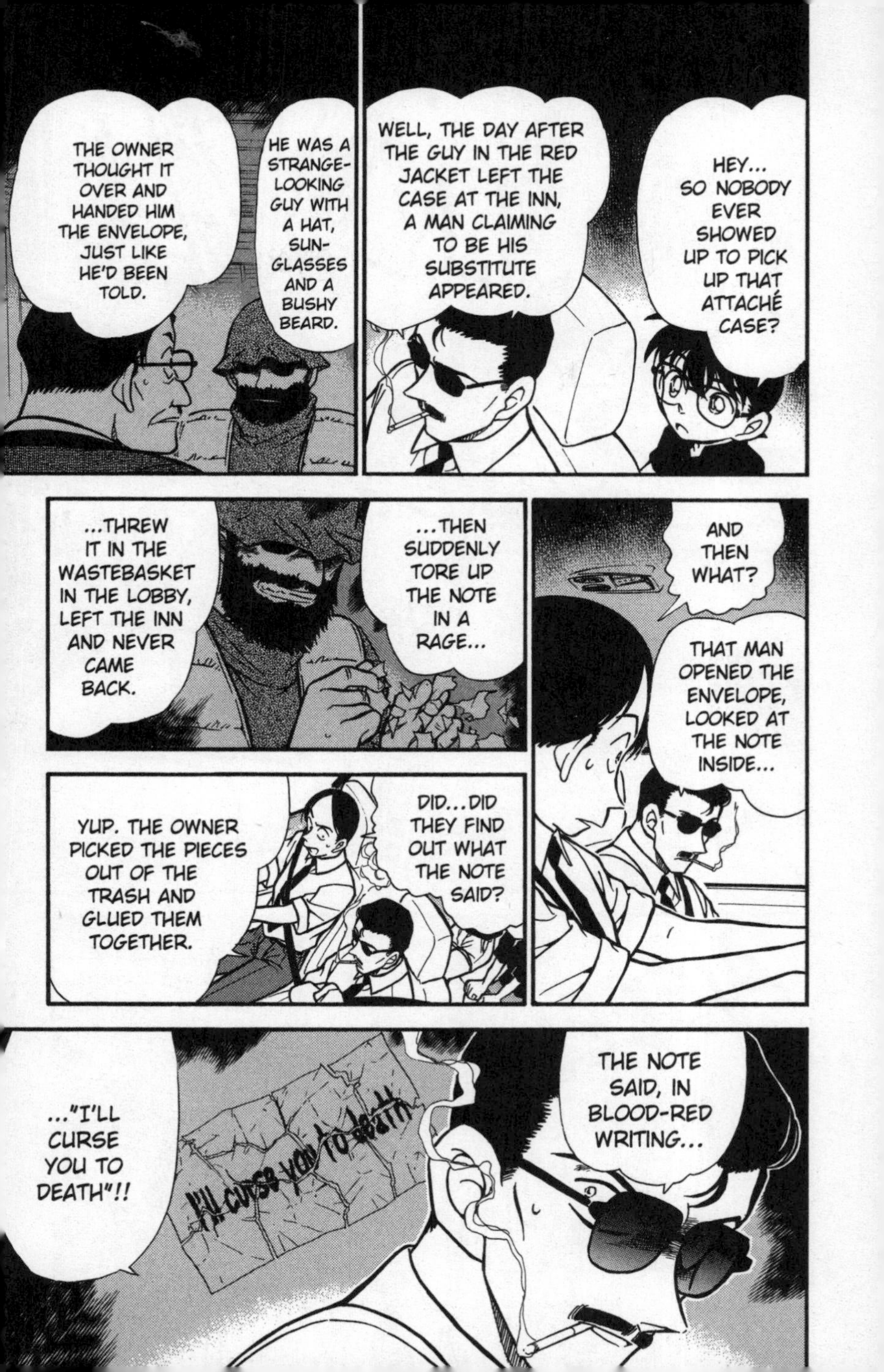
HEY... SO NOBODY EVER SHOWED UP TO PICK UP THAT ATTACHÉ CASE?
WELL, THE DAY AFTER THE GUY IN THE RED JACKET LEFT THE CASE AT THE INN, A MAN CLAIMING TO BE HIS SUBSTITUTE APPEARED.
HE WAS A STRANGE-LOOKING GUY WITH A HAT, SUN-GLASSES AND A BUSHY BEARD.
THE OWNER THOUGHT IT OVER AND HANDED HIM THE ENVELOPE, JUST LIKE HE'D BEEN TOLD.
AND THEN WHAT?
THAT MAN OPENED THE ENVELOPE, LOOKED AT THE NOTE INSIDE...
...THEN SUDDENLY TORE UP THE NOTE IN A RAGE...
...THREW IT IN THE WASTEBASKET IN THE LOBBY, LEFT THE INN AND NEVER CAME BACK.
DID...DID THEY FIND OUT WHAT THE NOTE SAID?
YUP. THE OWNER PICKED THE PIECES OUT OF THE TRASH AND GLUED THEM TOGETHER.
THE NOTE SAID, IN BLOOD-RED WRITING...
I'll curse you to death
..."I'LL CURSE YOU TO DEATH"!!

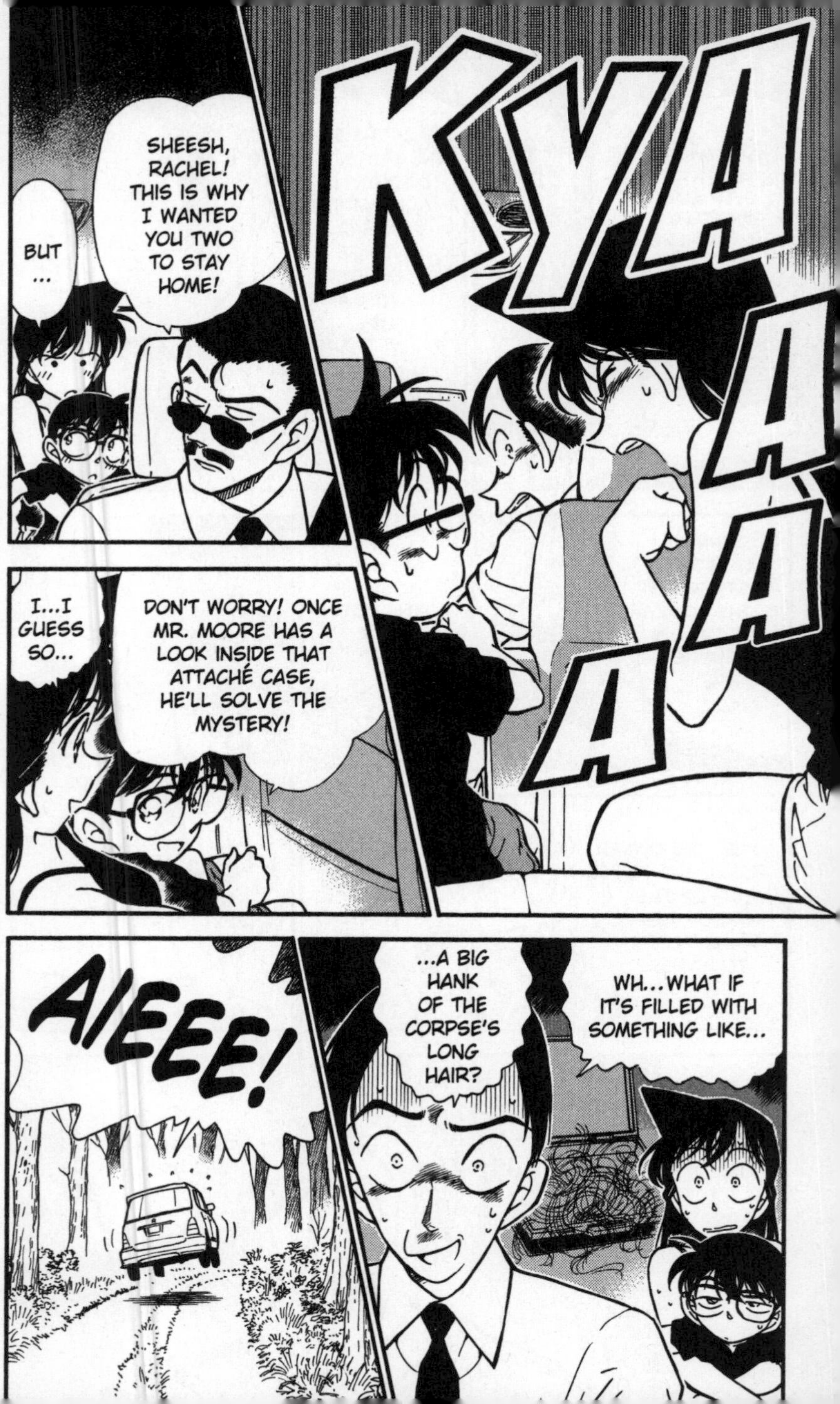
KYAAAAA
SHEESH, RACHEL! THIS IS WHY I WANTED YOU TWO TO STAY HOME!
BUT ...
DON'T WORRY! ONCE MR. MOORE HAS A LOOK INSIDE THAT ATTACHÉ CASE, HE'LL SOLVE THE MYSTERY!
I...I GUESS SO...
WH...WHAT IF IT'S FILLED WITH SOMETHING LIKE...
...A BIG HANK OF THE CORPSE'S LONG HAIR?
AIEEE!

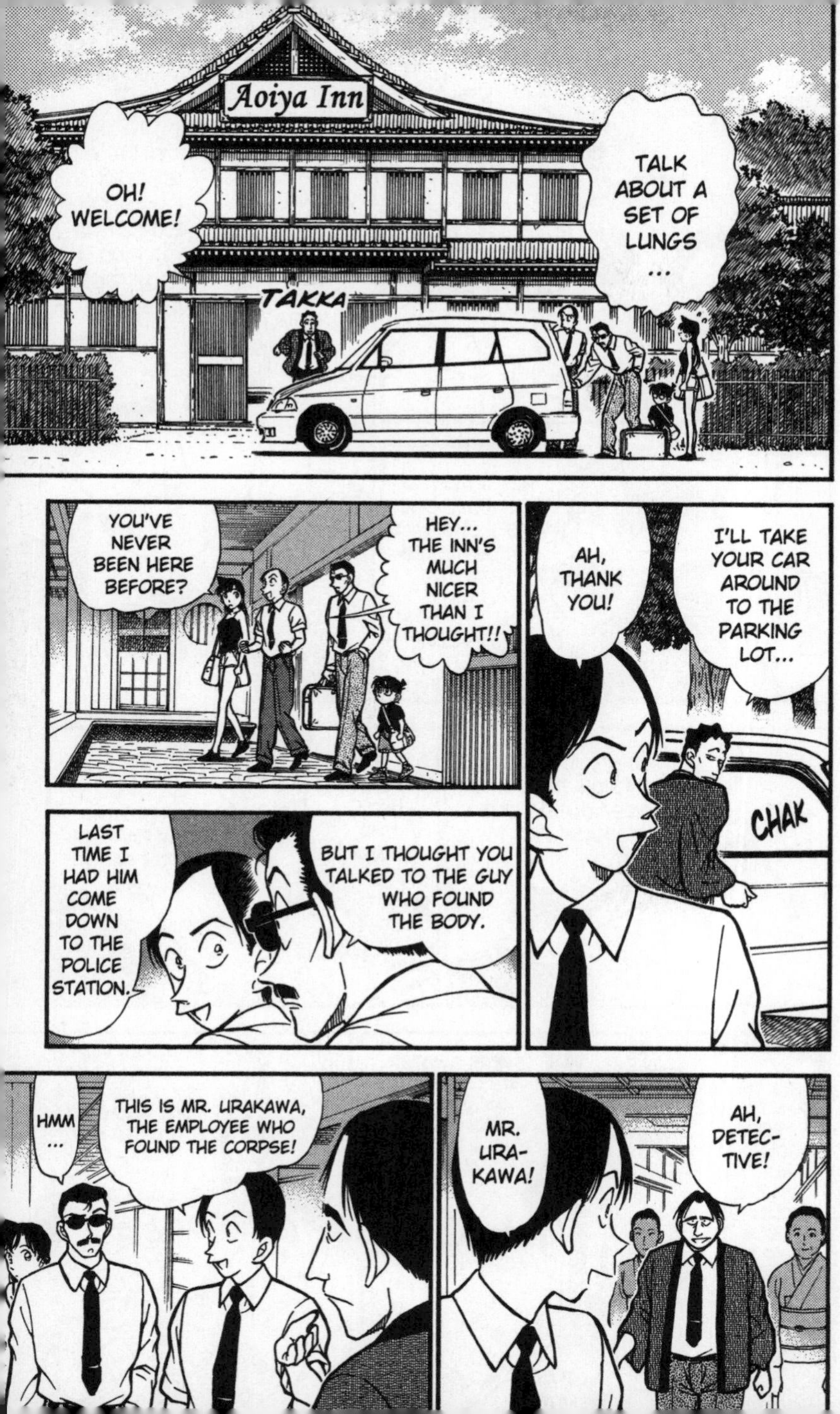
OH! WELCOME!
TALK ABOUT A SET OF LUNGS ...
TAKKA
I'LL TAKE YOUR CAR AROUND TO THE PARKING LOT...
AH, THANK YOU!
CHAK
HEY... THE INN'S MUCH NICER THAN I THOUGHT!!
YOU'VE NEVER BEEN HERE BEFORE?
BUT I THOUGHT YOU TALKED TO THE GUY WHO FOUND THE BODY.
LAST TIME I HAD HIM COME DOWN TO THE POLICE STATION.
AH, DETECTIVE!
MR. URAKAWA!
THIS IS MR. URAKAWA, THE EMPLOYEE WHO FOUND THE CORPSE!
HMM ...

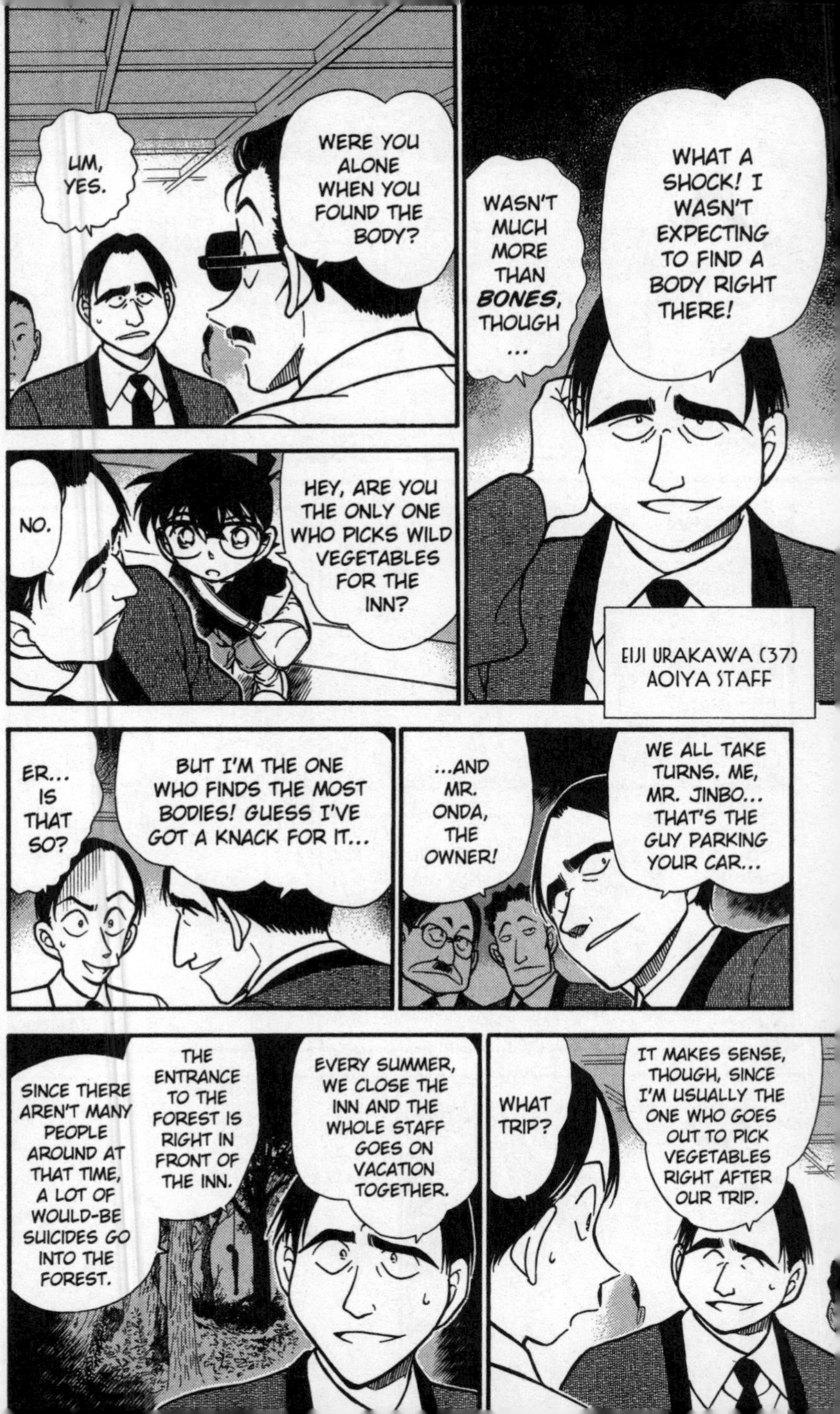
WHAT A SHOCK! I WASN'T EXPECTING TO FIND A BODY RIGHT THERE!
WASN'T MUCH MORE THAN BONES, THOUGH ...
EIJI URAKAWA (37) AOIYA STAFF
WERE YOU ALONE WHEN YOU FOUND THE BODY?
UM, YES.
HEY, ARE YOU THE ONLY ONE WHO PICKS WILD VEGETABLES FOR THE INN?
NO.
WE ALL TAKE TURNS. ME, MR. JINBO... THAT'S THE GUY PARKING YOUR CAR...
...AND MR. ONDA, THE OWNER!
BUT I'M THE ONE WHO FINDS THE MOST BODIES! GUESS I'VE GOT A KNACK FOR IT...
ER... IS THAT SO?
IT MAKES SENSE, THOUGH, SINCE I'M USUALLY THE ONE WHO GOES OUT TO PICK VEGETABLES RIGHT AFTER OUR TRIP.
WHAT TRIP?
EVERY SUMMER, WE CLOSE THE INN AND THE WHOLE STAFF GOES ON VACATION TOGETHER.
THE ENTRANCE TO THE FOREST IS RIGHT IN FRONT OF THE INN.
SINCE THERE AREN'T MANY PEOPLE AROUND AT THAT TIME, A LOT OF WOULD-BE SUICIDES GO INTO THE FOREST.

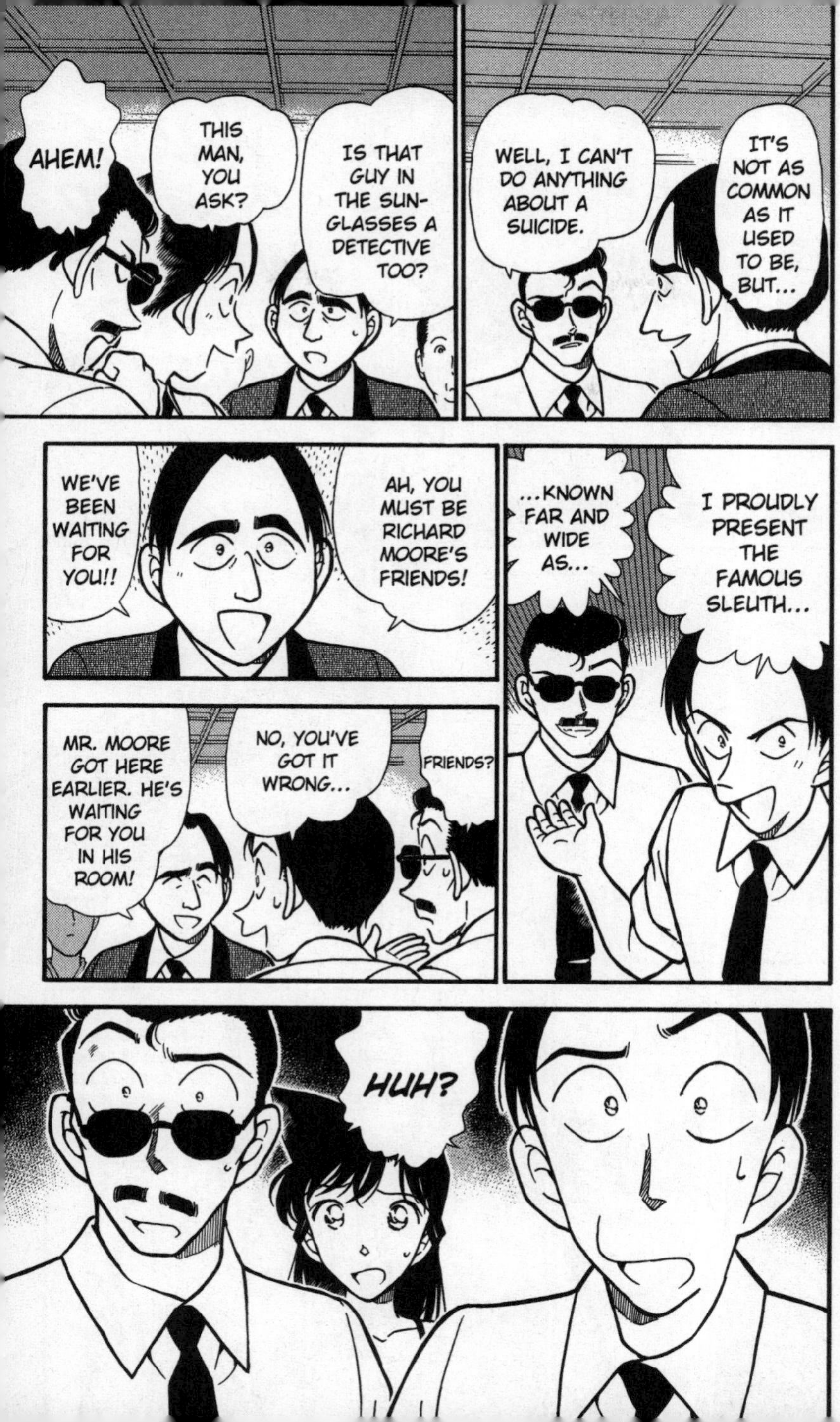
IT'S NOT AS COMMON AS IT USED TO BE, BUT...
WELL, I CAN'T DO ANYTHING ABOUT A SUICIDE.
IS THAT GUY IN THE SUN-GLASSES A DETECTIVE TOO?
THIS MAN, YOU ASK?
AHEM!
I PROUDLY PRESENT THE FAMOUS SLEUTH...
...KNOWN FAR AND WIDE AS...
AH, YOU MUST BE RICHARD MOORE'S FRIENDS!
WE'VE BEEN WAITING FOR YOU!!
FRIENDS?
NO, YOU'VE GOT IT WRONG...
MR. MOORE GOT HERE EARLIER. HE'S WAITING FOR YOU IN HIS ROOM!
HUH?

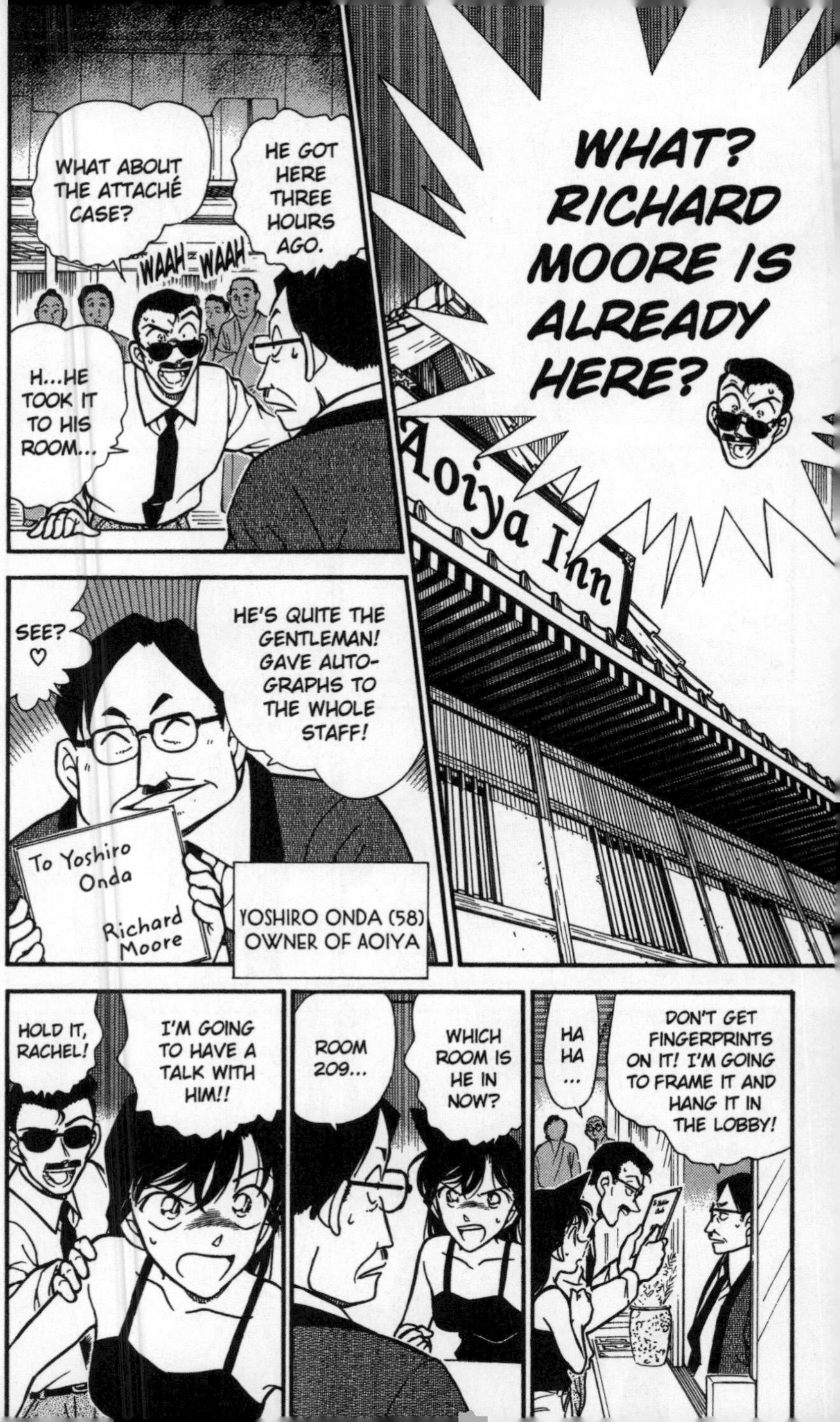
WHAT? RICHARD MOORE IS ALREADY HERE?
Aoiya Inn
HE GOT HERE THREE HOURS AGO.
WHAT ABOUT THE ATTACHÉ CASE?
WAAH WAAH
H...HE TOOK IT TO HIS ROOM...
HE'S QUITE THE GENTLEMAN! GAVE AUTO-GRAPHS TO THE WHOLE STAFF!
SEE? ♡
To Yoshiro Onda
Richard Moore
YOSHIRO ONDA (58) OWNER OF AOIYA
DON'T GET FINGERPRINTS ON IT! I'M GOING TO FRAME IT AND HANG IT IN THE LOBBY!
HA HA ...
WHICH ROOM IS HE IN NOW?
ROOM 209...
I'M GOING TO HAVE A TALK WITH HIM!!
HOLD IT, RACHEL!

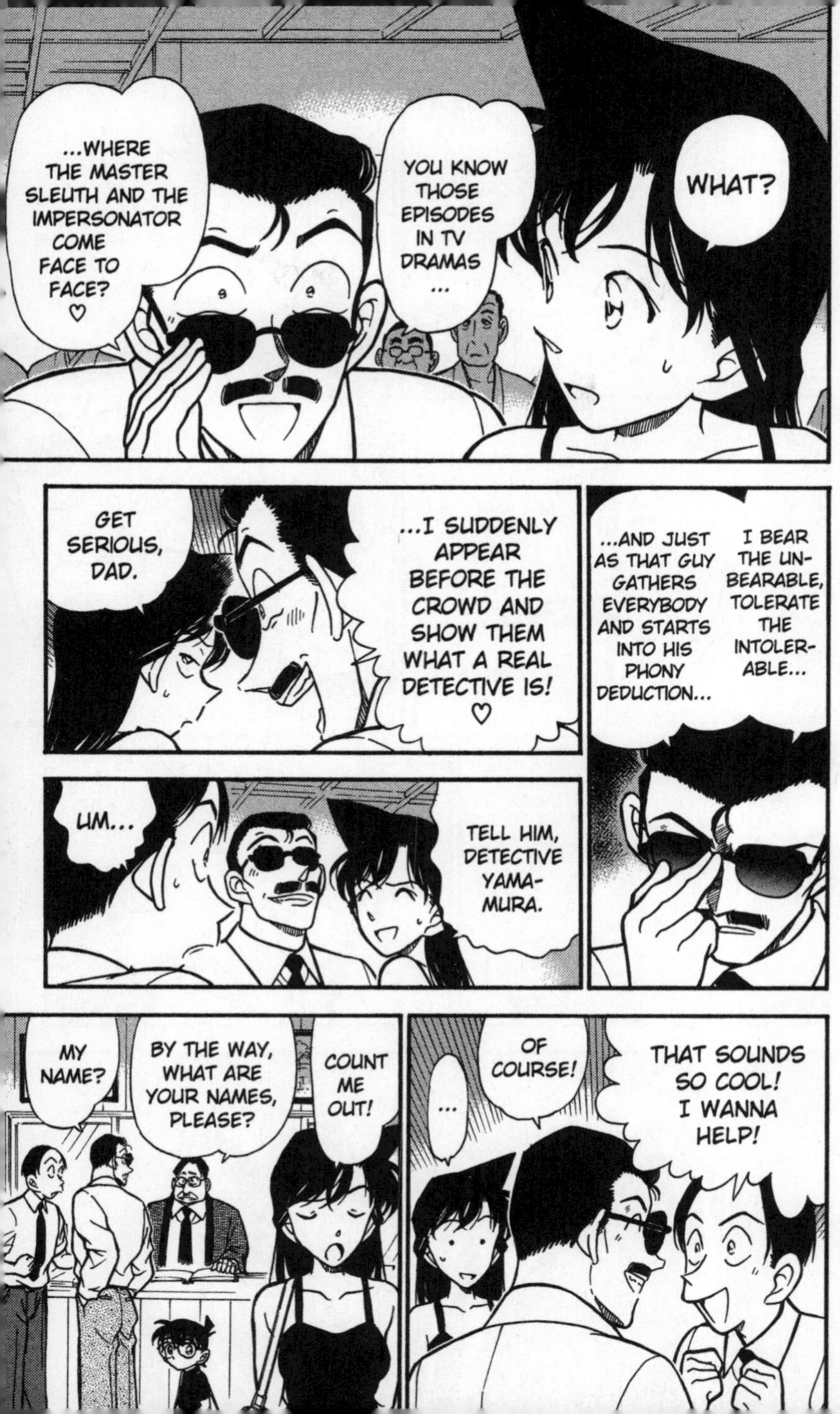
WHAT?
YOU KNOW THOSE EPISODES IN TV DRAMAS ...
...WHERE THE MASTER SLEUTH AND THE IMPERSONATOR COME FACE TO FACE? ♡
I BEAR THE UN-BEARABLE, TOLERATE THE INTOLER-ABLE...
...AND JUST AS THAT GUY GATHERS EVERYBODY AND STARTS INTO HIS PHONY DEDUCTION...
...I SUDDENLY APPEAR BEFORE THE CROWD AND SHOW THEM WHAT A REAL DETECTIVE IS! ♡
GET SERIOUS, DAD.
TELL HIM, DETECTIVE YAMA-MURA.
UM...
THAT SOUNDS SO COOL! I WANNA HELP!
OF COURSE!
...
COUNT ME OUT!
BY THE WAY, WHAT ARE YOUR NAMES, PLEASE?
MY NAME?

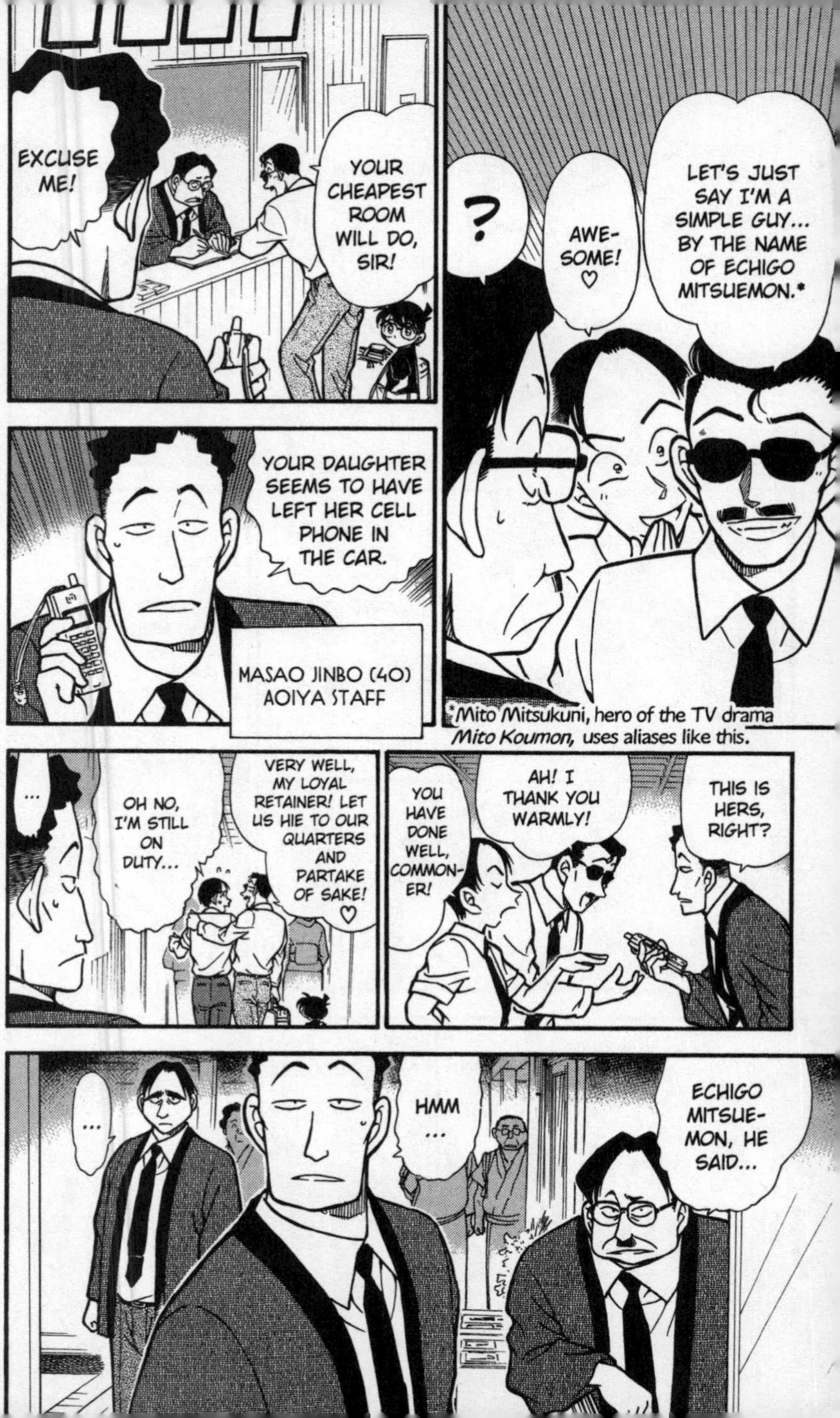
LET'S JUST SAY I'M A SIMPLE GUY... BY THE NAME OF ECHIGO MITSUEMON.*
AWE-SOME! ♡
?
YOUR CHEAPEST ROOM WILL DO, SIR!
EXCUSE ME!
YOUR DAUGHTER SEEMS TO HAVE LEFT HER CELL PHONE IN THE CAR.
MASAO JINBO (40) AOIYA STAFF
THIS IS HERS, RIGHT?
AH! I THANK YOU WARMLY!
YOU HAVE DONE WELL, COMMON-ER!
VERY WELL, MY LOYAL RETAINER! LET US HIE TO OUR QUARTERS AND PARTAKE OF SAKE! ♡
OH NO, I'M STILL ON DUTY...
...
ECHIGO MITSUE-MON, HE SAID...
HMM ...
...

*Mito Mitsukuni, hero of the TV drama *Mito Koumon,* uses aliases like this.

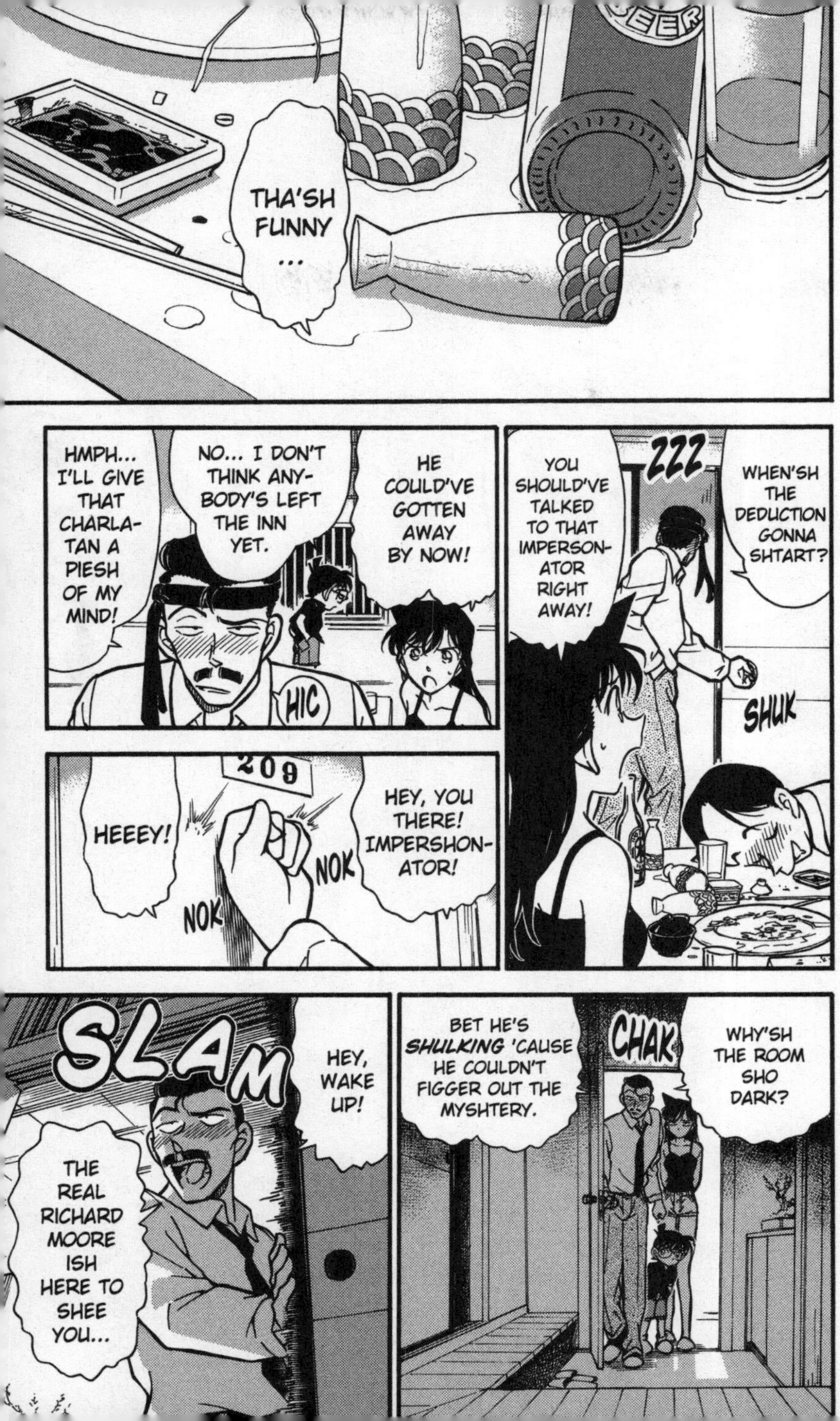
THA'SH FUNNY ...
WHEN'SH THE DEDUCTION GONNA SHTART?
ZZZ
YOU SHOULD'VE TALKED TO THAT IMPERSONATOR RIGHT AWAY!
SHUK
HE COULD'VE GOTTEN AWAY BY NOW!
NO... I DON'T THINK ANYBODY'S LEFT THE INN YET.
HMPH... I'LL GIVE THAT CHARLATAN A PIESH OF MY MIND!
HIC
209
HEY, YOU THERE! IMPERSHONATOR!
NOK
NOK
HEEEY!
WHY'SH THE ROOM SHO DARK?
CHAK
BET HE'S *SHULKING* 'CAUSE HE COULDN'T FIGGER OUT THE MYSHTERY.
SLAM
HEY, WAKE UP!
THE REAL RICHARD MOORE ISH HERE TO SHEE YOU...

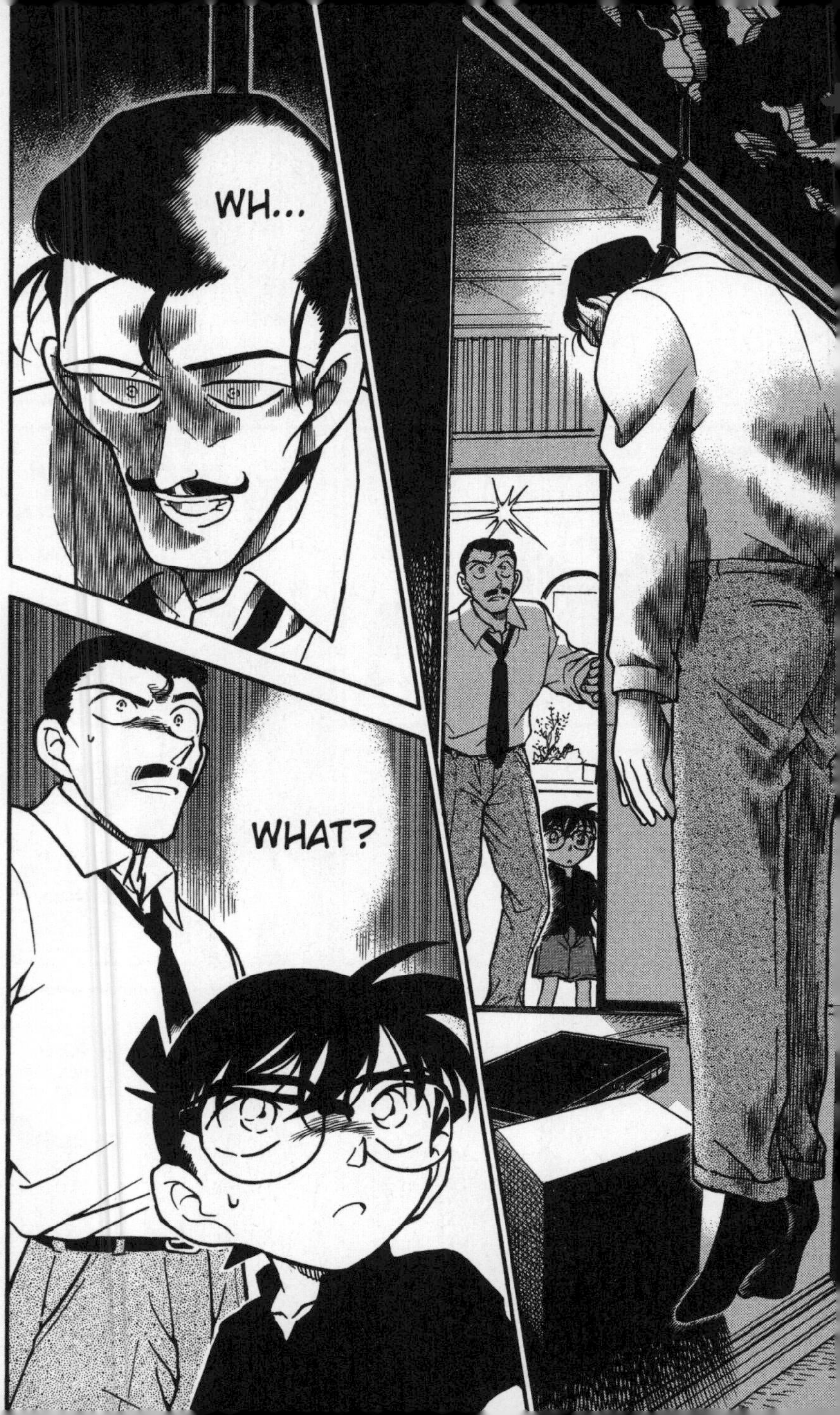
WH...
WHAT?

THE TRUTH REVEALED

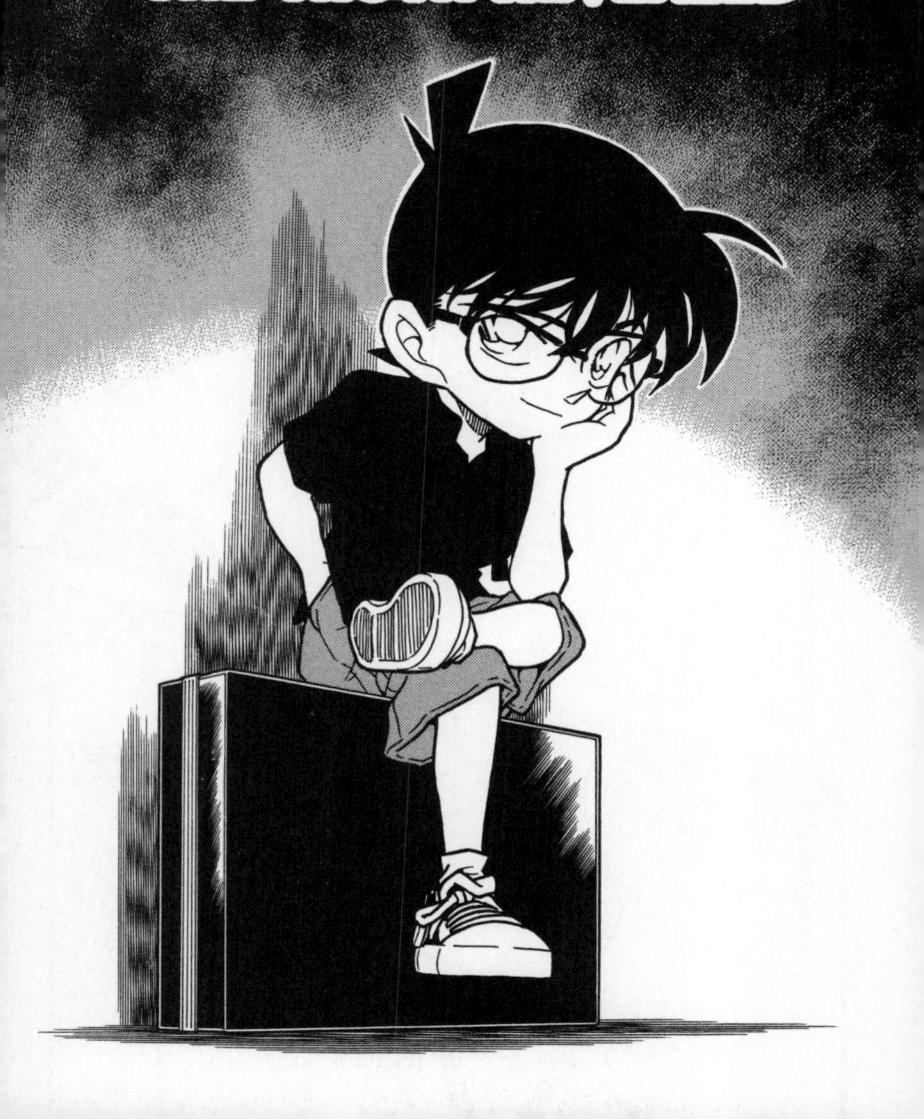

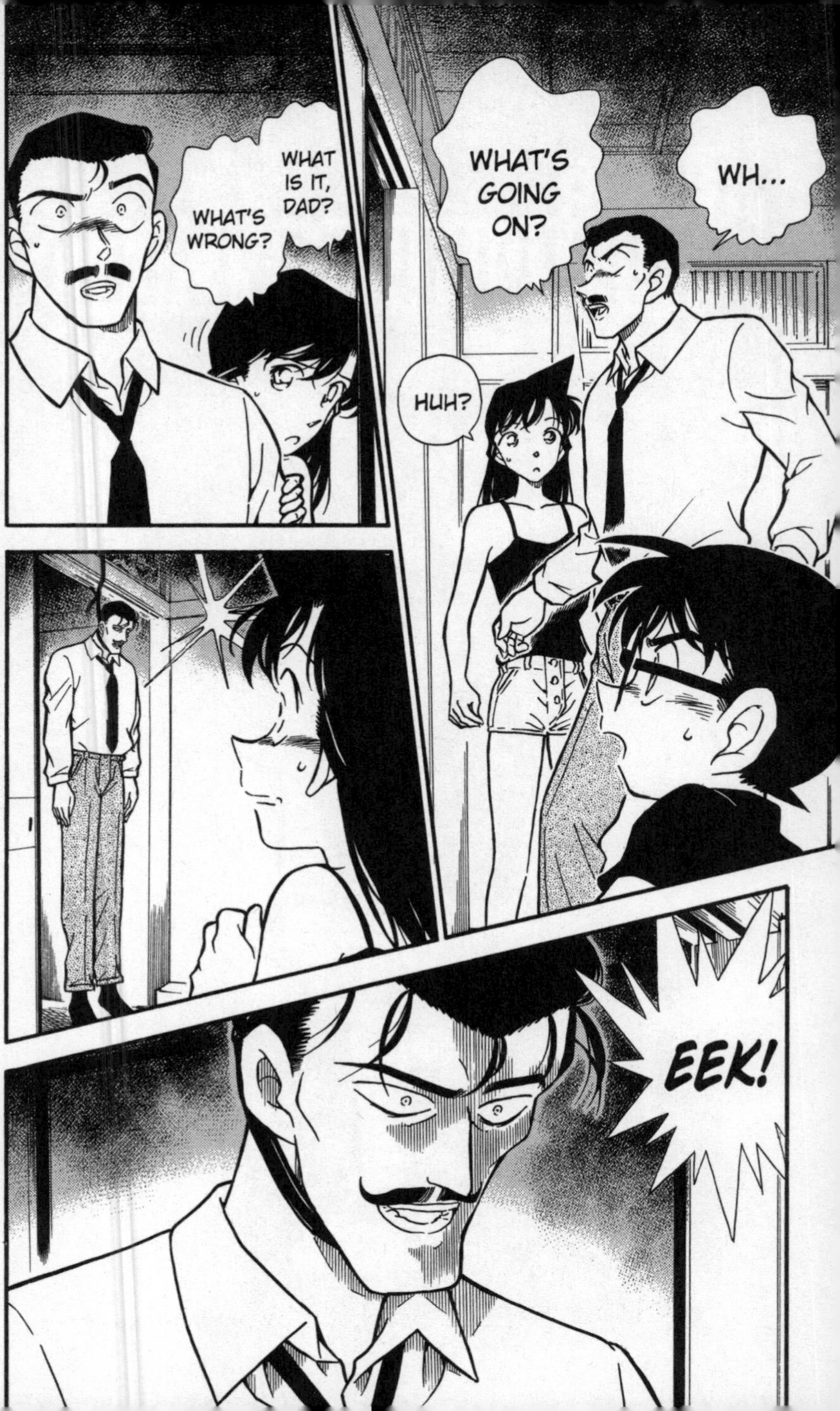
WH...
WHAT'S GOING ON?
HUH?
WHAT IS IT, DAD?
WHAT'S WRONG?
EEK!

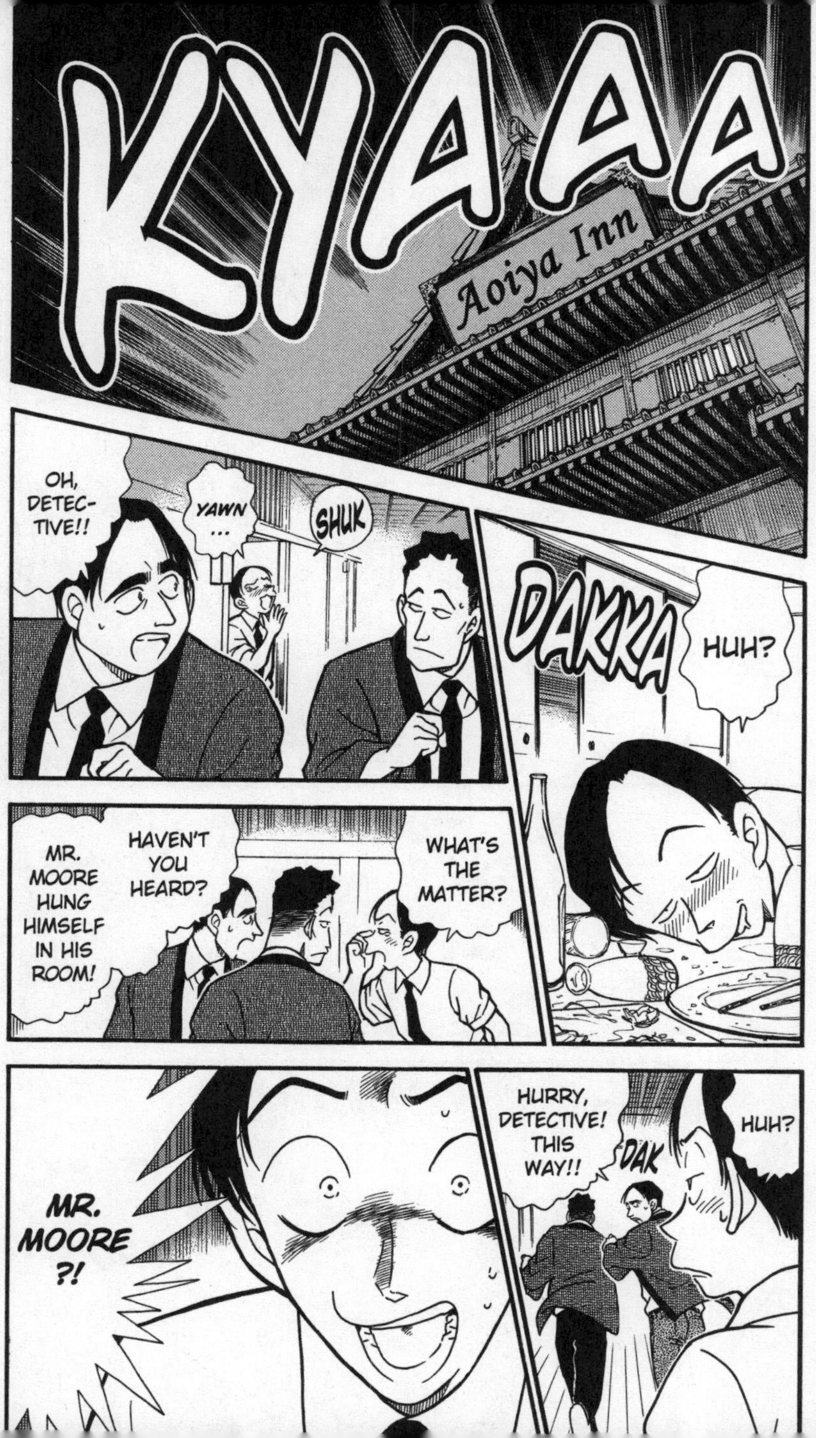
KYAAA
Aoiya Inn
DAKKA
HUH?
SHUK
YAWN ...
OH, DETECTIVE!!
WHAT'S THE MATTER?
HAVEN'T YOU HEARD?
MR. MOORE HUNG HIMSELF IN HIS ROOM!
HUH?
DAK
HURRY, DETECTIVE! THIS WAY!!
MR. MOORE ?!

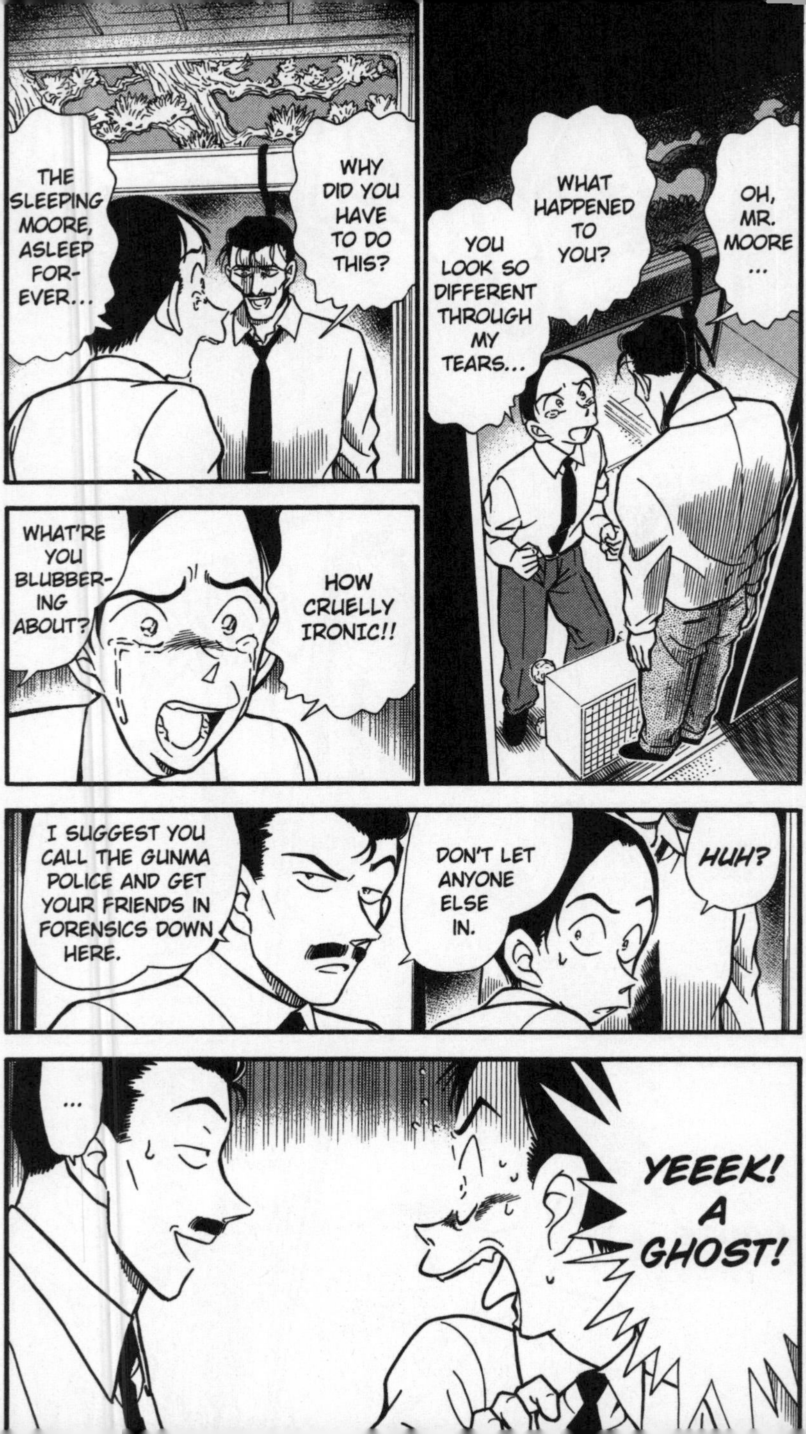
OH, MR. MOORE...
WHAT HAPPENED TO YOU?
YOU LOOK SO DIFFERENT THROUGH MY TEARS...
WHY DID YOU HAVE TO DO THIS?
THE SLEEPING MOORE, ASLEEP FOR-EVER...
HOW CRUELLY IRONIC!!
WHAT'RE YOU BLUBBER-ING ABOUT?
HUH?
DON'T LET ANYONE ELSE IN.
I SUGGEST YOU CALL THE GUNMA POLICE AND GET YOUR FRIENDS IN FORENSICS DOWN HERE.
YEEEK! A GHOST!
...

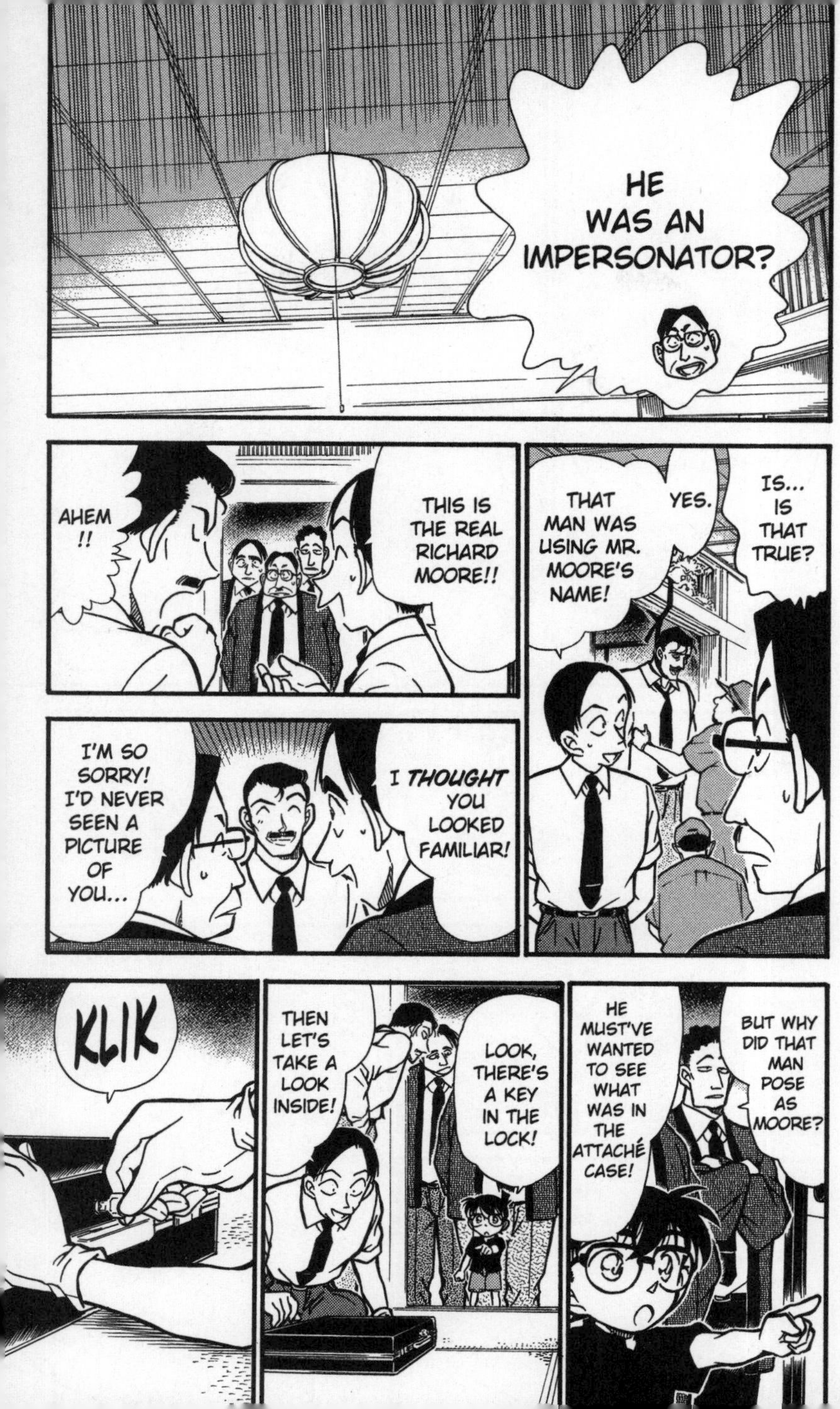
HE WAS AN IMPERSONATOR?
IS... IS THAT TRUE?
YES.
THAT MAN WAS USING MR. MOORE'S NAME!
THIS IS THE REAL RICHARD MOORE!!
AHEM !!
I *THOUGHT* YOU LOOKED FAMILIAR!
I'M SO SORRY! I'D NEVER SEEN A PICTURE OF YOU...
BUT WHY DID THAT MAN POSE AS MOORE?
HE MUST'VE WANTED TO SEE WHAT WAS IN THE ATTACHÉ CASE!
LOOK, THERE'S A KEY IN THE LOCK!
THEN LET'S TAKE A LOOK INSIDE!
KLIK

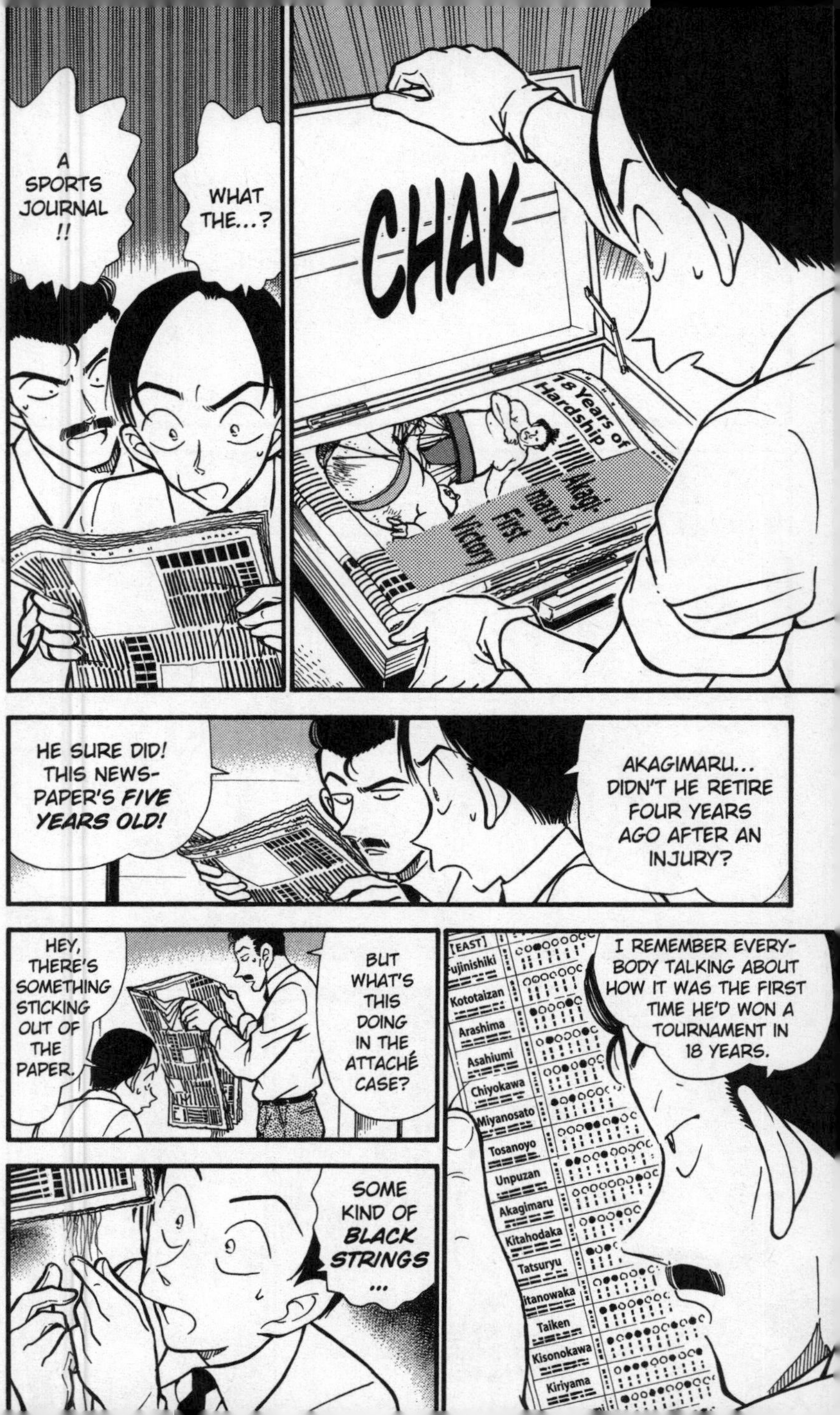
CHAK
18 Years of Hardship
Akagi-maru's First Victory
WHAT THE...?
A SPORTS JOURNAL !!
AKAGIMARU... DIDN'T HE RETIRE FOUR YEARS AGO AFTER AN INJURY?
HE SURE DID! THIS NEWS-PAPER'S *FIVE YEARS OLD!*
I REMEMBER EVERY-BODY TALKING ABOUT HOW IT WAS THE FIRST TIME HE'D WON A TOURNAMENT IN 18 YEARS.
EAST
Fujinishiki
Kototaizan
Arashima
Asahiumi
Chiyokawa
Miyanosato
Tosanoyo
Unpuzan
Akagimaru
Kitahodaka
Tatsuryu
Taiken
Kisonokawa
Kiriyama
BUT WHAT'S THIS DOING IN THE ATTACHÉ CASE?
HEY, THERE'S SOMETHING STICKING OUT OF THE PAPER.
SOME KIND OF *BLACK STRINGS* ...

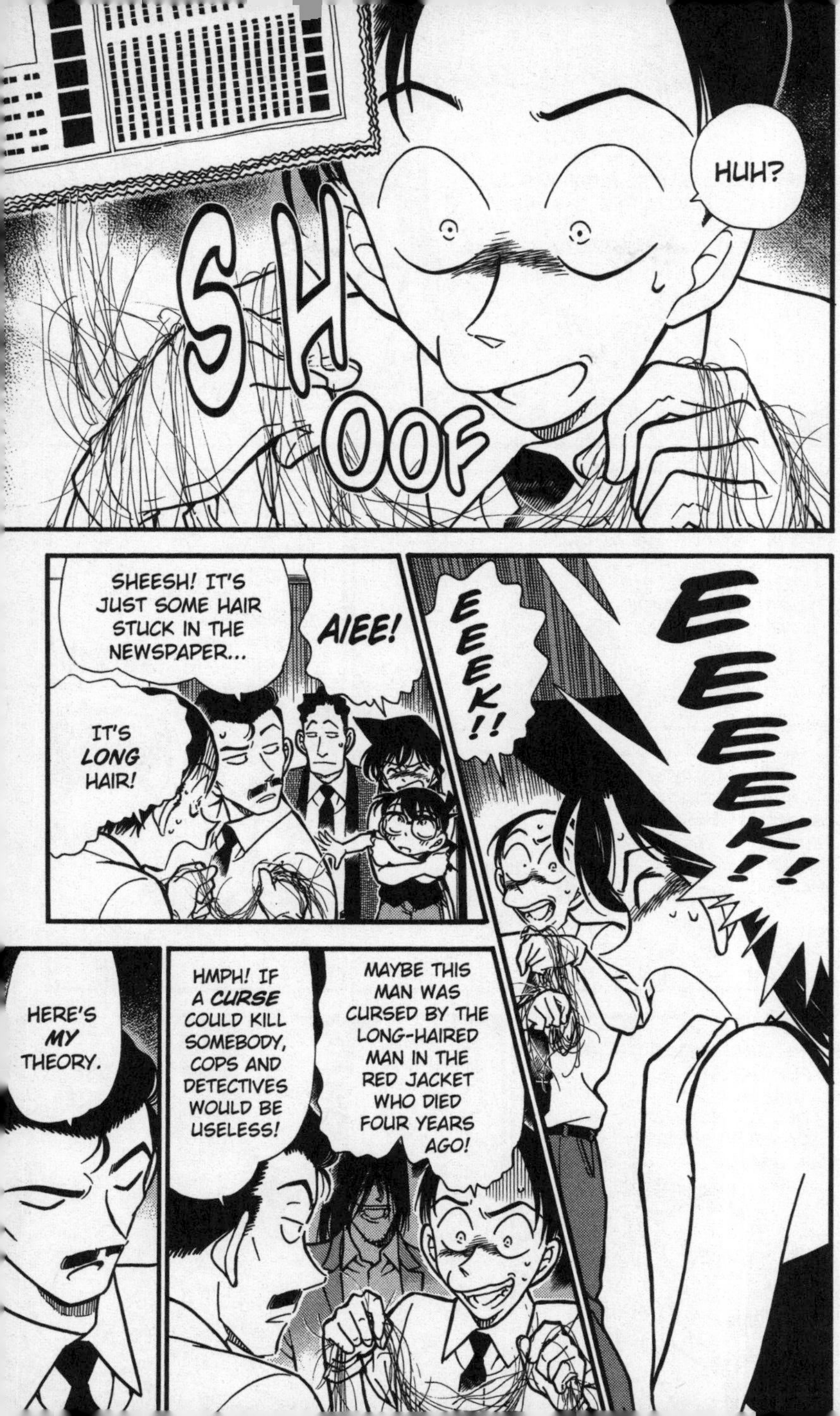
HUH?
SHOOOF
EEEEK!!
EEEEK!!
AIEE!
SHEESH! IT'S JUST SOME HAIR STUCK IN THE NEWSPAPER...
IT'S *LONG* HAIR!
MAYBE THIS MAN WAS CURSED BY THE LONG-HAIRED MAN IN THE RED JACKET WHO DIED FOUR YEARS AGO!
HMPH! IF A *CURSE* COULD KILL SOMEBODY, COPS AND DETECTIVES WOULD BE USELESS!
HERE'S *MY* THEORY.

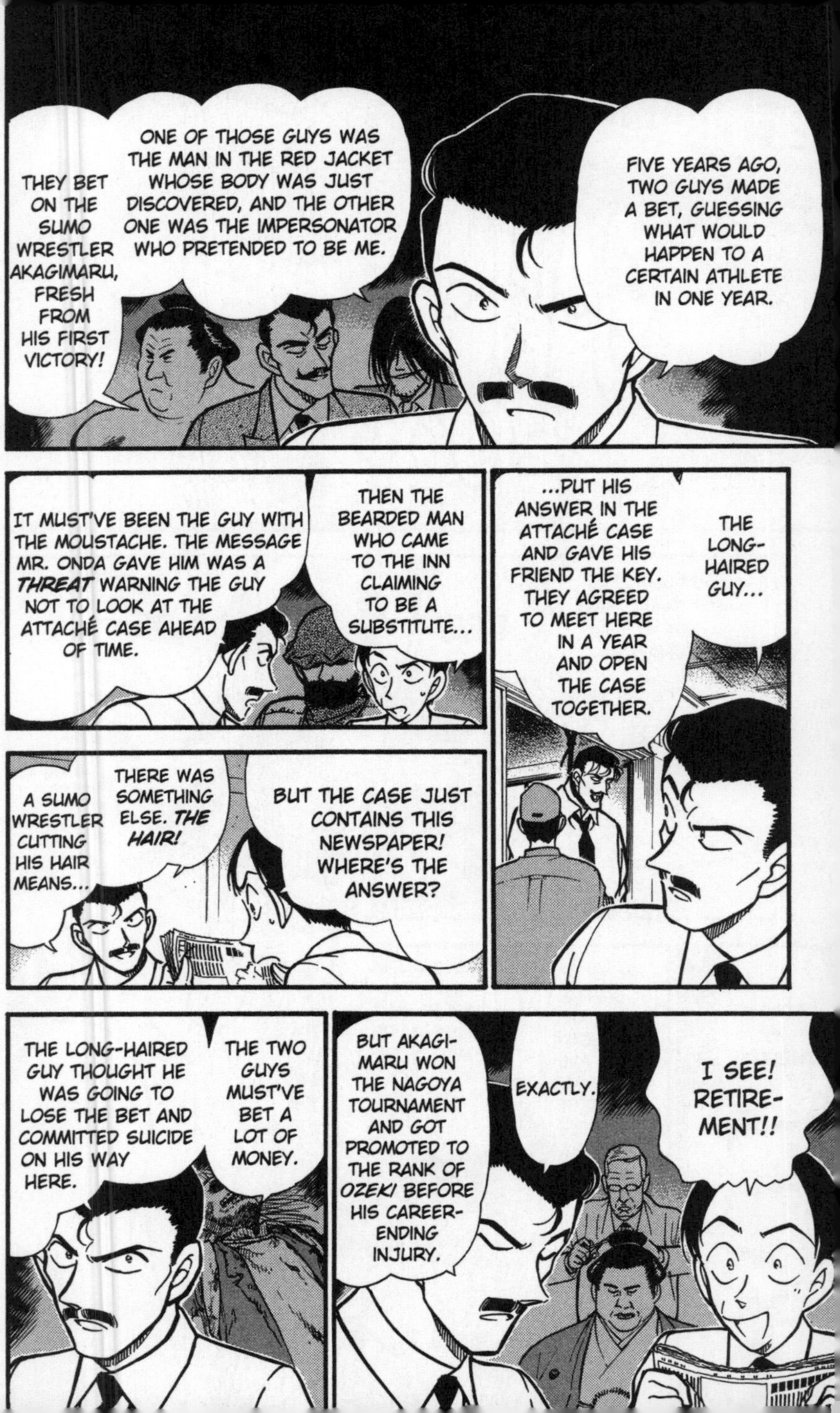
FIVE YEARS AGO, TWO GUYS MADE A BET, GUESSING WHAT WOULD HAPPEN TO A CERTAIN ATHLETE IN ONE YEAR.
ONE OF THOSE GUYS WAS THE MAN IN THE RED JACKET WHOSE BODY WAS JUST DISCOVERED, AND THE OTHER ONE WAS THE IMPERSONATOR WHO PRETENDED TO BE ME.
THEY BET ON THE SUMO WRESTLER AKAGIMARU, FRESH FROM HIS FIRST VICTORY!
THE LONG-HAIRED GUY...
...PUT HIS ANSWER IN THE ATTACHÉ CASE AND GAVE HIS FRIEND THE KEY. THEY AGREED TO MEET HERE IN A YEAR AND OPEN THE CASE TOGETHER.
THEN THE BEARDED MAN WHO CAME TO THE INN CLAIMING TO BE A SUBSTITUTE...
IT MUST'VE BEEN THE GUY WITH THE MOUSTACHE. THE MESSAGE MR. ONDA GAVE HIM WAS A *THREAT* WARNING THE GUY NOT TO LOOK AT THE ATTACHÉ CASE AHEAD OF TIME.
BUT THE CASE JUST CONTAINS THIS NEWSPAPER! WHERE'S THE ANSWER?
THERE WAS SOMETHING ELSE. *THE HAIR!*
A SUMO WRESTLER CUTTING HIS HAIR MEANS...
I SEE! RETIREMENT!!
EXACTLY.
BUT AKAGIMARU WON THE NAGOYA TOURNAMENT AND GOT PROMOTED TO THE RANK OF *OZEKI* BEFORE HIS CAREER-ENDING INJURY.
THE TWO GUYS MUST'VE BET A LOT OF MONEY.
THE LONG-HAIRED GUY THOUGHT HE WAS GOING TO LOSE THE BET AND COMMITTED SUICIDE ON HIS WAY HERE.

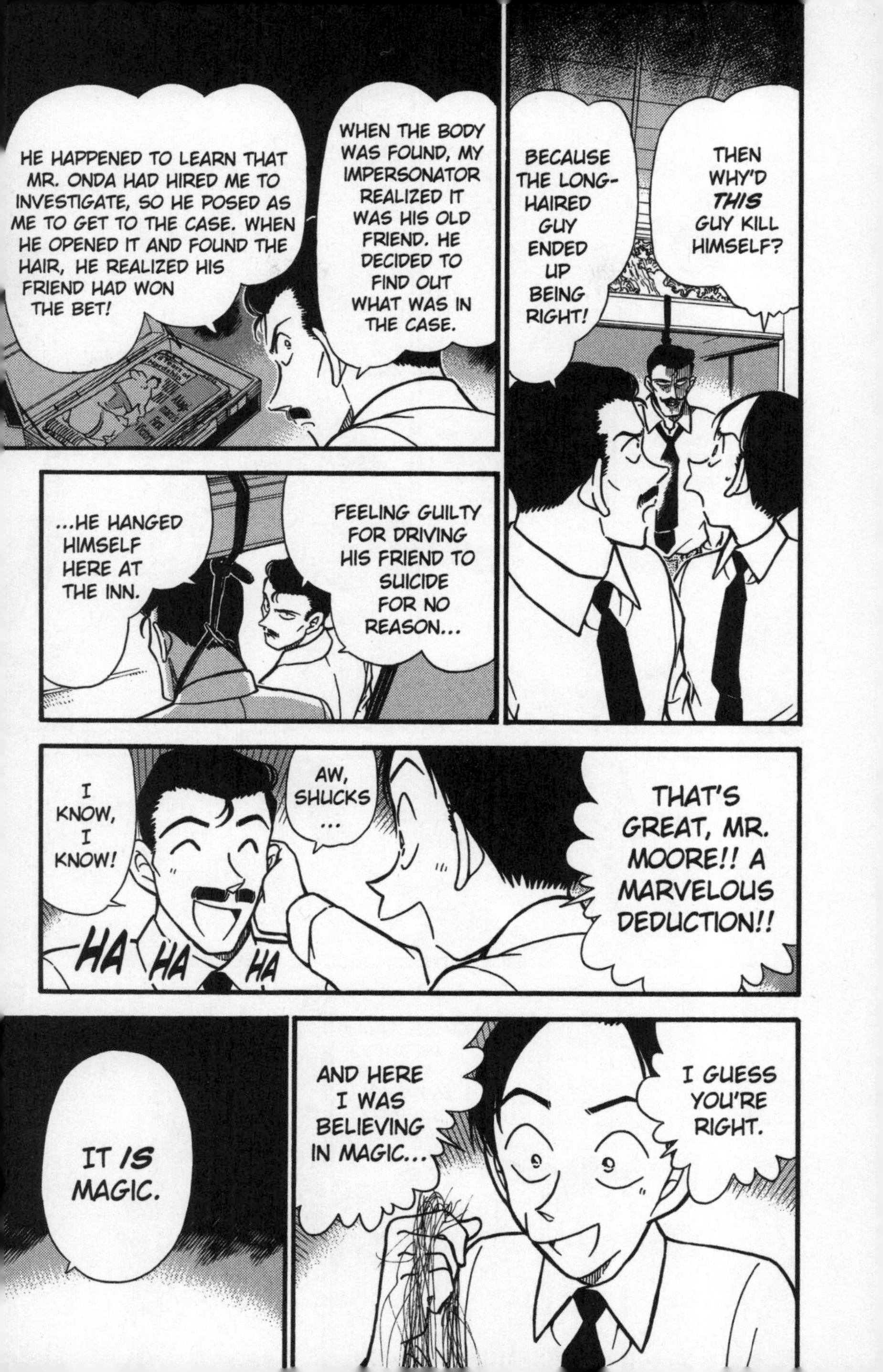
THEN WHY'D *THIS* GUY KILL HIMSELF?
BECAUSE THE LONG-HAIRED GUY ENDED UP BEING RIGHT!
WHEN THE BODY WAS FOUND, MY IMPERSONATOR REALIZED IT WAS HIS OLD FRIEND. HE DECIDED TO FIND OUT WHAT WAS IN THE CASE.
HE HAPPENED TO LEARN THAT MR. ONDA HAD HIRED ME TO INVESTIGATE, SO HE POSED AS ME TO GET TO THE CASE. WHEN HE OPENED IT AND FOUND THE HAIR, HE REALIZED HIS FRIEND HAD WON THE BET!
FEELING GUILTY FOR DRIVING HIS FRIEND TO SUICIDE FOR NO REASON...
...HE HANGED HIMSELF HERE AT THE INN.
THAT'S GREAT, MR. MOORE!! A MARVELOUS DEDUCTION!!
AW, SHUCKS ...
I KNOW, I KNOW!
HA HA HA
I GUESS YOU'RE RIGHT.
AND HERE I WAS BELIEVING IN MAGIC...
IT *IS* MAGIC.

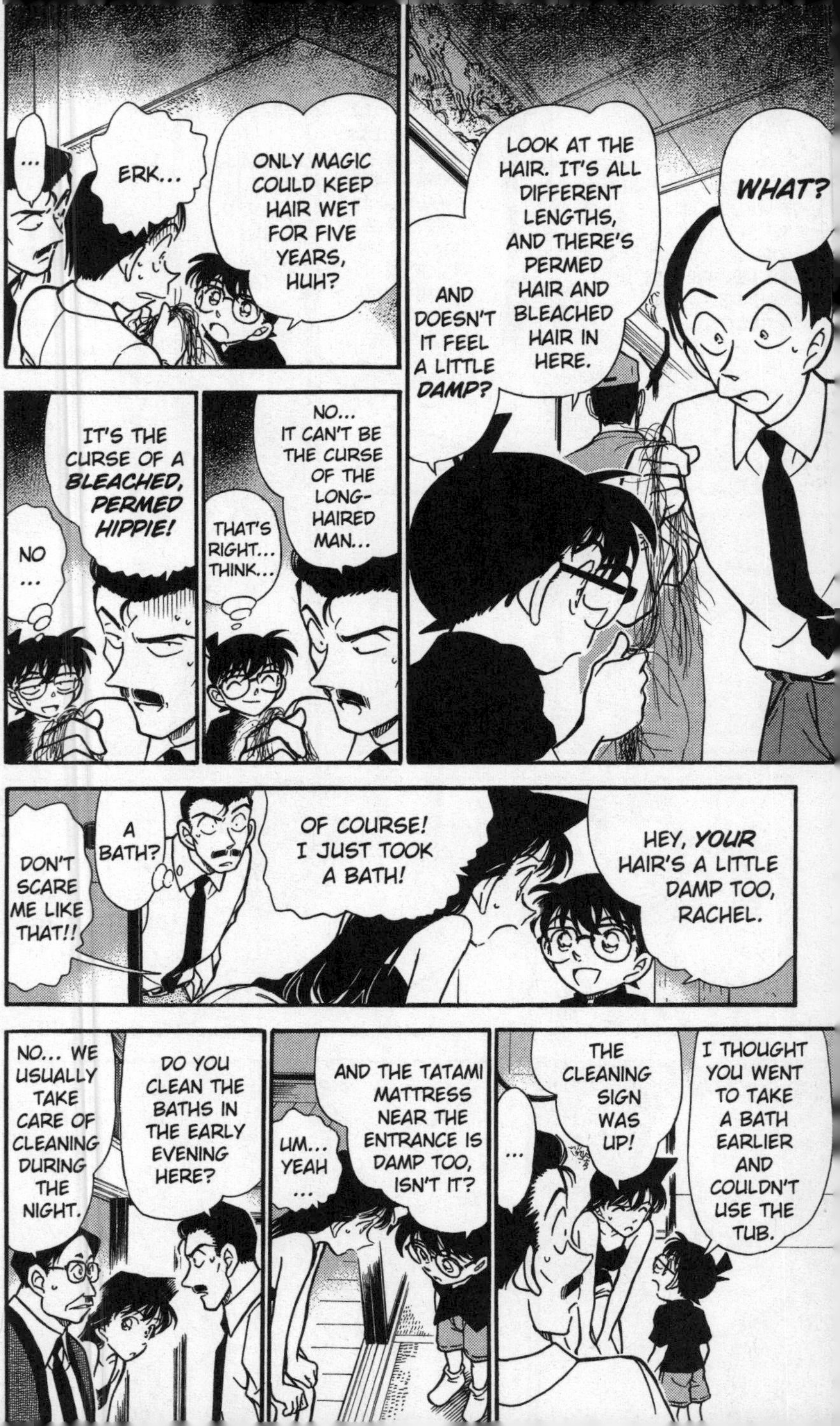
WHAT?
LOOK AT THE HAIR. IT'S ALL DIFFERENT LENGTHS, AND THERE'S PERMED HAIR AND BLEACHED HAIR IN HERE.
AND DOESN'T IT FEEL A LITTLE DAMP?
ONLY MAGIC COULD KEEP HAIR WET FOR FIVE YEARS, HUH?
ERK...
...
NO... IT CAN'T BE THE CURSE OF THE LONG-HAIRED MAN...
THAT'S RIGHT... THINK...
IT'S THE CURSE OF A BLEACHED, PERMED HIPPIE!
NO ...
HEY, YOUR HAIR'S A LITTLE DAMP TOO, RACHEL.
OF COURSE! I JUST TOOK A BATH!
A BATH?
DON'T SCARE ME LIKE THAT!!
I THOUGHT YOU WENT TO TAKE A BATH EARLIER AND COULDN'T USE THE TUB.
THE CLEANING SIGN WAS UP!
...
AND THE TATAMI MATTRESS NEAR THE ENTRANCE IS DAMP TOO, ISN'T IT?
UM... YEAH ...
DO YOU CLEAN THE BATHS IN THE EARLY EVENING HERE?
NO... WE USUALLY TAKE CARE OF CLEANING DURING THE NIGHT.

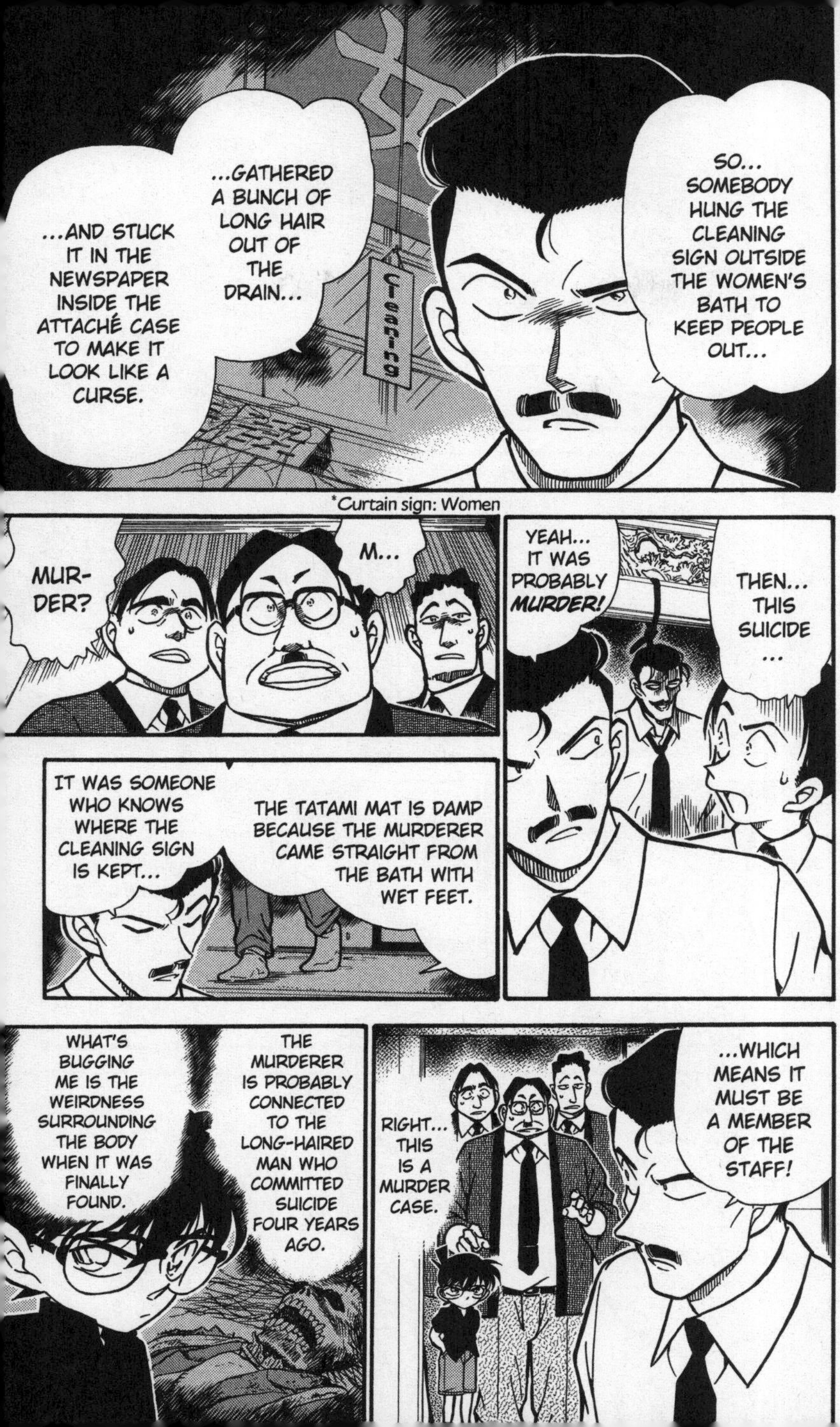
SO... SOMEBODY HUNG THE CLEANING SIGN OUTSIDE THE WOMEN'S BATH TO KEEP PEOPLE OUT...
...GATHERED A BUNCH OF LONG HAIR OUT OF THE DRAIN...
Cleaning
...AND STUCK IT IN THE NEWSPAPER INSIDE THE ATTACHÉ CASE TO MAKE IT LOOK LIKE A CURSE.
THEN... THIS SUICIDE ...
YEAH... IT WAS PROBABLY *MURDER!*
M...
MUR-DER?
THE TATAMI MAT IS DAMP BECAUSE THE MURDERER CAME STRAIGHT FROM THE BATH WITH WET FEET.
IT WAS SOMEONE WHO KNOWS WHERE THE CLEANING SIGN IS KEPT...
...WHICH MEANS IT MUST BE A MEMBER OF THE STAFF!
RIGHT... THIS IS A MURDER CASE.
THE MURDERER IS PROBABLY CONNECTED TO THE LONG-HAIRED MAN WHO COMMITTED SUICIDE FOUR YEARS AGO.
WHAT'S BUGGING ME IS THE WEIRDNESS SURROUNDING THE BODY WHEN IT WAS FINALLY FOUND.
*Curtain sign: Women

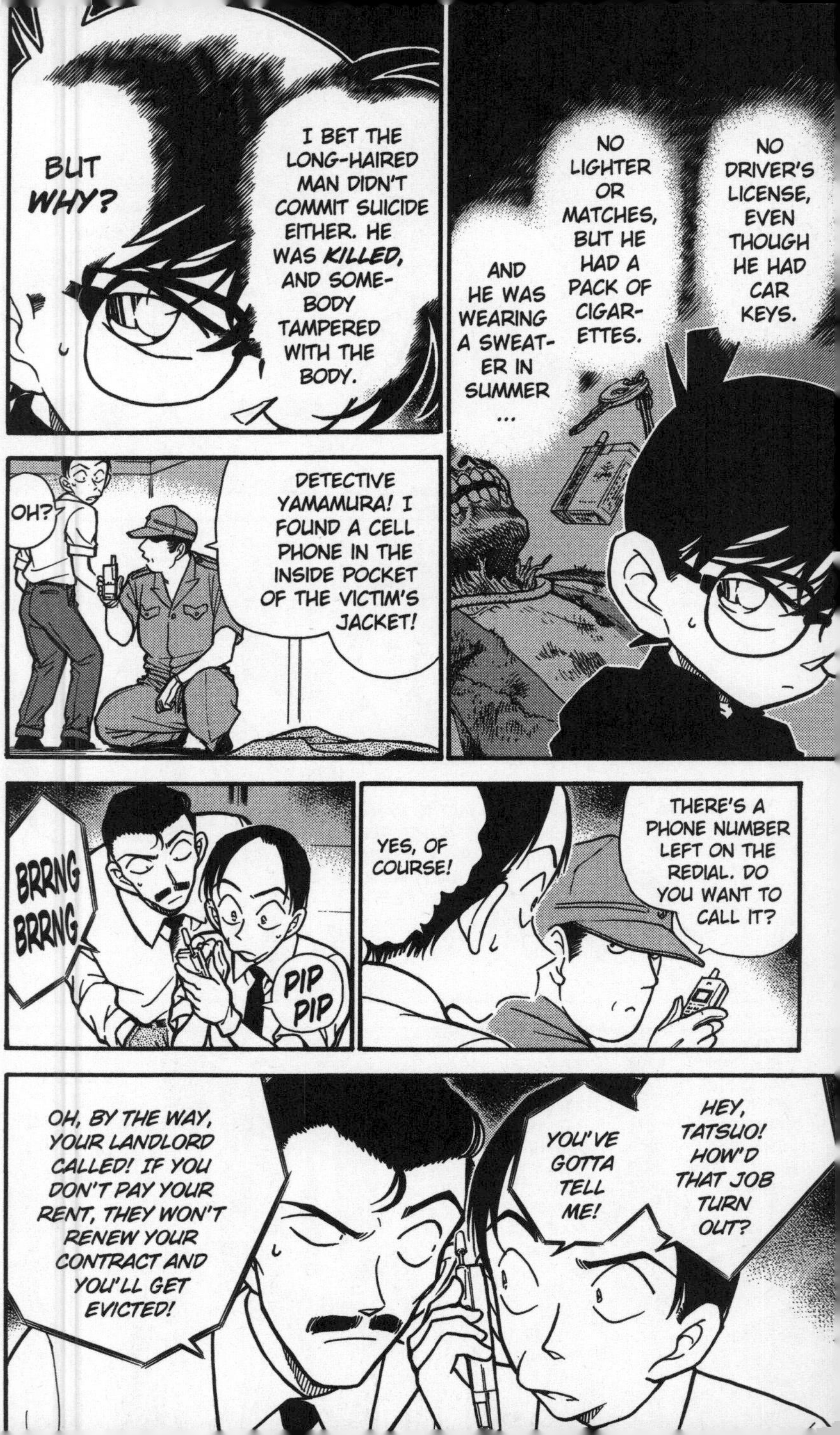
NO DRIVER'S LICENSE, EVEN THOUGH HE HAD CAR KEYS.
NO LIGHTER OR MATCHES, BUT HE HAD A PACK OF CIGARETTES.
AND HE WAS WEARING A SWEATER IN SUMMER ...
I BET THE LONG-HAIRED MAN DIDN'T COMMIT SUICIDE EITHER. HE WAS *KILLED,* AND SOMEBODY TAMPERED WITH THE BODY.
BUT *WHY?*
DETECTIVE YAMAMURA! I FOUND A CELL PHONE IN THE INSIDE POCKET OF THE VICTIM'S JACKET!
OH?
THERE'S A PHONE NUMBER LEFT ON THE REDIAL. DO YOU WANT TO CALL IT?
YES, OF COURSE!
PIP PIP
BRRNG BRRNG
HEY, TATSUO! HOW'D THAT JOB TURN OUT?
YOU'VE GOTTA TELL ME!
OH, BY THE WAY, YOUR LANDLORD CALLED! IF YOU DON'T PAY YOUR RENT, THEY WON'T RENEW YOUR CONTRACT AND YOU'LL GET EVICTED!

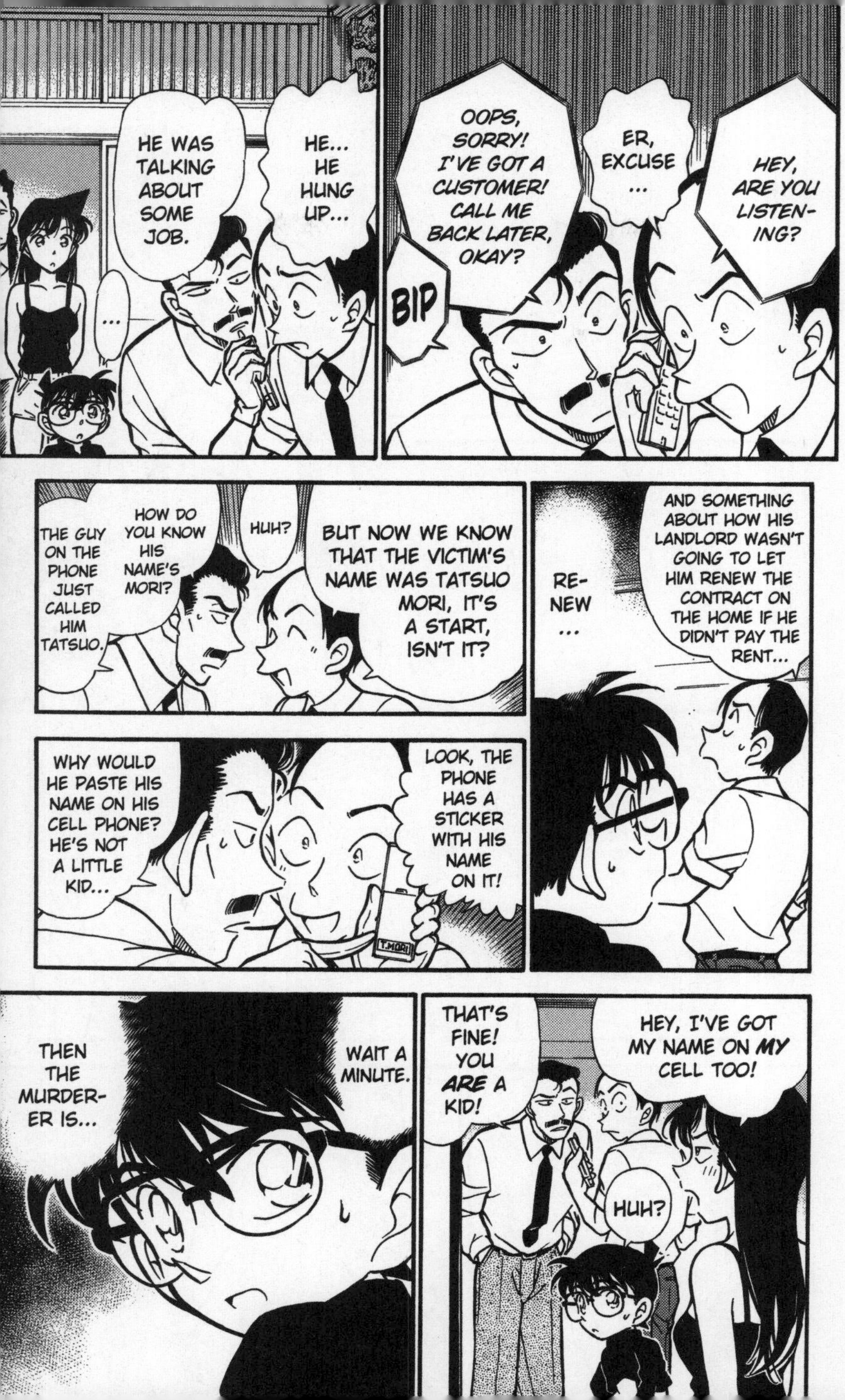
HEY, ARE YOU LISTEN-ING?
ER, EXCUSE ...
OOPS, SORRY! I'VE GOT A CUSTOMER! CALL ME BACK LATER, OKAY?
BIP
HE... HE HUNG UP...
HE WAS TALKING ABOUT SOME JOB.
...
AND SOMETHING ABOUT HOW HIS LANDLORD WASN'T GOING TO LET HIM RENEW THE CONTRACT ON THE HOME IF HE DIDN'T PAY THE RENT...
RE-NEW ...
BUT NOW WE KNOW THAT THE VICTIM'S NAME WAS TATSUO MORI, IT'S A START, ISN'T IT?
HUH?
HOW DO YOU KNOW HIS NAME'S MORI?
THE GUY ON THE PHONE JUST CALLED HIM TATSUO.
LOOK, THE PHONE HAS A STICKER WITH HIS NAME ON IT!
T.MORI
WHY WOULD HE PASTE HIS NAME ON HIS CELL PHONE? HE'S NOT A LITTLE KID...
HEY, I'VE GOT MY NAME ON *MY* CELL TOO!
THAT'S FINE! YOU ***ARE*** A KID!
HUH?
WAIT A MINUTE.
THEN THE MURDER-ER IS...

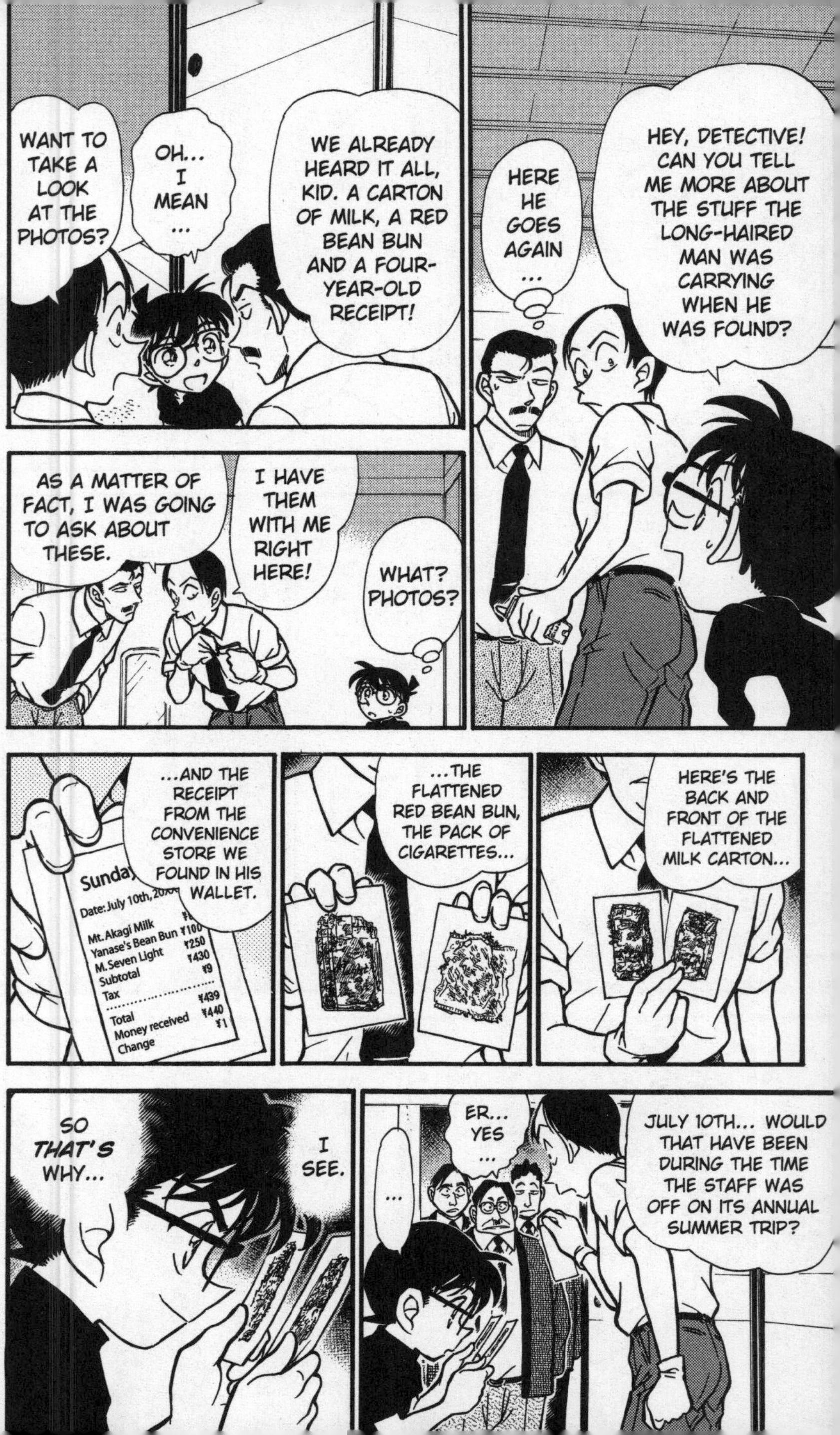

HEY, DETECTIVE! CAN YOU TELL ME MORE ABOUT THE STUFF THE LONG-HAIRED MAN WAS CARRYING WHEN HE WAS FOUND?
HERE HE GOES AGAIN...
WE ALREADY HEARD IT ALL, KID. A CARTON OF MILK, A RED BEAN BUN AND A FOUR-YEAR-OLD RECEIPT!
OH... I MEAN...
WANT TO TAKE A LOOK AT THE PHOTOS?
I HAVE THEM WITH ME RIGHT HERE!
WHAT? PHOTOS?
AS A MATTER OF FACT, I WAS GOING TO ASK ABOUT THESE.
HERE'S THE BACK AND FRONT OF THE FLATTENED MILK CARTON...
...THE FLATTENED RED BEAN BUN, THE PACK OF CIGARETTES...
...AND THE RECEIPT FROM THE CONVENIENCE STORE WE FOUND IN HIS WALLET.
Sunday
Date: July 10th, 20XX
Mt. Akagi Milk
Yanase's Bean Bun ¥100
M. Seven Light ¥250
Subtotal ¥430
Tax ¥9
Total ¥439
Money received ¥440
Change ¥1
JULY 10TH... WOULD THAT HAVE BEEN DURING THE TIME THE STAFF WAS OFF ON ITS ANNUAL SUMMER TRIP?
ER... YES...
...
I SEE.
SO *THAT'S* WHY...

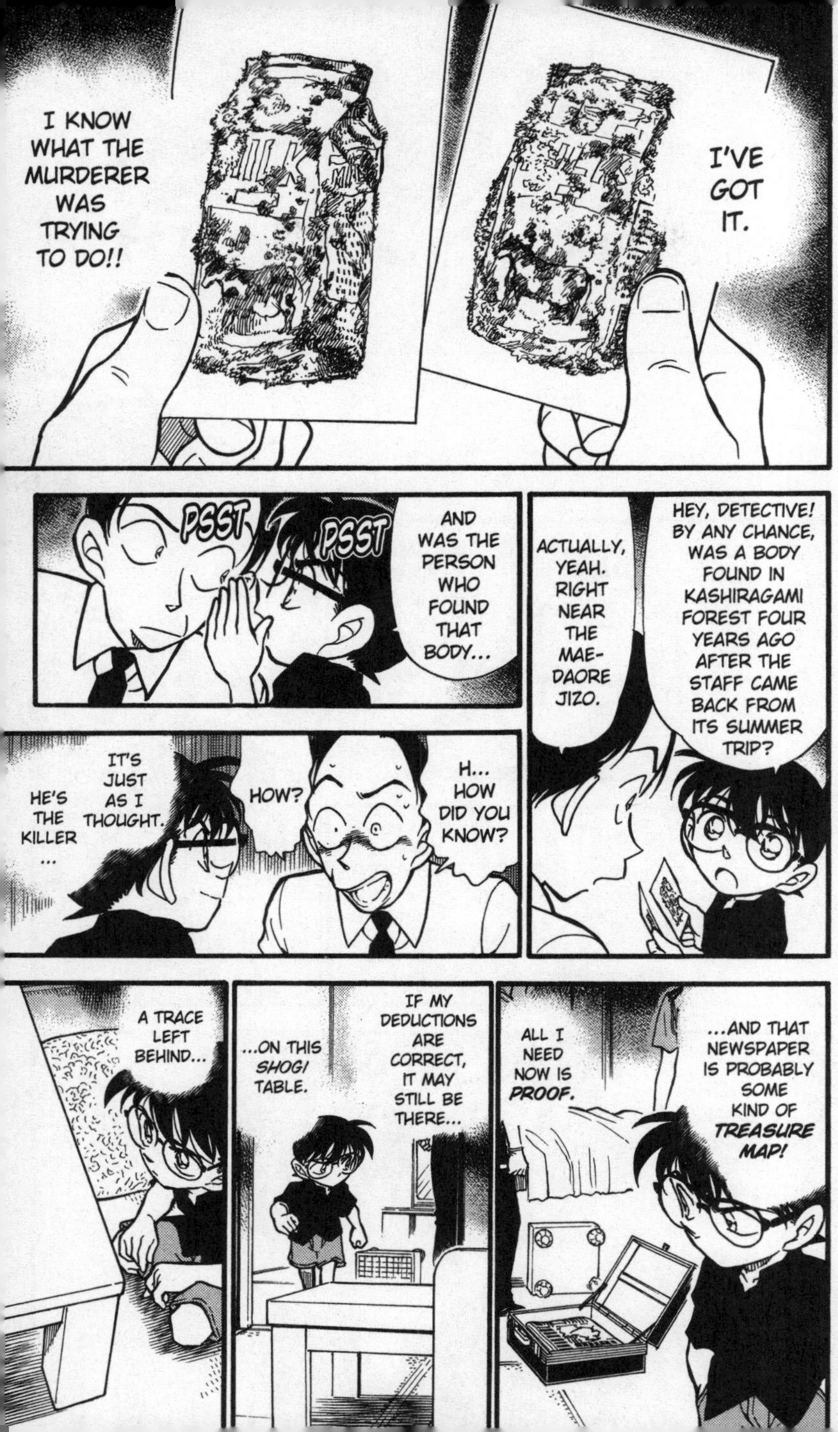
I'VE GOT IT.
I KNOW WHAT THE MURDERER WAS TRYING TO DO!!
HEY, DETECTIVE! BY ANY CHANCE, WAS A BODY FOUND IN KASHIRAGAMI FOREST FOUR YEARS AGO AFTER THE STAFF CAME BACK FROM ITS SUMMER TRIP?
ACTUALLY, YEAH. RIGHT NEAR THE MAE-DAORE JIZO.
AND WAS THE PERSON WHO FOUND THAT BODY...
PSST
PSST
H... HOW DID YOU KNOW?
HOW?
IT'S JUST AS I THOUGHT.
HE'S THE KILLER...
...AND THAT NEWSPAPER IS PROBABLY SOME KIND OF *TREASURE MAP!*
ALL I NEED NOW IS *PROOF.*
IF MY DEDUCTIONS ARE CORRECT, IT MAY STILL BE THERE...
...ON THIS *SHOGI* TABLE.
A TRACE LEFT BEHIND...

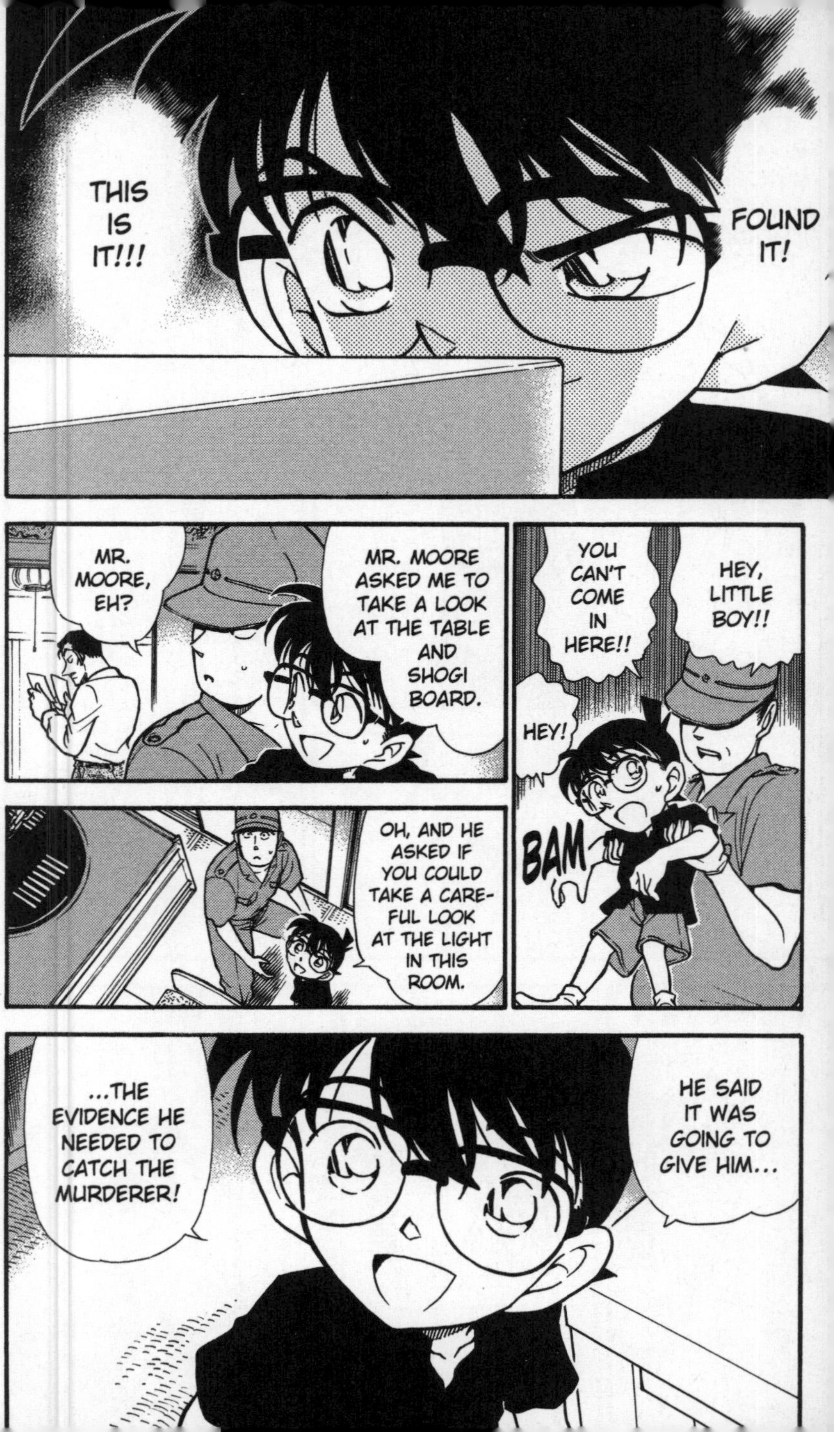
FOUND IT!
THIS IS IT!!!
HEY, LITTLE BOY!!
YOU CAN'T COME IN HERE!!
HEY!
BAM
MR. MOORE ASKED ME TO TAKE A LOOK AT THE TABLE AND SHOGI BOARD.
MR. MOORE, EH?
OH, AND HE ASKED IF YOU COULD TAKE A CARE-FUL LOOK AT THE LIGHT IN THIS ROOM.
HE SAID IT WAS GOING TO GIVE HIM...
...THE EVIDENCE HE NEEDED TO CATCH THE MURDERER!

A TIME OF DECEIT

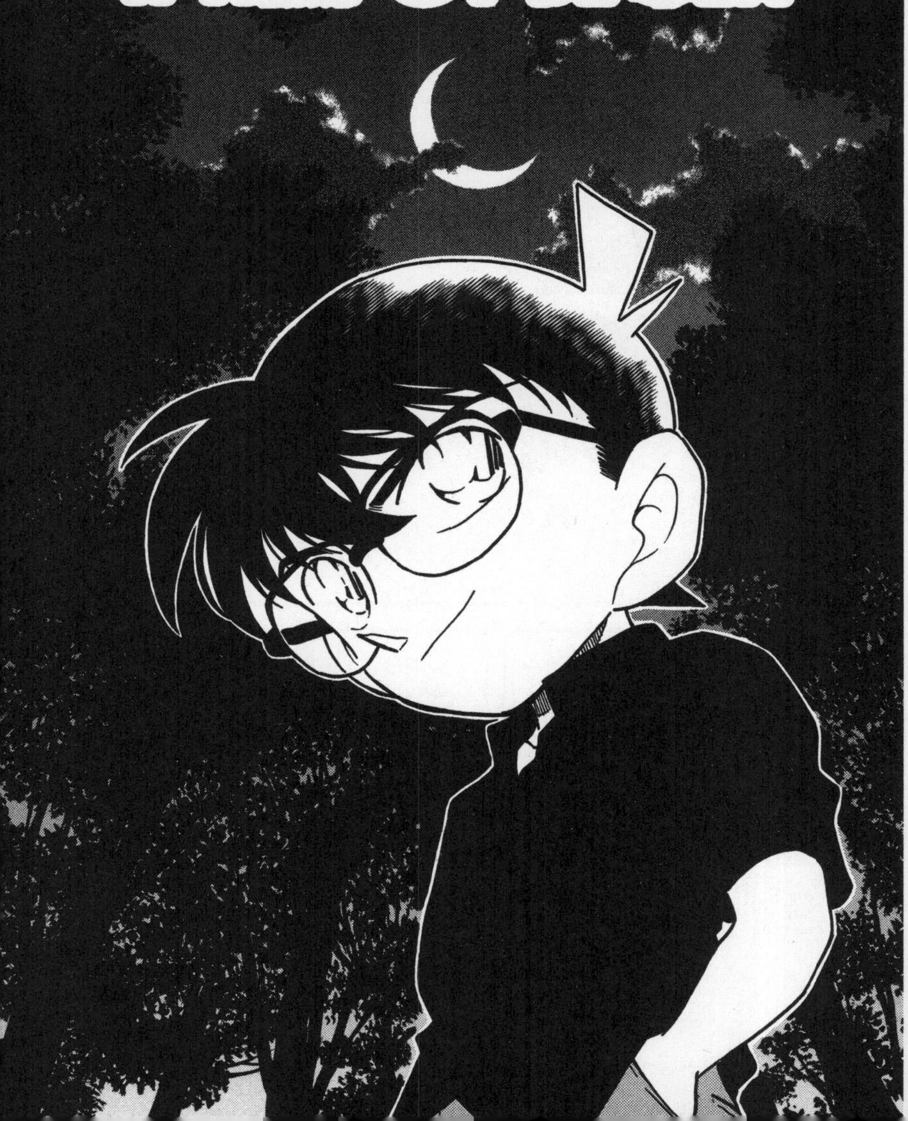

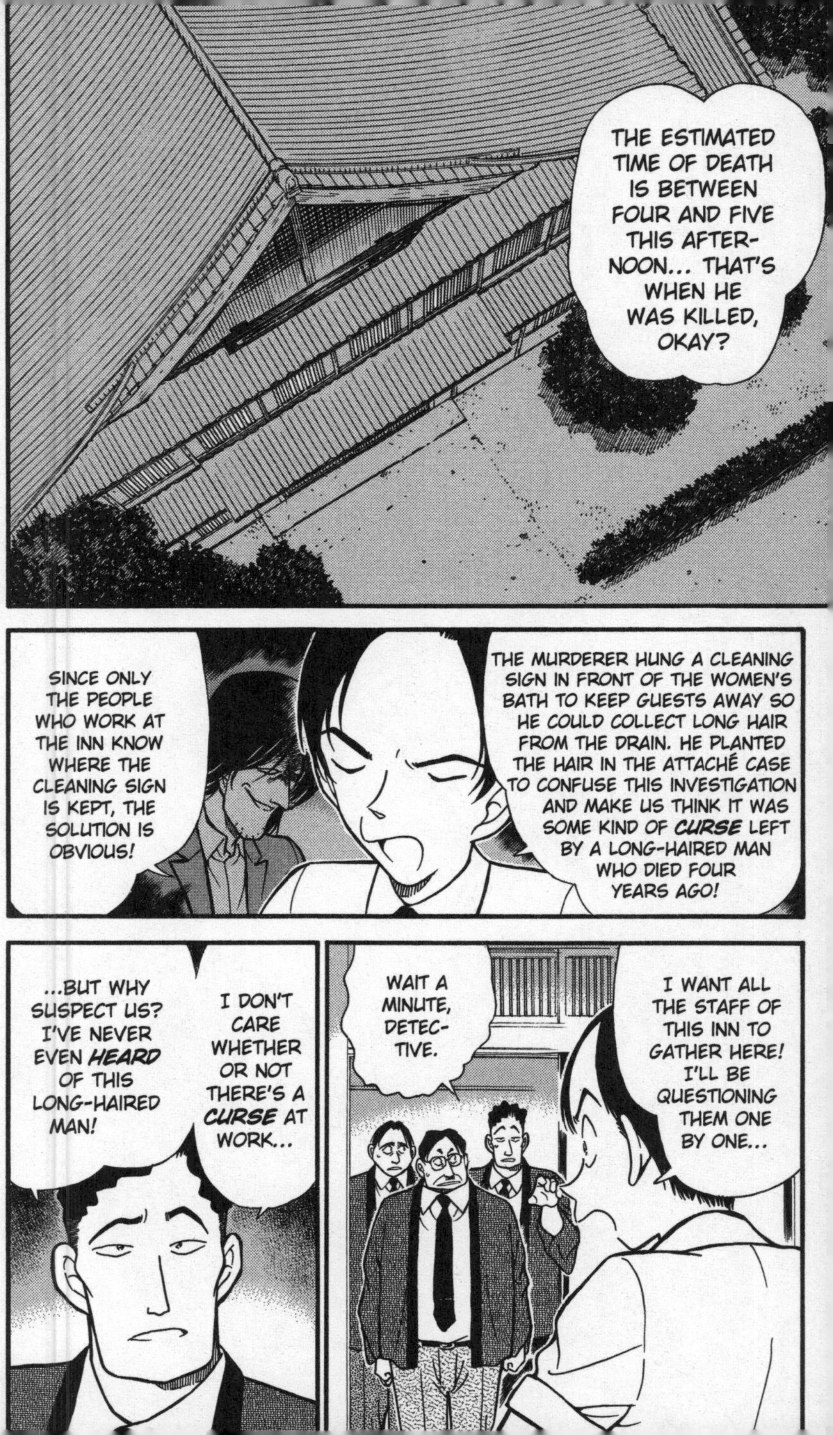
THE ESTIMATED TIME OF DEATH IS BETWEEN FOUR AND FIVE THIS AFTER-NOON... THAT'S WHEN HE WAS KILLED, OKAY?
THE MURDERER HUNG A CLEANING SIGN IN FRONT OF THE WOMEN'S BATH TO KEEP GUESTS AWAY SO HE COULD COLLECT LONG HAIR FROM THE DRAIN. HE PLANTED THE HAIR IN THE ATTACHÉ CASE TO CONFUSE THIS INVESTIGATION AND MAKE US THINK IT WAS SOME KIND OF CURSE LEFT BY A LONG-HAIRED MAN WHO DIED FOUR YEARS AGO!
SINCE ONLY THE PEOPLE WHO WORK AT THE INN KNOW WHERE THE CLEANING SIGN IS KEPT, THE SOLUTION IS OBVIOUS!
I WANT ALL THE STAFF OF THIS INN TO GATHER HERE! I'LL BE QUESTIONING THEM ONE BY ONE...
WAIT A MINUTE, DETEC-TIVE.
I DON'T CARE WHETHER OR NOT THERE'S A CURSE AT WORK...
...BUT WHY SUSPECT US? I'VE NEVER EVEN HEARD OF THIS LONG-HAIRED MAN!

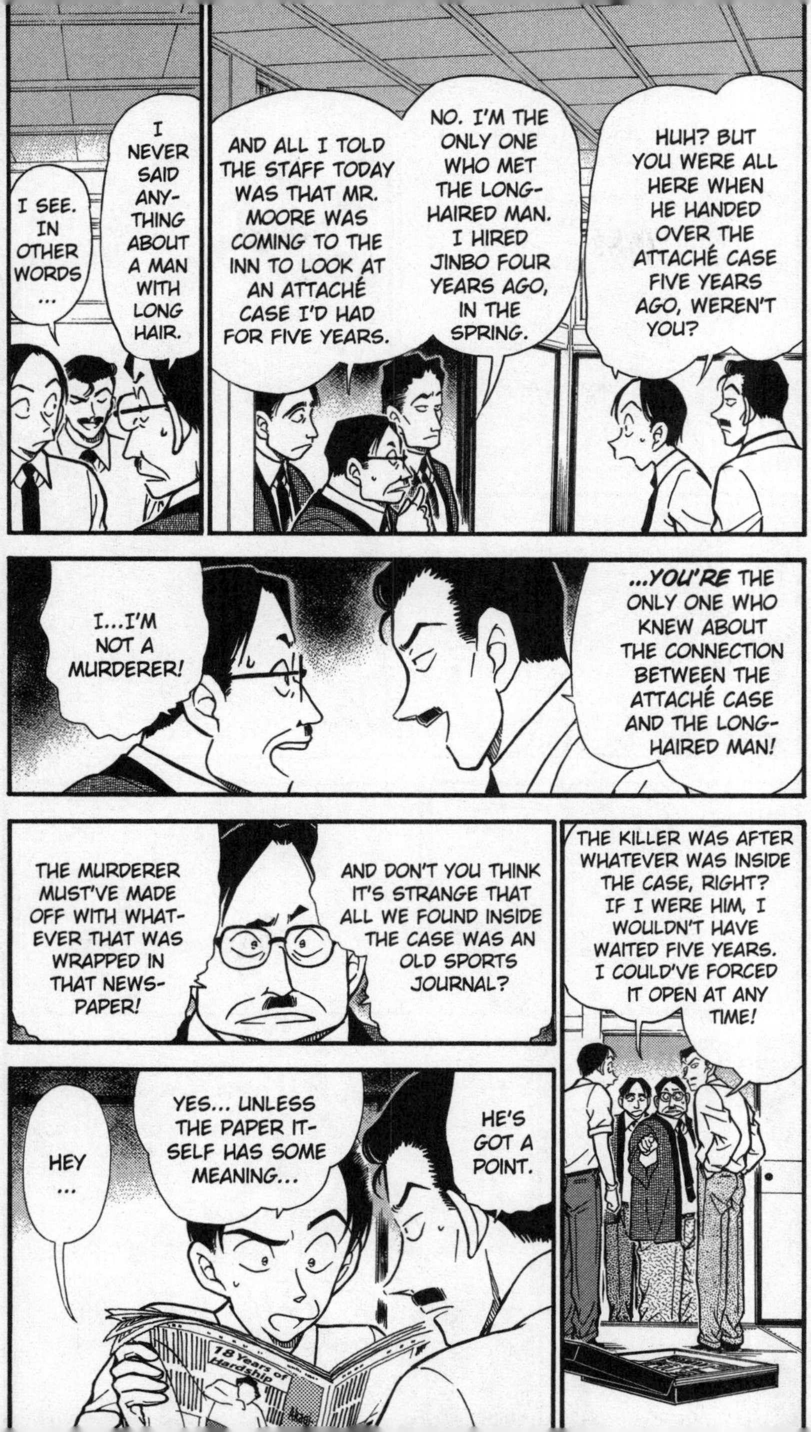
HUH? BUT YOU WERE ALL HERE WHEN HE HANDED OVER THE ATTACHÉ CASE FIVE YEARS AGO, WEREN'T YOU?
NO. I'M THE ONLY ONE WHO MET THE LONG-HAIRED MAN. I HIRED JINBO FOUR YEARS AGO, IN THE SPRING.
AND ALL I TOLD THE STAFF TODAY WAS THAT MR. MOORE WAS COMING TO THE INN TO LOOK AT AN ATTACHÉ CASE I'D HAD FOR FIVE YEARS.
I NEVER SAID ANY-THING ABOUT A MAN WITH LONG HAIR.
I SEE. IN OTHER WORDS ...
...YOU'RE THE ONLY ONE WHO KNEW ABOUT THE CONNECTION BETWEEN THE ATTACHÉ CASE AND THE LONG-HAIRED MAN!
I...I'M NOT A MURDERER!
THE KILLER WAS AFTER WHATEVER WAS INSIDE THE CASE, RIGHT? IF I WERE HIM, I WOULDN'T HAVE WAITED FIVE YEARS. I COULD'VE FORCED IT OPEN AT ANY TIME!
AND DON'T YOU THINK IT'S STRANGE THAT ALL WE FOUND INSIDE THE CASE WAS AN OLD SPORTS JOURNAL?
THE MURDERER MUST'VE MADE OFF WITH WHAT-EVER THAT WAS WRAPPED IN THAT NEWS-PAPER!
HE'S GOT A POINT.
YES... UNLESS THE PAPER IT-SELF HAS SOME MEANING...
HEY ...
18 Years of Hardship

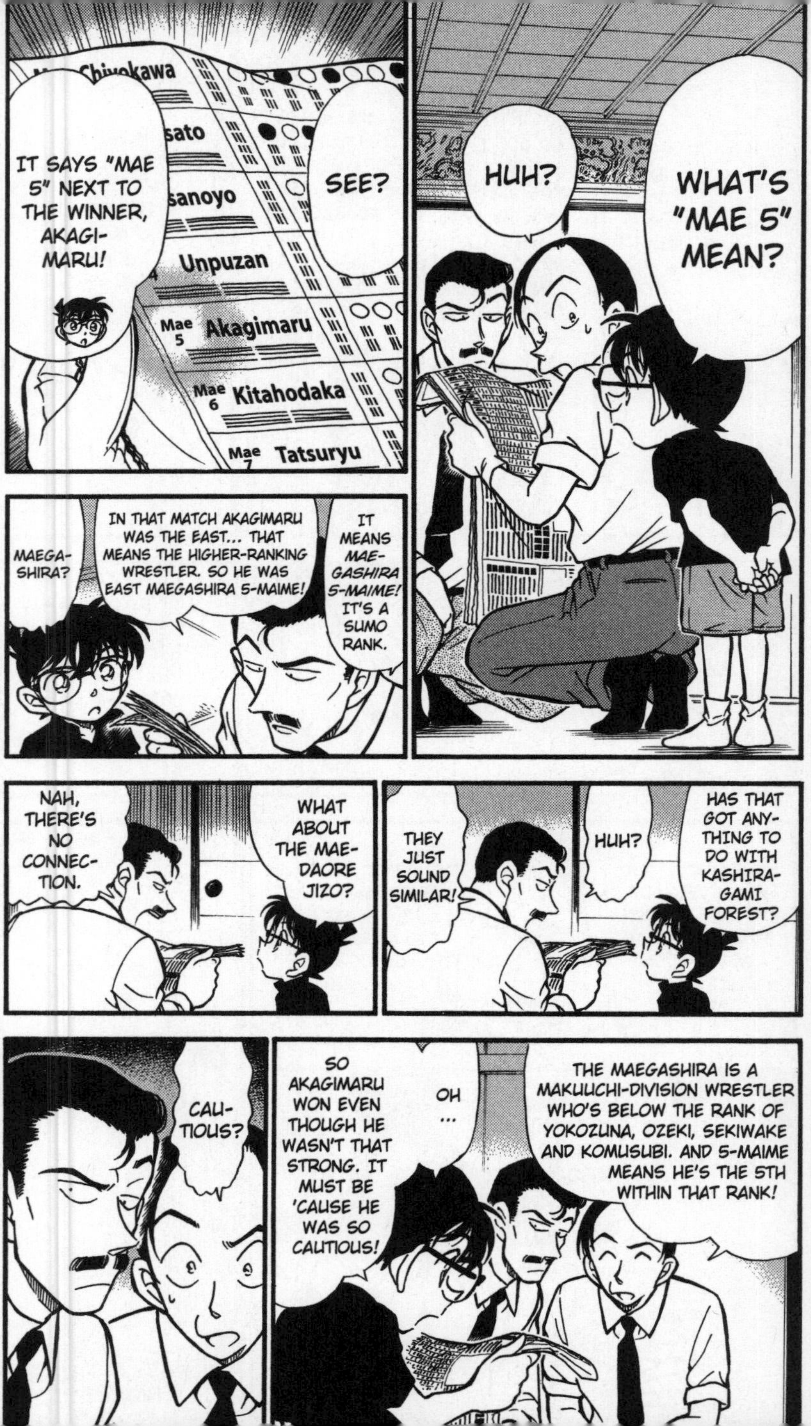
WHAT'S "MAE 5" MEAN?
HUH?
SEE?
IT SAYS "MAE 5" NEXT TO THE WINNER, AKAGIMARU!
Chiyokawa
sato
sanoyo
Unpuzan
Mae 5 Akagimaru
Mae 6 Kitahodaka
Mae 7 Tatsuryu
IT MEANS *MAEGASHIRA 5-MAIME!* IT'S A SUMO RANK.
IN THAT MATCH AKAGIMARU WAS THE EAST... THAT MEANS THE HIGHER-RANKING WRESTLER. SO HE WAS EAST MAEGASHIRA 5-MAIME!
MAEGASHIRA?
HAS THAT GOT ANYTHING TO DO WITH KASHIRAGAMI FOREST?
HUH?
THEY JUST SOUND SIMILAR!
WHAT ABOUT THE MAEDAORE JIZO?
NAH, THERE'S NO CONNECTION.
THE MAEGASHIRA IS A MAKUUCHI-DIVISION WRESTLER WHO'S BELOW THE RANK OF YOKOZUNA, OZEKI, SEKIWAKE AND KOMUSUBI. AND 5-MAIME MEANS HE'S THE 5TH WITHIN THAT RANK!
OH ...
SO AKAGIMARU WON EVEN THOUGH HE WASN'T THAT STRONG. IT MUST BE 'CAUSE HE WAS SO CAUTIOUS!
CAUTIOUS?

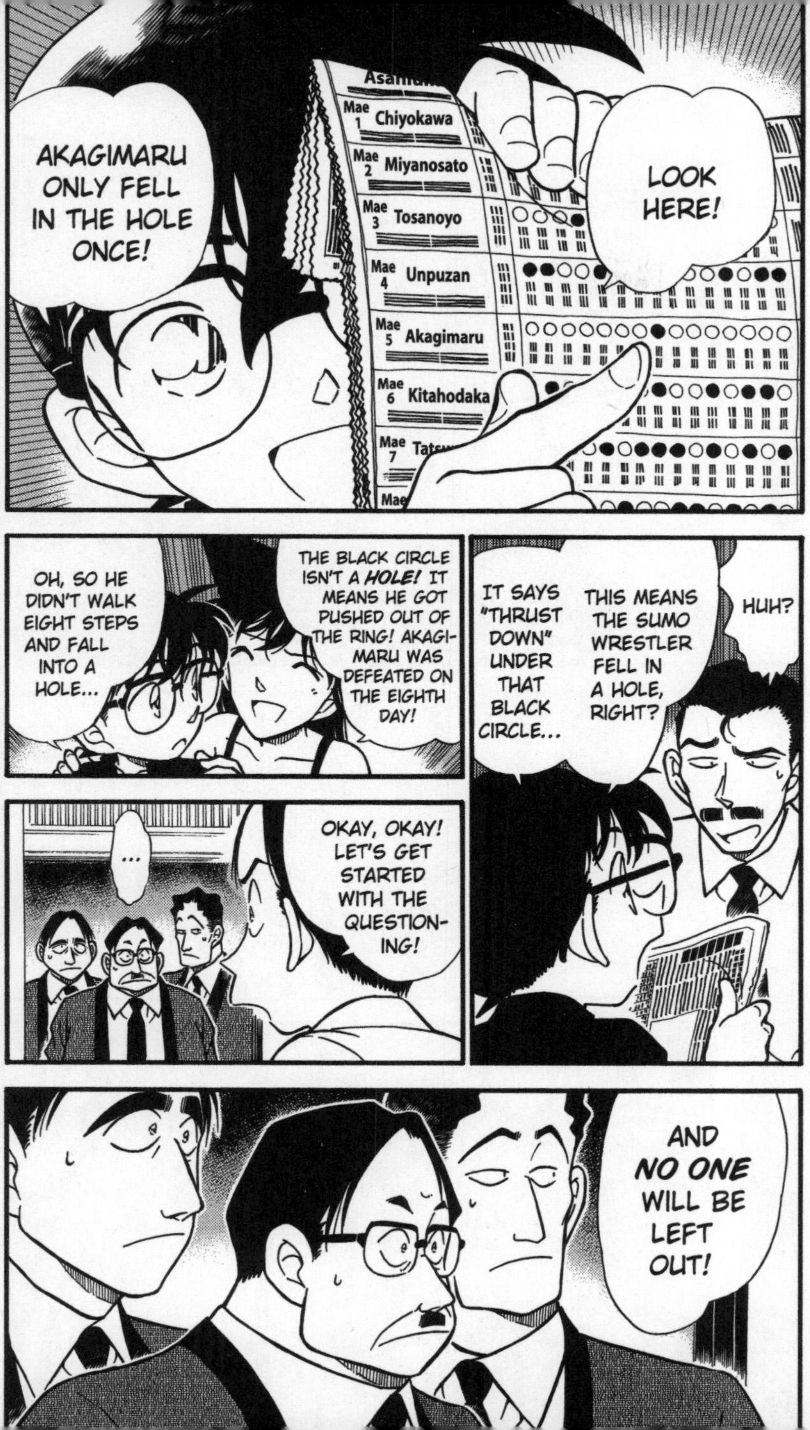
LOOK HERE!
AKAGIMARU ONLY FELL IN THE HOLE ONCE!
Mae 1 Chiyokawa
Mae 2 Miyanosato
Mae 3 Tosanoyo
Mae 4 Unpuzan
Mae 5 Akagimaru
Mae 6 Kitahodaka
HUH?
THIS MEANS THE SUMO WRESTLER FELL IN A HOLE, RIGHT?
IT SAYS "THRUST DOWN" UNDER THAT BLACK CIRCLE...
THE BLACK CIRCLE ISN'T A *HOLE!* IT MEANS HE GOT PUSHED OUT OF THE RING! AKAGIMARU WAS DEFEATED ON THE EIGHTH DAY!
OH, SO HE DIDN'T WALK EIGHT STEPS AND FALL INTO A HOLE...
OKAY, OKAY! LET'S GET STARTED WITH THE QUESTIONING!
...
AND *NO ONE* WILL BE LEFT OUT!

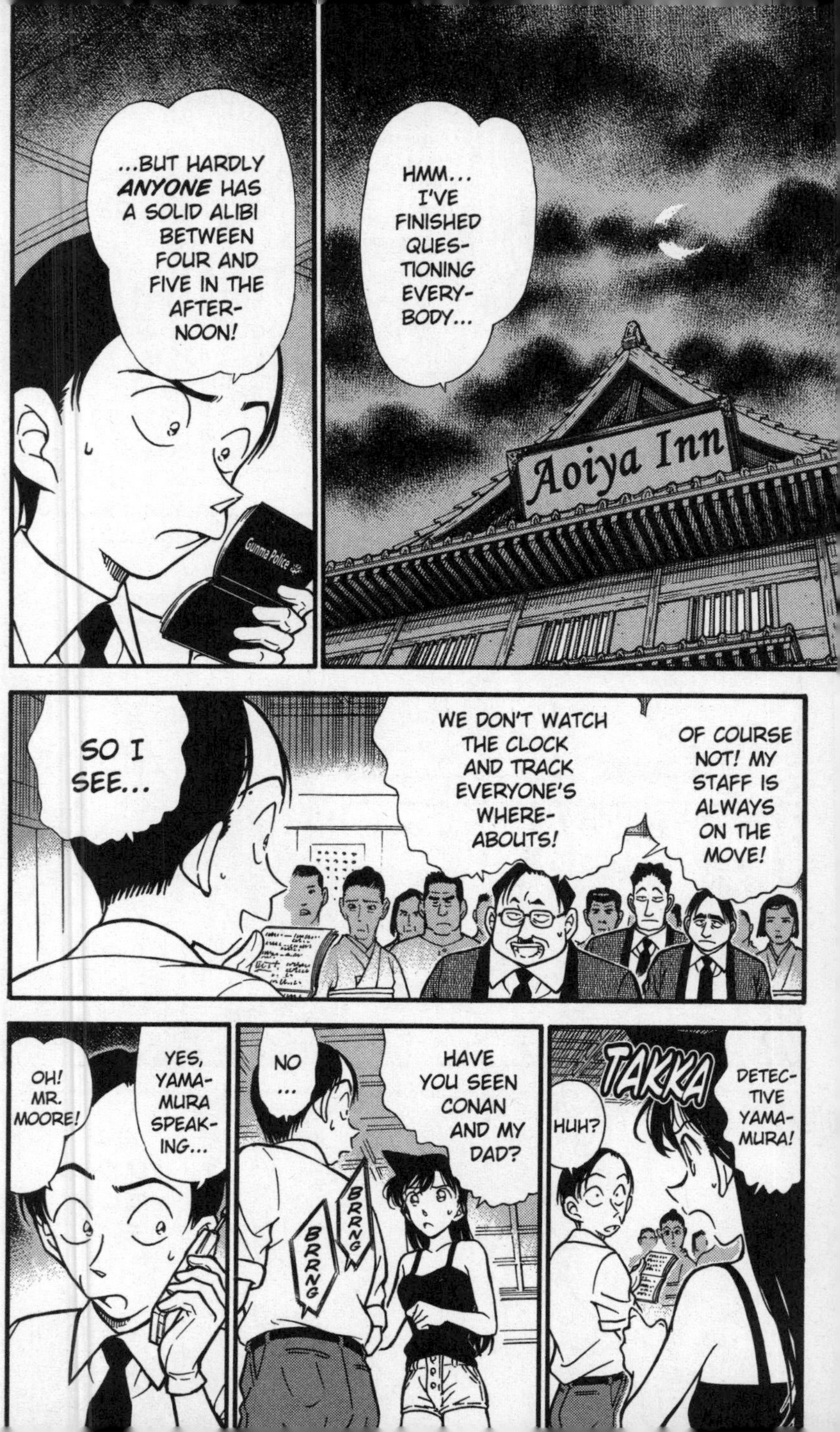
HMM... I'VE FINISHED QUES-TIONING EVERY-BODY...
Aoiya Inn
...BUT HARDLY ANYONE HAS A SOLID ALIBI BETWEEN FOUR AND FIVE IN THE AFTER-NOON!
Gunma Police
OF COURSE NOT! MY STAFF IS ALWAYS ON THE MOVE!
WE DON'T WATCH THE CLOCK AND TRACK EVERYONE'S WHERE-ABOUTS!
SO I SEE...
TAKKA
DETEC-TIVE YAMA-MURA!
HUH?
HAVE YOU SEEN CONAN AND MY DAD?
NO ...
BRRNG
BRRNG
YES, YAMA-MURA SPEAK-ING...
OH! MR. MOORE!

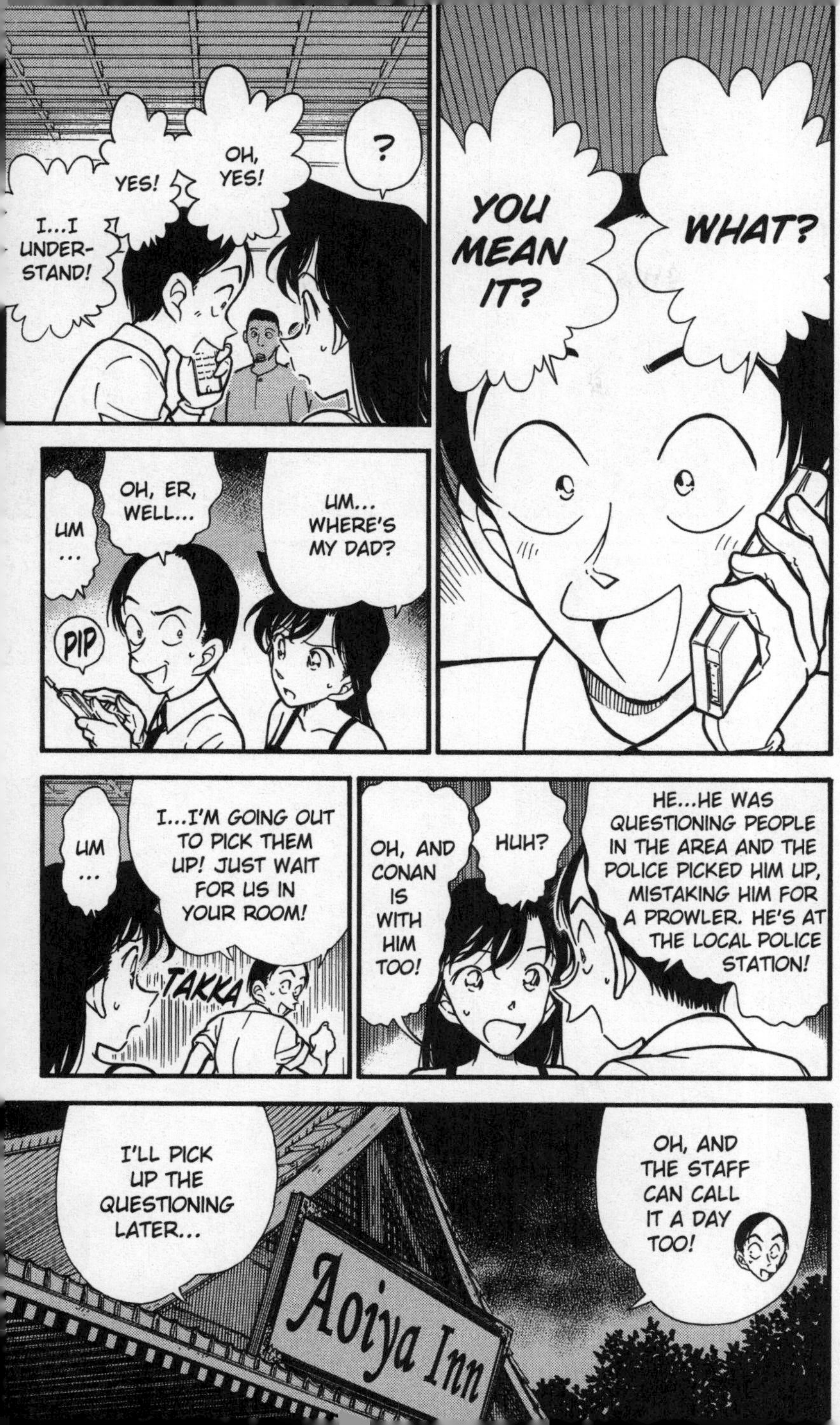
WHAT?
YOU MEAN IT?
?
OH, YES!
YES!
I...I UNDERSTAND!
UM... WHERE'S MY DAD?
OH, ER, WELL...
UM ...
PIP
HE...HE WAS QUESTIONING PEOPLE IN THE AREA AND THE POLICE PICKED HIM UP, MISTAKING HIM FOR A PROWLER. HE'S AT THE LOCAL POLICE STATION!
HUH?
OH, AND CONAN IS WITH HIM TOO!
I...I'M GOING OUT TO PICK THEM UP! JUST WAIT FOR US IN YOUR ROOM!
UM ...
TAKKA
OH, AND THE STAFF CAN CALL IT A DAY TOO!
I'LL PICK UP THE QUESTIONING LATER...
Aoiya Inn

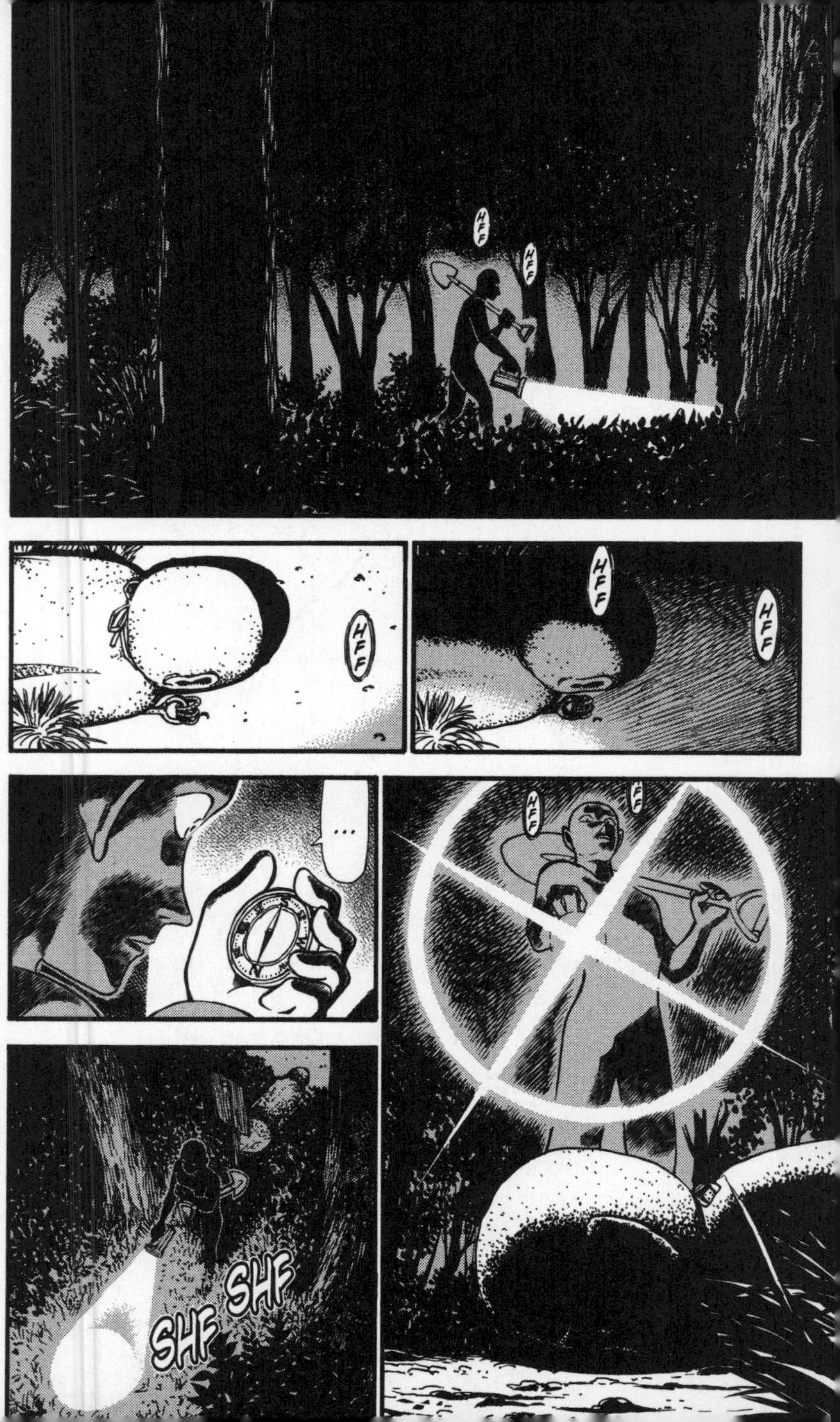
HFF
HFF
HFF
HFF
HFF
HFF
HFF
...
SHF
SHF

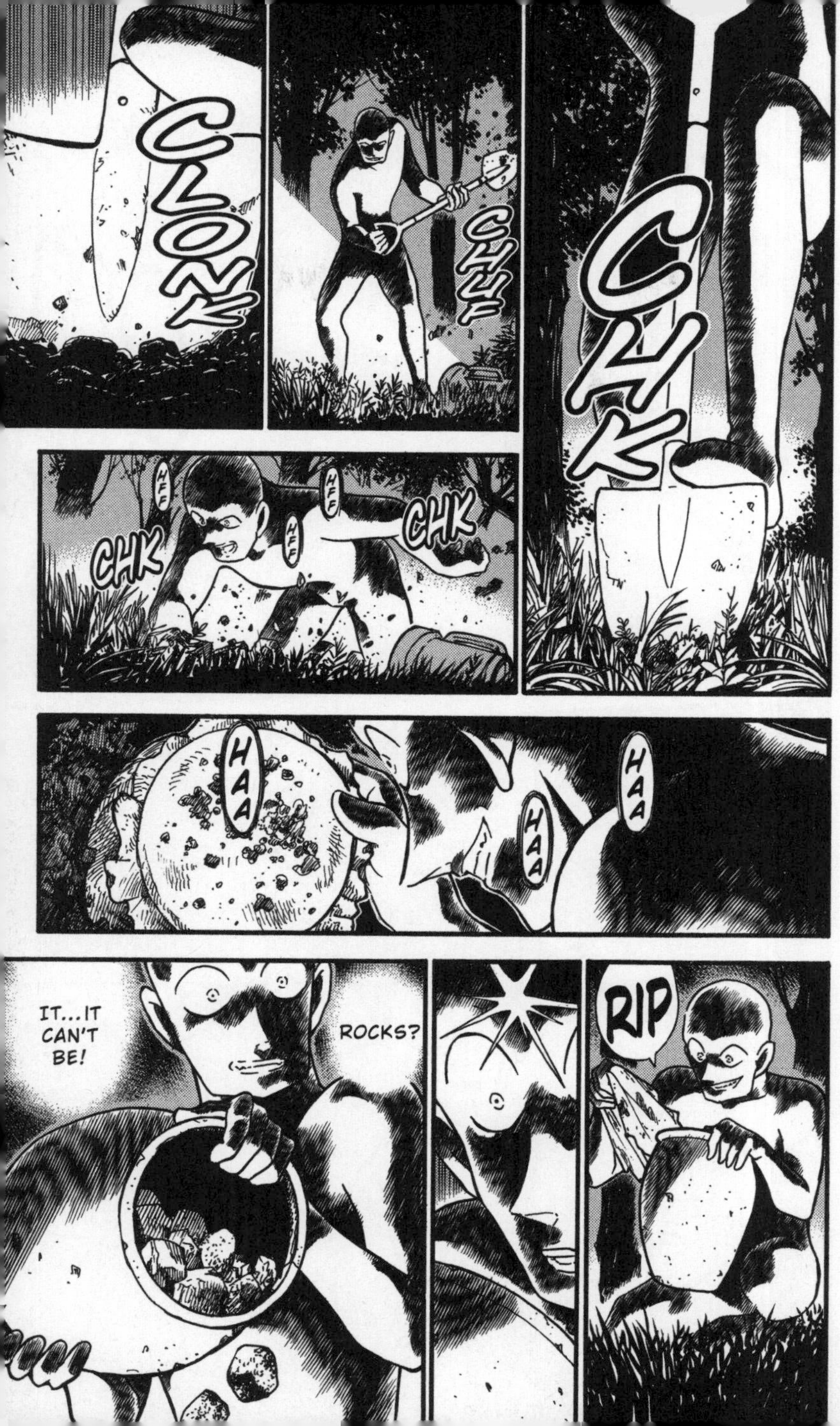
CHK
CHUF
CLONK
HFF
HFF
HFF
CHK
CHK
HAA
HAA
HAA
RIP
ROCKS?
IT...IT CAN'T BE!

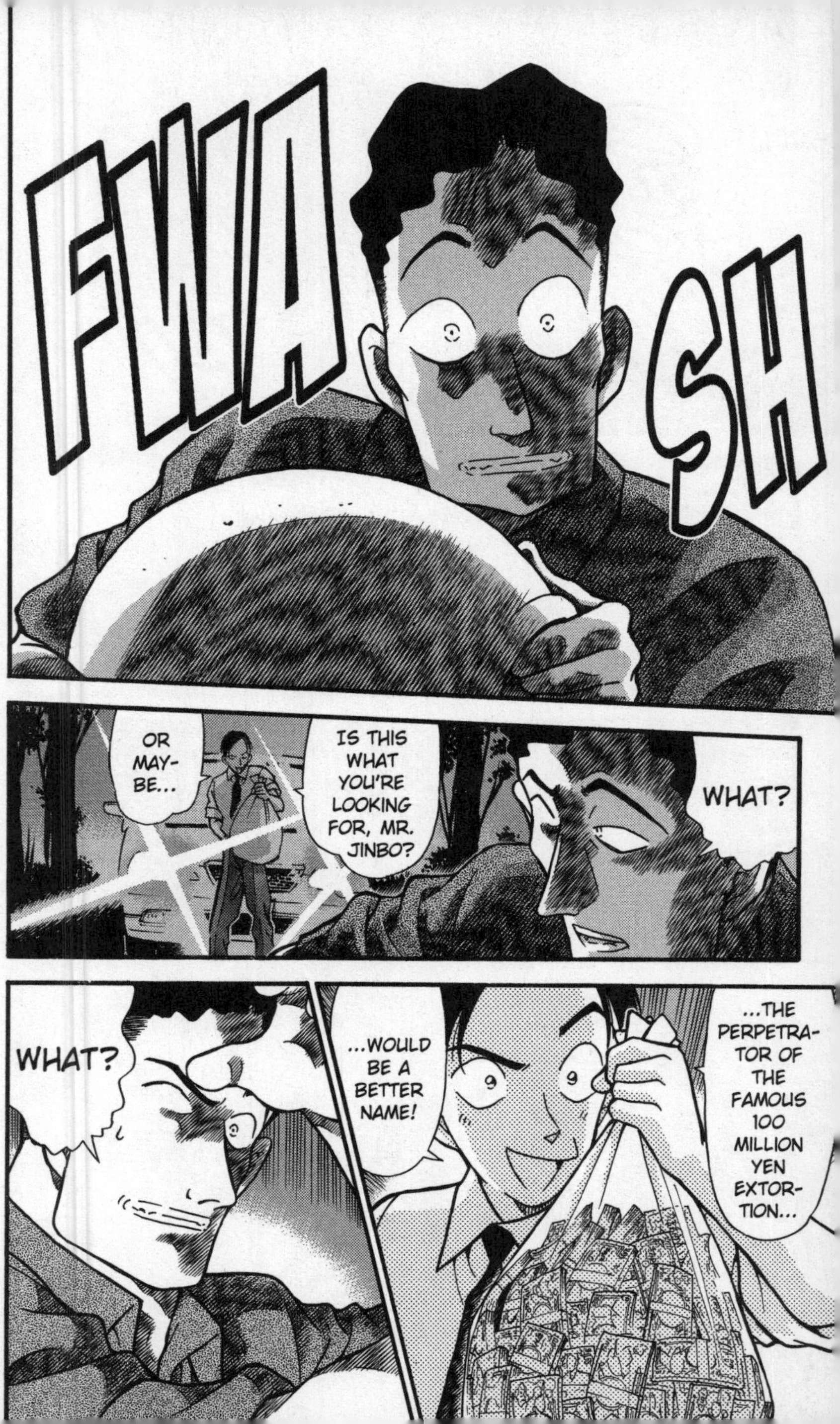
FWASH
WHAT?
IS THIS WHAT YOU'RE LOOKING FOR, MR. JINBO?
OR MAYBE...
...THE PERPETRATOR OF THE FAMOUS 100 MILLION YEN EXTORTION...
...WOULD BE A BETTER NAME!
WHAT?

THE SPORTS JOURNAL INSIDE WAS A MAP TO THE LOCATION OF THE MONEY!

...AND THE OTHER WAS THE LONG-HAIRED MAN WHO HANDED THE ATTACHÉ CASE TO MR. ONDA.

ONE OF THOSE CROOKS WAS YOU...

I CHECKED THE SERIAL NUMBERS ON THESE 10,000 YEN NOTES. THIS IS THE MONEY TWO CROOKS EXTORTED FROM A CANDY COMPANY FIVE YEARS AGO!

"MAEGASHIRA" IS THE KEYWORD POINTING TO THE MAEDAORE JIZO AT KASHIRA-GAMI FOREST!

8 Years of Hardship
Akagimaru's First Victory

AKAGIMARU, WHOSE NAME IS ON THE HEADLINE HERE, WAS AN EAST MAEGA-SHIRA 5-MAIME.

...TO THE BLACK CIRCLE ON THE EIGHTH DAY, AKAGIMARU'S ONLY LOSS!

West	Mae 1							
	Mae 2							
	Mae 3							
	Mae 4							
East	Mae 5							

...THEN MOVE EIGHT STEPS TO THE RIGHT, JUST LIKE ON AKAGIMARU'S TOURNAMENT RESULTS...

YOU START FROM THE MAEDAORE JIZO AND MOVE FIVE STEPS TO THE EAST...

...WAS BECAUSE HE HAD A SUSPI-CION.

THE REASON THE LONG-HAIRED MAN PUT THE SPORTS JOURNAL IN THE ATTACHE CASE AND LEFT IT WITH MR. ONDA FOR SAFE-KEEPING...

RIGHT.

ISN'T THAT RIGHT, MR. MOORE?

...

IF YOU DUG AT THAT SPOT, YOU'D FIND A JAR PACKED WITH MONEY!

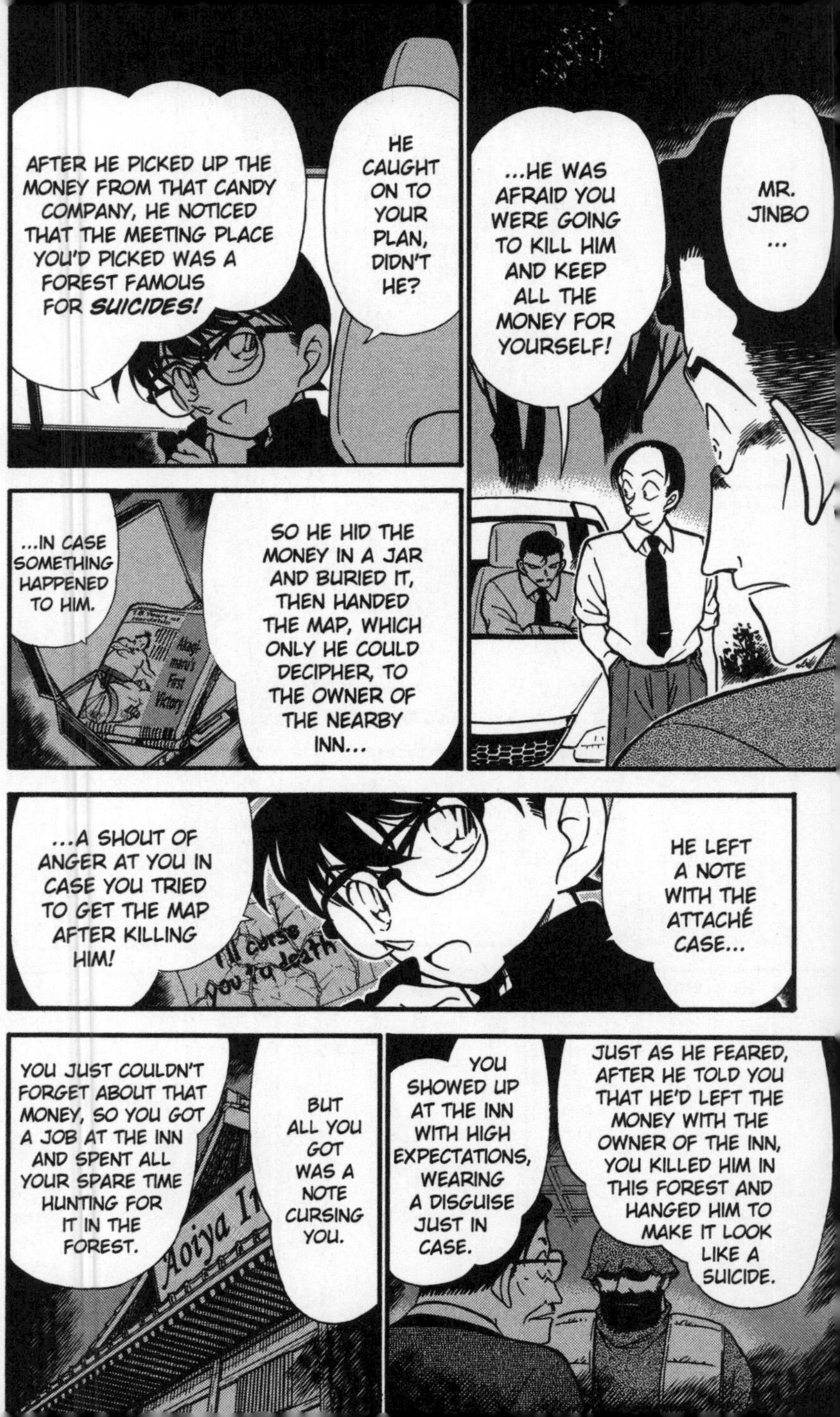
MR. JINBO ...
...HE WAS AFRAID YOU WERE GOING TO KILL HIM AND KEEP ALL THE MONEY FOR YOURSELF!
HE CAUGHT ON TO YOUR PLAN, DIDN'T HE?
AFTER HE PICKED UP THE MONEY FROM THAT CANDY COMPANY, HE NOTICED THAT THE MEETING PLACE YOU'D PICKED WAS A FOREST FAMOUS FOR ***SUICIDES!***
SO HE HID THE MONEY IN A JAR AND BURIED IT, THEN HANDED THE MAP, WHICH ONLY HE COULD DECIPHER, TO THE OWNER OF THE NEARBY INN...
...IN CASE SOMETHING HAPPENED TO HIM.
Akagi-maru's First Victory
HE LEFT A NOTE WITH THE ATTACHÉ CASE...
I'll curse you to death
...A SHOUT OF ANGER AT YOU IN CASE YOU TRIED TO GET THE MAP AFTER KILLING HIM!
JUST AS HE FEARED, AFTER HE TOLD YOU THAT HE'D LEFT THE MONEY WITH THE OWNER OF THE INN, YOU KILLED HIM IN THIS FOREST AND HANGED HIM TO MAKE IT LOOK LIKE A SUICIDE.
YOU SHOWED UP AT THE INN WITH HIGH EXPECTATIONS, WEARING A DISGUISE JUST IN CASE.
BUT ALL YOU GOT WAS A NOTE CURSING YOU.
YOU JUST COULDN'T FORGET ABOUT THAT MONEY, SO YOU GOT A JOB AT THE INN AND SPENT ALL YOUR SPARE TIME HUNTING FOR IT IN THE FOREST.
Aoiya In

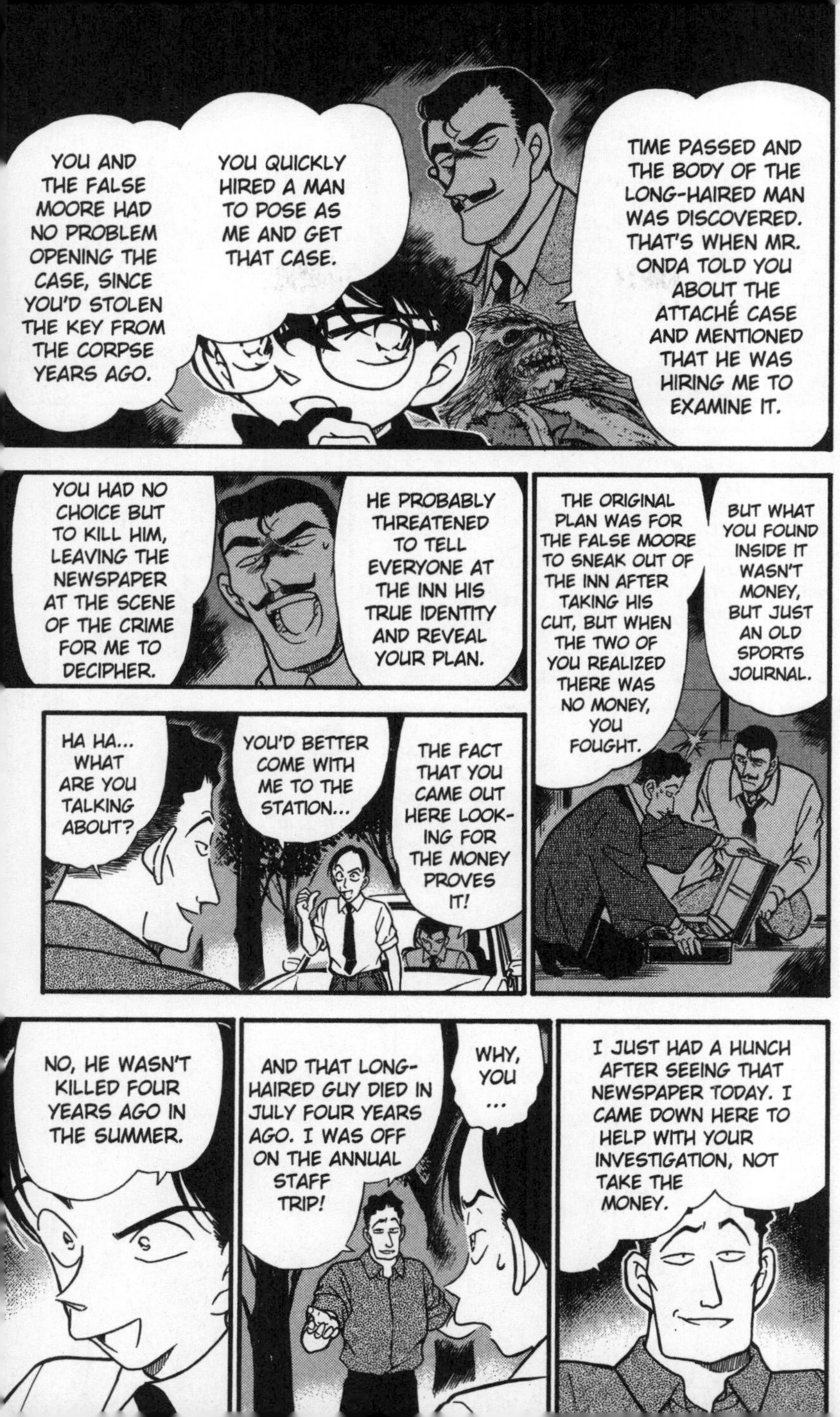
TIME PASSED AND THE BODY OF THE LONG-HAIRED MAN WAS DISCOVERED. THAT'S WHEN MR. ONDA TOLD YOU ABOUT THE ATTACHÉ CASE AND MENTIONED THAT HE WAS HIRING ME TO EXAMINE IT.
YOU QUICKLY HIRED A MAN TO POSE AS ME AND GET THAT CASE.
YOU AND THE FALSE MOORE HAD NO PROBLEM OPENING THE CASE, SINCE YOU'D STOLEN THE KEY FROM THE CORPSE YEARS AGO.
BUT WHAT YOU FOUND INSIDE IT WASN'T MONEY, BUT JUST AN OLD SPORTS JOURNAL.
THE ORIGINAL PLAN WAS FOR THE FALSE MOORE TO SNEAK OUT OF THE INN AFTER TAKING HIS CUT, BUT WHEN THE TWO OF YOU REALIZED THERE WAS NO MONEY, YOU FOUGHT.
HE PROBABLY THREATENED TO TELL EVERYONE AT THE INN HIS TRUE IDENTITY AND REVEAL YOUR PLAN.
YOU HAD NO CHOICE BUT TO KILL HIM, LEAVING THE NEWSPAPER AT THE SCENE OF THE CRIME FOR ME TO DECIPHER.
THE FACT THAT YOU CAME OUT HERE LOOKING FOR THE MONEY PROVES IT!
YOU'D BETTER COME WITH ME TO THE STATION...
HA HA... WHAT ARE YOU TALKING ABOUT?
I JUST HAD A HUNCH AFTER SEEING THAT NEWSPAPER TODAY. I CAME DOWN HERE TO HELP WITH YOUR INVESTIGATION, NOT TAKE THE MONEY.
WHY, YOU ...
AND THAT LONG-HAIRED GUY DIED IN JULY FOUR YEARS AGO. I WAS OFF ON THE ANNUAL STAFF TRIP!
NO, HE WASN'T KILLED FOUR YEARS AGO IN THE SUMMER.

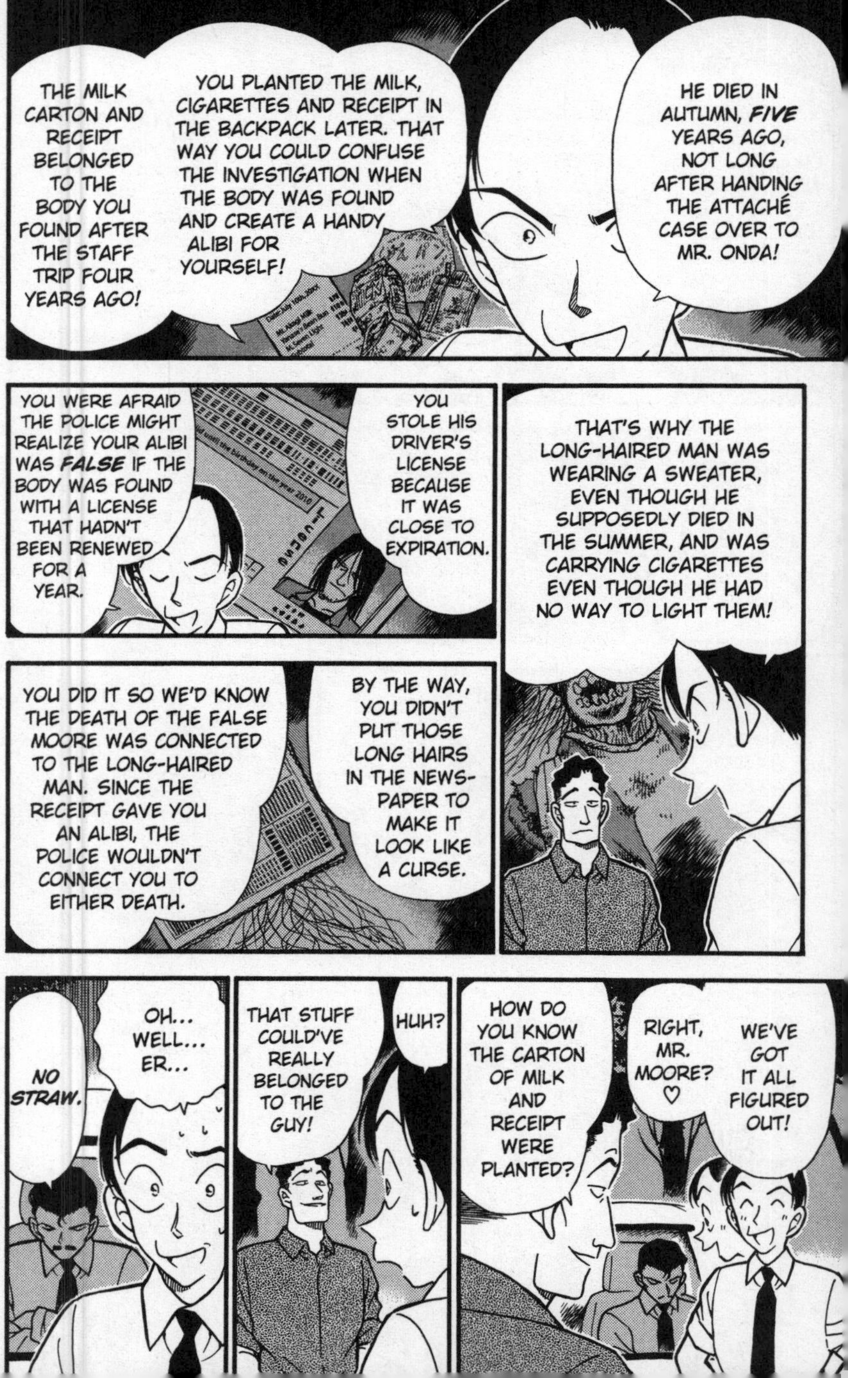
HE DIED IN AUTUMN, ***FIVE*** YEARS AGO, NOT LONG AFTER HANDING THE ATTACHÉ CASE OVER TO MR. ONDA!
YOU PLANTED THE MILK, CIGARETTES AND RECEIPT IN THE BACKPACK LATER. THAT WAY YOU COULD CONFUSE THE INVESTIGATION WHEN THE BODY WAS FOUND AND CREATE A HANDY ALIBI FOR YOURSELF!
THE MILK CARTON AND RECEIPT BELONGED TO THE BODY YOU FOUND AFTER THE STAFF TRIP FOUR YEARS AGO!
THAT'S WHY THE LONG-HAIRED MAN WAS WEARING A SWEATER, EVEN THOUGH HE SUPPOSEDLY DIED IN THE SUMMER, AND WAS CARRYING CIGARETTES EVEN THOUGH HE HAD NO WAY TO LIGHT THEM!
YOU STOLE HIS DRIVER'S LICENSE BECAUSE IT WAS CLOSE TO EXPIRATION.
YOU WERE AFRAID THE POLICE MIGHT REALIZE YOUR ALIBI WAS ***FALSE*** IF THE BODY WAS FOUND WITH A LICENSE THAT HADN'T BEEN RENEWED FOR A YEAR.
BY THE WAY, YOU DIDN'T PUT THOSE LONG HAIRS IN THE NEWS-PAPER TO MAKE IT LOOK LIKE A CURSE.
YOU DID IT SO WE'D KNOW THE DEATH OF THE FALSE MOORE WAS CONNECTED TO THE LONG-HAIRED MAN. SINCE THE RECEIPT GAVE YOU AN ALIBI, THE POLICE WOULDN'T CONNECT YOU TO EITHER DEATH.
WE'VE GOT IT ALL FIGURED OUT!
RIGHT, MR. MOORE? ♡
HOW DO YOU KNOW THE CARTON OF MILK AND RECEIPT WERE PLANTED?
HUH?
THAT STUFF COULD'VE REALLY BELONGED TO THE GUY!
OH... WELL... ER...
NO STRAW.

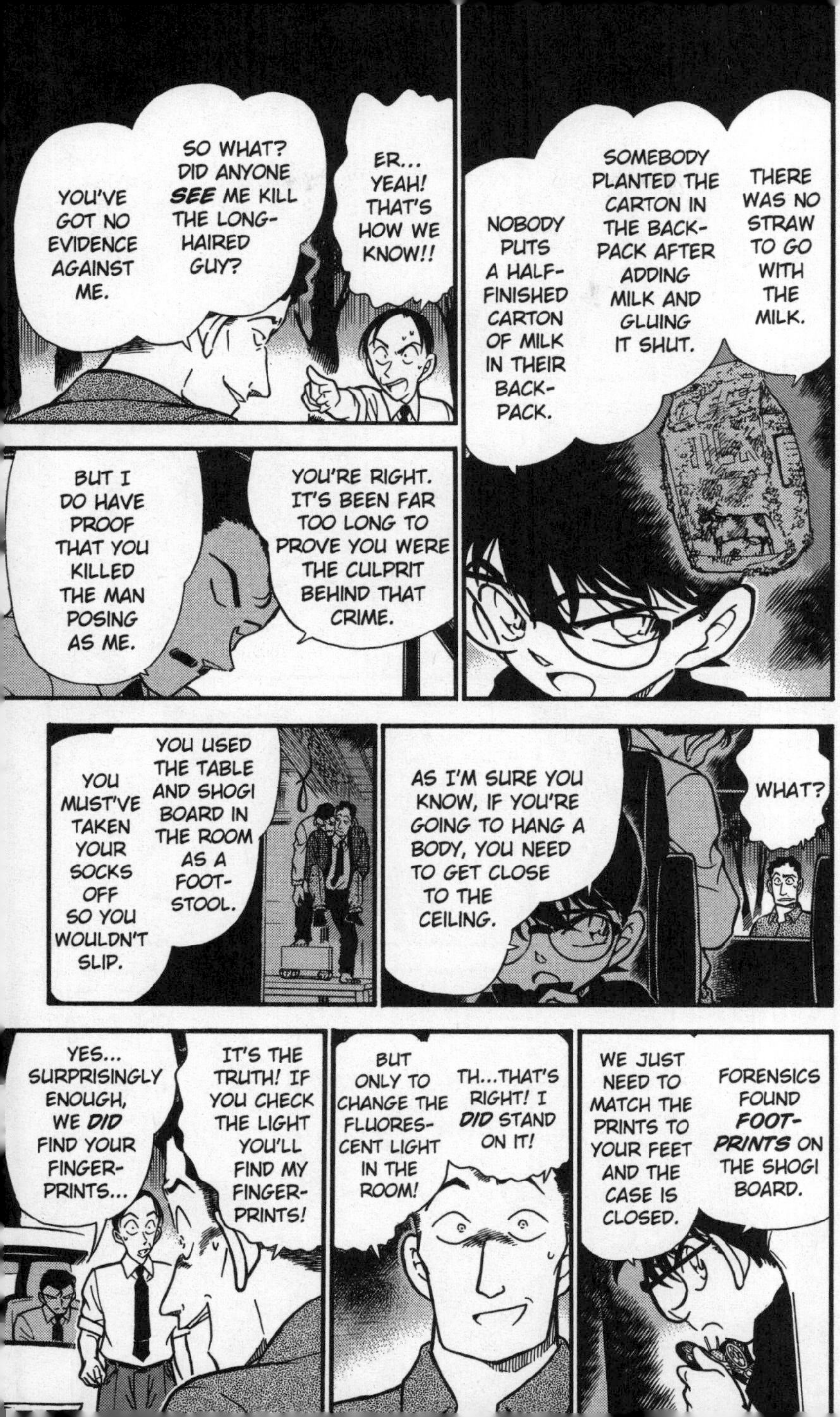
THERE WAS NO STRAW TO GO WITH THE MILK.
SOMEBODY PLANTED THE CARTON IN THE BACK-PACK AFTER ADDING MILK AND GLUING IT SHUT.
NOBODY PUTS A HALF-FINISHED CARTON OF MILK IN THEIR BACK-PACK.
ER... YEAH! THAT'S HOW WE KNOW!!
SO WHAT? DID ANYONE *SEE* ME KILL THE LONG-HAIRED GUY?
YOU'VE GOT NO EVIDENCE AGAINST ME.
YOU'RE RIGHT. IT'S BEEN FAR TOO LONG TO PROVE YOU WERE THE CULPRIT BEHIND THAT CRIME.
BUT I DO HAVE PROOF THAT YOU KILLED THE MAN POSING AS ME.
WHAT?
AS I'M SURE YOU KNOW, IF YOU'RE GOING TO HANG A BODY, YOU NEED TO GET CLOSE TO THE CEILING.
YOU USED THE TABLE AND SHOGI BOARD IN THE ROOM AS A FOOT-STOOL.
YOU MUST'VE TAKEN YOUR SOCKS OFF SO YOU WOULDN'T SLIP.
FORENSICS FOUND *FOOT-PRINTS* ON THE SHOGI BOARD.
WE JUST NEED TO MATCH THE PRINTS TO YOUR FEET AND THE CASE IS CLOSED.
TH...THAT'S RIGHT! I *DID* STAND ON IT!
BUT ONLY TO CHANGE THE FLUORES-CENT LIGHT IN THE ROOM!
IT'S THE TRUTH! IF YOU CHECK THE LIGHT YOU'LL FIND MY FINGER-PRINTS!
YES... SURPRISINGLY ENOUGH, WE *DID* FIND YOUR FINGER-PRINTS...

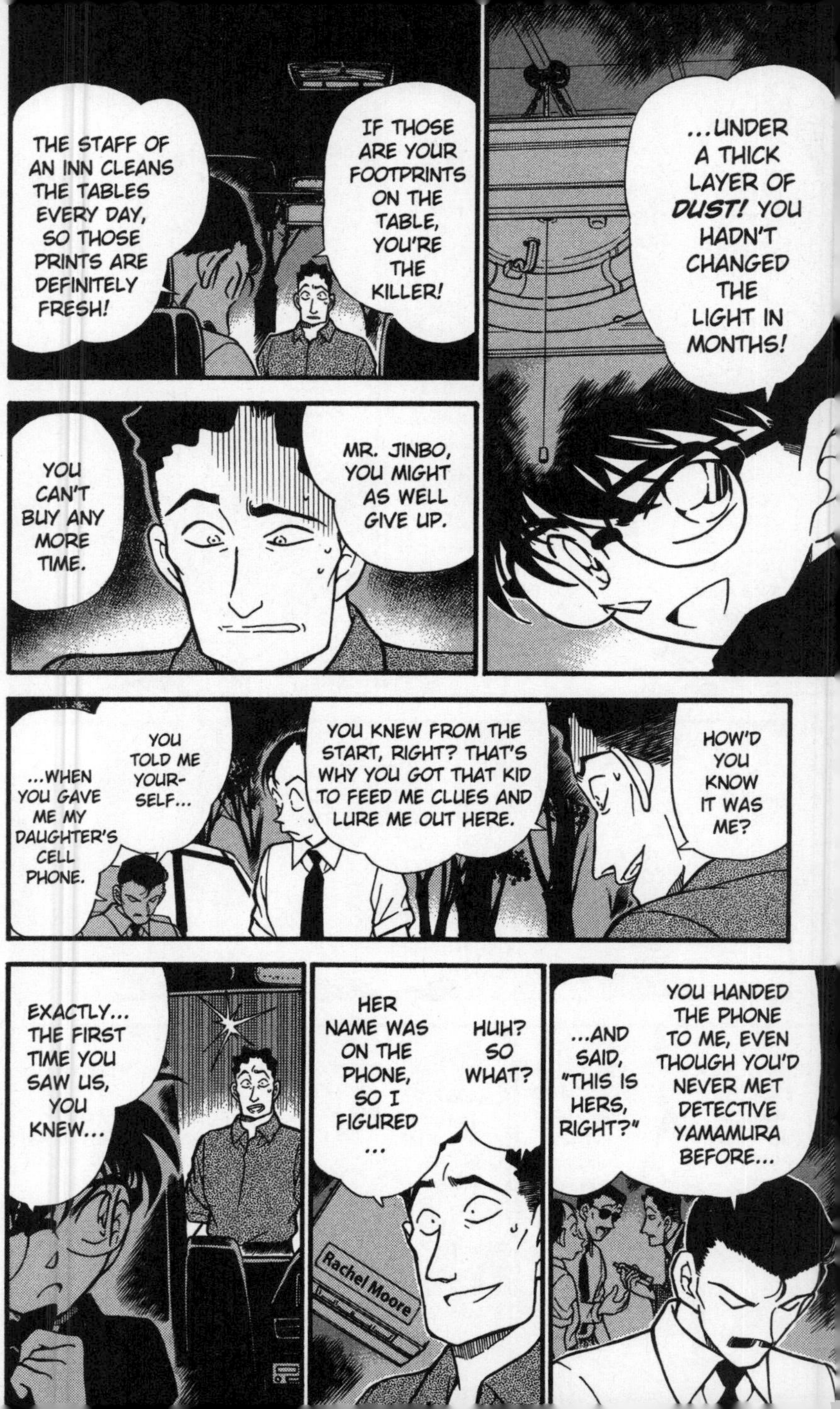
...UNDER A THICK LAYER OF DUST! YOU HADN'T CHANGED THE LIGHT IN MONTHS!
IF THOSE ARE YOUR FOOTPRINTS ON THE TABLE, YOU'RE THE KILLER!
THE STAFF OF AN INN CLEANS THE TABLES EVERY DAY, SO THOSE PRINTS ARE DEFINITELY FRESH!
MR. JINBO, YOU MIGHT AS WELL GIVE UP.
YOU CAN'T BUY ANY MORE TIME.
HOW'D YOU KNOW IT WAS ME?
YOU KNEW FROM THE START, RIGHT? THAT'S WHY YOU GOT THAT KID TO FEED ME CLUES AND LURE ME OUT HERE.
YOU TOLD ME YOURSELF...
...WHEN YOU GAVE ME MY DAUGHTER'S CELL PHONE.
YOU HANDED THE PHONE TO ME, EVEN THOUGH YOU'D NEVER MET DETECTIVE YAMAMURA BEFORE...
...AND SAID, "THIS IS HERS, RIGHT?"
HUH? SO WHAT?
HER NAME WAS ON THE PHONE, SO I FIGURED ...
Rachel Moore
EXACTLY... THE FIRST TIME YOU SAW US, YOU KNEW...

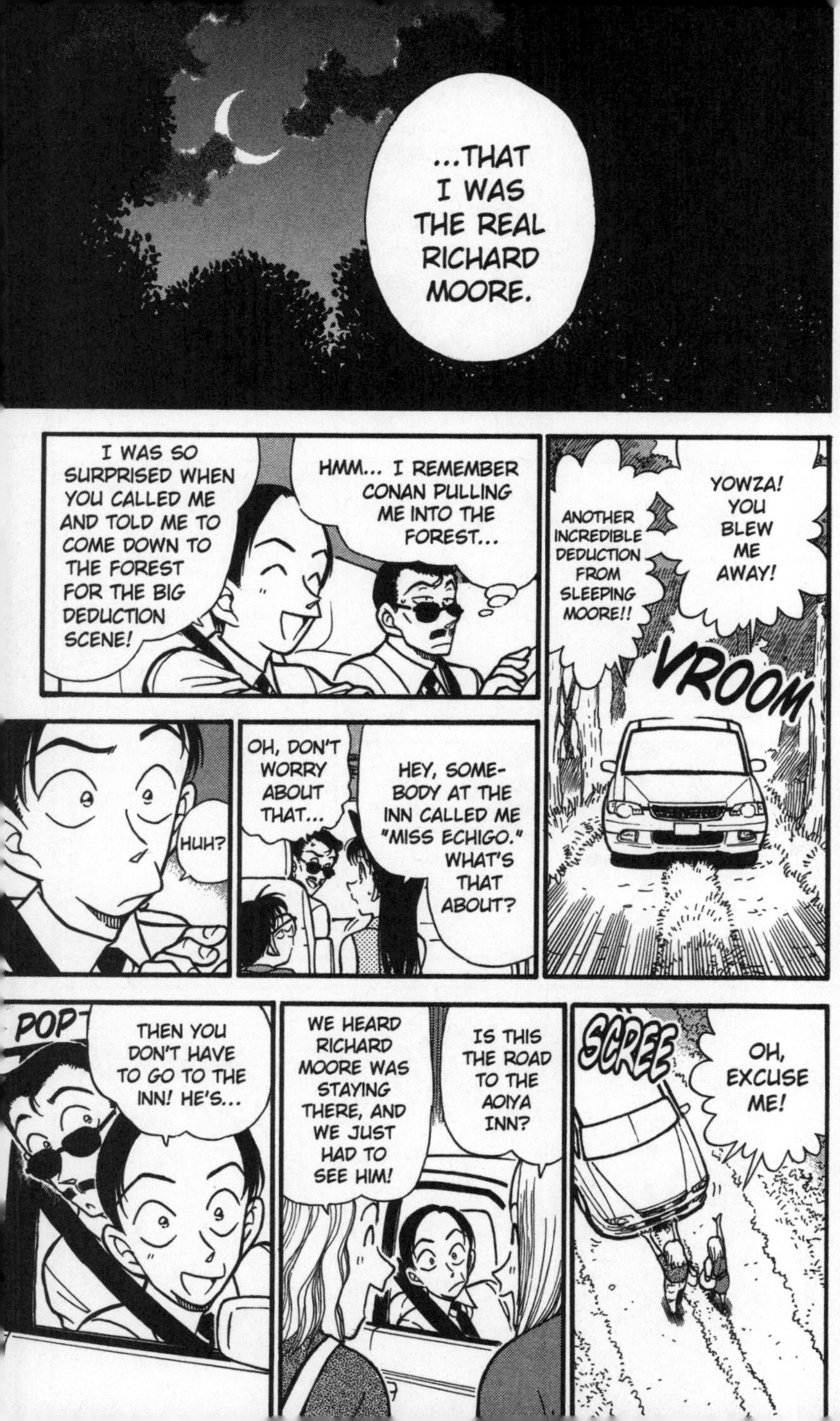
...THAT I WAS THE REAL RICHARD MOORE.
YOWZA! YOU BLEW ME AWAY!
ANOTHER INCREDIBLE DEDUCTION FROM SLEEPING MOORE!!
VROOM
HMM... I REMEMBER CONAN PULLING ME INTO THE FOREST...
I WAS SO SURPRISED WHEN YOU CALLED ME AND TOLD ME TO COME DOWN TO THE FOREST FOR THE BIG DEDUCTION SCENE!
HEY, SOME-BODY AT THE INN CALLED ME "MISS ECHIGO." WHAT'S THAT ABOUT?
OH, DON'T WORRY ABOUT THAT...
HUH?
SCREE
OH, EXCUSE ME!
IS THIS THE ROAD TO THE AOIYA INN?
WE HEARD RICHARD MOORE WAS STAYING THERE, AND WE JUST HAD TO SEE HIM!
THEN YOU DON'T HAVE TO GO TO THE INN! HE'S...
POP

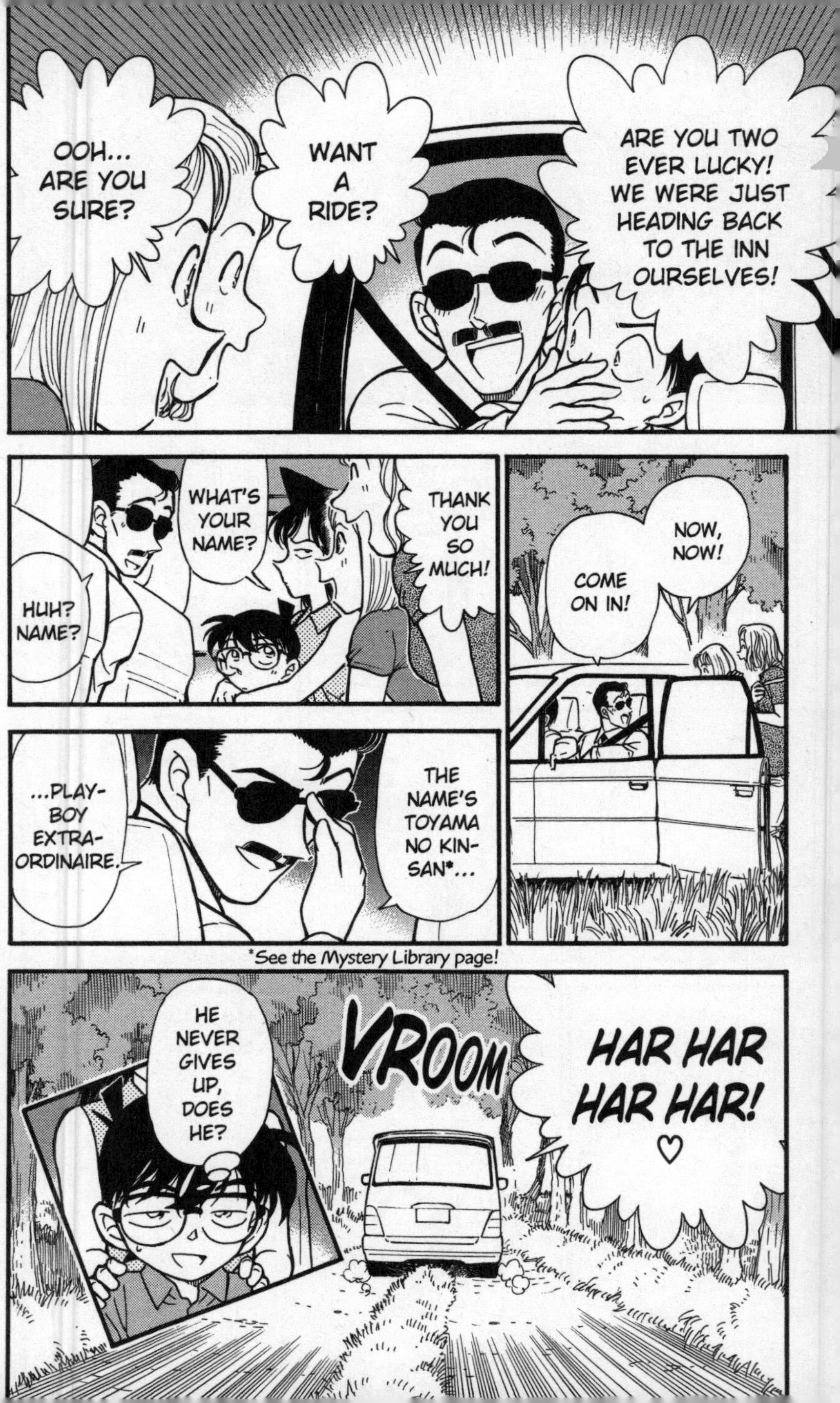
ARE YOU TWO EVER LUCKY! WE WERE JUST HEADING BACK TO THE INN OURSELVES!
WANT A RIDE?
OOH... ARE YOU SURE?
NOW, NOW!
COME ON IN!
THANK YOU SO MUCH!
WHAT'S YOUR NAME?
HUH? NAME?
THE NAME'S TOYAMA NO KIN-SAN*...
...PLAY-BOY EXTRA-ORDINAIRE.
HAR HAR HAR HAR! ♡
VROOM
HE NEVER GIVES UP, DOES HE?

*See the *Mystery Library* page!

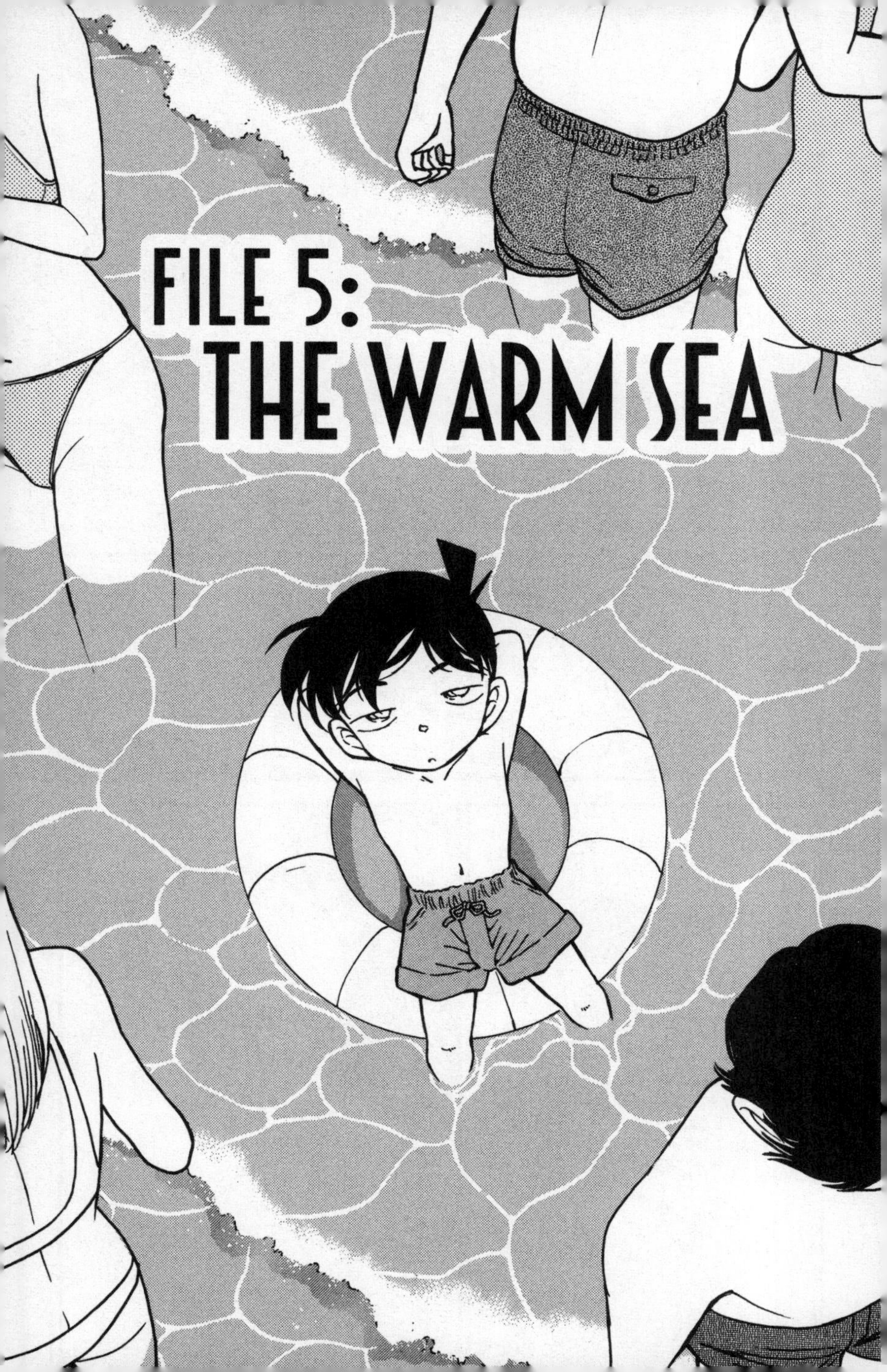
FILE 5:
THE WARM SEA

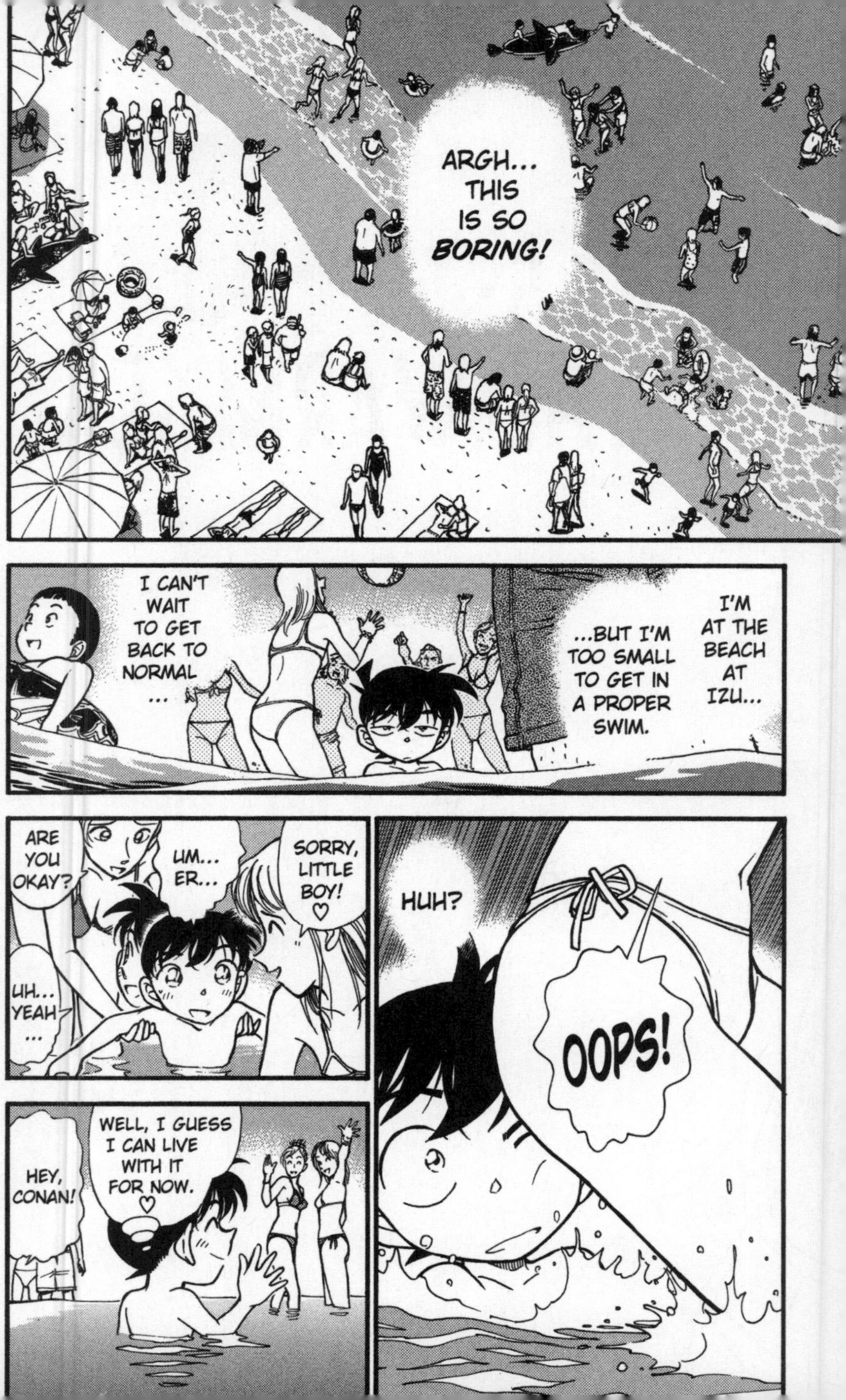
ARGH... THIS IS SO BORING!
I'M AT THE BEACH AT IZU...
...BUT I'M TOO SMALL TO GET IN A PROPER SWIM.
I CAN'T WAIT TO GET BACK TO NORMAL...
HUH?
OOPS!
SORRY, LITTLE BOY! ♡
UM... ER...
ARE YOU OKAY?
UH... YEAH...
WELL, I GUESS I CAN LIVE WITH IT FOR NOW. ♡
HEY, CONAN!

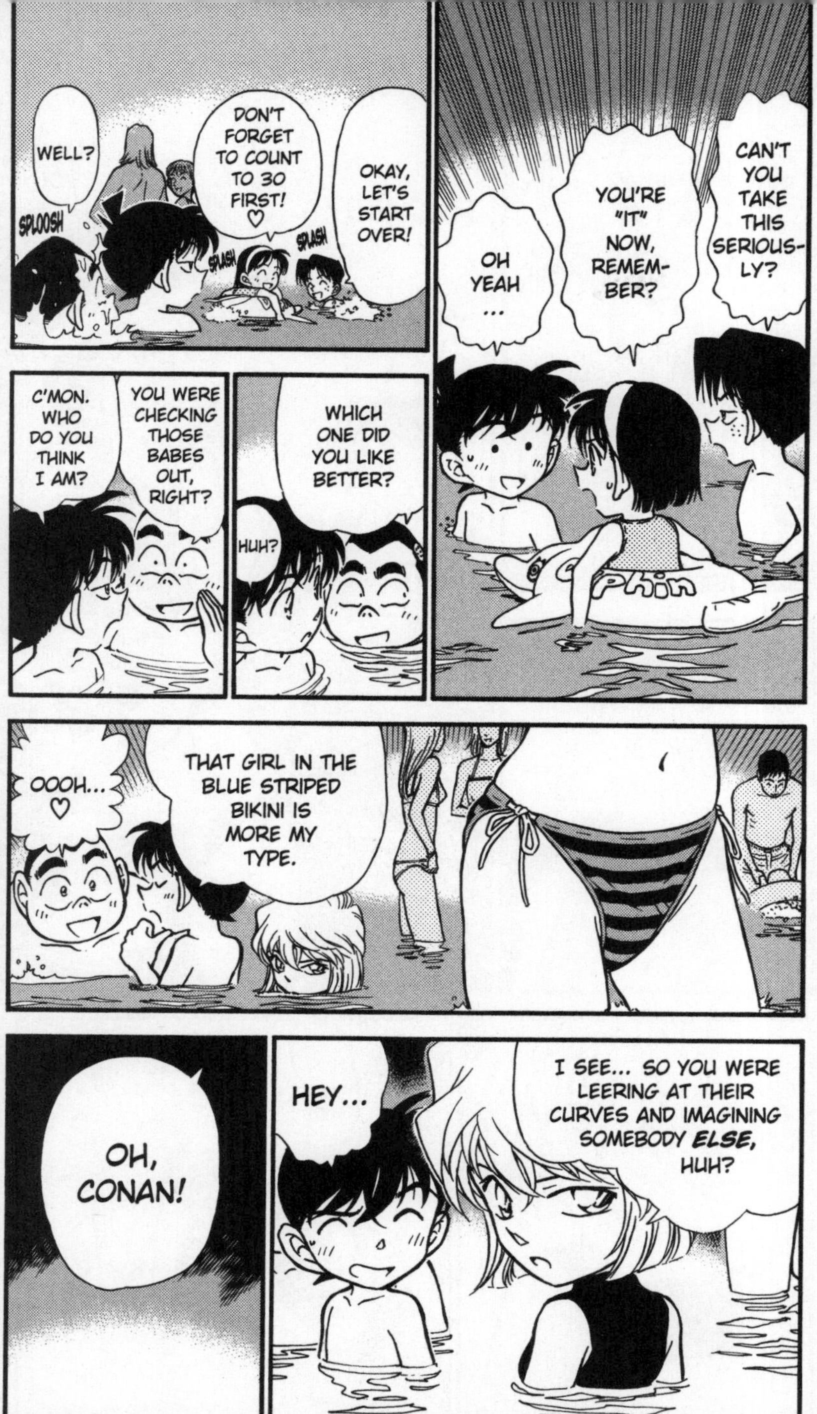
CAN'T YOU TAKE THIS SERIOUS-LY?
YOU'RE "IT" NOW, REMEM-BER?
OH YEAH ...
OKAY, LET'S START OVER!
DON'T FORGET TO COUNT TO 30 FIRST! ♡
SPLASH
WELL?
SPLASH
SPLOOSH
WHICH ONE DID YOU LIKE BETTER?
HUH?
YOU WERE CHECKING THOSE BABES OUT, RIGHT?
C'MON. WHO DO YOU THINK I AM?
THAT GIRL IN THE BLUE STRIPED BIKINI IS MORE MY TYPE.
OOOH... ♡
I SEE... SO YOU WERE LEERING AT THEIR CURVES AND IMAGINING SOMEBODY *ELSE*, HUH?
HEY...
OH, CONAN!

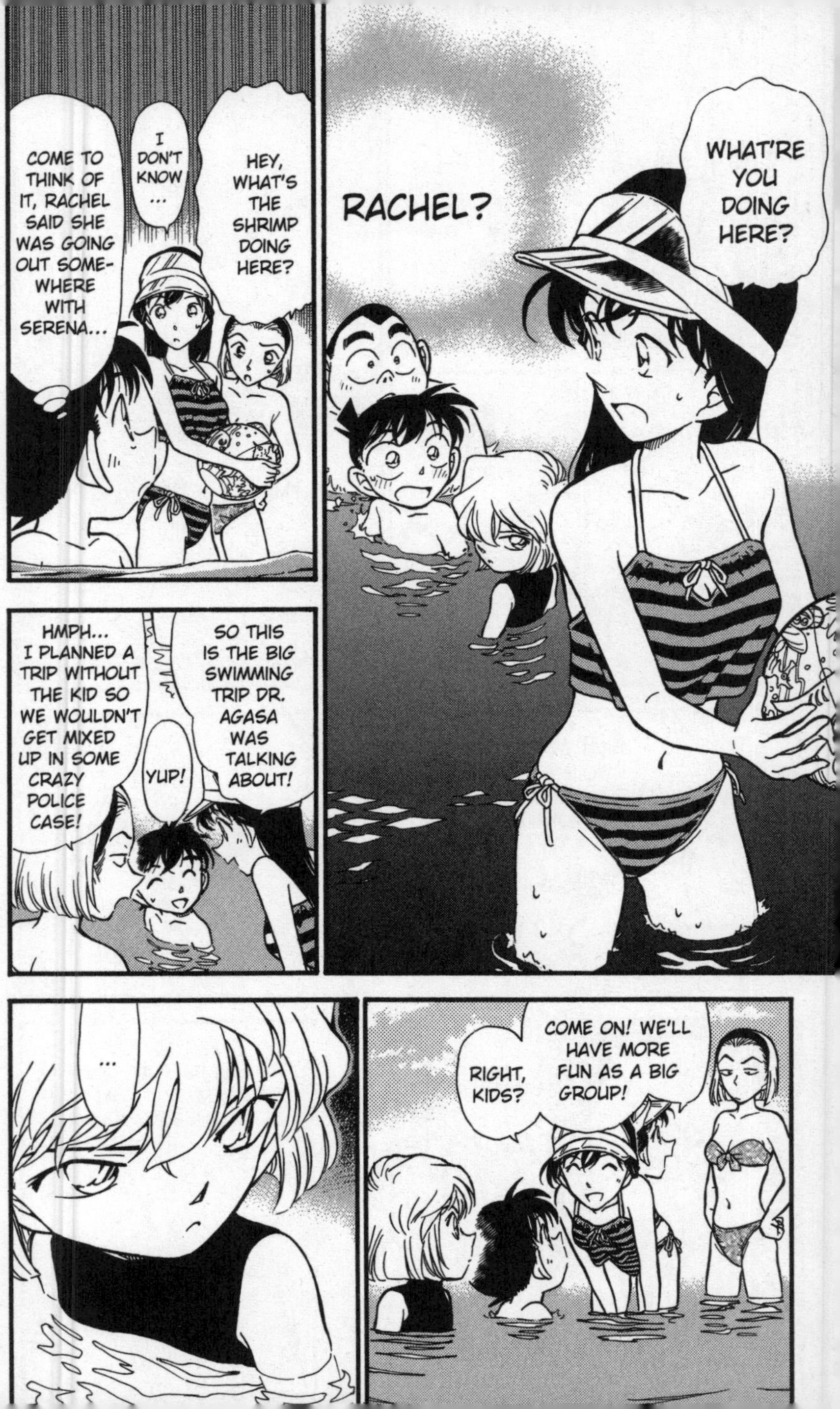
WHAT'RE YOU DOING HERE?
RACHEL?
HEY, WHAT'S THE SHRIMP DOING HERE?
I DON'T KNOW ...
COME TO THINK OF IT, RACHEL SAID SHE WAS GOING OUT SOME-WHERE WITH SERENA...
SO THIS IS THE BIG SWIMMING TRIP DR. AGASA WAS TALKING ABOUT!
YUP!
HMPH... I PLANNED A TRIP WITHOUT THE KID SO WE WOULDN'T GET MIXED UP IN SOME CRAZY POLICE CASE!
COME ON! WE'LL HAVE MORE FUN AS A BIG GROUP!
RIGHT, KIDS?
...

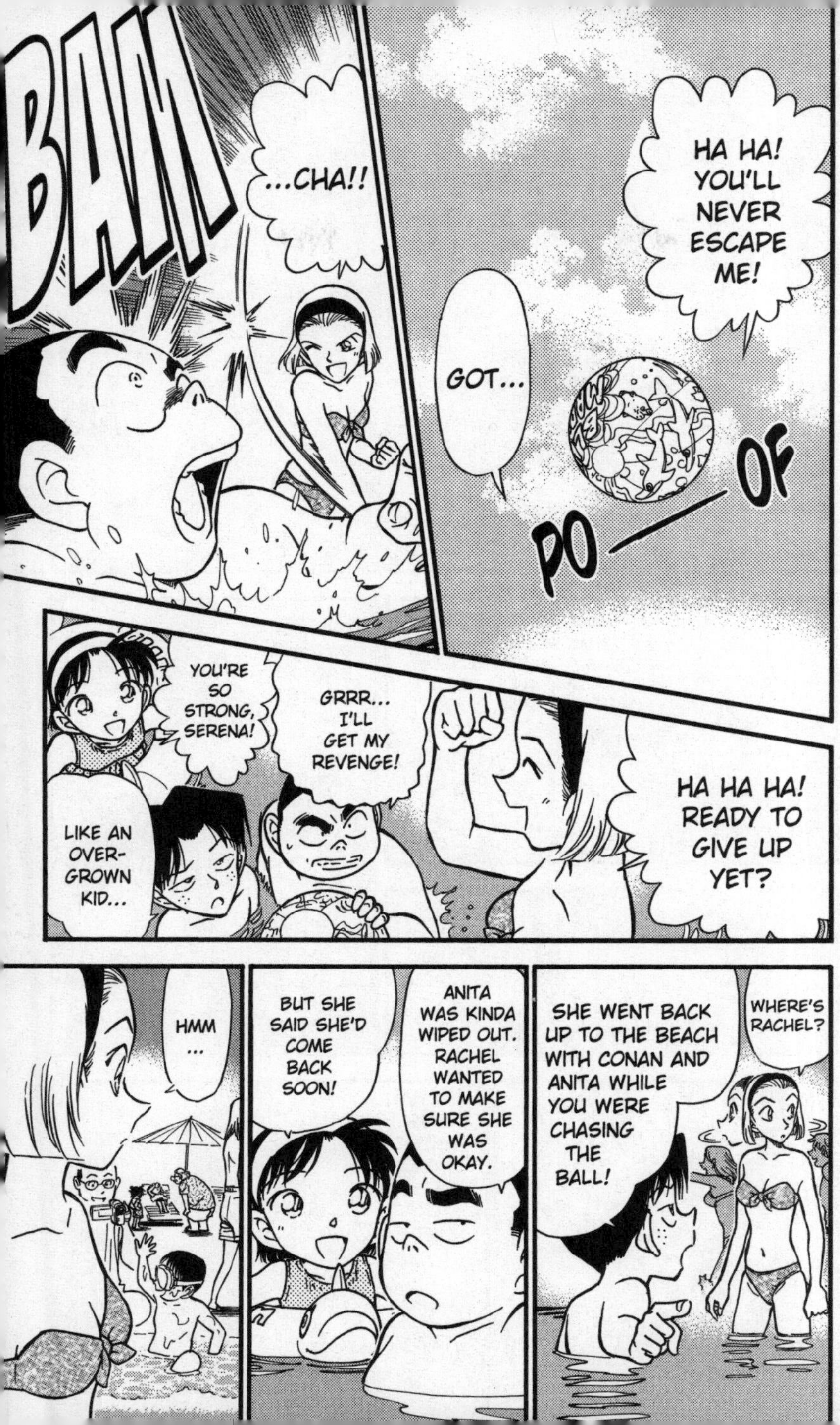
HA HA! YOU'LL NEVER ESCAPE ME!
GOT...
PO—OF
...CHA!!
BAM
HA HA HA! READY TO GIVE UP YET?
GRRR... I'LL GET MY REVENGE!
YOU'RE SO STRONG, SERENA!
LIKE AN OVER-GROWN KID...
WHERE'S RACHEL?
SHE WENT BACK UP TO THE BEACH WITH CONAN AND ANITA WHILE YOU WERE CHASING THE BALL!
ANITA WAS KINDA WIPED OUT. RACHEL WANTED TO MAKE SURE SHE WAS OKAY.
BUT SHE SAID SHE'D COME BACK SOON!
HMM...

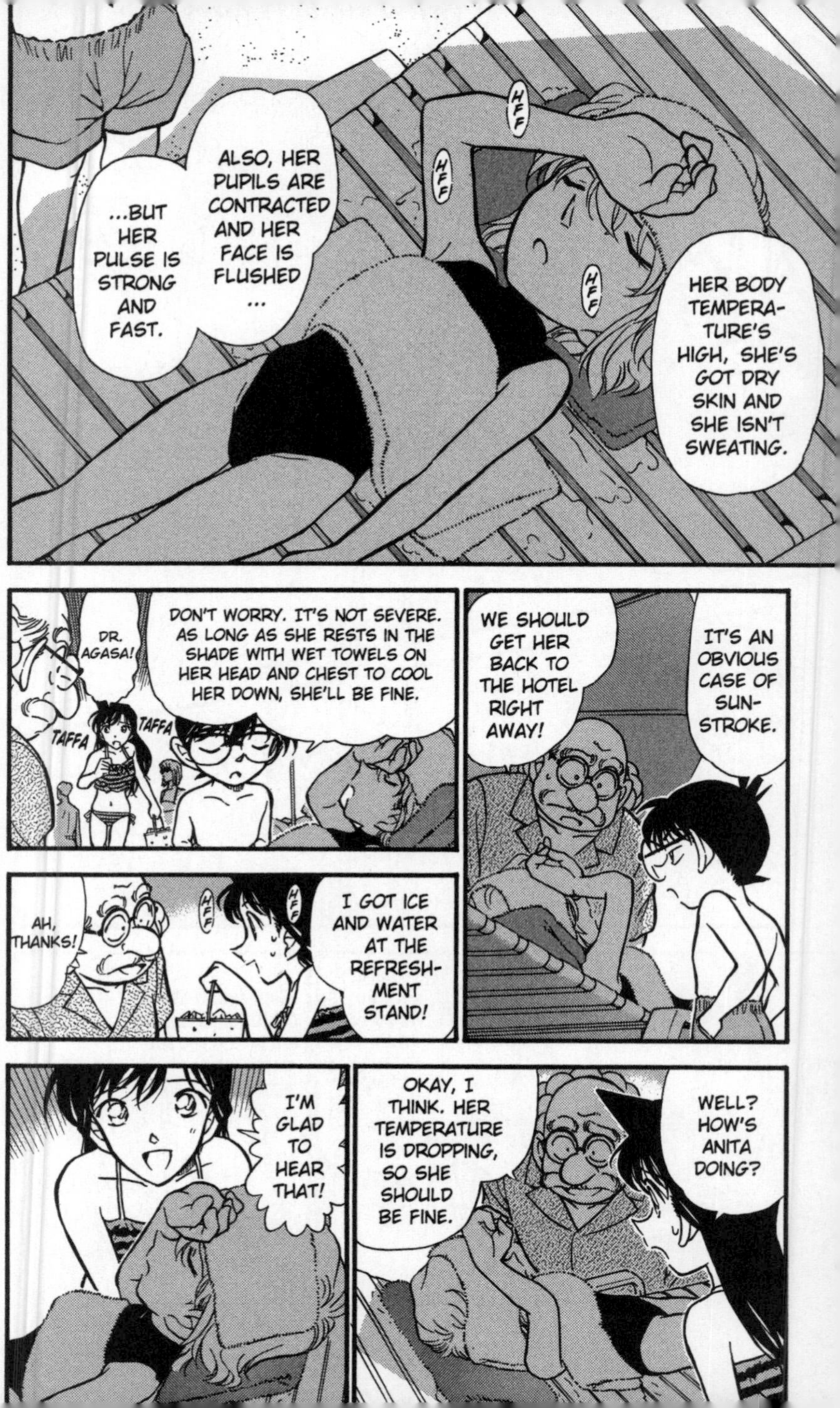
HFF
HFF
HFF
HER BODY TEMPERA-TURE'S HIGH, SHE'S GOT DRY SKIN AND SHE ISN'T SWEATING.
ALSO, HER PUPILS ARE CONTRACTED AND HER FACE IS FLUSHED ...
...BUT HER PULSE IS STRONG AND FAST.
IT'S AN OBVIOUS CASE OF SUN-STROKE.
WE SHOULD GET HER BACK TO THE HOTEL RIGHT AWAY!
DON'T WORRY. IT'S NOT SEVERE. AS LONG AS SHE RESTS IN THE SHADE WITH WET TOWELS ON HER HEAD AND CHEST TO COOL HER DOWN, SHE'LL BE FINE.
DR. AGASA!
TAFFA
TAFFA
I GOT ICE AND WATER AT THE REFRESH-MENT STAND!
HFF
HFF
AH, THANKS!
WELL? HOW'S ANITA DOING?
OKAY, I THINK. HER TEMPERATURE IS DROPPING, SO SHE SHOULD BE FINE.
I'M GLAD TO HEAR THAT!

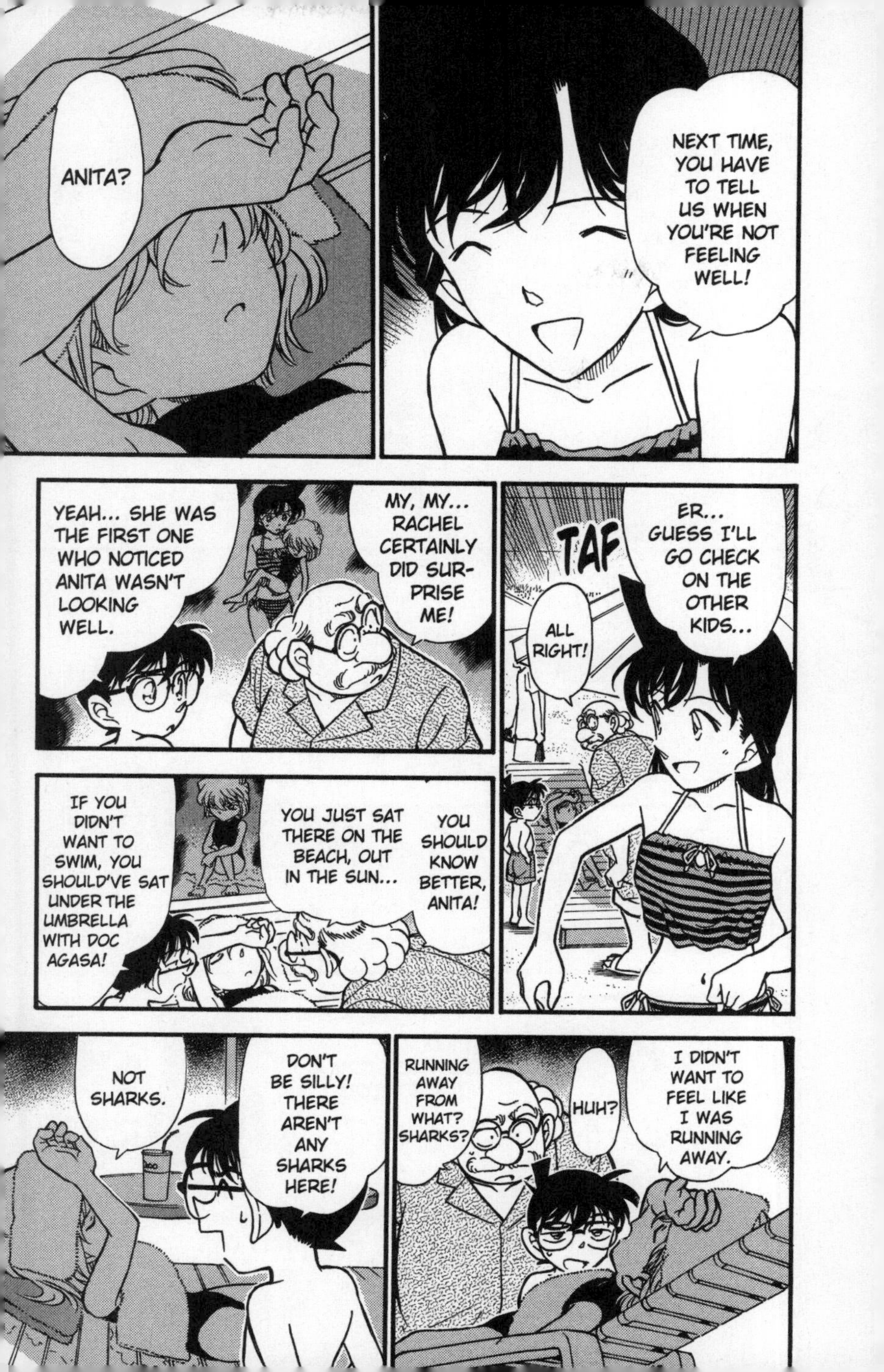
NEXT TIME, YOU HAVE TO TELL US WHEN YOU'RE NOT FEELING WELL!
ANITA?
ER... GUESS I'LL GO CHECK ON THE OTHER KIDS...
TAF
ALL RIGHT!
MY, MY... RACHEL CERTAINLY DID SUR-PRISE ME!
YEAH... SHE WAS THE FIRST ONE WHO NOTICED ANITA WASN'T LOOKING WELL.
YOU SHOULD KNOW BETTER, ANITA!
YOU JUST SAT THERE ON THE BEACH, OUT IN THE SUN...
IF YOU DIDN'T WANT TO SWIM, YOU SHOULD'VE SAT UNDER THE UMBRELLA WITH DOC AGASA!
I DIDN'T WANT TO FEEL LIKE I WAS RUNNING AWAY.
HUH?
RUNNING AWAY FROM WHAT? SHARKS?
DON'T BE SILLY! THERE AREN'T ANY SHARKS HERE!
NOT SHARKS.

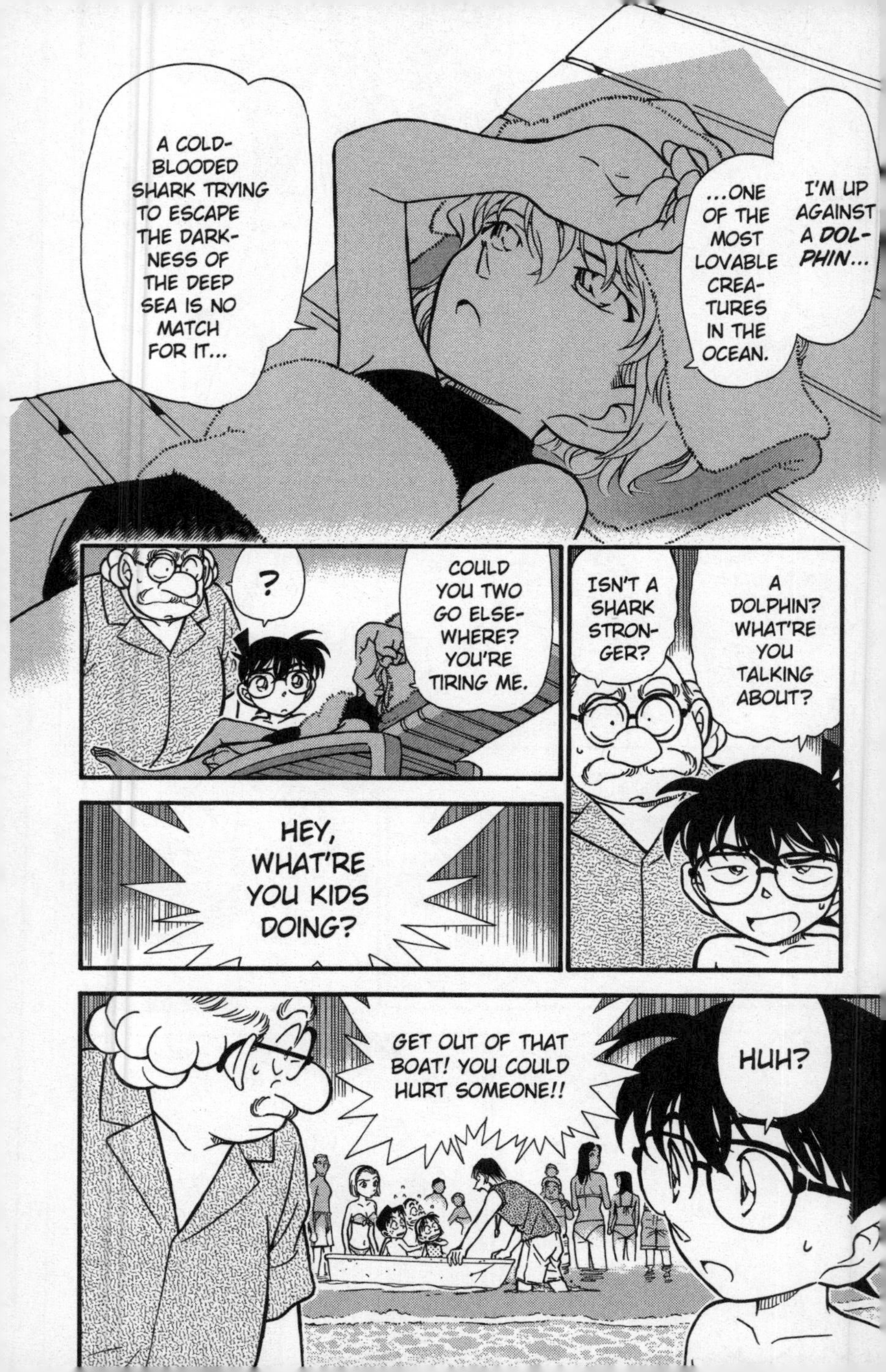
I'M UP AGAINST A DOLPHIN...
...ONE OF THE MOST LOVABLE CREATURES IN THE OCEAN.
A COLD-BLOODED SHARK TRYING TO ESCAPE THE DARKNESS OF THE DEEP SEA IS NO MATCH FOR IT...
A DOLPHIN? WHAT'RE YOU TALKING ABOUT?
ISN'T A SHARK STRONGER?
COULD YOU TWO GO ELSEWHERE? YOU'RE TIRING ME.
?
HEY, WHAT'RE YOU KIDS DOING?
HUH?
GET OUT OF THAT BOAT! YOU COULD HURT SOMEONE!!

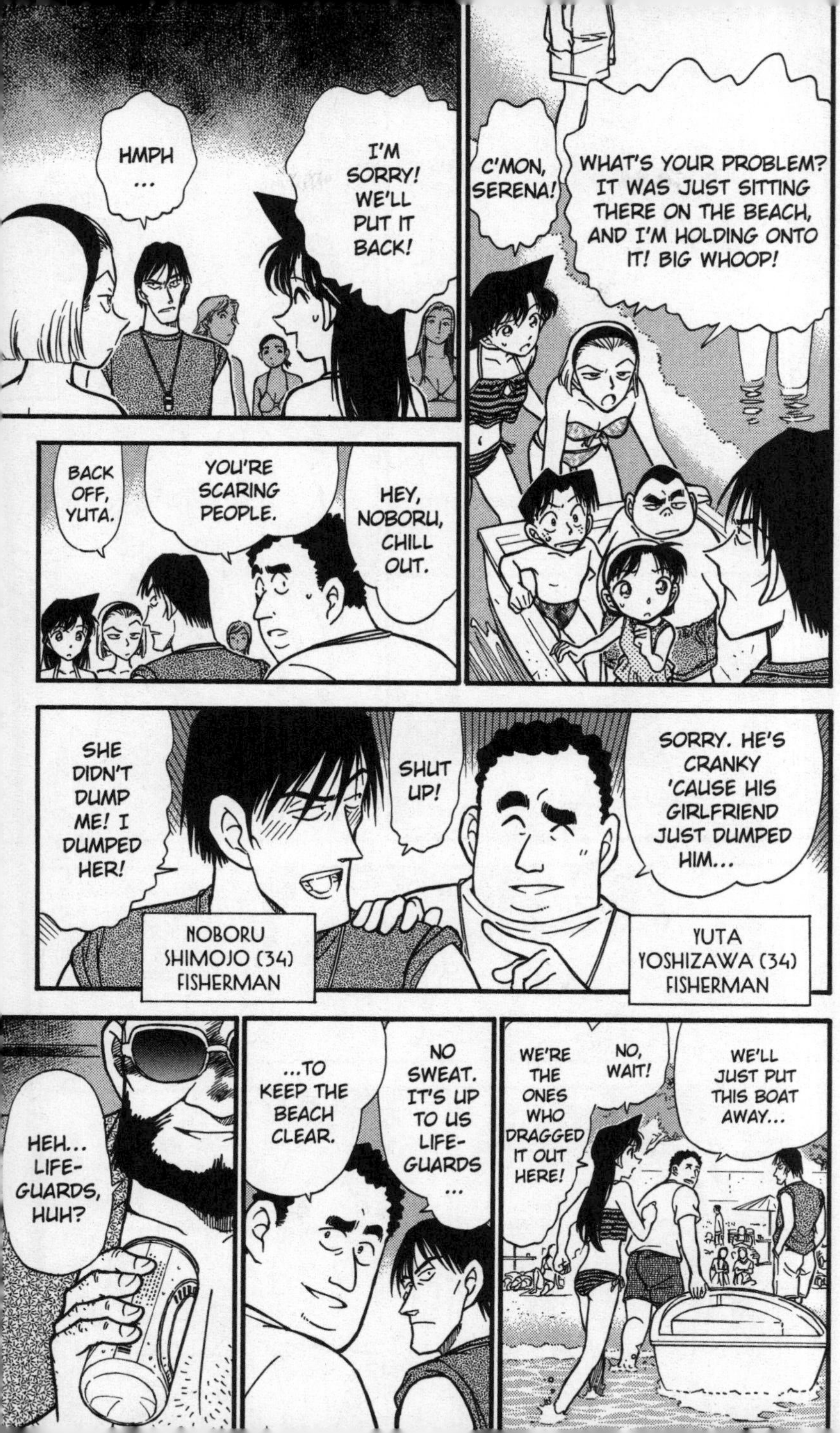
WHAT'S YOUR PROBLEM? IT WAS JUST SITTING THERE ON THE BEACH, AND I'M HOLDING ONTO IT! BIG WHOOP!
C'MON, SERENA!
I'M SORRY! WE'LL PUT IT BACK!
HMPH ...
HEY, NOBORU, CHILL OUT.
YOU'RE SCARING PEOPLE.
BACK OFF, YUTA.
SORRY. HE'S CRANKY 'CAUSE HIS GIRLFRIEND JUST DUMPED HIM...
YUTA YOSHIZAWA (34) FISHERMAN
SHUT UP!
SHE DIDN'T DUMP ME! I DUMPED HER!
NOBORU SHIMOJO (34) FISHERMAN
WE'LL JUST PUT THIS BOAT AWAY...
NO, WAIT!
WE'RE THE ONES WHO DRAGGED IT OUT HERE!
NO SWEAT. IT'S UP TO US LIFE-GUARDS ...
...TO KEEP THE BEACH CLEAR.
HEH... LIFE-GUARDS, HUH?

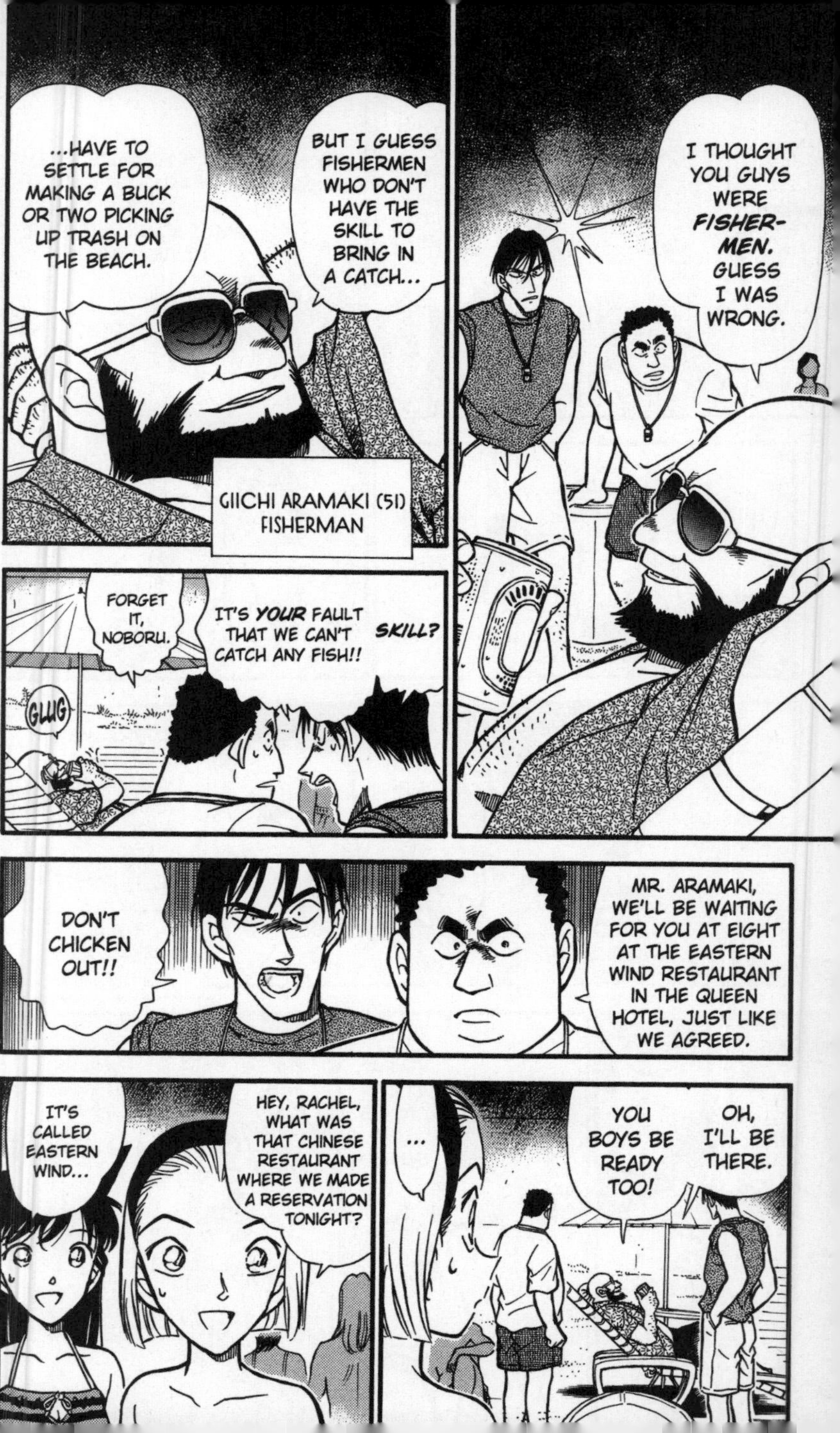
I THOUGHT YOU GUYS WERE **FISHERMEN.** GUESS I WAS WRONG.
BUT I GUESS FISHERMEN WHO DON'T HAVE THE SKILL TO BRING IN A CATCH...
...HAVE TO SETTLE FOR MAKING A BUCK OR TWO PICKING UP TRASH ON THE BEACH.
GIICHI ARAMAKI (51) FISHERMAN
SKILL?
IT'S ***YOUR*** FAULT THAT WE CAN'T CATCH ANY FISH!!
FORGET IT, NOBORU.
GLUG
MR. ARAMAKI, WE'LL BE WAITING FOR YOU AT EIGHT AT THE EASTERN WIND RESTAURANT IN THE QUEEN HOTEL, JUST LIKE WE AGREED.
DON'T CHICKEN OUT!!
OH, I'LL BE THERE.
YOU BOYS BE READY TOO!
...
HEY, RACHEL, WHAT WAS THAT CHINESE RESTAURANT WHERE WE MADE A RESERVATION TONIGHT?
IT'S CALLED EASTERN WIND...

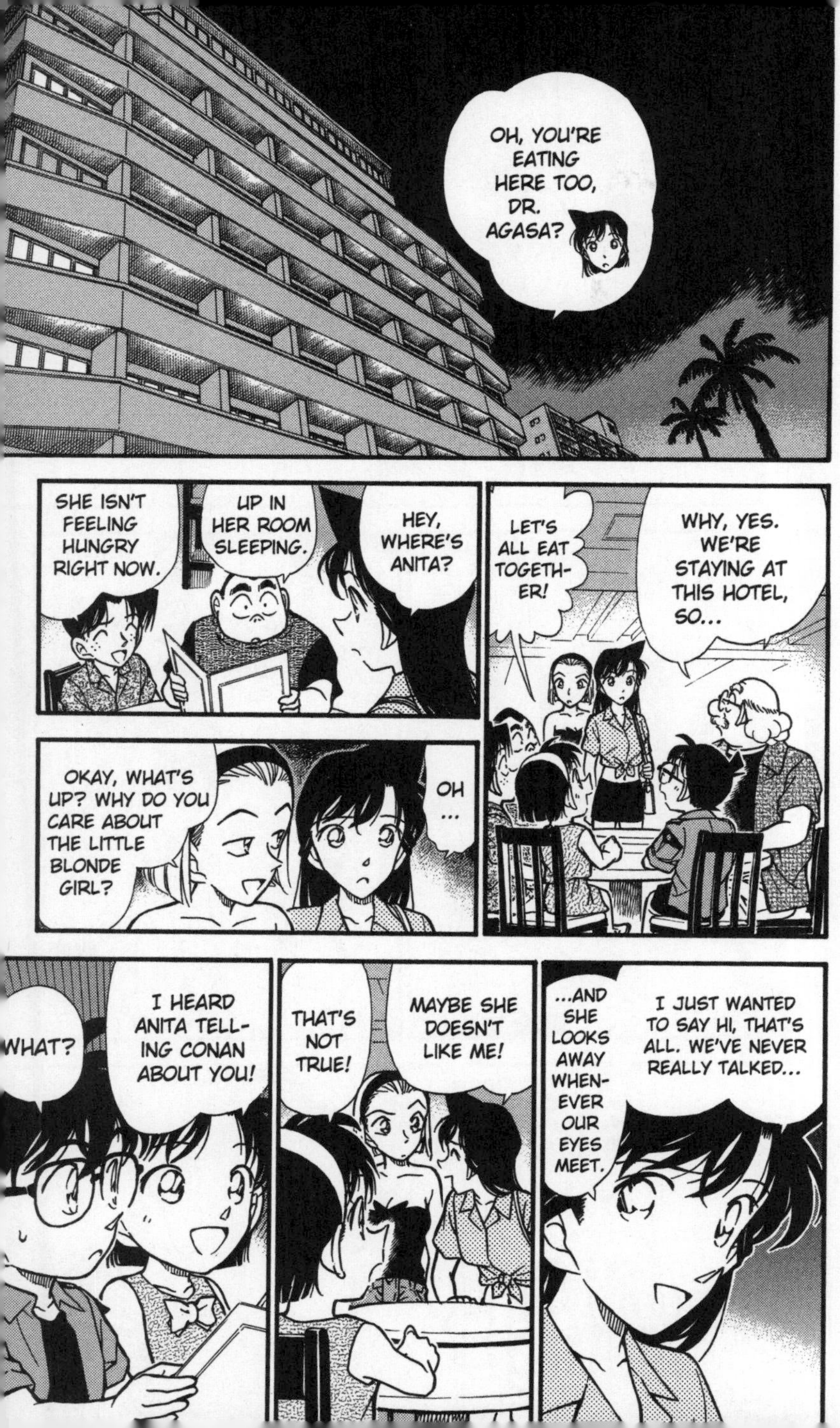
OH, YOU'RE EATING HERE TOO, DR. AGASA?
WHY, YES. WE'RE STAYING AT THIS HOTEL, SO...
LET'S ALL EAT TOGETH-ER!
HEY, WHERE'S ANITA?
UP IN HER ROOM SLEEPING.
SHE ISN'T FEELING HUNGRY RIGHT NOW.
OH ...
OKAY, WHAT'S UP? WHY DO YOU CARE ABOUT THE LITTLE BLONDE GIRL?
I JUST WANTED TO SAY HI, THAT'S ALL. WE'VE NEVER REALLY TALKED...
...AND SHE LOOKS AWAY WHEN-EVER OUR EYES MEET.
MAYBE SHE DOESN'T LIKE ME!
THAT'S NOT TRUE!
I HEARD ANITA TELL-ING CONAN ABOUT YOU!
WHAT?

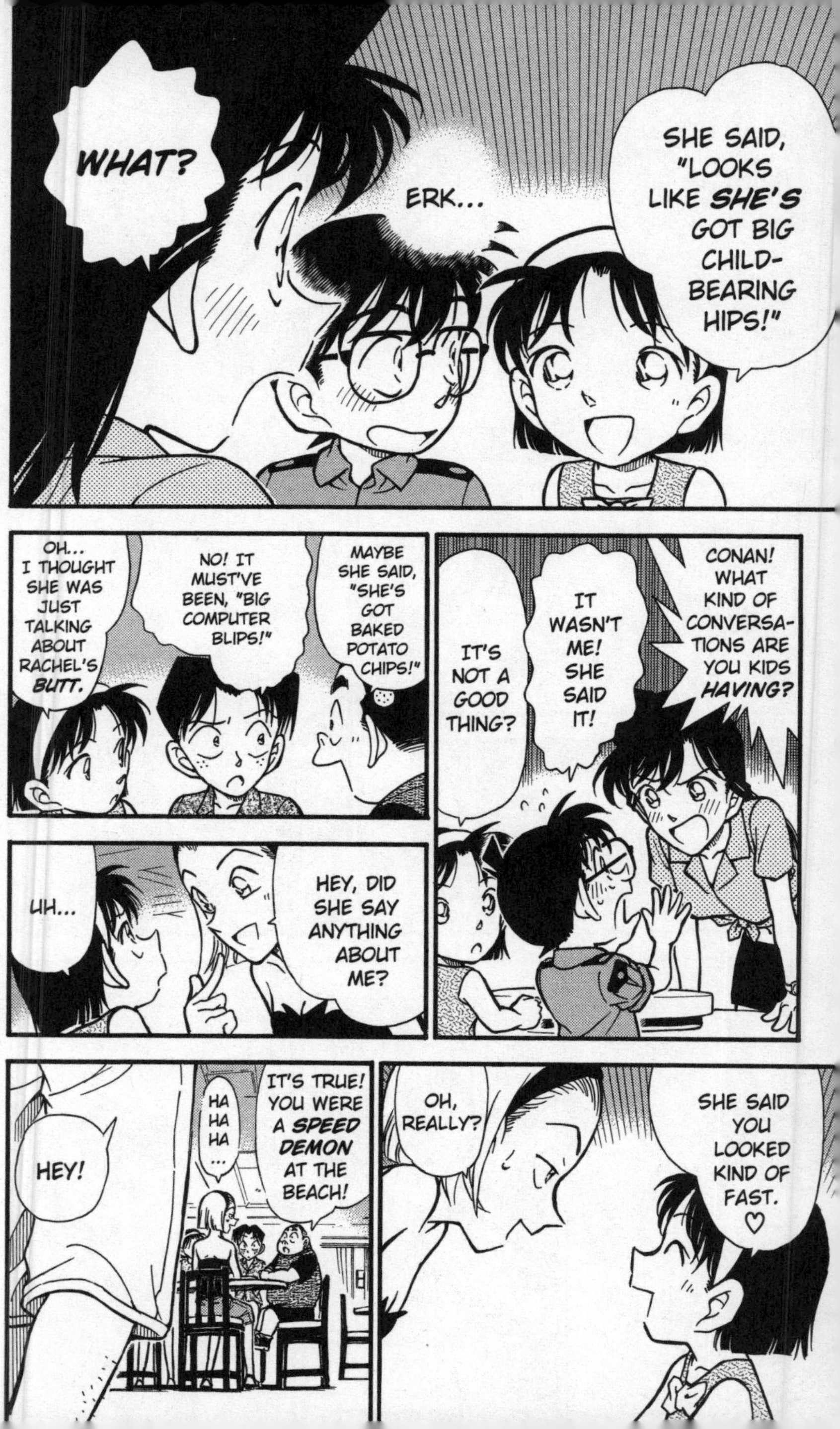
SHE SAID, "LOOKS LIKE SHE'S GOT BIG CHILD-BEARING HIPS!"
ERK...
WHAT?
CONAN! WHAT KIND OF CONVERSA-TIONS ARE YOU KIDS HAVING?
IT WASN'T ME! SHE SAID IT!
IT'S NOT A GOOD THING?
MAYBE SHE SAID, "SHE'S GOT BAKED POTATO CHIPS!"
NO! IT MUST'VE BEEN, "BIG COMPUTER BLIPS!"
OH... I THOUGHT SHE WAS JUST TALKING ABOUT RACHEL'S BUTT.
HEY, DID SHE SAY ANYTHING ABOUT ME?
UH...
SHE SAID YOU LOOKED KIND OF FAST. ♡
OH, REALLY?
IT'S TRUE! YOU WERE A SPEED DEMON AT THE BEACH!
HA HA HA ...
HEY!

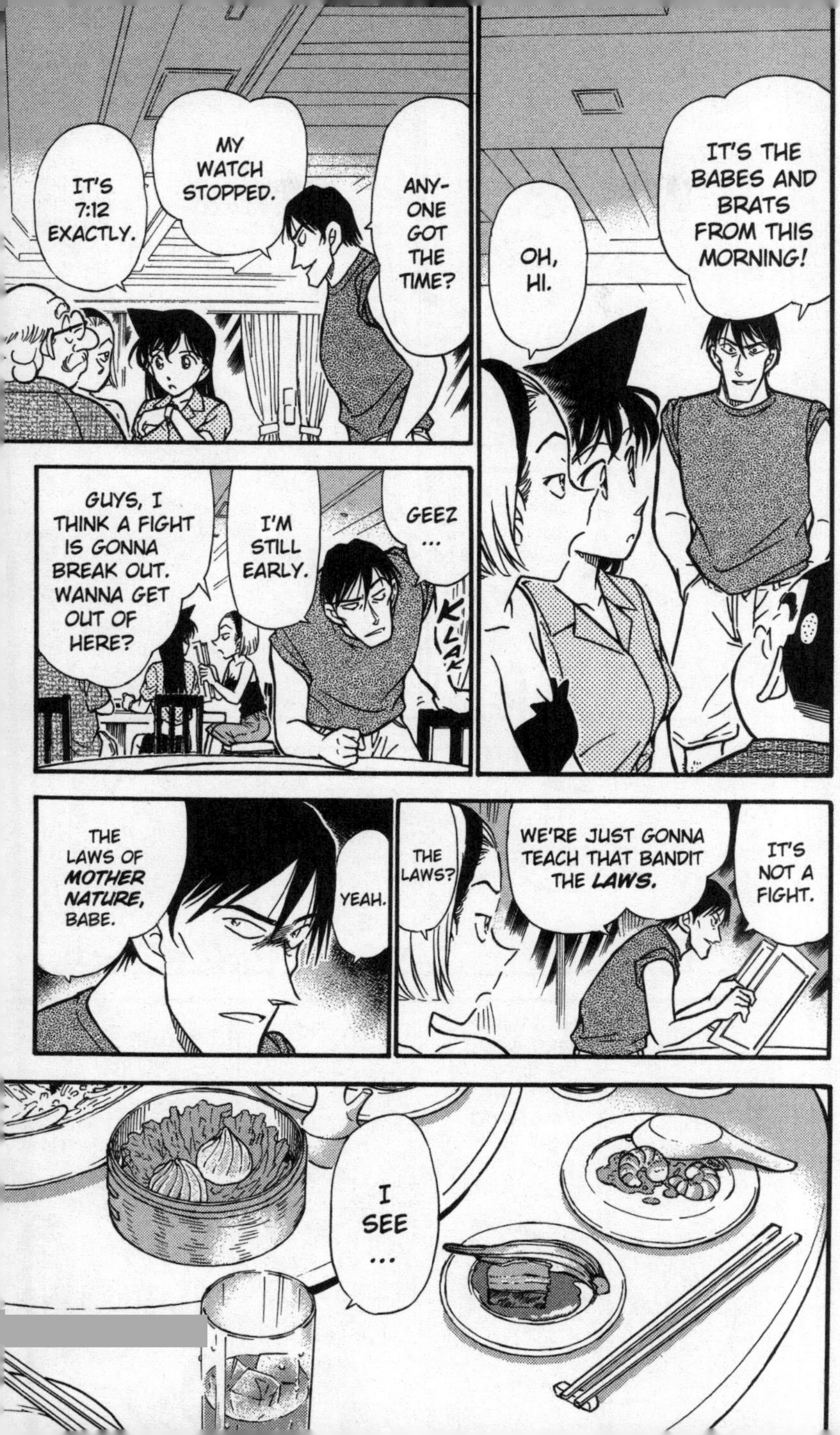
IT'S THE BABES AND BRATS FROM THIS MORNING!
OH, HI.
ANY-ONE GOT THE TIME?
MY WATCH STOPPED.
IT'S 7:12 EXACTLY.
GEEZ ...
KLAK
I'M STILL EARLY.
GUYS, I THINK A FIGHT IS GONNA BREAK OUT. WANNA GET OUT OF HERE?
IT'S NOT A FIGHT.
WE'RE JUST GONNA TEACH THAT BANDIT THE ***LAWS.***
THE LAWS?
YEAH.
THE LAWS OF ***MOTHER NATURE,*** BABE.
I SEE ...

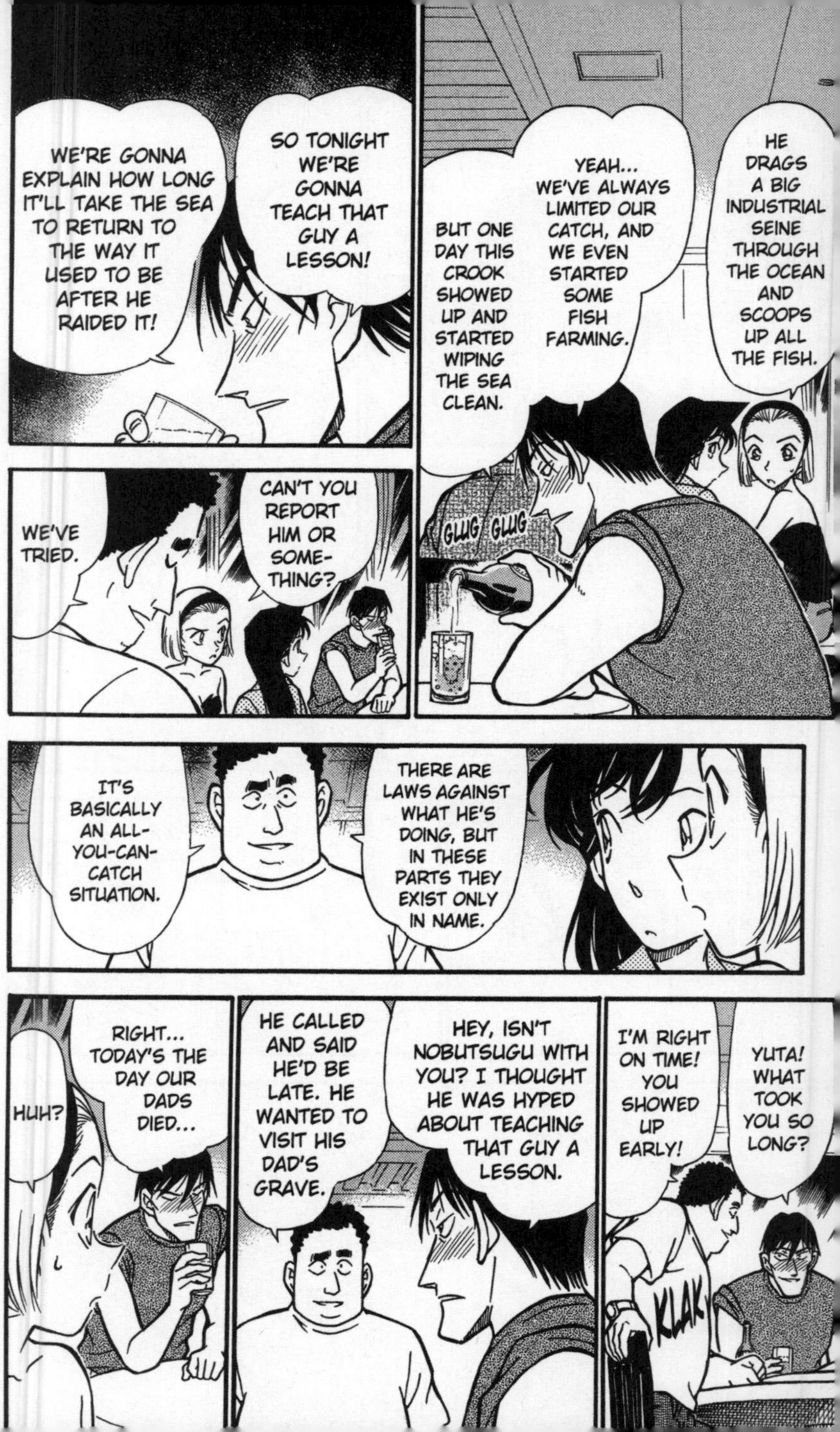
HE DRAGS A BIG INDUSTRIAL SEINE THROUGH THE OCEAN AND SCOOPS UP ALL THE FISH.
YEAH... WE'VE ALWAYS LIMITED OUR CATCH, AND WE EVEN STARTED SOME FISH FARMING.
BUT ONE DAY THIS CROOK SHOWED UP AND STARTED WIPING THE SEA CLEAN.
GLUG GLUG
SO TONIGHT WE'RE GONNA TEACH THAT GUY A LESSON!
WE'RE GONNA EXPLAIN HOW LONG IT'LL TAKE THE SEA TO RETURN TO THE WAY IT USED TO BE AFTER HE RAIDED IT!
CAN'T YOU REPORT HIM OR SOME-THING?
WE'VE TRIED.
THERE ARE LAWS AGAINST WHAT HE'S DOING, BUT IN THESE PARTS THEY EXIST ONLY IN NAME.
IT'S BASICALLY AN ALL-YOU-CAN-CATCH SITUATION.
YUTA! WHAT TOOK YOU SO LONG?
I'M RIGHT ON TIME! YOU SHOWED UP EARLY!
KLAK
HEY, ISN'T NOBUTSUGU WITH YOU? I THOUGHT HE WAS HYPED ABOUT TEACHING THAT GUY A LESSON.
HE CALLED AND SAID HE'D BE LATE. HE WANTED TO VISIT HIS DAD'S GRAVE.
RIGHT... TODAY'S THE DAY OUR DADS DIED...
HUH?

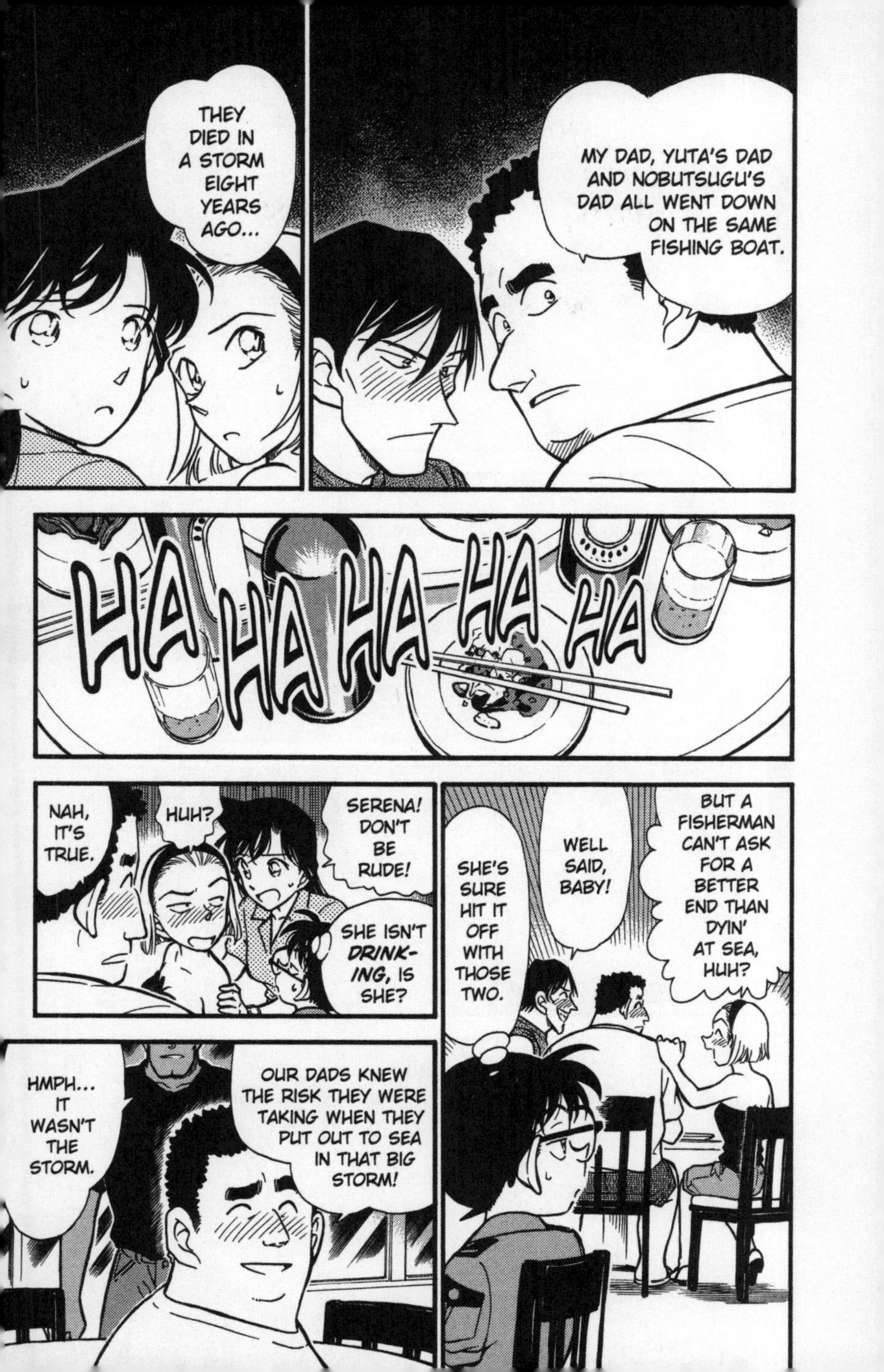
MY DAD, YUTA'S DAD AND NOBUTSUGU'S DAD ALL WENT DOWN ON THE SAME FISHING BOAT.
THEY DIED IN A STORM EIGHT YEARS AGO...
HA HA HA HA HA HA
BUT A FISHERMAN CAN'T ASK FOR A BETTER END THAN DYIN' AT SEA, HUH?
WELL SAID, BABY!
SHE'S SURE HIT IT OFF WITH THOSE TWO.
SERENA! DON'T BE RUDE!
HUH?
NAH, IT'S TRUE.
SHE ISN'T *DRINKING*, IS SHE?
OUR DADS KNEW THE RISK THEY WERE TAKING WHEN THEY PUT OUT TO SEA IN THAT BIG STORM!
HMPH... IT WASN'T THE STORM.

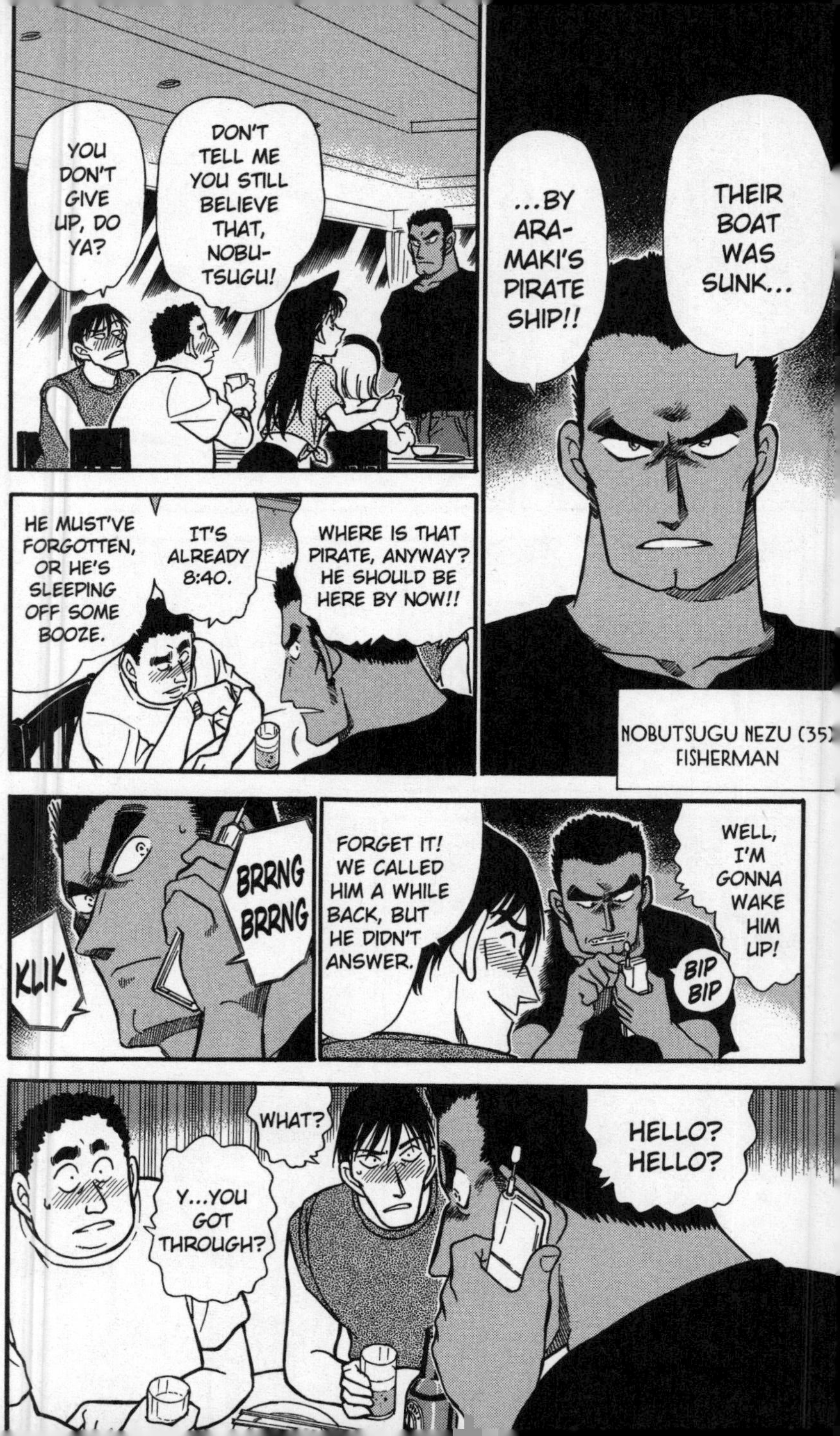
THEIR BOAT WAS SUNK...
...BY ARA-MAKI'S PIRATE SHIP!!
NOBUTSUGU NEZU (35)
FISHERMAN
DON'T TELL ME YOU STILL BELIEVE THAT, NOBU-TSUGU!
YOU DON'T GIVE UP, DO YA?
WHERE IS THAT PIRATE, ANYWAY? HE SHOULD BE HERE BY NOW!!
IT'S ALREADY 8:40.
HE MUST'VE FORGOTTEN, OR HE'S SLEEPING OFF SOME BOOZE.
WELL, I'M GONNA WAKE HIM UP!
BIP BIP
FORGET IT! WE CALLED HIM A WHILE BACK, BUT HE DIDN'T ANSWER.
BRRNG BRRNG
KLIK
HELLO? HELLO?
WHAT?
Y...YOU GOT THROUGH?

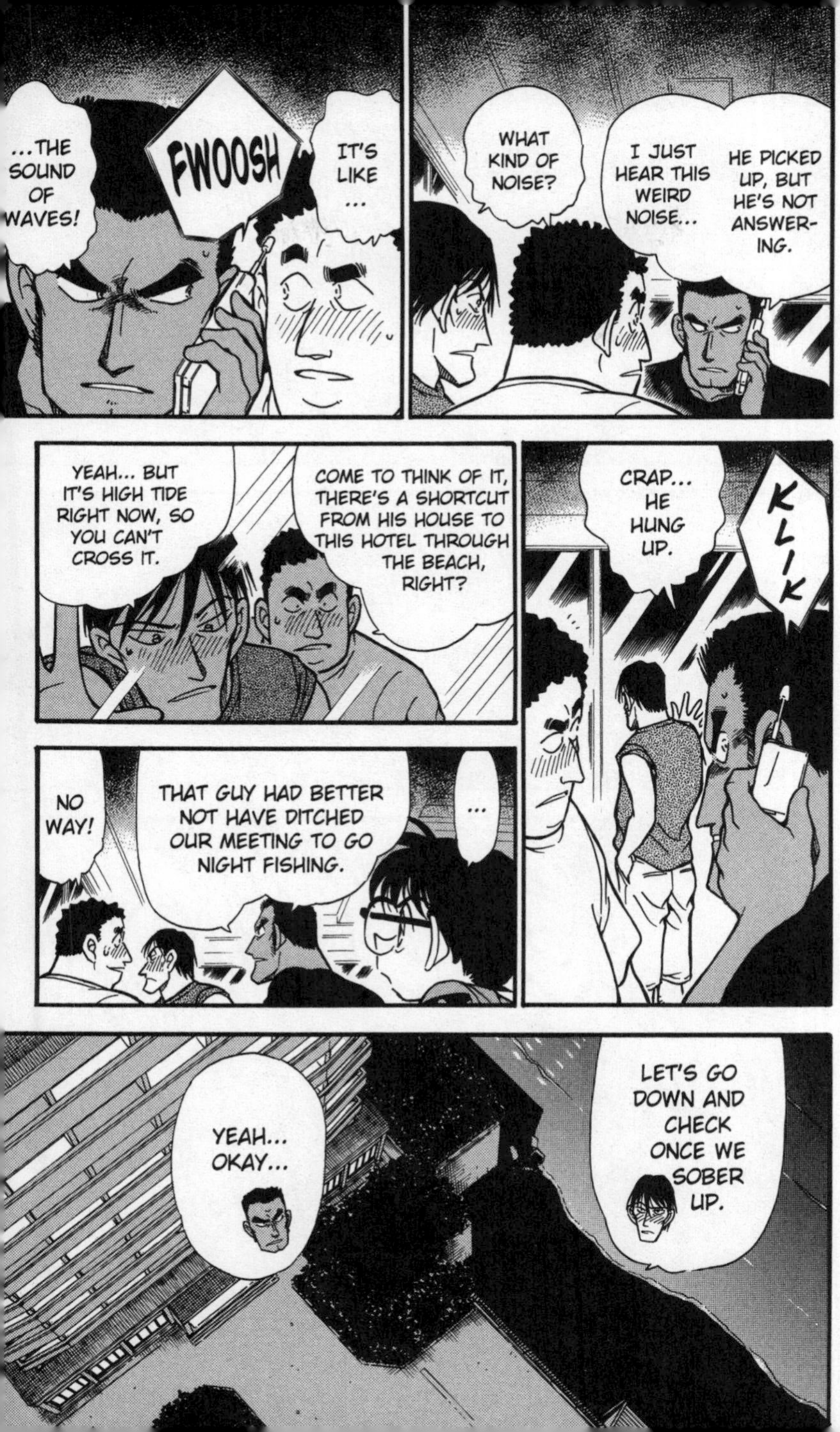
HE PICKED UP, BUT HE'S NOT ANSWER-ING.
I JUST HEAR THIS WEIRD NOISE...
WHAT KIND OF NOISE?
IT'S LIKE ...
FWOOSH
...THE SOUND OF WAVES!
KLIK
CRAP... HE HUNG UP.
COME TO THINK OF IT, THERE'S A SHORTCUT FROM HIS HOUSE TO THIS HOTEL THROUGH THE BEACH, RIGHT?
YEAH... BUT IT'S HIGH TIDE RIGHT NOW, SO YOU CAN'T CROSS IT.
...
THAT GUY HAD BETTER NOT HAVE DITCHED OUR MEETING TO GO NIGHT FISHING.
NO WAY!
LET'S GO DOWN AND CHECK ONCE WE SOBER UP.
YEAH... OKAY...

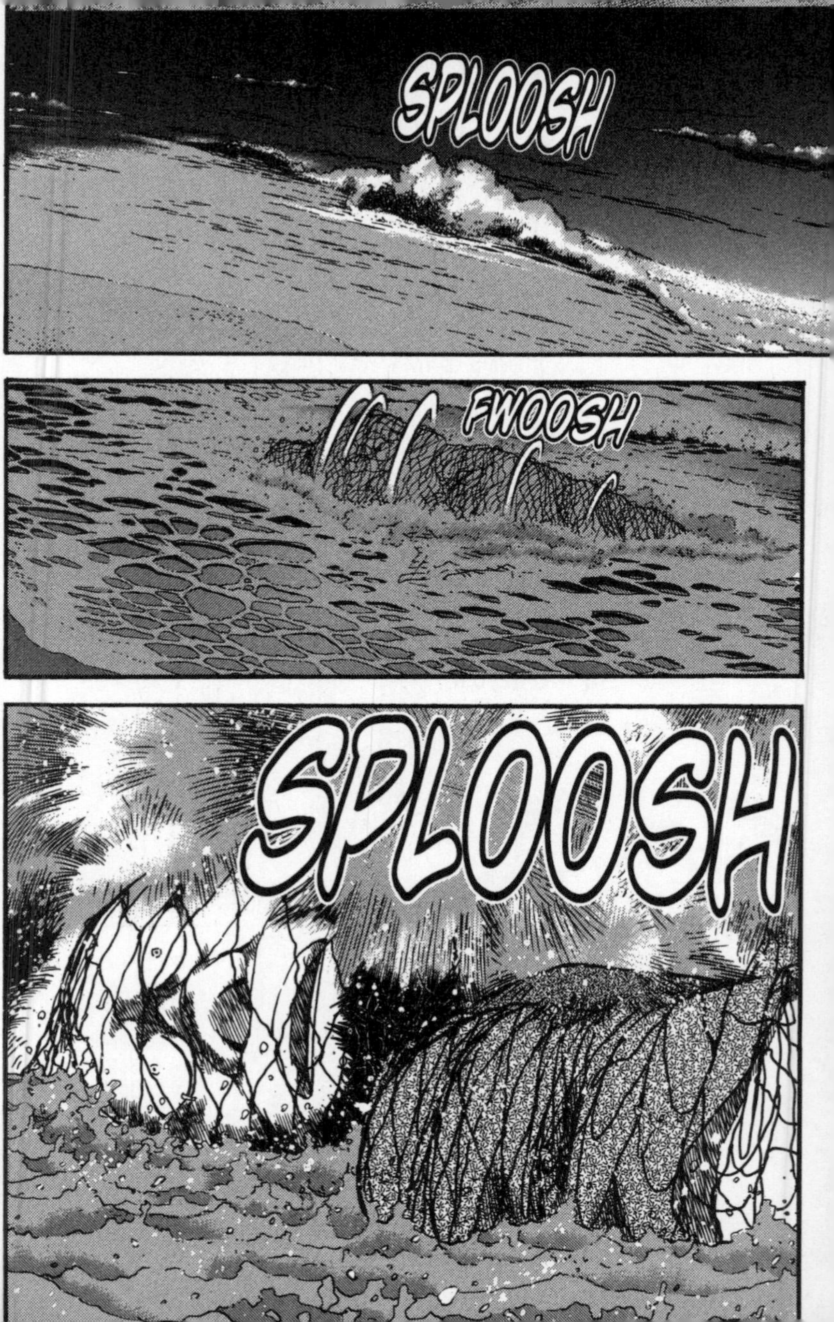
SPLOOSH
FWOOSH
SPLOOSH

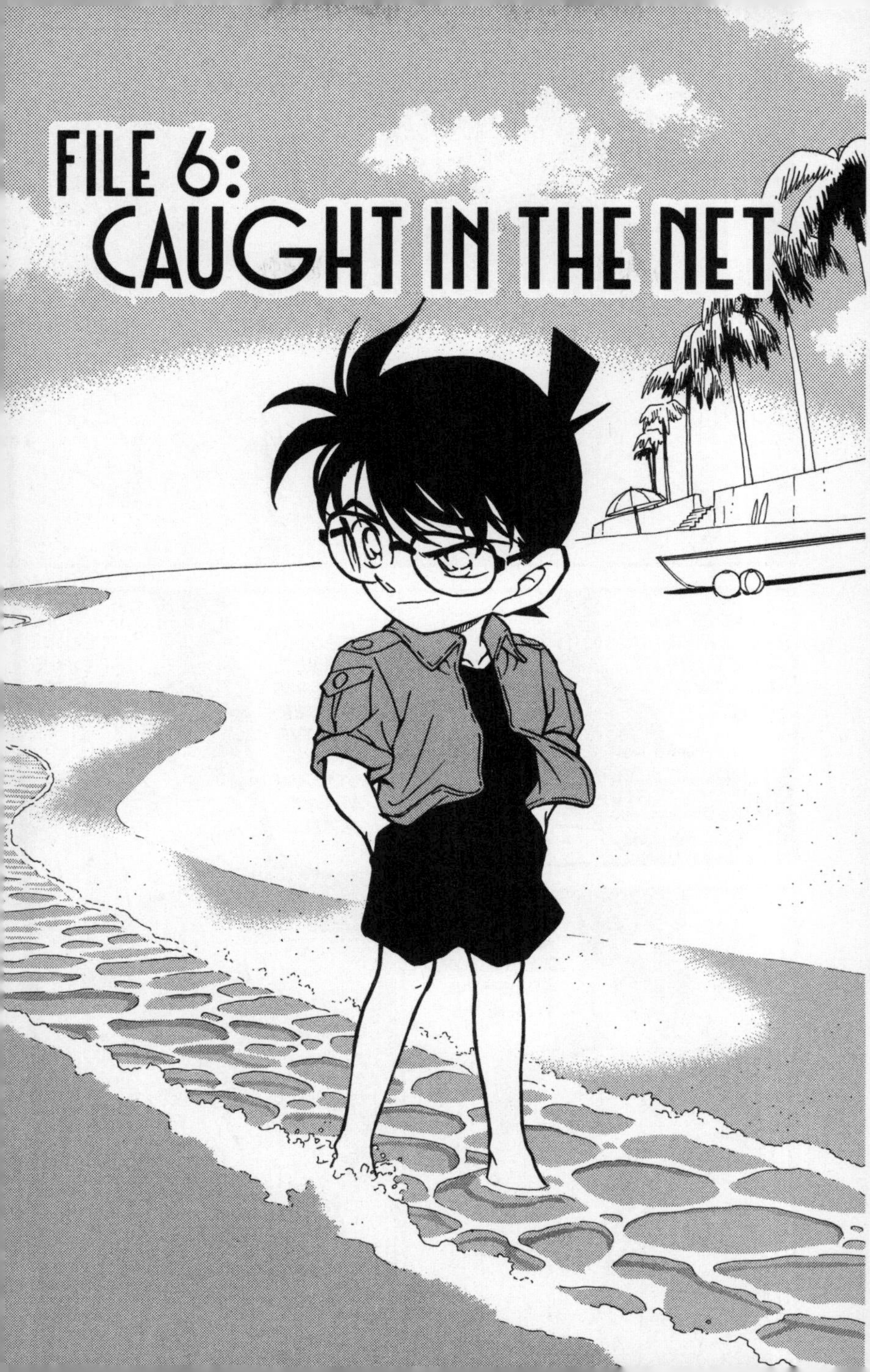
FILE 6:
CAUGHT IN THE NET

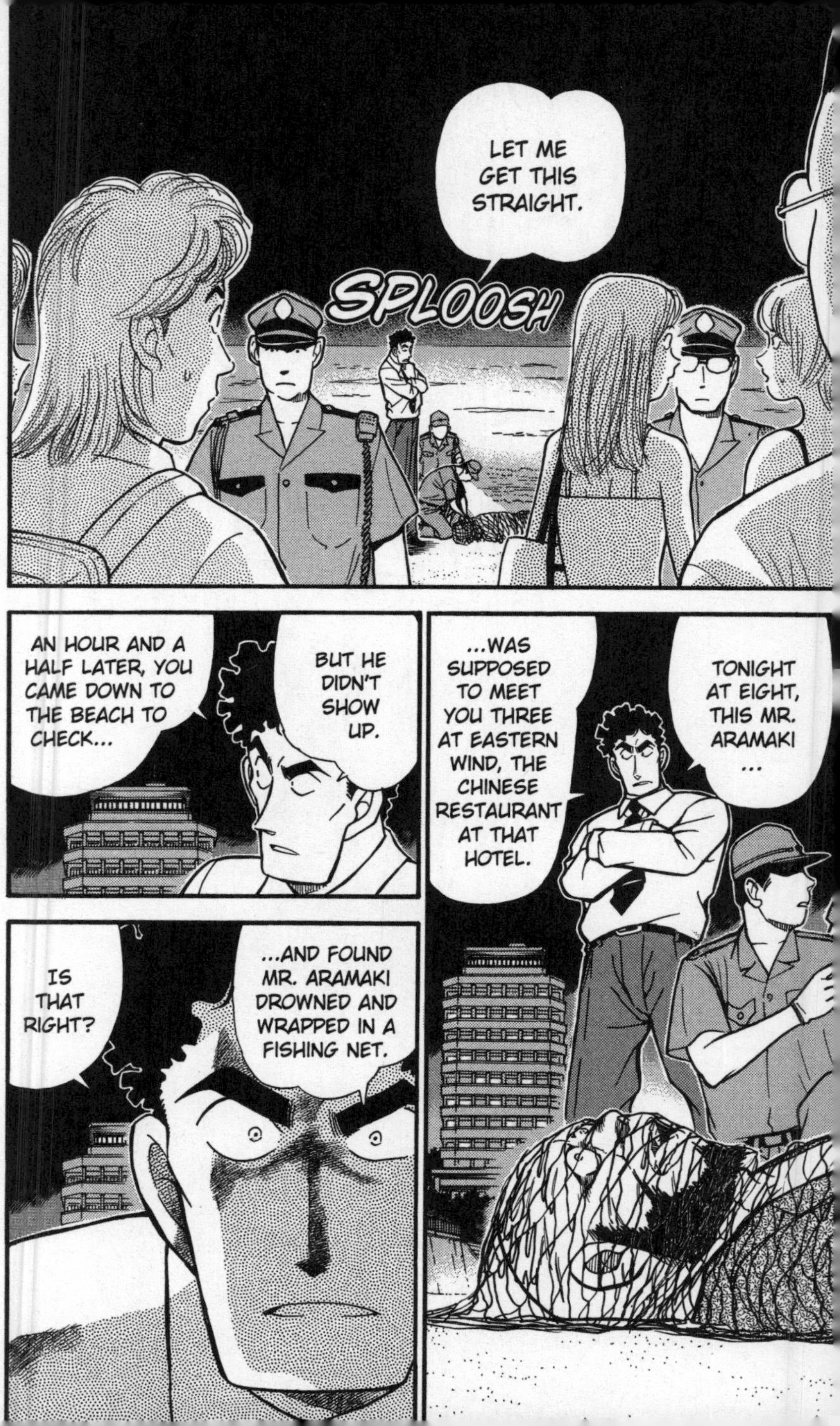
LET ME GET THIS STRAIGHT.
SPLOOSH
TONIGHT AT EIGHT, THIS MR. ARAMAKI ...
...WAS SUPPOSED TO MEET YOU THREE AT EASTERN WIND, THE CHINESE RESTAURANT AT THAT HOTEL.
BUT HE DIDN'T SHOW UP.
AN HOUR AND A HALF LATER, YOU CAME DOWN TO THE BEACH TO CHECK...
...AND FOUND MR. ARAMAKI DROWNED AND WRAPPED IN A FISHING NET.
IS THAT RIGHT?

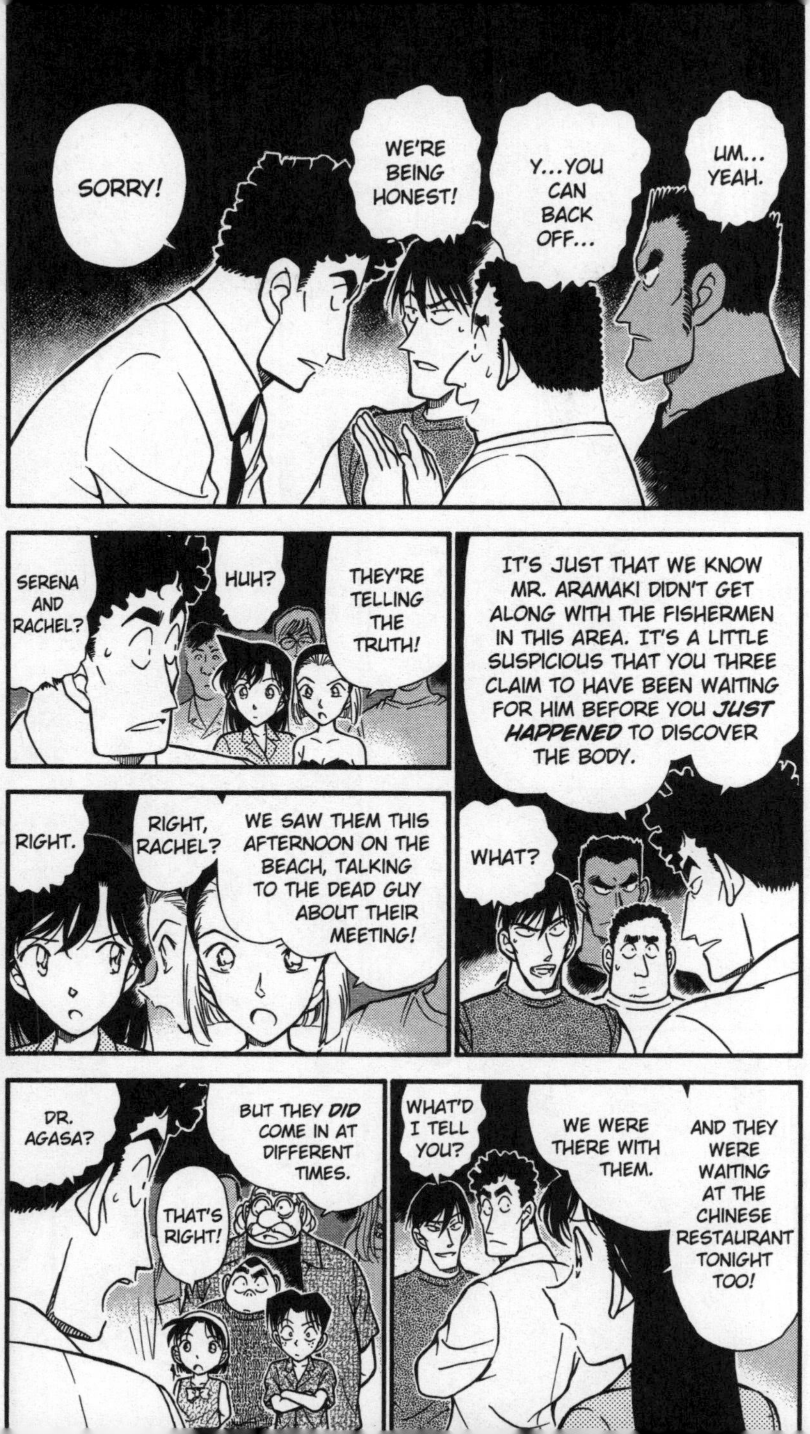
UM... YEAH.
Y...YOU CAN BACK OFF...
WE'RE BEING HONEST!
SORRY!
IT'S JUST THAT WE KNOW MR. ARAMAKI DIDN'T GET ALONG WITH THE FISHERMEN IN THIS AREA. IT'S A LITTLE SUSPICIOUS THAT YOU THREE CLAIM TO HAVE BEEN WAITING FOR HIM BEFORE YOU *JUST HAPPENED* TO DISCOVER THE BODY.
WHAT?
THEY'RE TELLING THE TRUTH!
HUH?
SERENA AND RACHEL?
WE SAW THEM THIS AFTERNOON ON THE BEACH, TALKING TO THE DEAD GUY ABOUT THEIR MEETING!
RIGHT, RACHEL?
RIGHT.
AND THEY WERE WAITING AT THE CHINESE RESTAURANT TONIGHT TOO!
WE WERE THERE WITH THEM.
WHAT'D I TELL YOU?
DR. AGASA?
THAT'S RIGHT!
BUT THEY *DID* COME IN AT DIFFERENT TIMES.

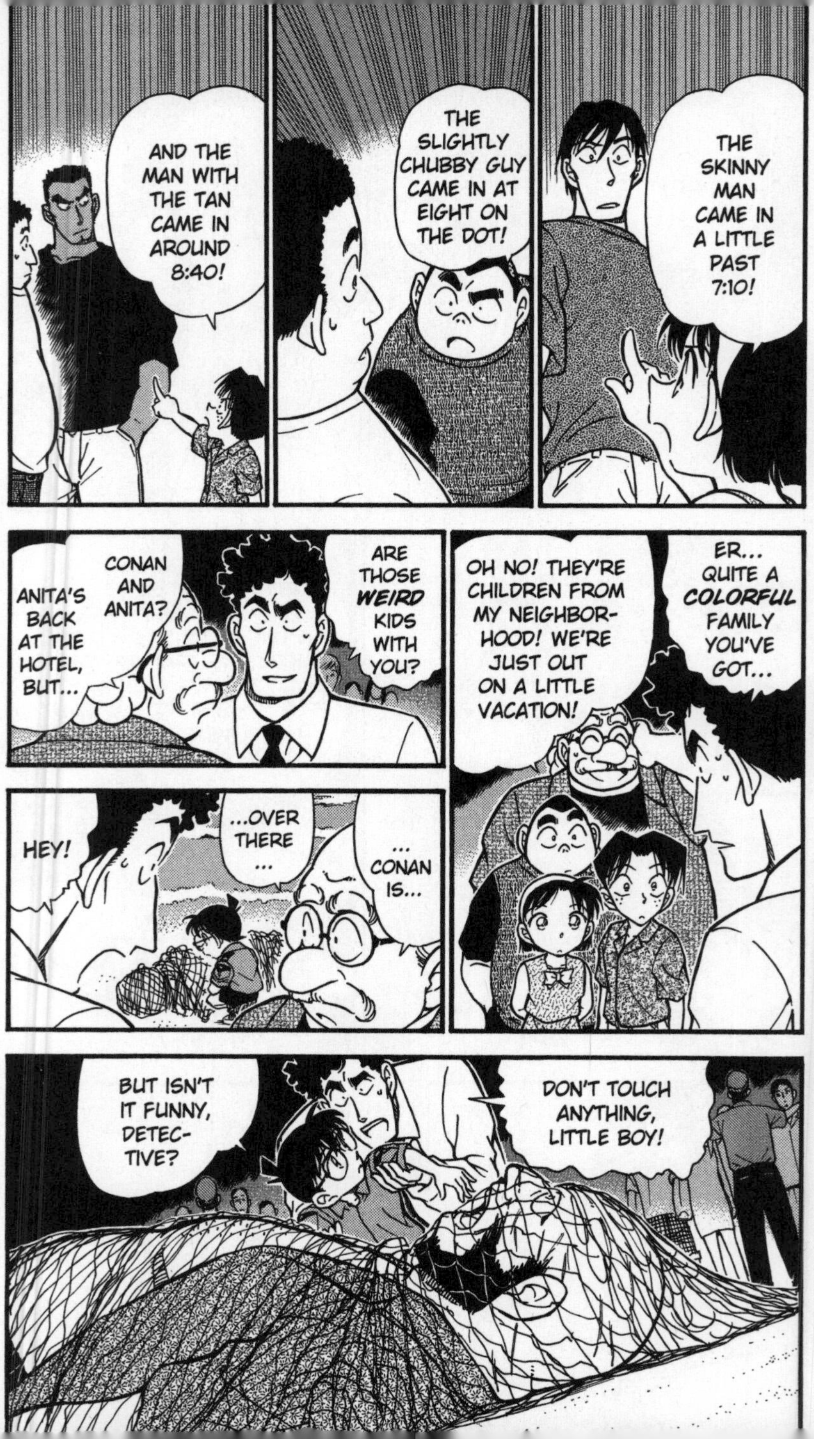
THE SKINNY MAN CAME IN A LITTLE PAST 7:10!
THE SLIGHTLY CHUBBY GUY CAME IN AT EIGHT ON THE DOT!
AND THE MAN WITH THE TAN CAME IN AROUND 8:40!
ER... QUITE A COLORFUL FAMILY YOU'VE GOT...
OH NO! THEY'RE CHILDREN FROM MY NEIGHBOR-HOOD! WE'RE JUST OUT ON A LITTLE VACATION!
ARE THOSE WEIRD KIDS WITH YOU?
CONAN AND ANITA?
ANITA'S BACK AT THE HOTEL, BUT...
... CONAN IS...
...OVER THERE ...
HEY!
DON'T TOUCH ANYTHING, LITTLE BOY!
BUT ISN'T IT FUNNY, DETEC-TIVE?

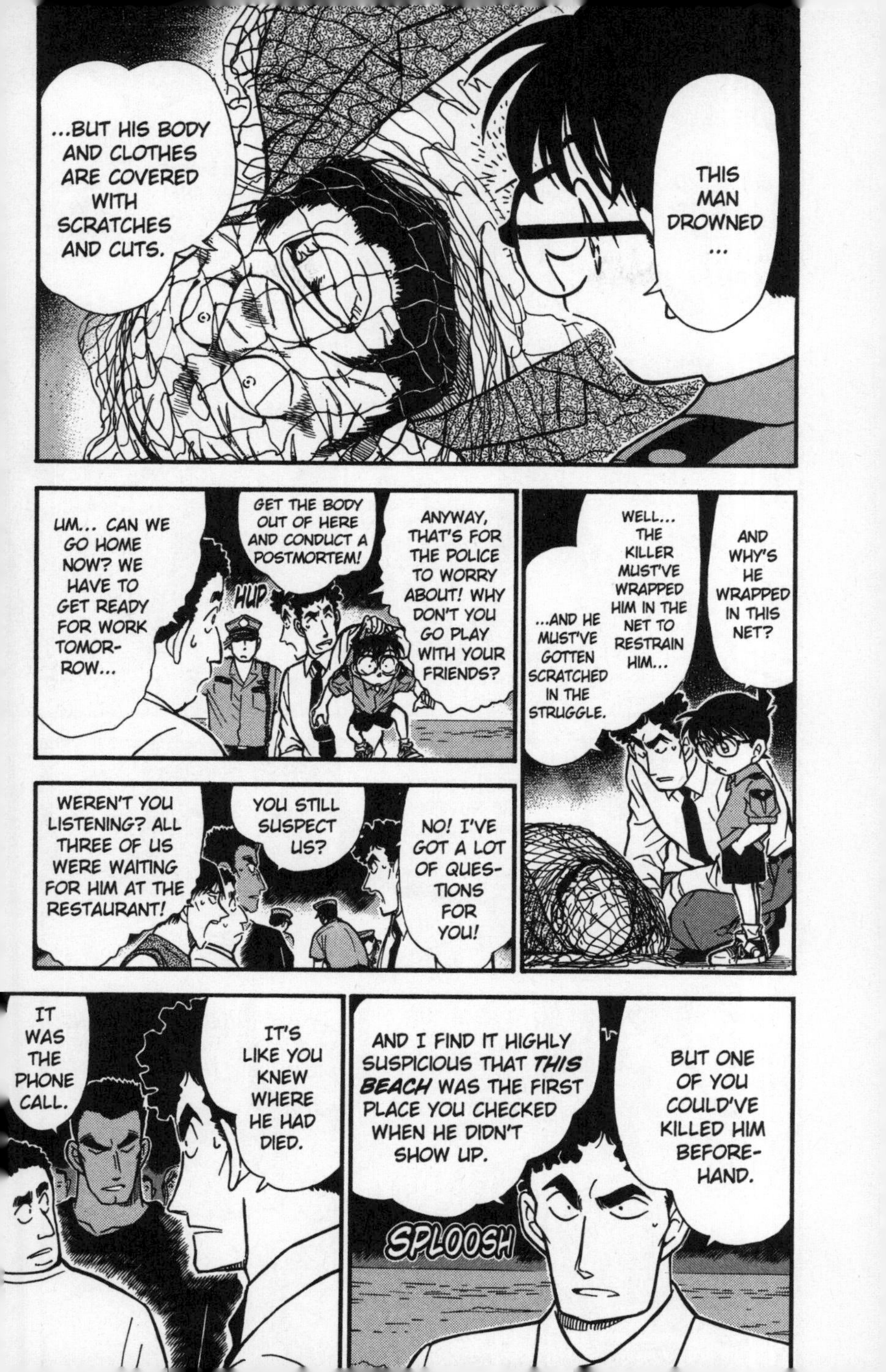
THIS MAN DROWNED ...
...BUT HIS BODY AND CLOTHES ARE COVERED WITH SCRATCHES AND CUTS.
AND WHY'S HE WRAPPED IN THIS NET?
WELL... THE KILLER MUST'VE WRAPPED HIM IN THE NET TO RESTRAIN HIM...
...AND HE MUST'VE GOTTEN SCRATCHED IN THE STRUGGLE.
ANYWAY, THAT'S FOR THE POLICE TO WORRY ABOUT! WHY DON'T YOU GO PLAY WITH YOUR FRIENDS?
GET THE BODY OUT OF HERE AND CONDUCT A POSTMORTEM!
HUP
UM... CAN WE GO HOME NOW? WE HAVE TO GET READY FOR WORK TOMOR-ROW...
NO! I'VE GOT A LOT OF QUES-TIONS FOR YOU!
YOU STILL SUSPECT US?
WEREN'T YOU LISTENING? ALL THREE OF US WERE WAITING FOR HIM AT THE RESTAURANT!
BUT ONE OF YOU COULD'VE KILLED HIM BEFORE-HAND.
AND I FIND IT HIGHLY SUSPICIOUS THAT *THIS BEACH* WAS THE FIRST PLACE YOU CHECKED WHEN HE DIDN'T SHOW UP.
SPLOOSH
IT'S LIKE YOU KNEW WHERE HE HAD DIED.
IT WAS THE PHONE CALL.

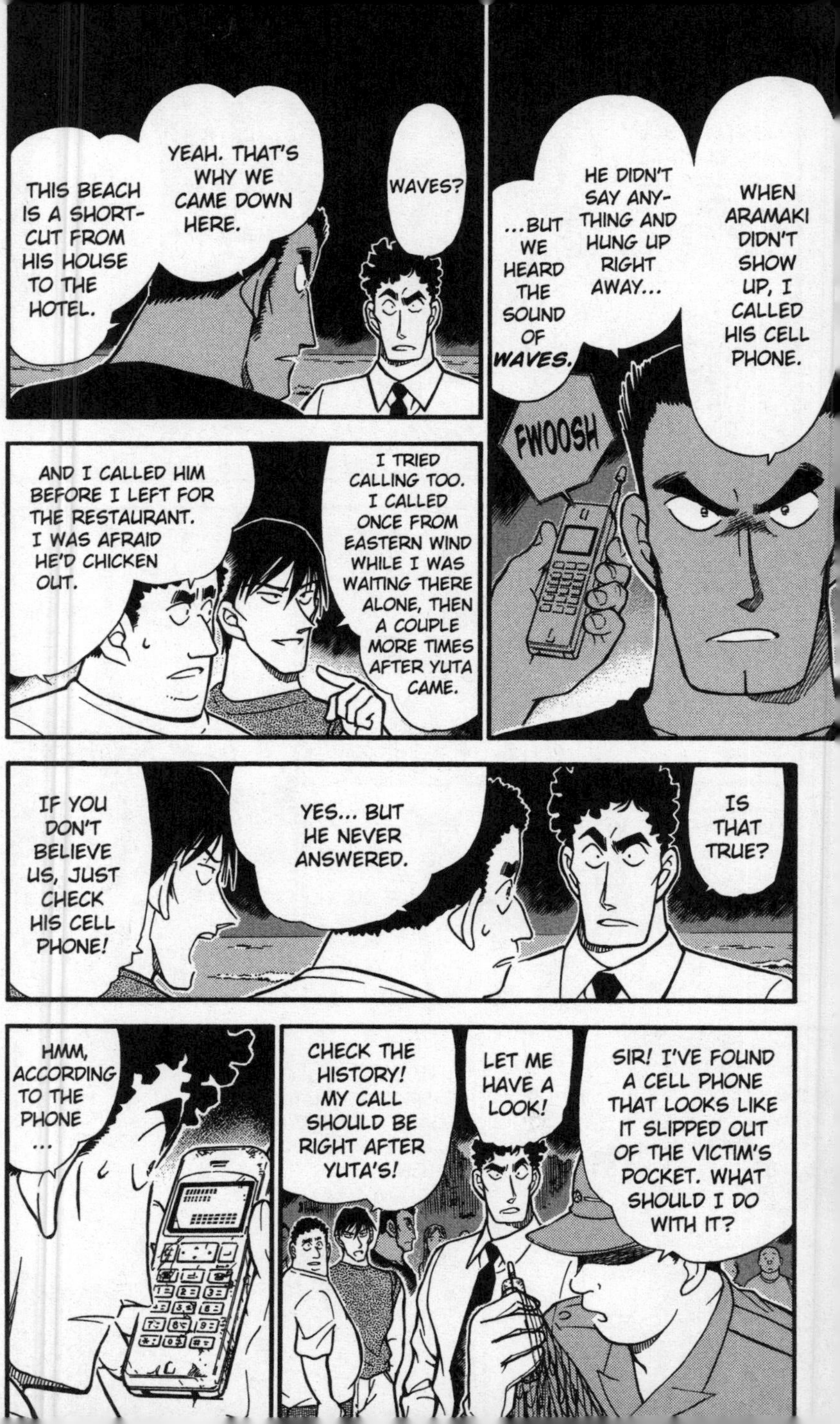
WHEN ARAMAKI DIDN'T SHOW UP, I CALLED HIS CELL PHONE.
HE DIDN'T SAY ANY-THING AND HUNG UP RIGHT AWAY...
...BUT WE HEARD THE SOUND OF WAVES.
FWOOSH
WAVES?
YEAH. THAT'S WHY WE CAME DOWN HERE.
THIS BEACH IS A SHORT-CUT FROM HIS HOUSE TO THE HOTEL.
I TRIED CALLING TOO. I CALLED ONCE FROM EASTERN WIND WHILE I WAS WAITING THERE ALONE, THEN A COUPLE MORE TIMES AFTER YUTA CAME.
AND I CALLED HIM BEFORE I LEFT FOR THE RESTAURANT. I WAS AFRAID HE'D CHICKEN OUT.
IS THAT TRUE?
YES... BUT HE NEVER ANSWERED.
IF YOU DON'T BELIEVE US, JUST CHECK HIS CELL PHONE!
SIR! I'VE FOUND A CELL PHONE THAT LOOKS LIKE IT SLIPPED OUT OF THE VICTIM'S POCKET. WHAT SHOULD I DO WITH IT?
LET ME HAVE A LOOK!
CHECK THE HISTORY! MY CALL SHOULD BE RIGHT AFTER YUTA'S!
HMM, ACCORDING TO THE PHONE ...

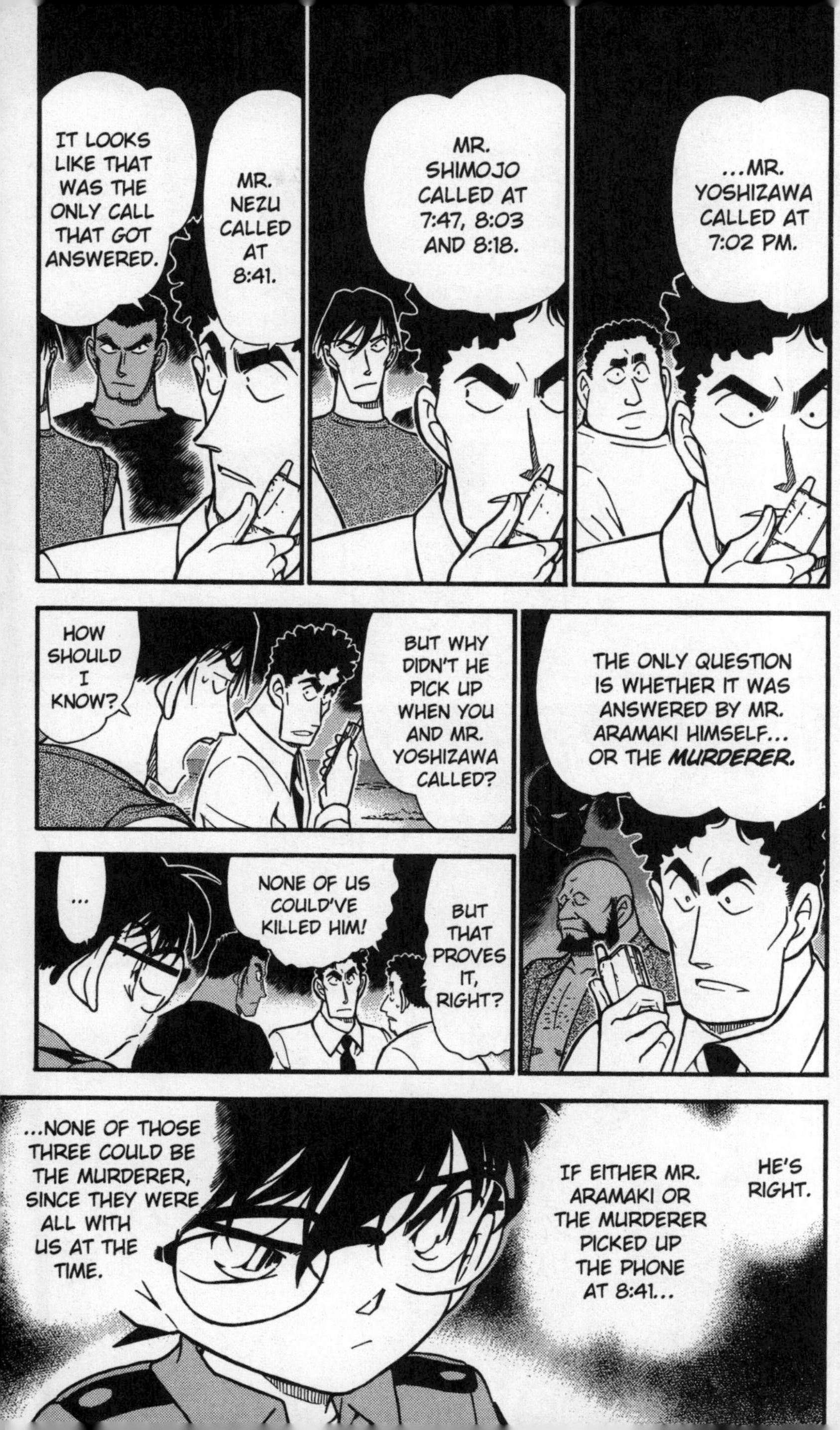
...MR. YOSHIZAWA CALLED AT 7:02 PM.
MR. SHIMOJO CALLED AT 7:47, 8:03 AND 8:18.
MR. NEZU CALLED AT 8:41.
IT LOOKS LIKE THAT WAS THE ONLY CALL THAT GOT ANSWERED.
THE ONLY QUESTION IS WHETHER IT WAS ANSWERED BY MR. ARAMAKI HIMSELF... OR THE *MURDERER.*
BUT WHY DIDN'T HE PICK UP WHEN YOU AND MR. YOSHIZAWA CALLED?
HOW SHOULD I KNOW?
BUT THAT PROVES IT, RIGHT?
NONE OF US COULD'VE KILLED HIM!
...
HE'S RIGHT.
IF EITHER MR. ARAMAKI OR THE MURDERER PICKED UP THE PHONE AT 8:41...
...NONE OF THOSE THREE COULD BE THE MURDERER, SINCE THEY WERE ALL WITH US AT THE TIME.

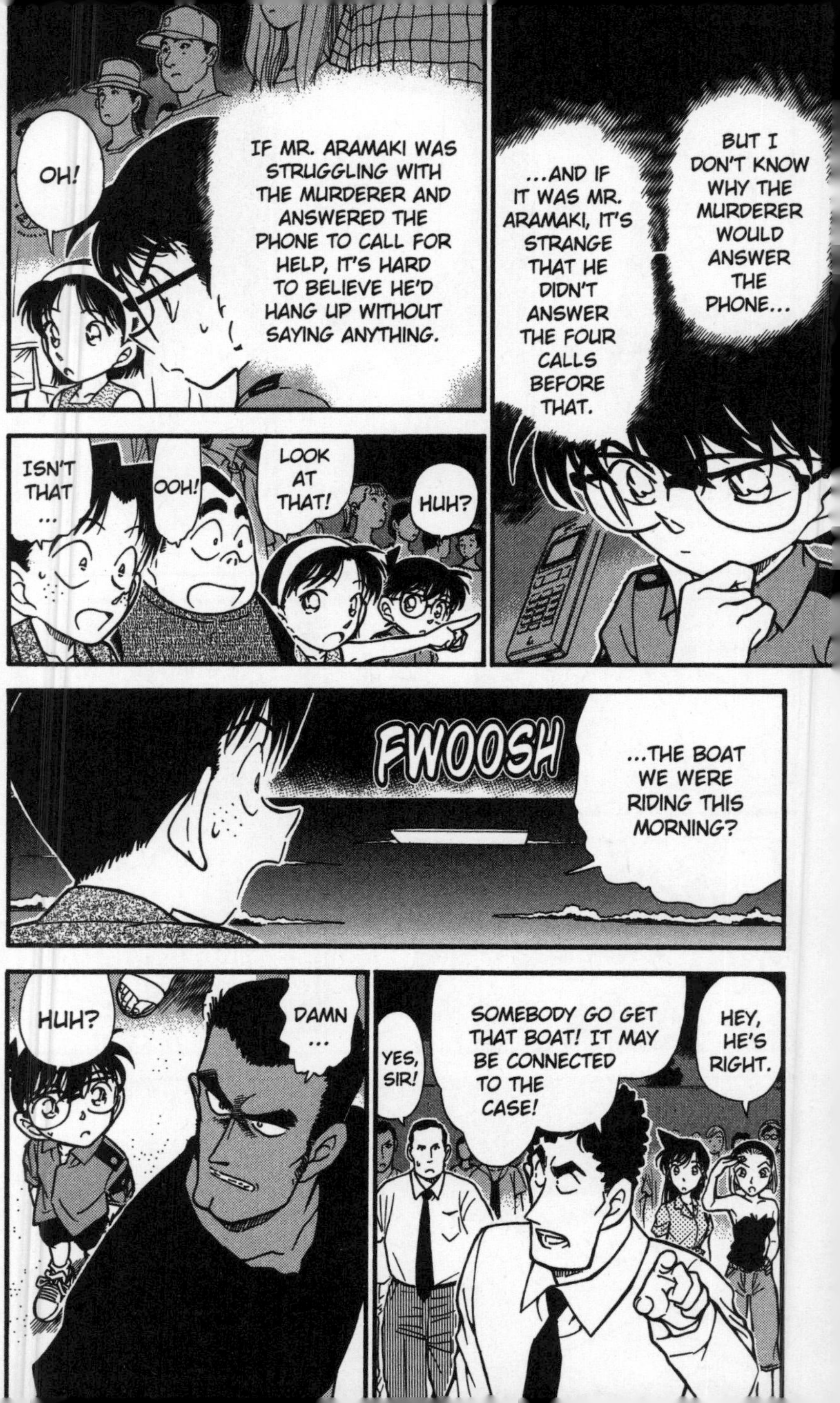
BUT I DON'T KNOW WHY THE MURDERER WOULD ANSWER THE PHONE...
...AND IF IT WAS MR. ARAMAKI, IT'S STRANGE THAT HE DIDN'T ANSWER THE FOUR CALLS BEFORE THAT.
IF MR. ARAMAKI WAS STRUGGLING WITH THE MURDERER AND ANSWERED THE PHONE TO CALL FOR HELP, IT'S HARD TO BELIEVE HE'D HANG UP WITHOUT SAYING ANYTHING.
OH!
HUH?
LOOK AT THAT!
OOH!
ISN'T THAT ...
...THE BOAT WE WERE RIDING THIS MORNING?
FWOOSH
HEY, HE'S RIGHT.
SOMEBODY GO GET THAT BOAT! IT MAY BE CONNECTED TO THE CASE!
YES, SIR!
DAMN ...
HUH?

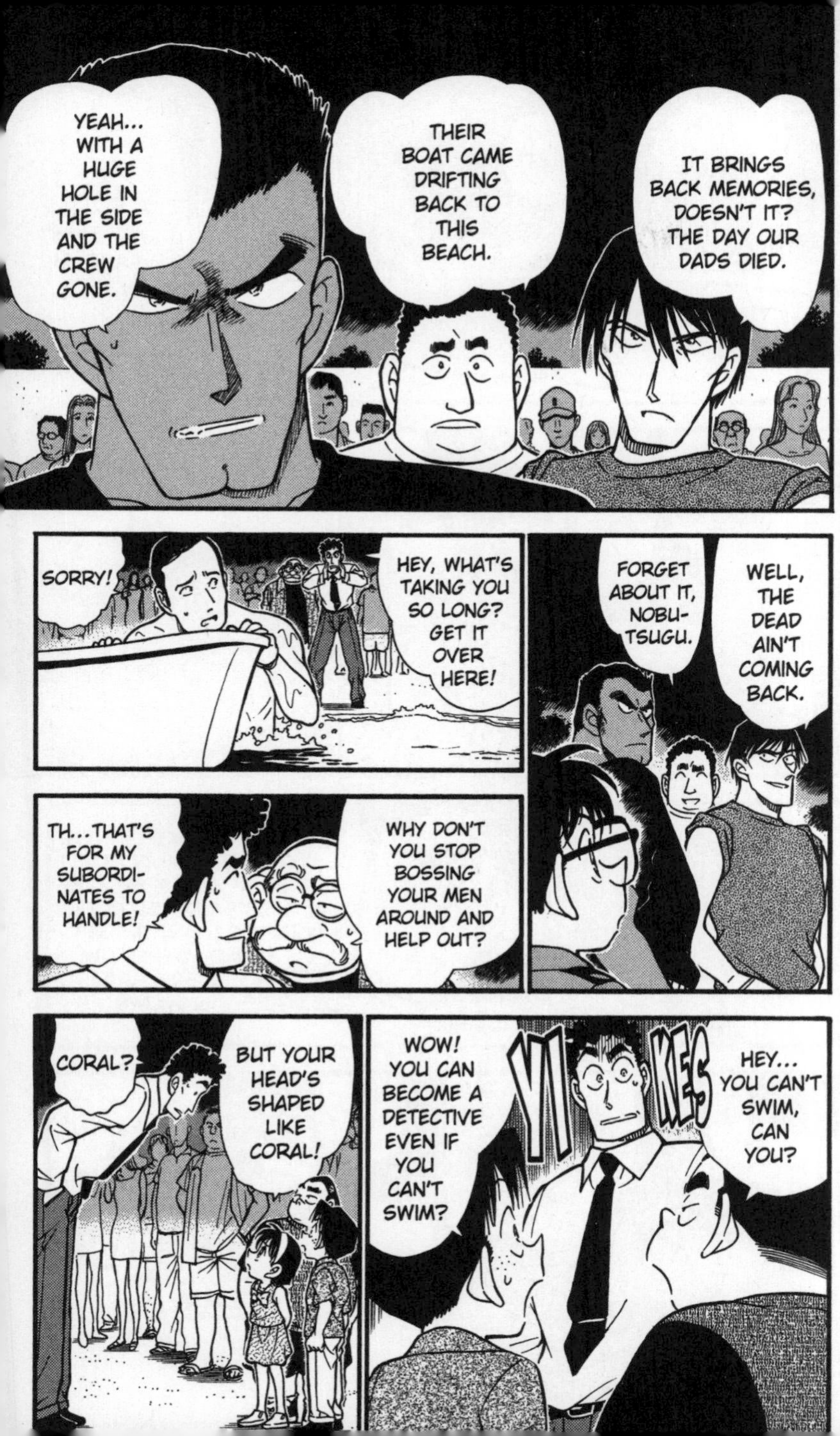
IT BRINGS BACK MEMORIES, DOESN'T IT? THE DAY OUR DADS DIED.
THEIR BOAT CAME DRIFTING BACK TO THIS BEACH.
YEAH... WITH A HUGE HOLE IN THE SIDE AND THE CREW GONE.
WELL, THE DEAD AIN'T COMING BACK.
FORGET ABOUT IT, NOBU-TSUGU.
HEY, WHAT'S TAKING YOU SO LONG? GET IT OVER HERE!
SORRY!
WHY DON'T YOU STOP BOSSING YOUR MEN AROUND AND HELP OUT?
TH...THAT'S FOR MY SUBORDI-NATES TO HANDLE!
HEY... YOU CAN'T SWIM, CAN YOU?
YIKES
WOW! YOU CAN BECOME A DETECTIVE EVEN IF YOU CAN'T SWIM?
BUT YOUR HEAD'S SHAPED LIKE CORAL!
CORAL?

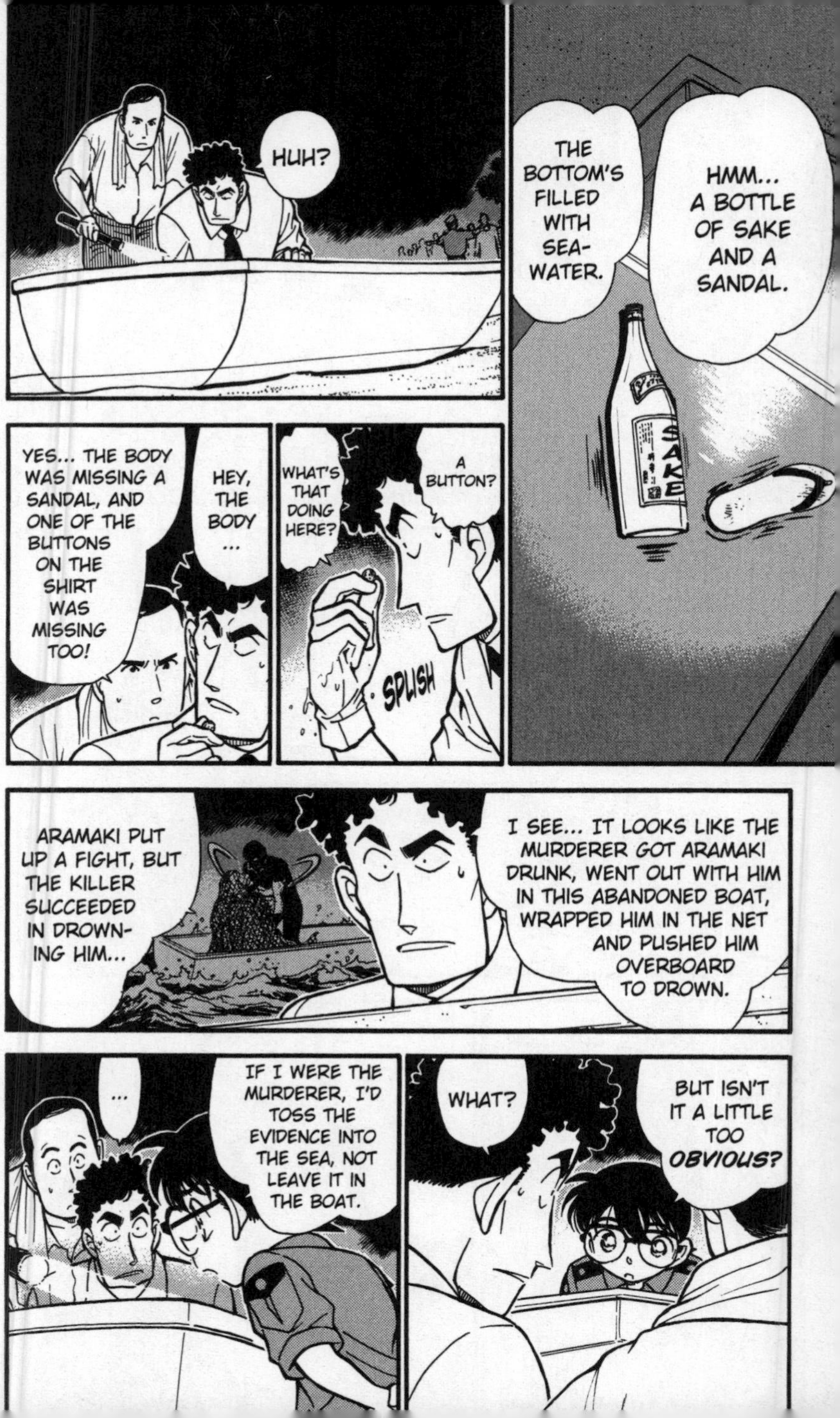
HMM... A BOTTLE OF SAKE AND A SANDAL.
THE BOTTOM'S FILLED WITH SEA-WATER.
SAKE
HUH?
A BUTTON?
WHAT'S THAT DOING HERE?
SPLISH
HEY, THE BODY ...
YES... THE BODY WAS MISSING A SANDAL, AND ONE OF THE BUTTONS ON THE SHIRT WAS MISSING TOO!
I SEE... IT LOOKS LIKE THE MURDERER GOT ARAMAKI DRUNK, WENT OUT WITH HIM IN THIS ABANDONED BOAT, WRAPPED HIM IN THE NET AND PUSHED HIM OVERBOARD TO DROWN.
ARAMAKI PUT UP A FIGHT, BUT THE KILLER SUCCEEDED IN DROWNING HIM...
BUT ISN'T IT A LITTLE TOO *OBVIOUS?*
WHAT?
IF I WERE THE MURDERER, I'D TOSS THE EVIDENCE INTO THE SEA, NOT LEAVE IT IN THE BOAT.
...

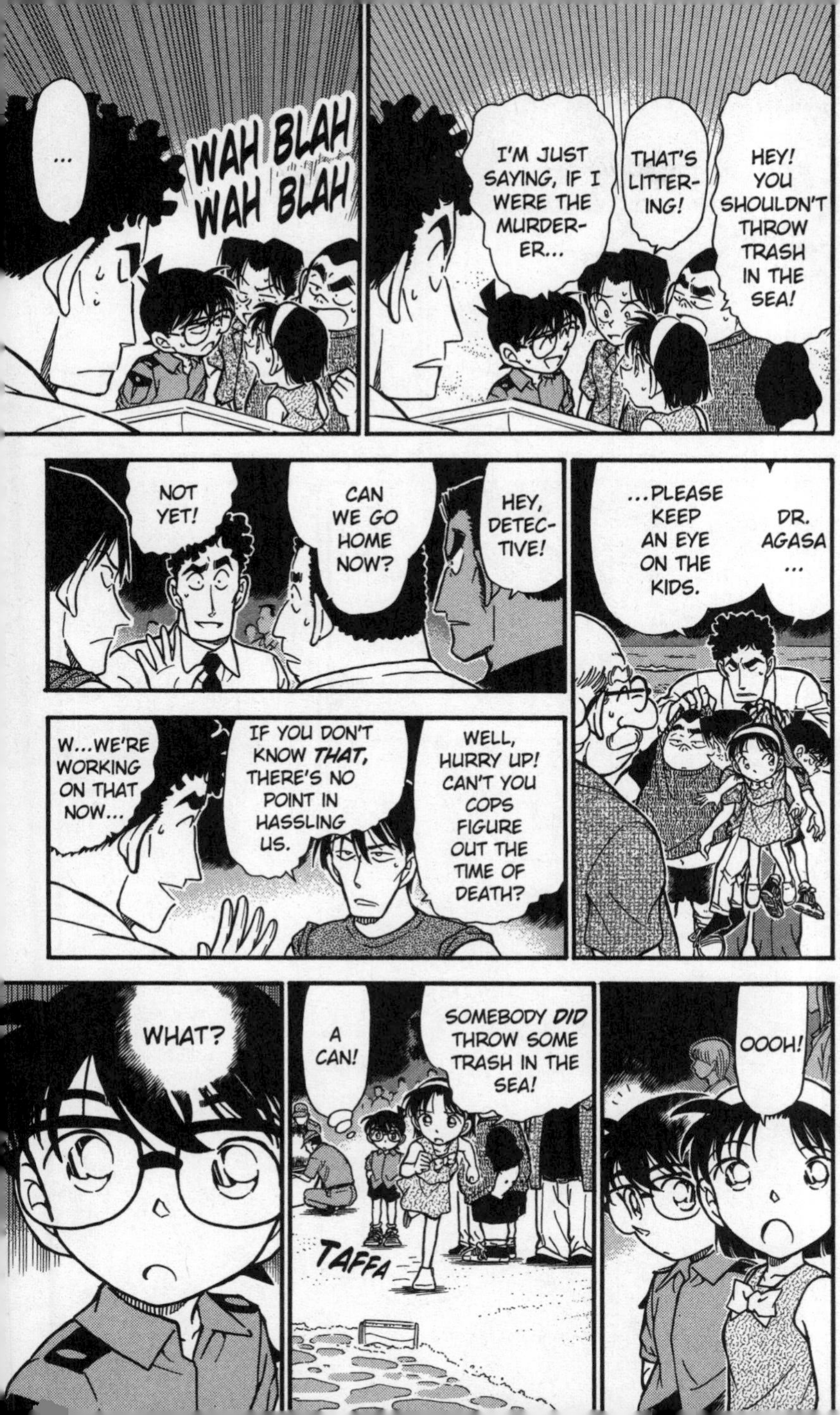
HEY! YOU SHOULDN'T THROW TRASH IN THE SEA!
THAT'S LITTER-ING!
I'M JUST SAYING, IF I WERE THE MURDER-ER...
WAH BLAH WAH BLAH
...
DR. AGASA ...
...PLEASE KEEP AN EYE ON THE KIDS.
HEY, DETEC-TIVE!
CAN WE GO HOME NOW?
NOT YET!
WELL, HURRY UP! CAN'T YOU COPS FIGURE OUT THE TIME OF DEATH?
IF YOU DON'T KNOW *THAT,* THERE'S NO POINT IN HASSLING US.
W...WE'RE WORKING ON THAT NOW...
OOOH!
SOMEBODY *DID* THROW SOME TRASH IN THE SEA!
A CAN!
TAFFA
WHAT?

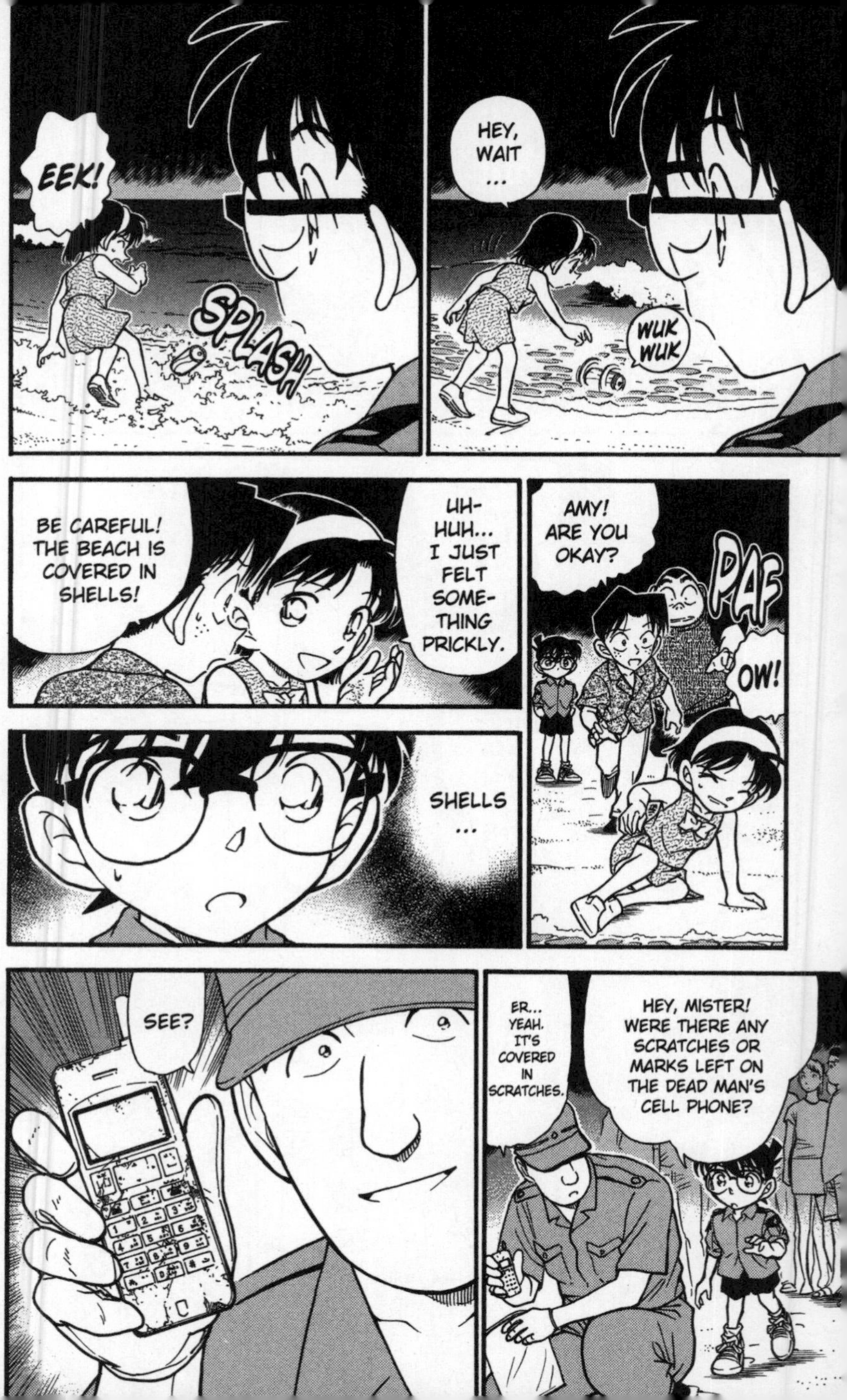
HEY, WAIT ...
WUK WUK
EEK!
SPLASH
AMY! ARE YOU OKAY?
PAF
OW!
UH-HUH... I JUST FELT SOMETHING PRICKLY.
BE CAREFUL! THE BEACH IS COVERED IN SHELLS!
SHELLS ...
HEY, MISTER! WERE THERE ANY SCRATCHES OR MARKS LEFT ON THE DEAD MAN'S CELL PHONE?
ER... YEAH. IT'S COVERED IN SCRATCHES.
SEE?

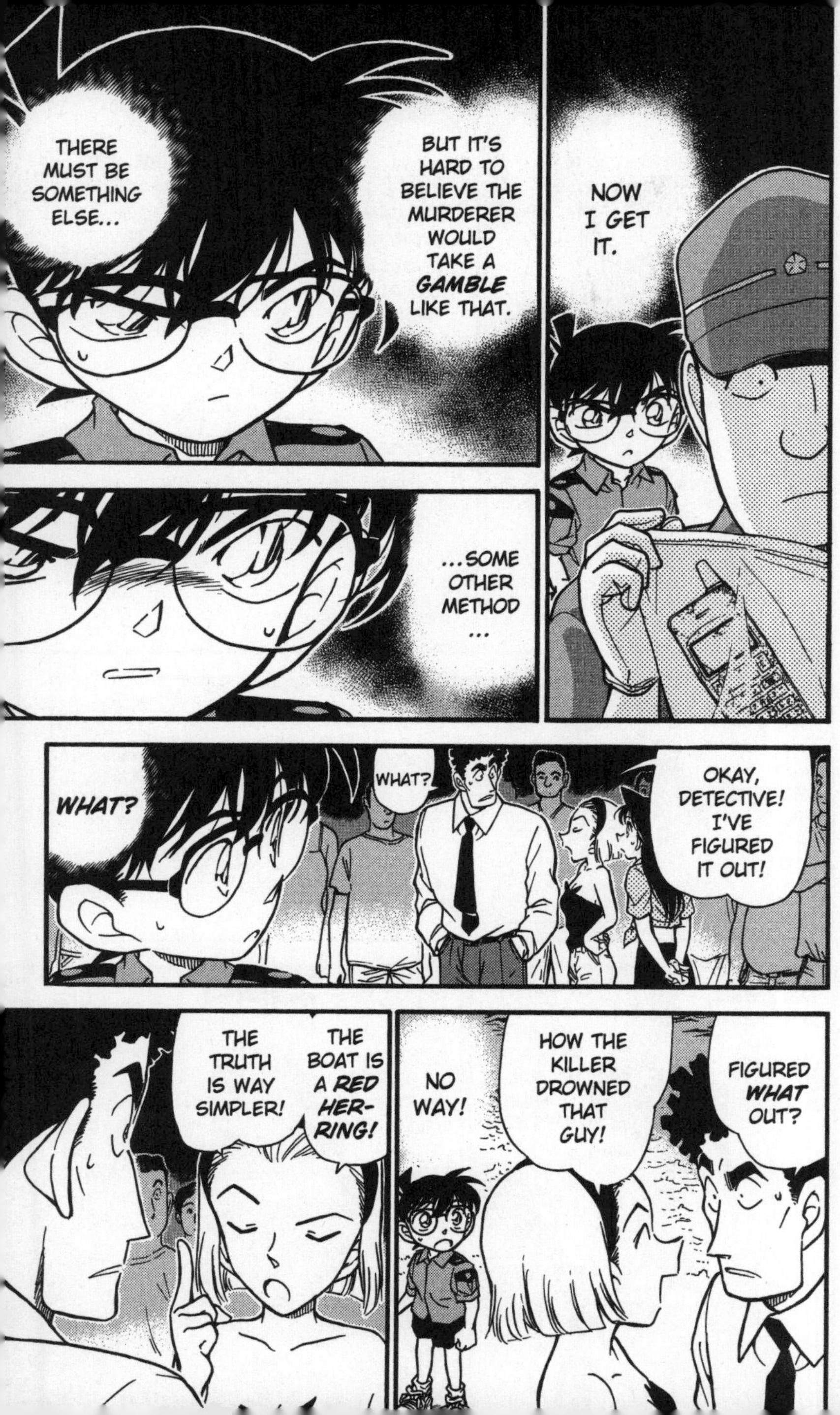
NOW I GET IT.
BUT IT'S HARD TO BELIEVE THE MURDERER WOULD TAKE A *GAMBLE* LIKE THAT.
THERE MUST BE SOMETHING ELSE...
...SOME OTHER METHOD...
OKAY, DETECTIVE! I'VE FIGURED IT OUT!
WHAT?
WHAT?
FIGURED *WHAT* OUT?
HOW THE KILLER DROWNED THAT GUY!
NO WAY!
THE BOAT IS A *RED HER-RING!*
THE TRUTH IS WAY SIMPLER!

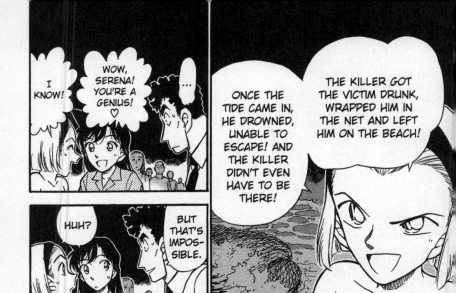

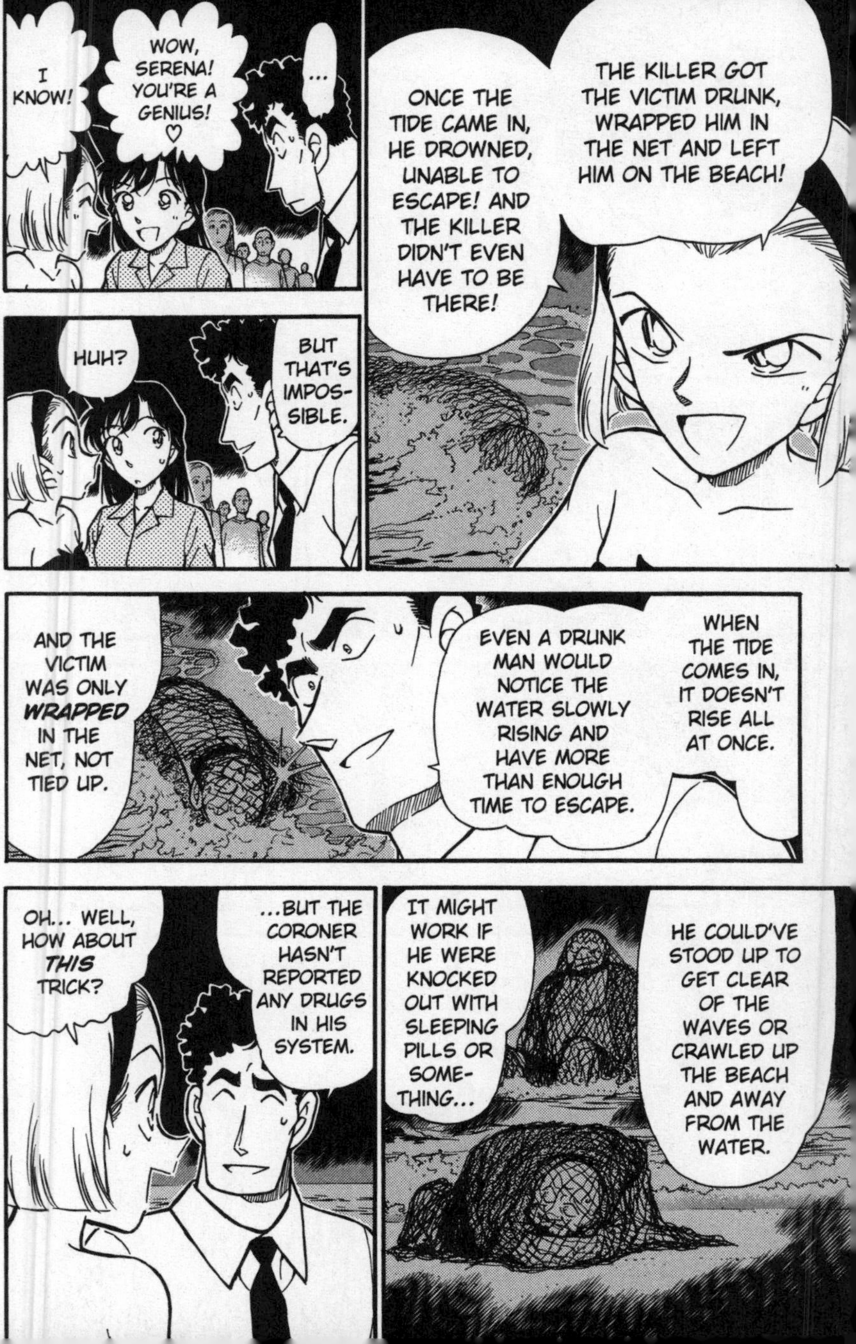
THE KILLER GOT THE VICTIM DRUNK, WRAPPED HIM IN THE NET AND LEFT HIM ON THE BEACH!
ONCE THE TIDE CAME IN, HE DROWNED, UNABLE TO ESCAPE! AND THE KILLER DIDN'T EVEN HAVE TO BE THERE!
...
WOW, SERENA! YOU'RE A GENIUS! ♡
I KNOW!
BUT THAT'S IMPOS-SIBLE.
HUH?
WHEN THE TIDE COMES IN, IT DOESN'T RISE ALL AT ONCE.
EVEN A DRUNK MAN WOULD NOTICE THE WATER SLOWLY RISING AND HAVE MORE THAN ENOUGH TIME TO ESCAPE.
AND THE VICTIM WAS ONLY *WRAPPED* IN THE NET, NOT TIED UP.
HE COULD'VE STOOD UP TO GET CLEAR OF THE WAVES OR CRAWLED UP THE BEACH AND AWAY FROM THE WATER.
IT MIGHT WORK IF HE WERE KNOCKED OUT WITH SLEEPING PILLS OR SOME-THING...
...BUT THE CORONER HASN'T REPORTED ANY DRUGS IN HIS SYSTEM.
OH... WELL, HOW ABOUT *THIS* TRICK?

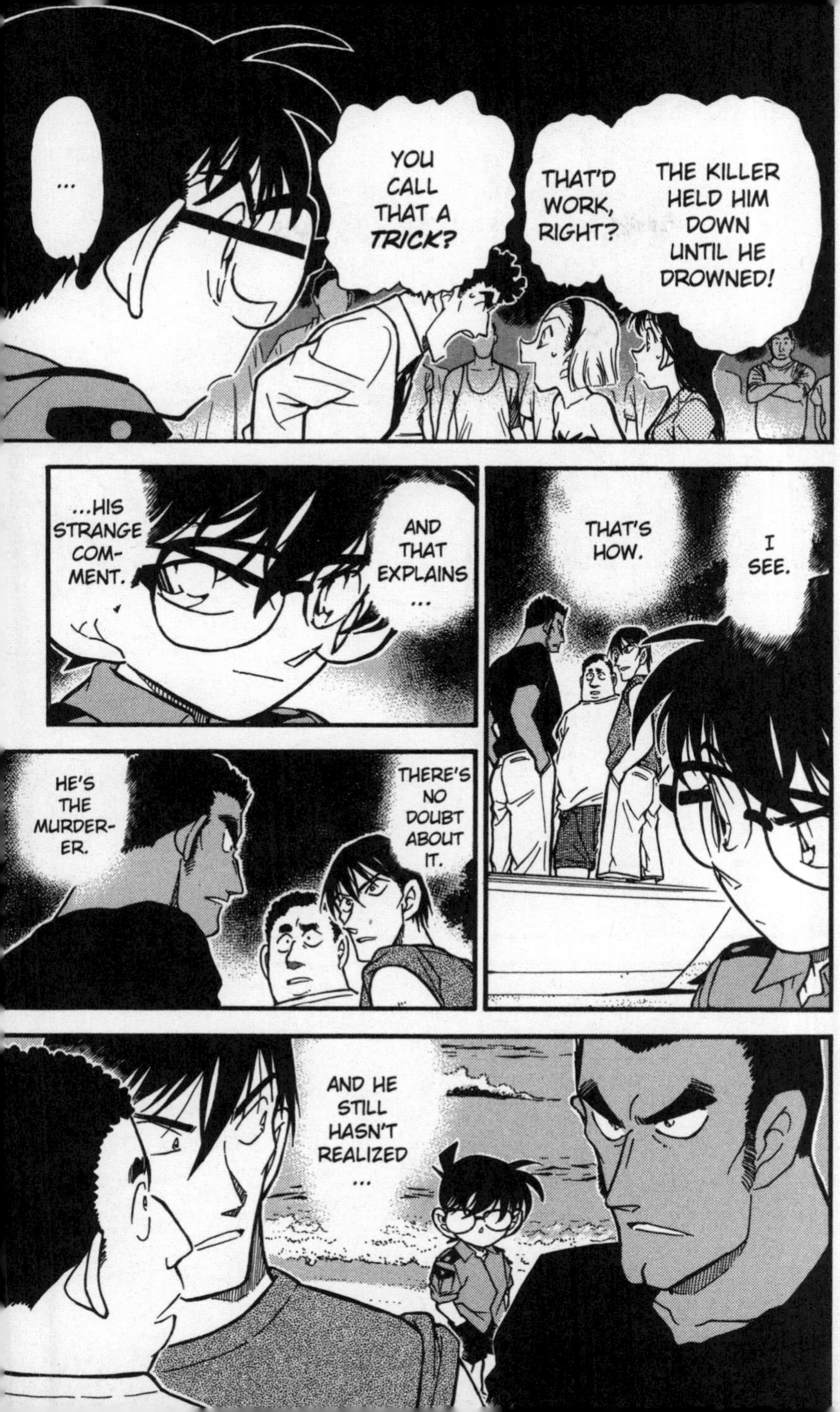
THE KILLER HELD HIM DOWN UNTIL HE DROWNED!
THAT'D WORK, RIGHT?
YOU CALL THAT A *TRICK*?
...
I SEE.
THAT'S HOW.
AND THAT EXPLAINS ...
...HIS STRANGE COM-MENT.
THERE'S NO DOUBT ABOUT IT.
HE'S THE MURDER-ER.
AND HE STILL HASN'T REALIZED ...

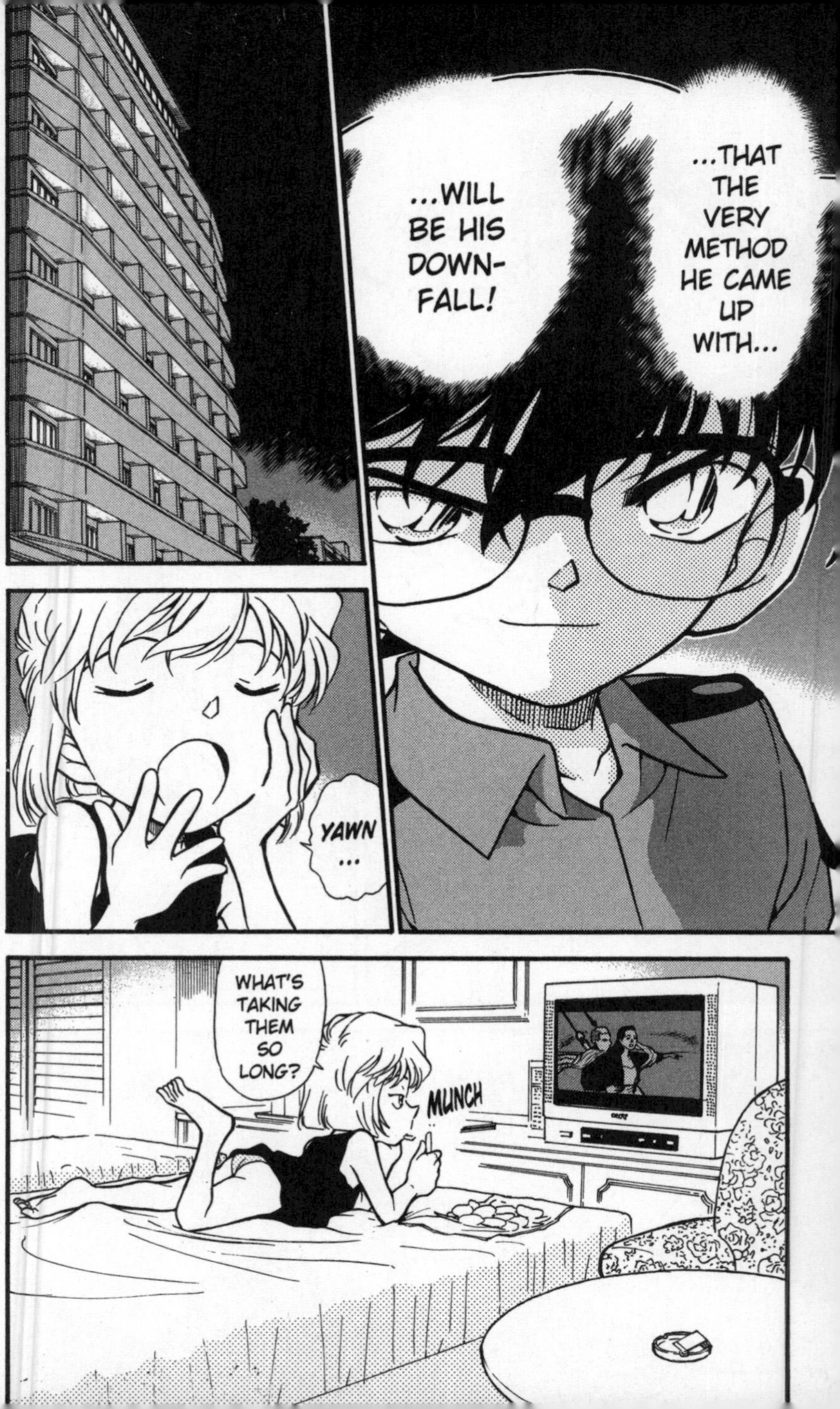
...THAT THE VERY METHOD HE CAME UP WITH...
...WILL BE HIS DOWN-FALL!
YAWN ...
WHAT'S TAKING THEM SO LONG?
MUNCH

FILE 7: A COURAGEOUS CHOICE

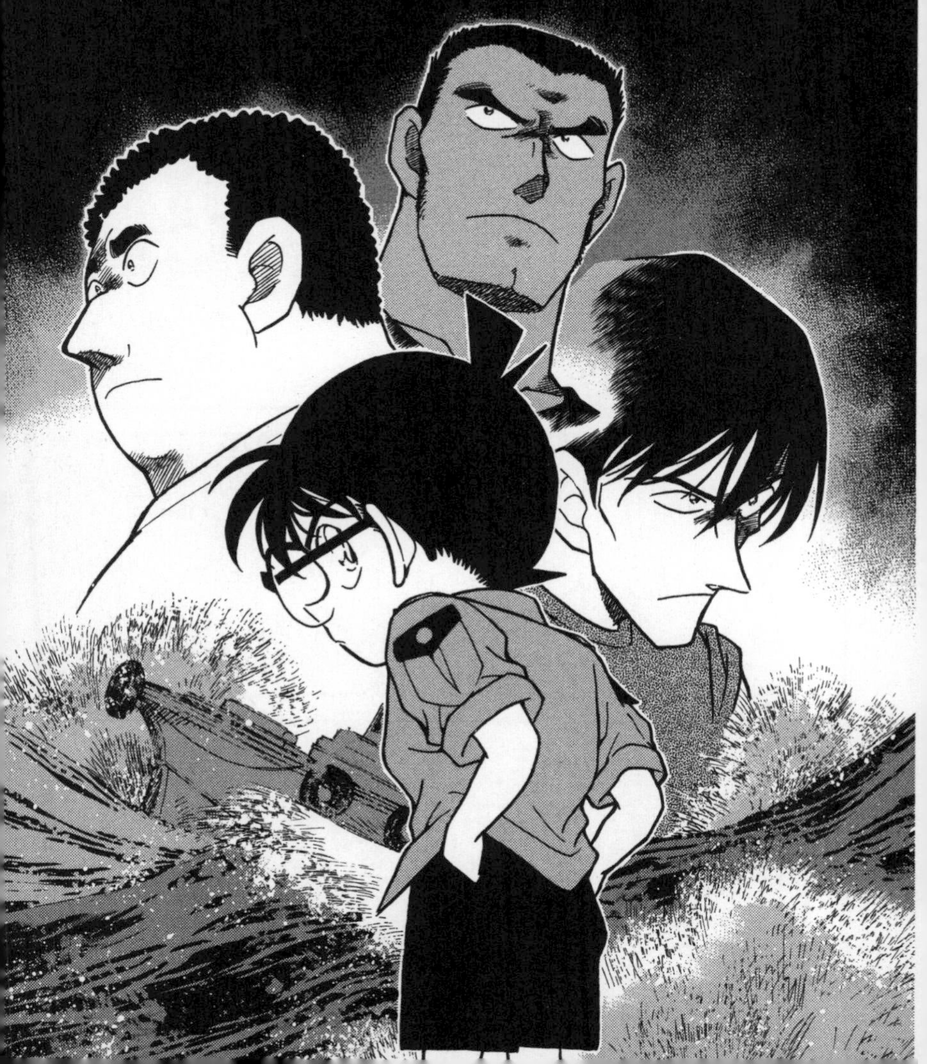

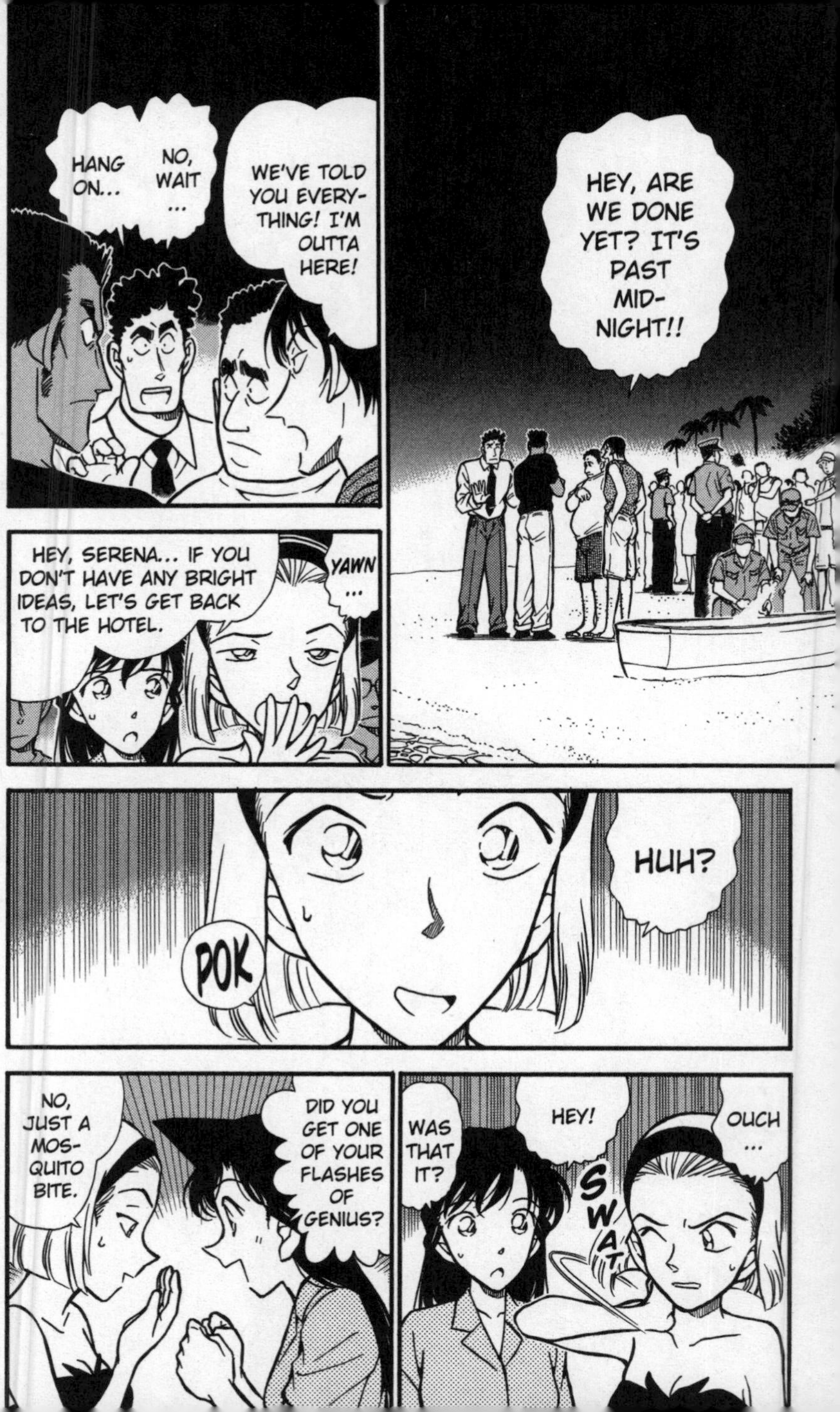
HEY, ARE WE DONE YET? IT'S PAST MID-NIGHT!!
WE'VE TOLD YOU EVERY-THING! I'M OUTTA HERE!
NO, WAIT ...
HANG ON...
YAWN ...
HEY, SERENA... IF YOU DON'T HAVE ANY BRIGHT IDEAS, LET'S GET BACK TO THE HOTEL.
HUH?
POK
OUCH ...
HEY!
SWAT
WAS THAT IT?
DID YOU GET ONE OF YOUR FLASHES OF GENIUS?
NO, JUST A MOS-QUITO BITE.

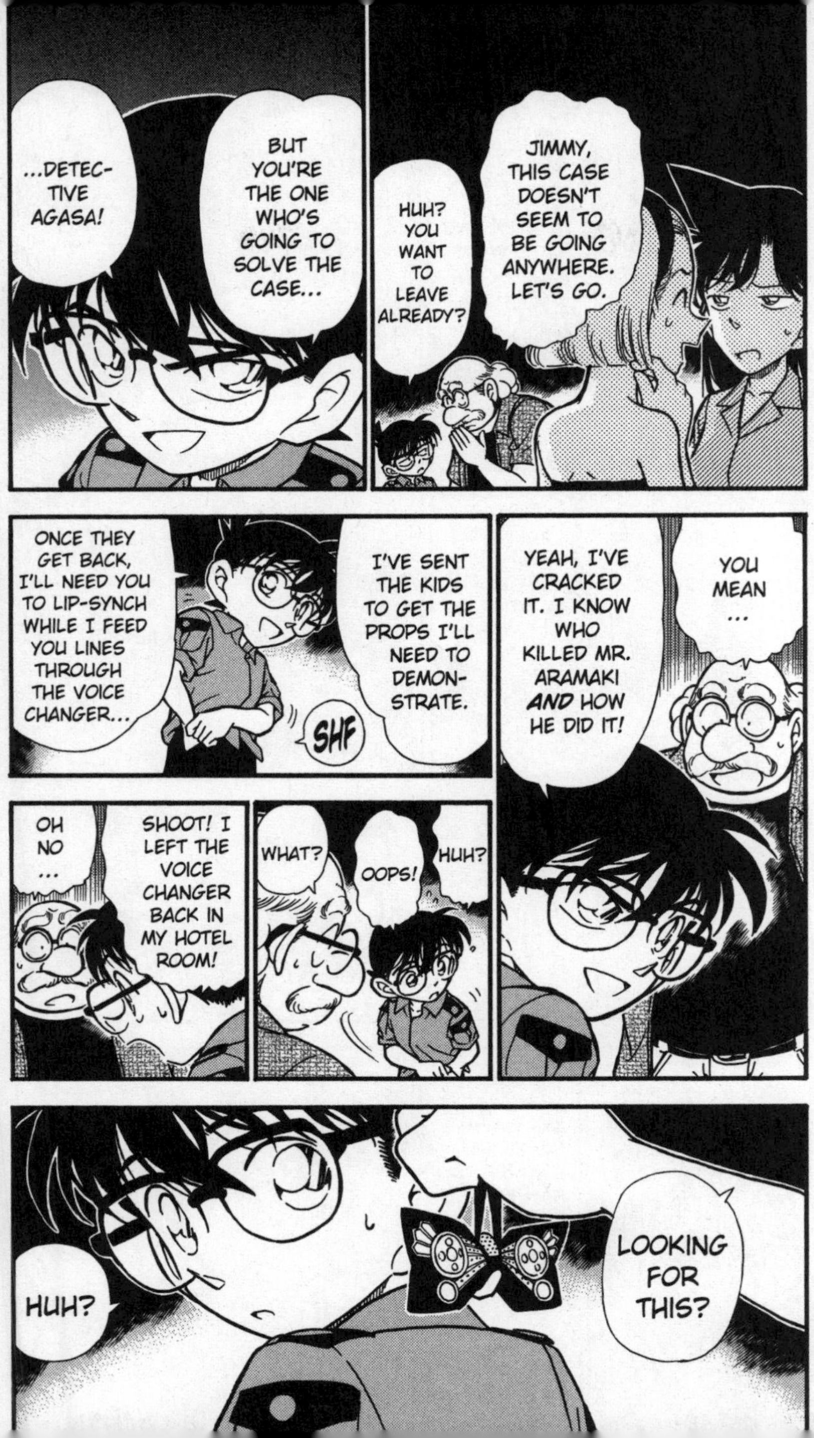
JIMMY, THIS CASE DOESN'T SEEM TO BE GOING ANYWHERE. LET'S GO.
HUH? YOU WANT TO LEAVE ALREADY?
BUT YOU'RE THE ONE WHO'S GOING TO SOLVE THE CASE...
...DETECTIVE AGASA!
YOU MEAN ...
YEAH, I'VE CRACKED IT. I KNOW WHO KILLED MR. ARAMAKI AND HOW HE DID IT!
I'VE SENT THE KIDS TO GET THE PROPS I'LL NEED TO DEMONSTRATE.
SHF
ONCE THEY GET BACK, I'LL NEED YOU TO LIP-SYNCH WHILE I FEED YOU LINES THROUGH THE VOICE CHANGER...
HUH?
OOPS!
WHAT?
SHOOT! I LEFT THE VOICE CHANGER BACK IN MY HOTEL ROOM!
OH NO ...
LOOKING FOR THIS?
HUH?

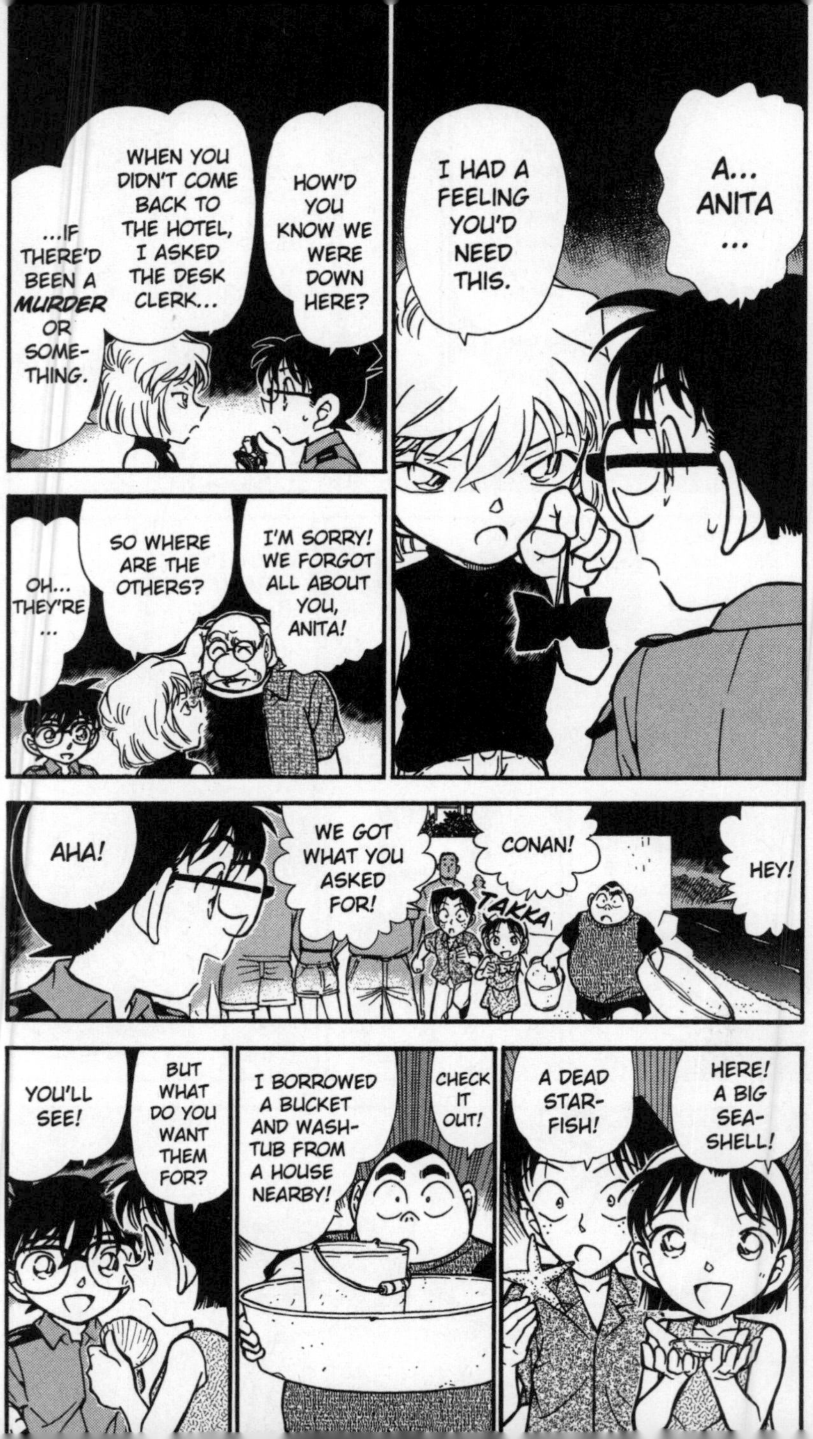
A... ANITA ...
I HAD A FEELING YOU'D NEED THIS.
HOW'D YOU KNOW WE WERE DOWN HERE?
WHEN YOU DIDN'T COME BACK TO THE HOTEL, I ASKED THE DESK CLERK...
...IF THERE'D BEEN A *MURDER* OR SOME-THING.
I'M SORRY! WE FORGOT ALL ABOUT YOU, ANITA!
SO WHERE ARE THE OTHERS?
OH... THEY'RE ...
HEY!
CONAN!
TAKKA
WE GOT WHAT YOU ASKED FOR!
AHA!
HERE! A BIG SEA-SHELL!
A DEAD STAR-FISH!
CHECK IT OUT!
I BORROWED A BUCKET AND WASH-TUB FROM A HOUSE NEARBY!
BUT WHAT DO YOU WANT THEM FOR?
YOU'LL SEE!

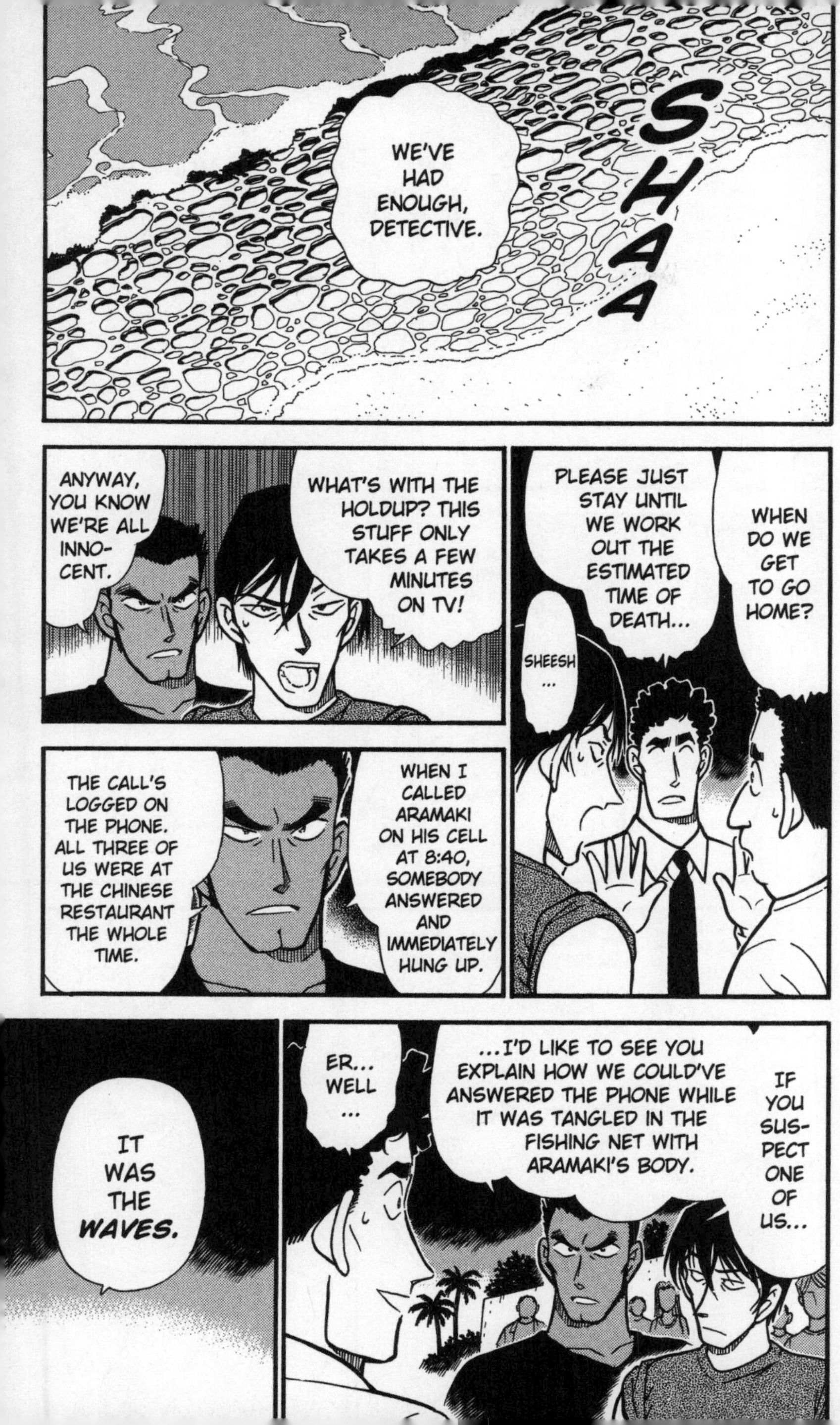
SHAA
WE'VE HAD ENOUGH, DETECTIVE.
WHEN DO WE GET TO GO HOME?
PLEASE JUST STAY UNTIL WE WORK OUT THE ESTIMATED TIME OF DEATH...
SHEESH...
WHAT'S WITH THE HOLDUP? THIS STUFF ONLY TAKES A FEW MINUTES ON TV!
ANYWAY, YOU KNOW WE'RE ALL INNO-CENT.
WHEN I CALLED ARAMAKI ON HIS CELL AT 8:40, SOMEBODY ANSWERED AND IMMEDIATELY HUNG UP.
THE CALL'S LOGGED ON THE PHONE. ALL THREE OF US WERE AT THE CHINESE RESTAURANT THE WHOLE TIME.
IF YOU SUSPECT ONE OF US...
...I'D LIKE TO SEE YOU EXPLAIN HOW WE COULD'VE ANSWERED THE PHONE WHILE IT WAS TANGLED IN THE FISHING NET WITH ARAMAKI'S BODY.
ER... WELL...
IT WAS THE *WAVES.*

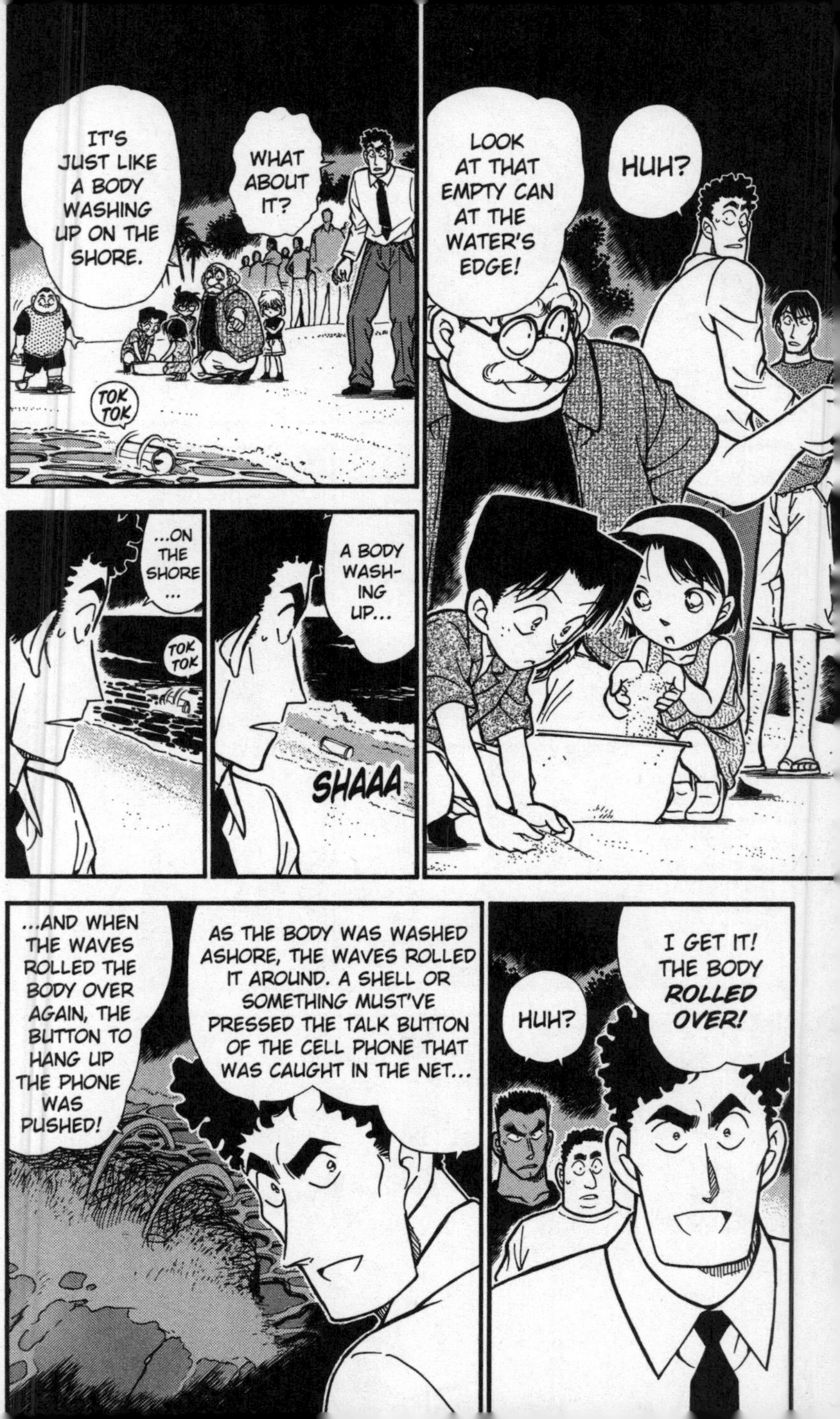
LOOK AT THAT EMPTY CAN AT THE WATER'S EDGE!
HUH?
IT'S JUST LIKE A BODY WASHING UP ON THE SHORE.
WHAT ABOUT IT?
TOK TOK
A BODY WASH-ING UP...
SHAAA
...ON THE SHORE...
TOK TOK
I GET IT! THE BODY *ROLLED OVER!*
HUH?
AS THE BODY WAS WASHED ASHORE, THE WAVES ROLLED IT AROUND. A SHELL OR SOMETHING MUST'VE PRESSED THE TALK BUTTON OF THE CELL PHONE THAT WAS CAUGHT IN THE NET...
...AND WHEN THE WAVES ROLLED THE BODY OVER AGAIN, THE BUTTON TO HANG UP THE PHONE WAS PUSHED!

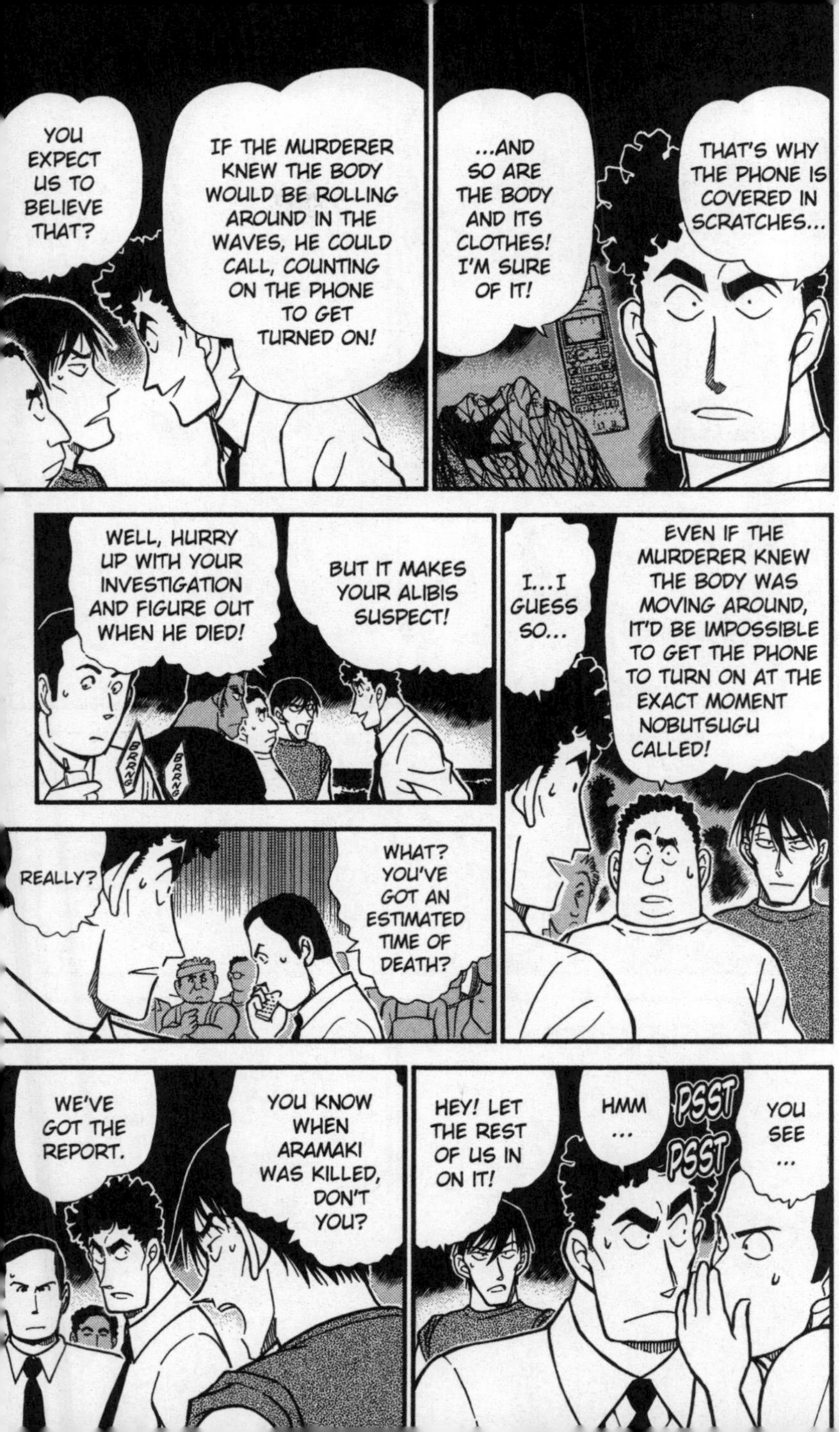
THAT'S WHY THE PHONE IS COVERED IN SCRATCHES...
...AND SO ARE THE BODY AND ITS CLOTHES! I'M SURE OF IT!
IF THE MURDERER KNEW THE BODY WOULD BE ROLLING AROUND IN THE WAVES, HE COULD CALL, COUNTING ON THE PHONE TO GET TURNED ON!
YOU EXPECT US TO BELIEVE THAT?
EVEN IF THE MURDERER KNEW THE BODY WAS MOVING AROUND, IT'D BE IMPOSSIBLE TO GET THE PHONE TO TURN ON AT THE EXACT MOMENT NOBUTSUGU CALLED!
I...I GUESS SO...
BUT IT MAKES YOUR ALIBIS SUSPECT!
WELL, HURRY UP WITH YOUR INVESTIGATION AND FIGURE OUT WHEN HE DIED!
BRRNG
BRRNG
WHAT? YOU'VE GOT AN ESTIMATED TIME OF DEATH?
REALLY?
YOU SEE...
PSST
PSST
HMM...
HEY! LET THE REST OF US IN ON IT!
YOU KNOW WHEN ARAMAKI WAS KILLED, DON'T YOU?
WE'VE GOT THE REPORT.

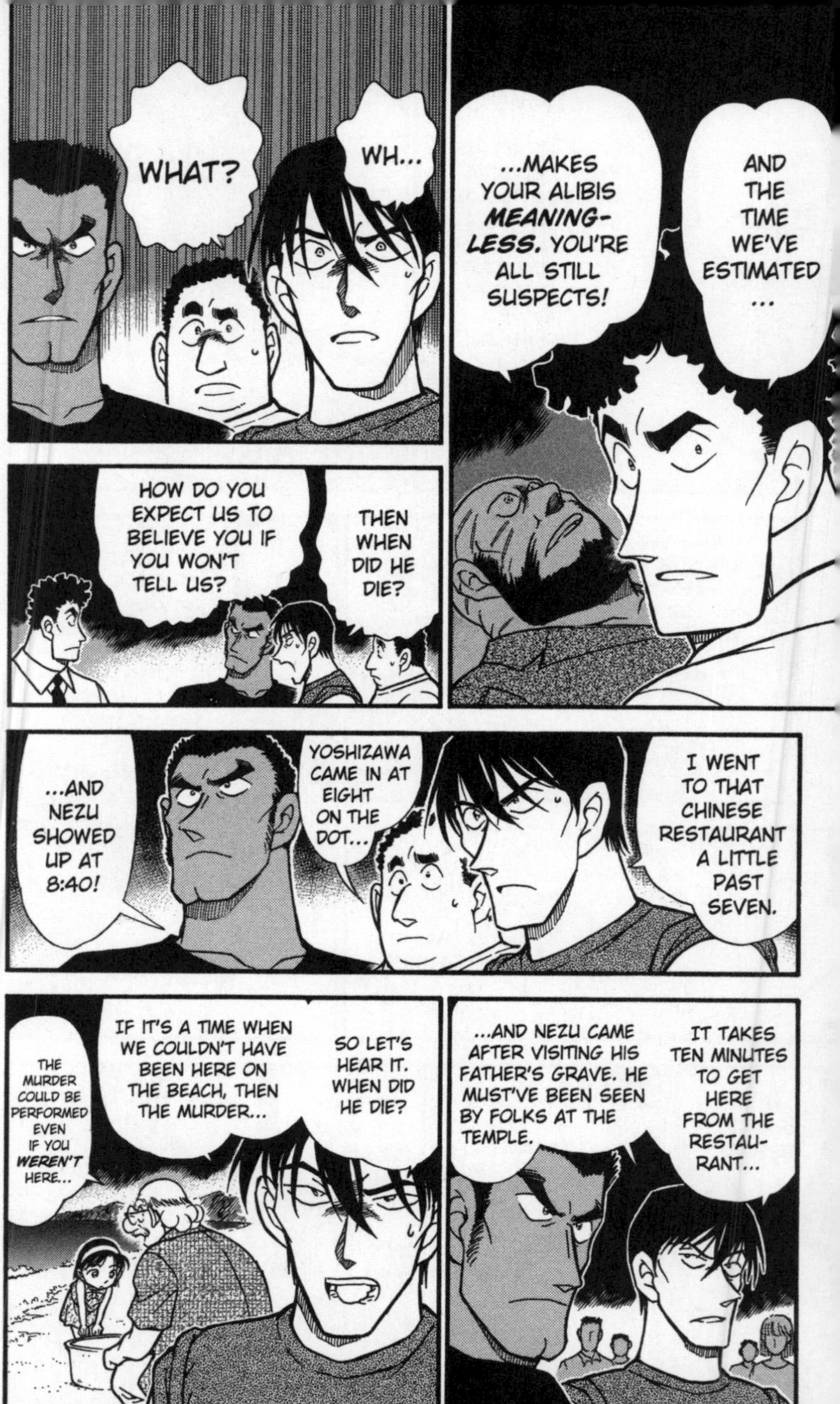
AND THE TIME WE'VE ESTIMATED...
...MAKES YOUR ALIBIS MEANINGLESS. YOU'RE ALL STILL SUSPECTS!
WH...
WHAT?
THEN WHEN DID HE DIE?
HOW DO YOU EXPECT US TO BELIEVE YOU IF YOU WON'T TELL US?
I WENT TO THAT CHINESE RESTAURANT A LITTLE PAST SEVEN.
YOSHIZAWA CAME IN AT EIGHT ON THE DOT...
...AND NEZU SHOWED UP AT 8:40!
IT TAKES TEN MINUTES TO GET HERE FROM THE RESTAURANT...
...AND NEZU CAME AFTER VISITING HIS FATHER'S GRAVE. HE MUST'VE BEEN SEEN BY FOLKS AT THE TEMPLE.
SO LET'S HEAR IT. WHEN DID HE DIE?
IF IT'S A TIME WHEN WE COULDN'T HAVE BEEN HERE ON THE BEACH, THEN THE MURDER...
THE MURDER COULD BE PERFORMED EVEN IF YOU WEREN'T HERE...

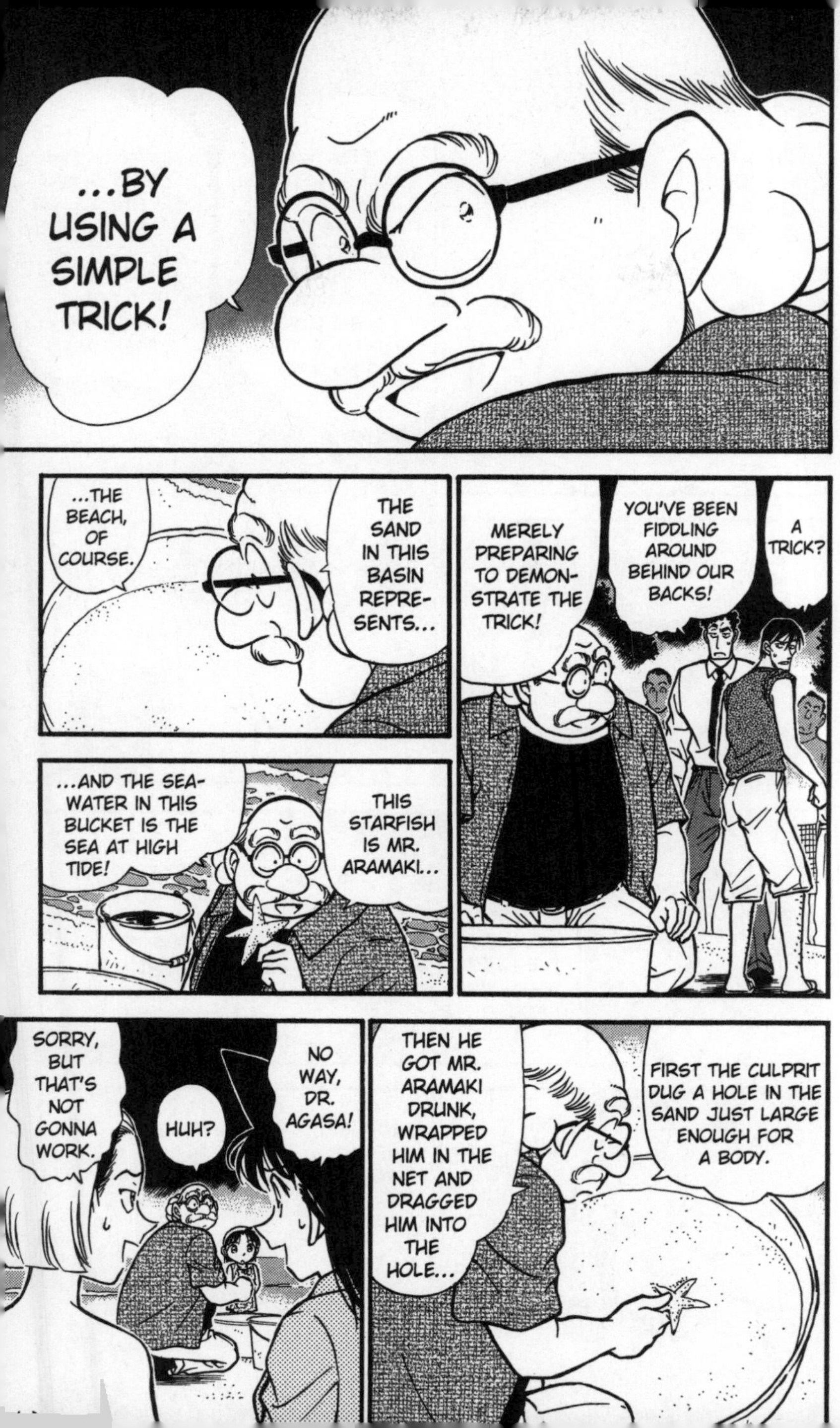
...BY USING A SIMPLE TRICK!
A TRICK?
YOU'VE BEEN FIDDLING AROUND BEHIND OUR BACKS!
MERELY PREPARING TO DEMON-STRATE THE TRICK!
THE SAND IN THIS BASIN REPRE-SENTS...
...THE BEACH, OF COURSE.
THIS STARFISH IS MR. ARAMAKI...
...AND THE SEA-WATER IN THIS BUCKET IS THE SEA AT HIGH TIDE!
FIRST THE CULPRIT DUG A HOLE IN THE SAND JUST LARGE ENOUGH FOR A BODY.
THEN HE GOT MR. ARAMAKI DRUNK, WRAPPED HIM IN THE NET AND DRAGGED HIM INTO THE HOLE...
NO WAY, DR. AGASA!
HUH?
SORRY, BUT THAT'S NOT GONNA WORK.

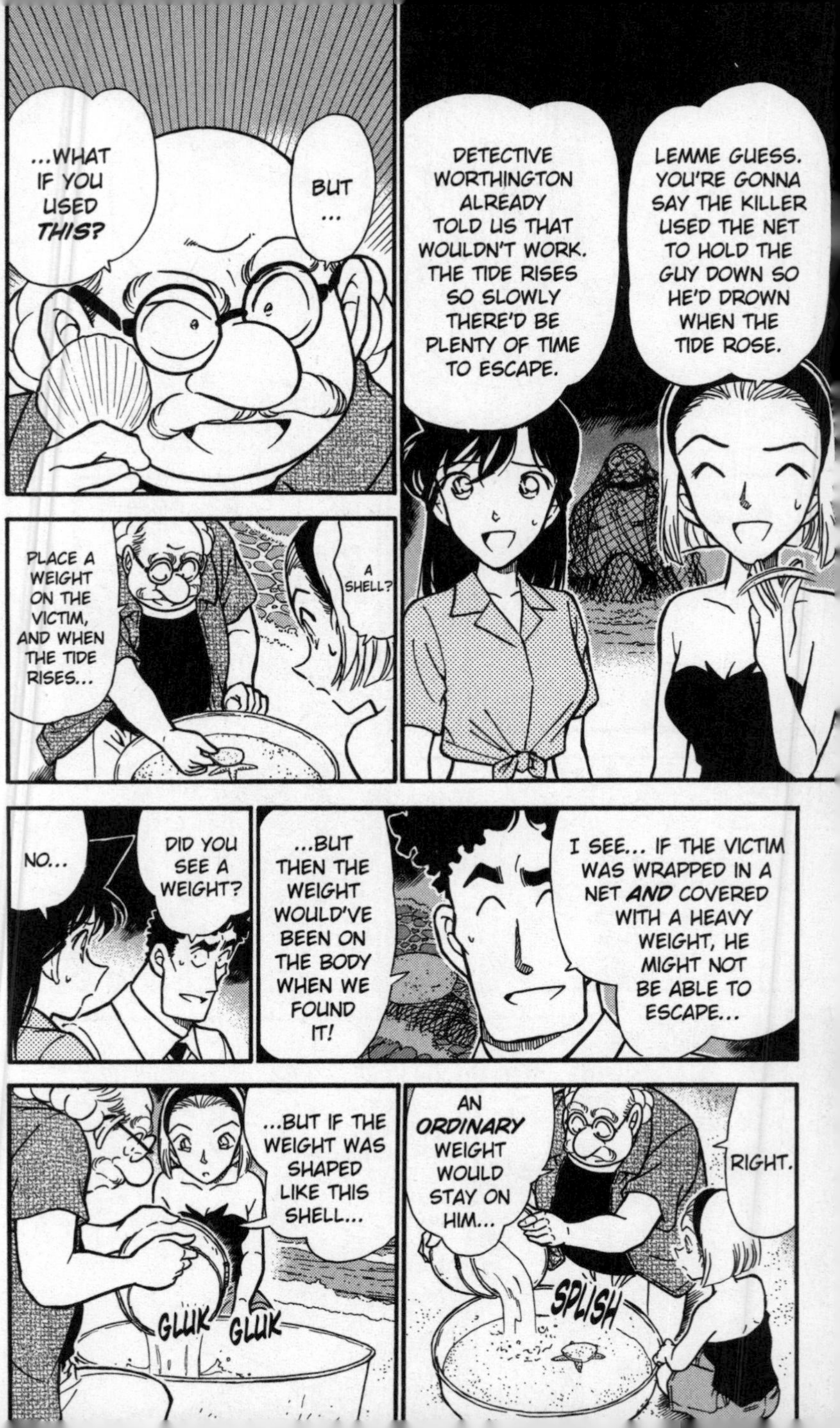
LEMME GUESS. YOU'RE GONNA SAY THE KILLER USED THE NET TO HOLD THE GUY DOWN SO HE'D DROWN WHEN THE TIDE ROSE.
DETECTIVE WORTHINGTON ALREADY TOLD US THAT WOULDN'T WORK. THE TIDE RISES SO SLOWLY THERE'D BE PLENTY OF TIME TO ESCAPE.
BUT ...
...WHAT IF YOU USED *THIS?*
A SHELL?
PLACE A WEIGHT ON THE VICTIM, AND WHEN THE TIDE RISES...
I SEE... IF THE VICTIM WAS WRAPPED IN A NET *AND* COVERED WITH A HEAVY WEIGHT, HE MIGHT NOT BE ABLE TO ESCAPE...
...BUT THEN THE WEIGHT WOULD'VE BEEN ON THE BODY WHEN WE FOUND IT!
DID YOU SEE A WEIGHT?
NO...
RIGHT.
AN *ORDINARY* WEIGHT WOULD STAY ON HIM...
SPLISH
...BUT IF THE WEIGHT WAS SHAPED LIKE THIS SHELL...
GLUK GLUK

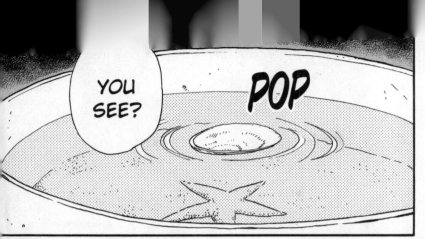

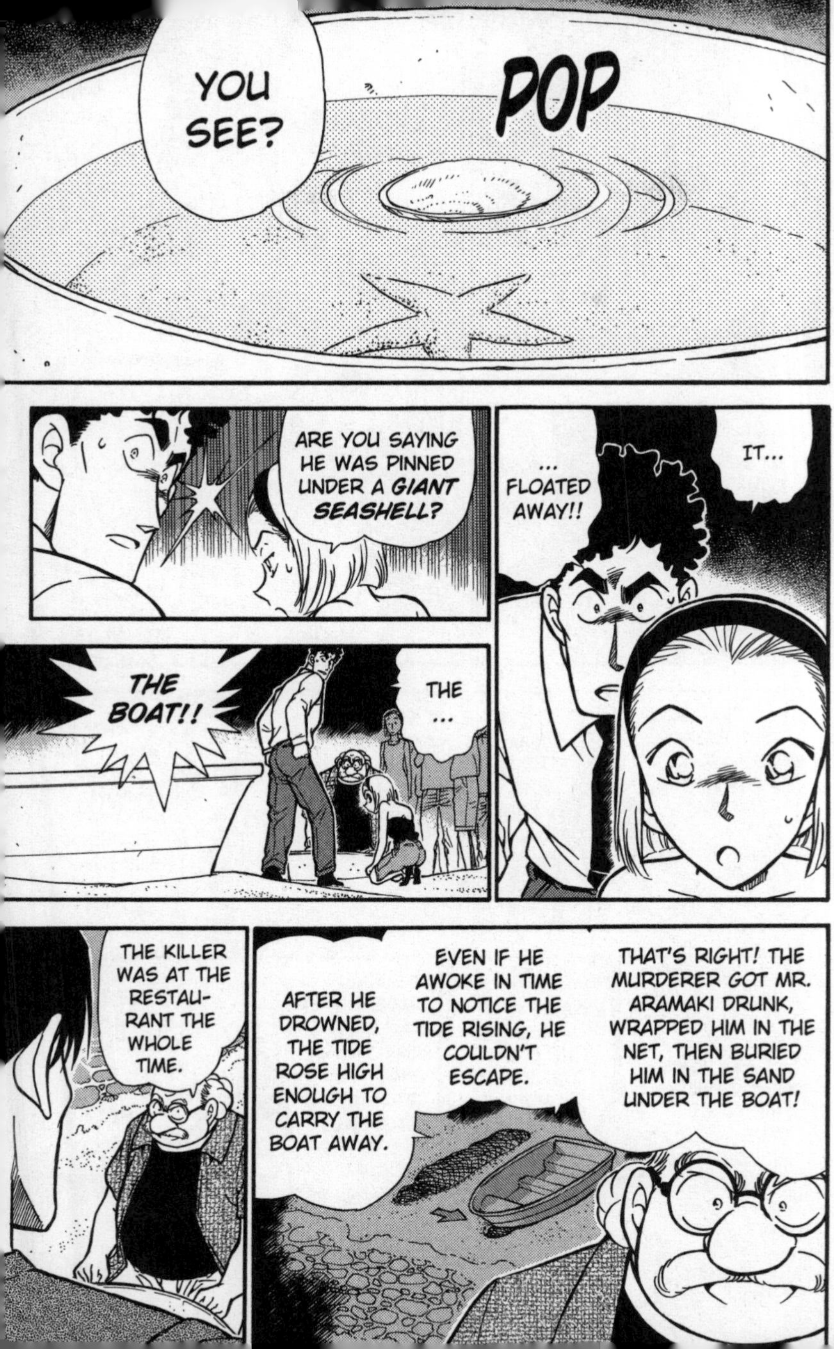
YOU SEE?
POP
IT...
...FLOATED AWAY!!
ARE YOU SAYING HE WAS PINNED UNDER A GIANT SEASHELL?
THE ...
THE BOAT!!
THAT'S RIGHT! THE MURDERER GOT MR. ARAMAKI DRUNK, WRAPPED HIM IN THE NET, THEN BURIED HIM IN THE SAND UNDER THE BOAT!
EVEN IF HE AWOKE IN TIME TO NOTICE THE TIDE RISING, HE COULDN'T ESCAPE.
AFTER HE DROWNED, THE TIDE ROSE HIGH ENOUGH TO CARRY THE BOAT AWAY.
THE KILLER WAS AT THE RESTAU-RANT THE WHOLE TIME.

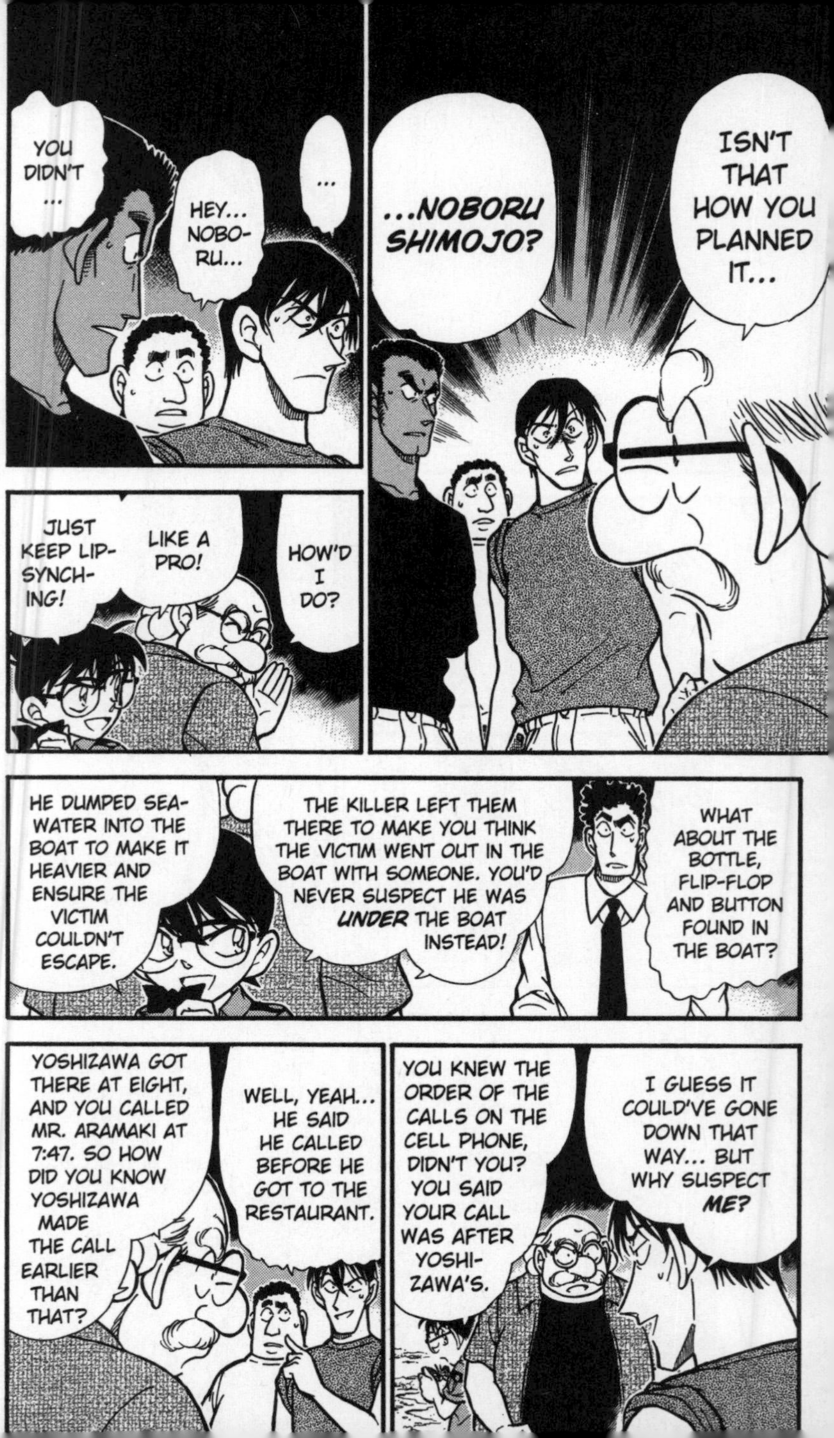
ISN'T THAT HOW YOU PLANNED IT...
...NOBORU SHIMOJO?
...
HEY... NOBORU...
YOU DIDN'T ...
HOW'D I DO?
LIKE A PRO!
JUST KEEP LIP-SYNCHING!
WHAT ABOUT THE BOTTLE, FLIP-FLOP AND BUTTON FOUND IN THE BOAT?
THE KILLER LEFT THEM THERE TO MAKE YOU THINK THE VICTIM WENT OUT IN THE BOAT WITH SOMEONE. YOU'D NEVER SUSPECT HE WAS *UNDER* THE BOAT INSTEAD!
HE DUMPED SEAWATER INTO THE BOAT TO MAKE IT HEAVIER AND ENSURE THE VICTIM COULDN'T ESCAPE.
I GUESS IT COULD'VE GONE DOWN THAT WAY... BUT WHY SUSPECT *ME?*
YOU KNEW THE ORDER OF THE CALLS ON THE CELL PHONE, DIDN'T YOU? YOU SAID YOUR CALL WAS AFTER YOSHIZAWA'S.
WELL, YEAH... HE SAID HE CALLED BEFORE HE GOT TO THE RESTAURANT.
YOSHIZAWA GOT THERE AT EIGHT, AND YOU CALLED MR. ARAMAKI AT 7:47. SO HOW DID YOU KNOW YOSHIZAWA MADE THE CALL EARLIER THAN THAT?

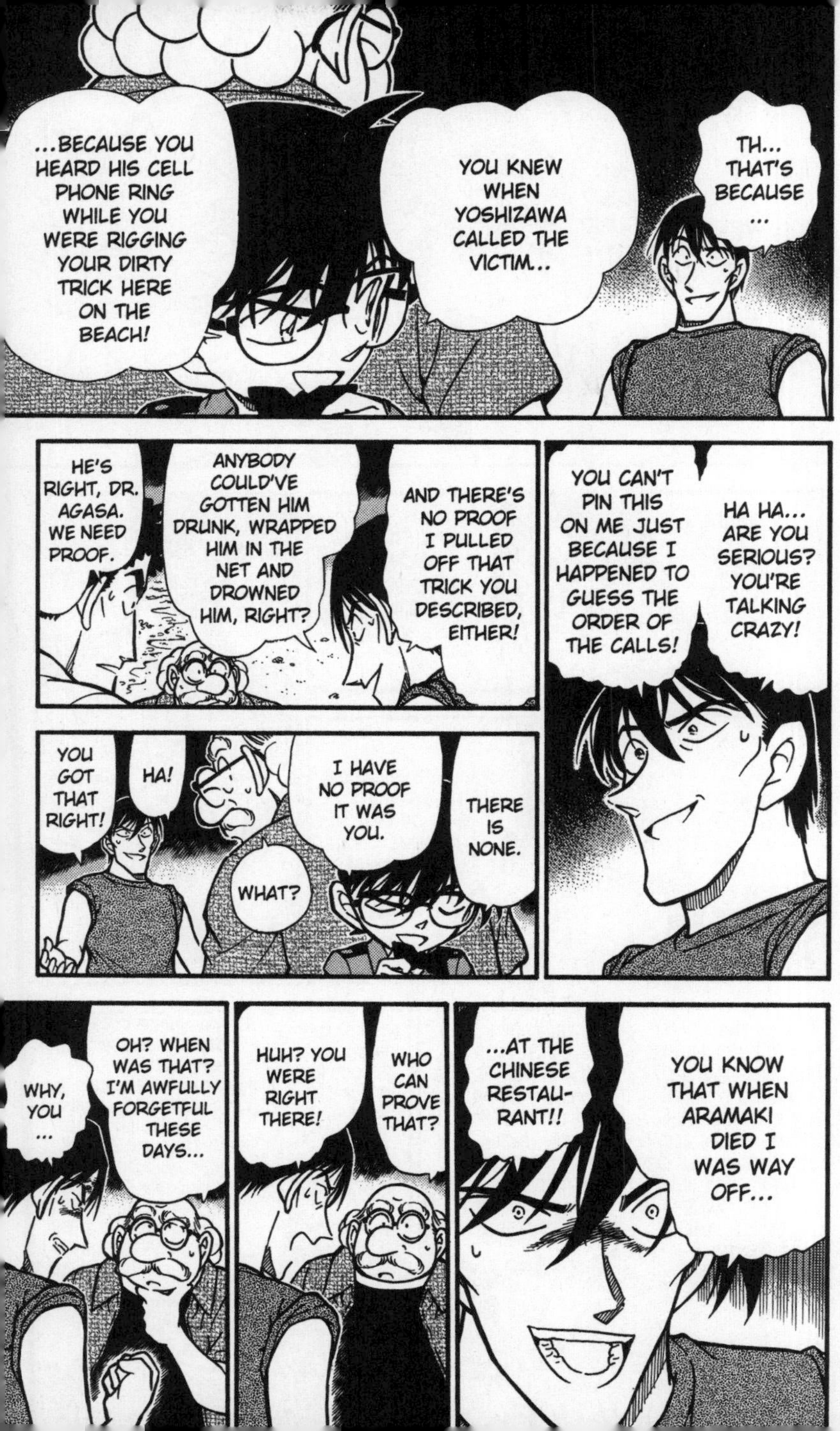
TH... THAT'S BECAUSE ...
YOU KNEW WHEN YOSHIZAWA CALLED THE VICTIM...
...BECAUSE YOU HEARD HIS CELL PHONE RING WHILE YOU WERE RIGGING YOUR DIRTY TRICK HERE ON THE BEACH!
HA HA... ARE YOU SERIOUS? YOU'RE TALKING CRAZY!
YOU CAN'T PIN THIS ON ME JUST BECAUSE I HAPPENED TO GUESS THE ORDER OF THE CALLS!
AND THERE'S NO PROOF I PULLED OFF THAT TRICK YOU DESCRIBED, EITHER!
ANYBODY COULD'VE GOTTEN HIM DRUNK, WRAPPED HIM IN THE NET AND DROWNED HIM, RIGHT?
HE'S RIGHT, DR. AGASA. WE NEED PROOF.
THERE IS NONE.
I HAVE NO PROOF IT WAS YOU.
WHAT?
HA!
YOU GOT THAT RIGHT!
YOU KNOW THAT WHEN ARAMAKI DIED I WAS WAY OFF...
...AT THE CHINESE RESTAU-RANT!!
WHO CAN PROVE THAT?
HUH? YOU WERE RIGHT THERE!
OH? WHEN WAS THAT? I'M AWFULLY FORGETFUL THESE DAYS...
WHY, YOU ...

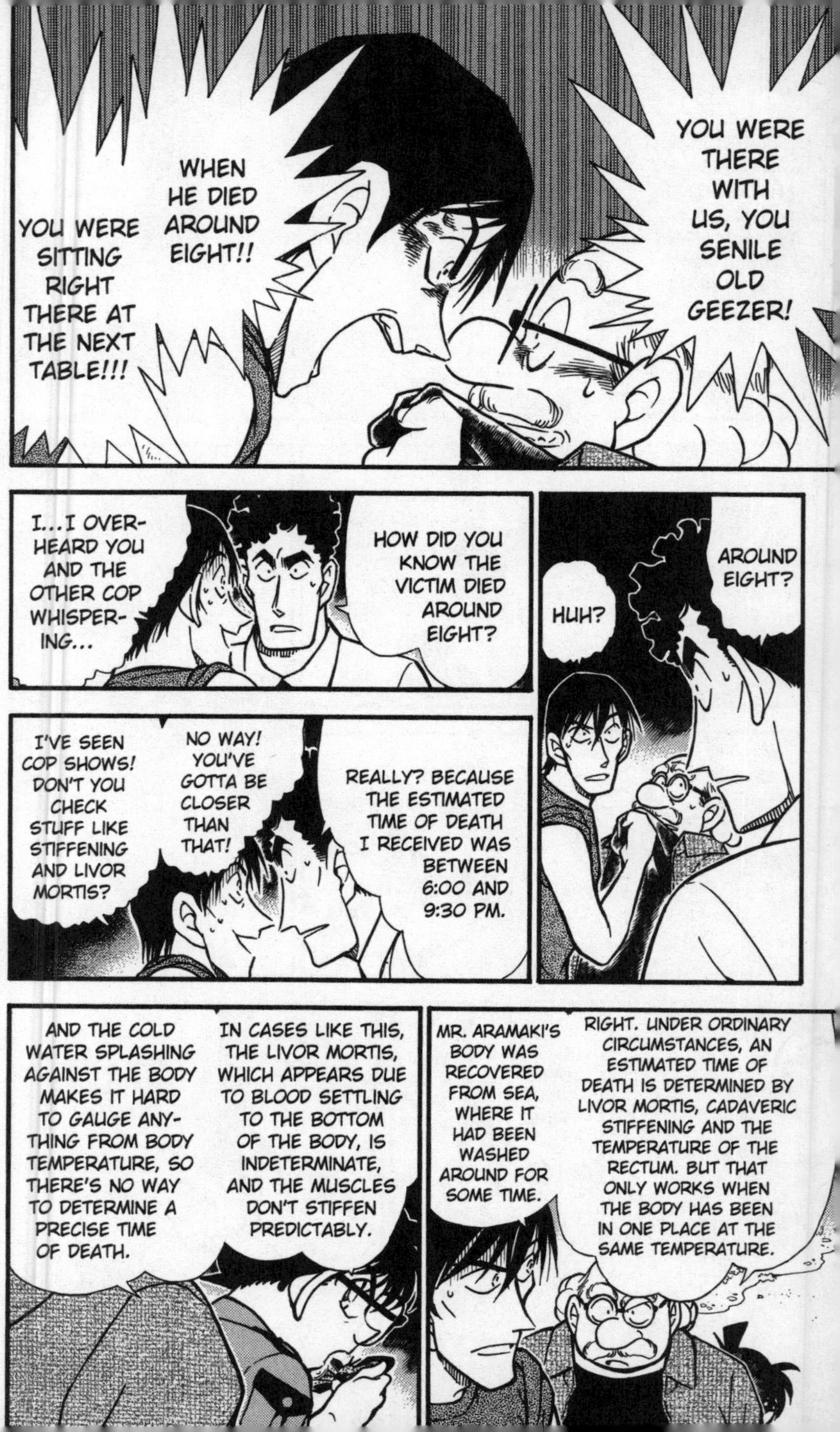
YOU WERE THERE WITH US, YOU SENILE OLD GEEZER!
WHEN HE DIED AROUND EIGHT!!
YOU WERE SITTING RIGHT THERE AT THE NEXT TABLE!!!
AROUND EIGHT?
HUH?
HOW DID YOU KNOW THE VICTIM DIED AROUND EIGHT?
I...I OVERHEARD YOU AND THE OTHER COP WHISPERING...
REALLY? BECAUSE THE ESTIMATED TIME OF DEATH I RECEIVED WAS BETWEEN 6:00 AND 9:30 PM.
NO WAY! YOU'VE GOTTA BE CLOSER THAN THAT!
I'VE SEEN COP SHOWS! DON'T YOU CHECK STUFF LIKE STIFFENING AND LIVOR MORTIS?
RIGHT. UNDER ORDINARY CIRCUMSTANCES, AN ESTIMATED TIME OF DEATH IS DETERMINED BY LIVOR MORTIS, CADAVERIC STIFFENING AND THE TEMPERATURE OF THE RECTUM. BUT THAT ONLY WORKS WHEN THE BODY HAS BEEN IN ONE PLACE AT THE SAME TEMPERATURE.
MR. ARAMAKI'S BODY WAS RECOVERED FROM SEA, WHERE IT HAD BEEN WASHED AROUND FOR SOME TIME.
IN CASES LIKE THIS, THE LIVOR MORTIS, WHICH APPEARS DUE TO BLOOD SETTLING TO THE BOTTOM OF THE BODY, IS INDETERMINATE, AND THE MUSCLES DON'T STIFFEN PREDICTABLY.
AND THE COLD WATER SPLASHING AGAINST THE BODY MAKES IT HARD TO GAUGE ANYTHING FROM BODY TEMPERATURE, SO THERE'S NO WAY TO DETERMINE A PRECISE TIME OF DEATH.

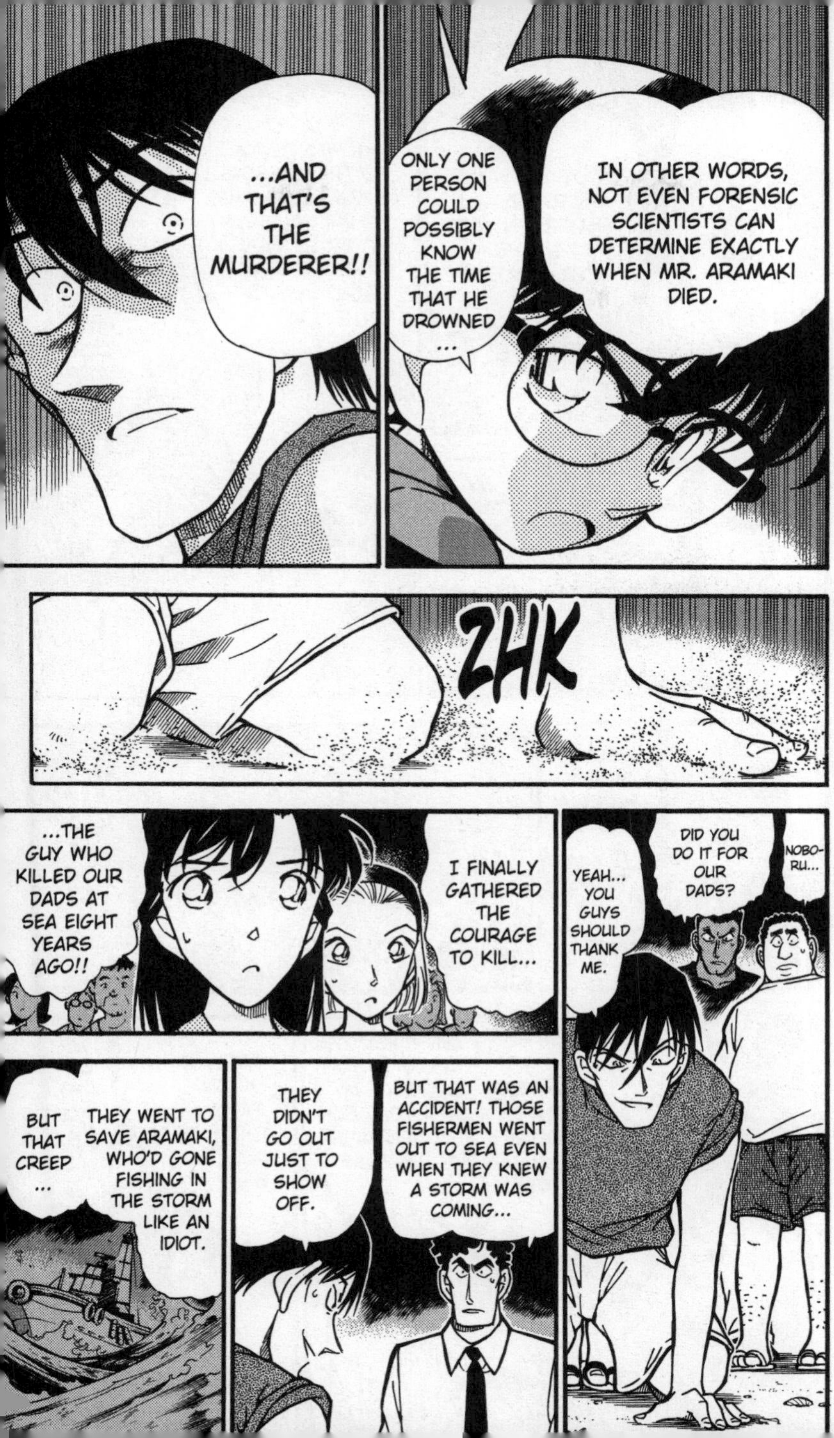
IN OTHER WORDS, NOT EVEN FORENSIC SCIENTISTS CAN DETERMINE EXACTLY WHEN MR. ARAMAKI DIED.
ONLY ONE PERSON COULD POSSIBLY KNOW THE TIME THAT HE DROWNED ...
...AND THAT'S THE MURDERER!!
ZHK
NOBO-RU...
DID YOU DO IT FOR OUR DADS?
YEAH... YOU GUYS SHOULD THANK ME.
I FINALLY GATHERED THE COURAGE TO KILL...
...THE GUY WHO KILLED OUR DADS AT SEA EIGHT YEARS AGO!!
BUT THAT WAS AN ACCIDENT! THOSE FISHERMEN WENT OUT TO SEA EVEN WHEN THEY KNEW A STORM WAS COMING...
THEY DIDN'T GO OUT JUST TO SHOW OFF.
THEY WENT TO SAVE ARAMAKI, WHO'D GONE FISHING IN THE STORM LIKE AN IDIOT.
BUT THAT CREEP ...

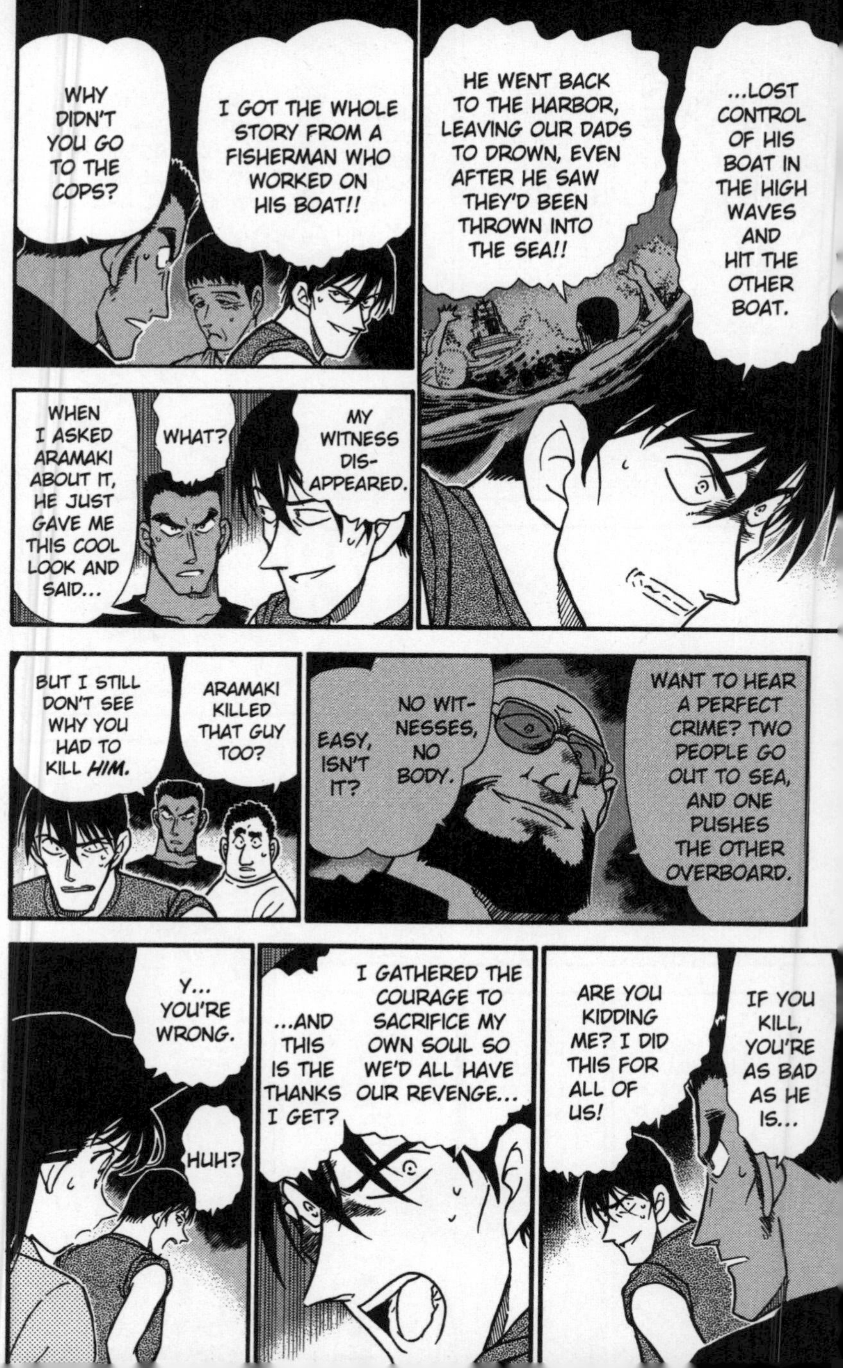
...LOST CONTROL OF HIS BOAT IN THE HIGH WAVES AND HIT THE OTHER BOAT.
HE WENT BACK TO THE HARBOR, LEAVING OUR DADS TO DROWN, EVEN AFTER HE SAW THEY'D BEEN THROWN INTO THE SEA!!
I GOT THE WHOLE STORY FROM A FISHERMAN WHO WORKED ON HIS BOAT!!
WHY DIDN'T YOU GO TO THE COPS?
MY WITNESS DIS-APPEARED.
WHAT?
WHEN I ASKED ARAMAKI ABOUT IT, HE JUST GAVE ME THIS COOL LOOK AND SAID...
WANT TO HEAR A PERFECT CRIME? TWO PEOPLE GO OUT TO SEA, AND ONE PUSHES THE OTHER OVERBOARD.
NO WIT-NESSES, NO BODY.
EASY, ISN'T IT?
ARAMAKI KILLED THAT GUY TOO?
BUT I STILL DON'T SEE WHY YOU HAD TO KILL *HIM*.
IF YOU KILL, YOU'RE AS BAD AS HE IS...
ARE YOU KIDDING ME? I DID THIS FOR ALL OF US!
I GATHERED THE COURAGE TO SACRIFICE MY OWN SOUL SO WE'D ALL HAVE OUR REVENGE...
...AND THIS IS THE THANKS I GET?
Y... YOU'RE WRONG.
HUH?

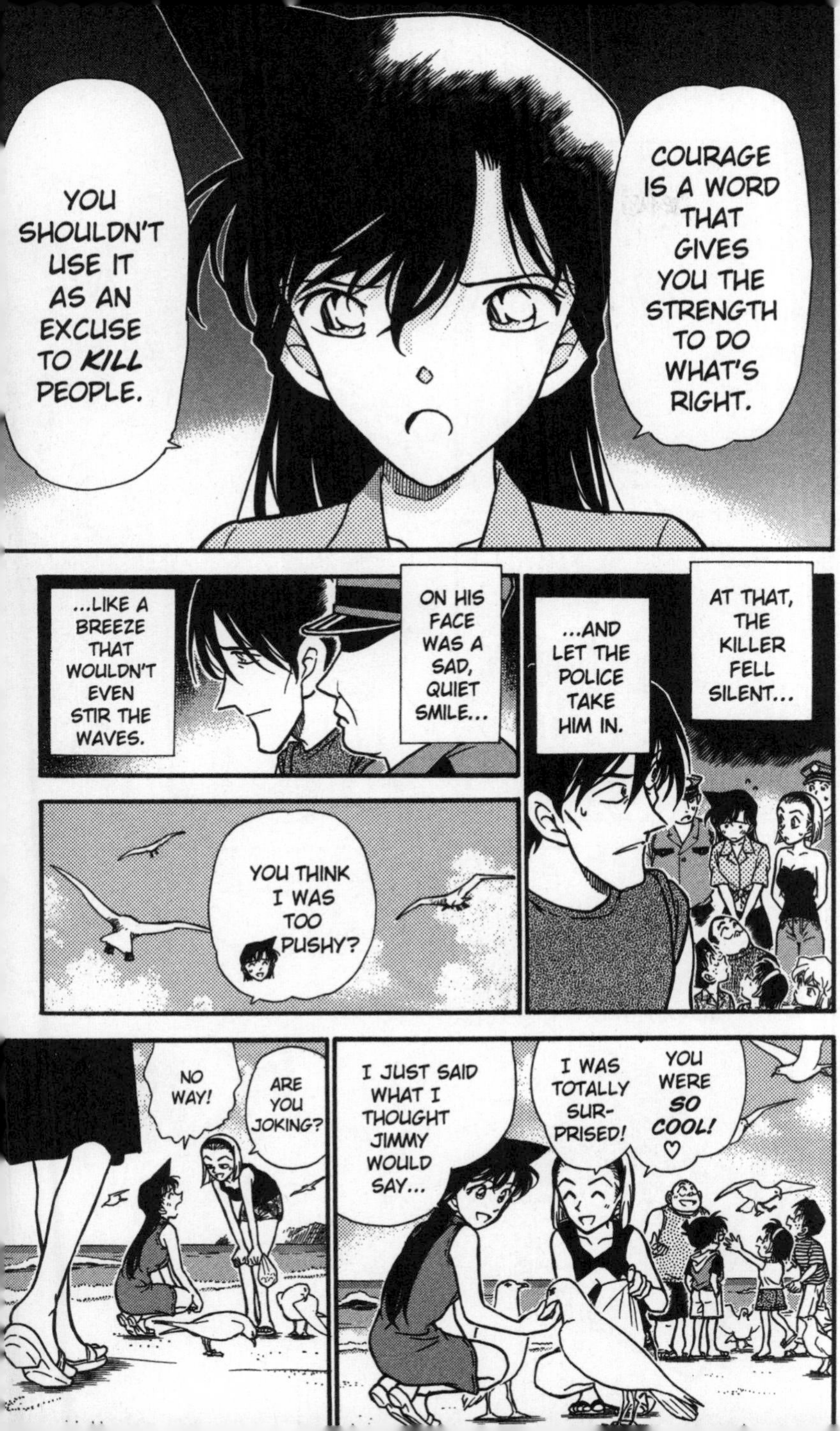
COURAGE IS A WORD THAT GIVES YOU THE STRENGTH TO DO WHAT'S RIGHT.
YOU SHOULDN'T USE IT AS AN EXCUSE TO *KILL* PEOPLE.
AT THAT, THE KILLER FELL SILENT...
...AND LET THE POLICE TAKE HIM IN.
ON HIS FACE WAS A SAD, QUIET SMILE...
...LIKE A BREEZE THAT WOULDN'T EVEN STIR THE WAVES.
YOU THINK I WAS TOO PUSHY?
YOU WERE *SO COOL!* ♡
I WAS TOTALLY SURPRISED!
I JUST SAID WHAT I THOUGHT JIMMY WOULD SAY...
ARE YOU JOKING?
NO WAY!

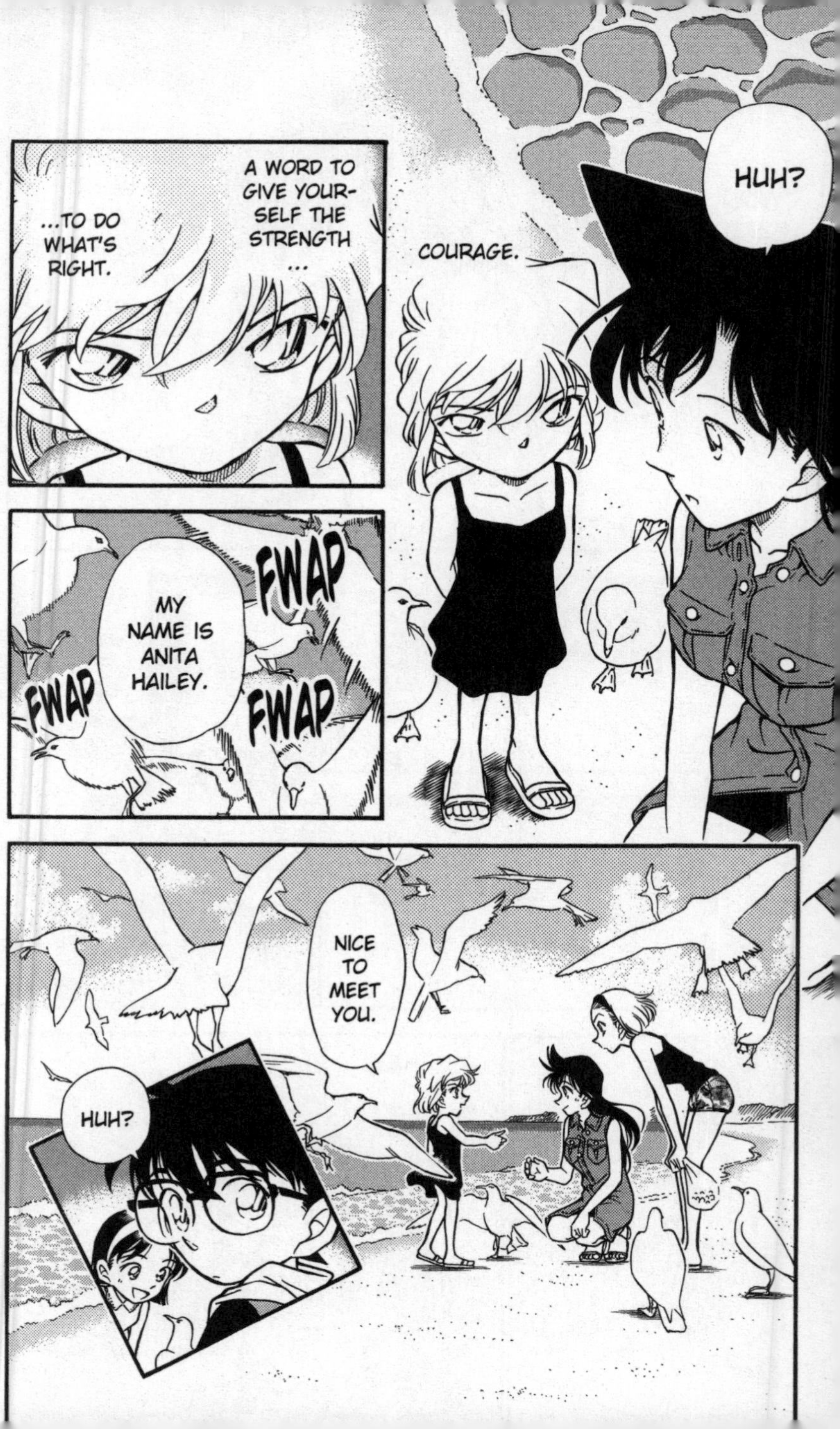
HUH?
COURAGE.
A WORD TO GIVE YOURSELF THE STRENGTH...
...TO DO WHAT'S RIGHT.
FWAP
MY NAME IS ANITA HAILEY.
FWAP
FWAP
NICE TO MEET YOU.
HUH?

FILE 8: THE SWORDSMAN FROM OSAKA

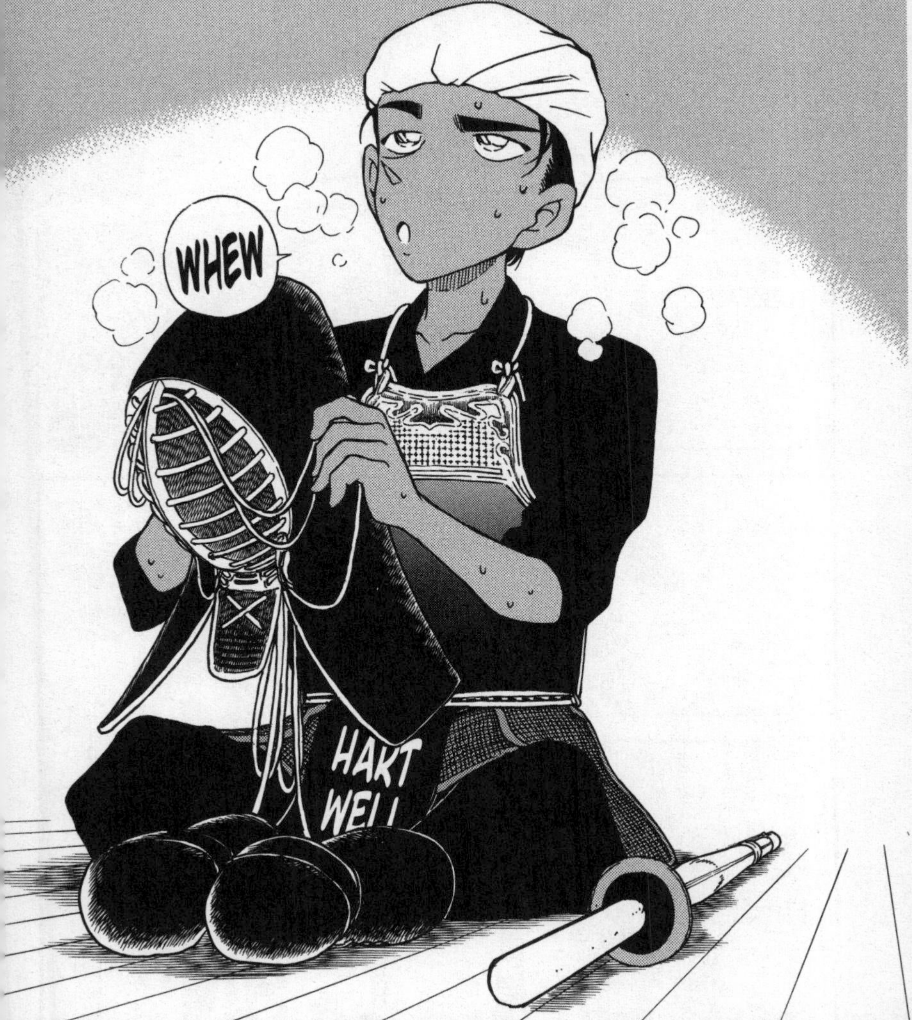
WHEW
HAKT

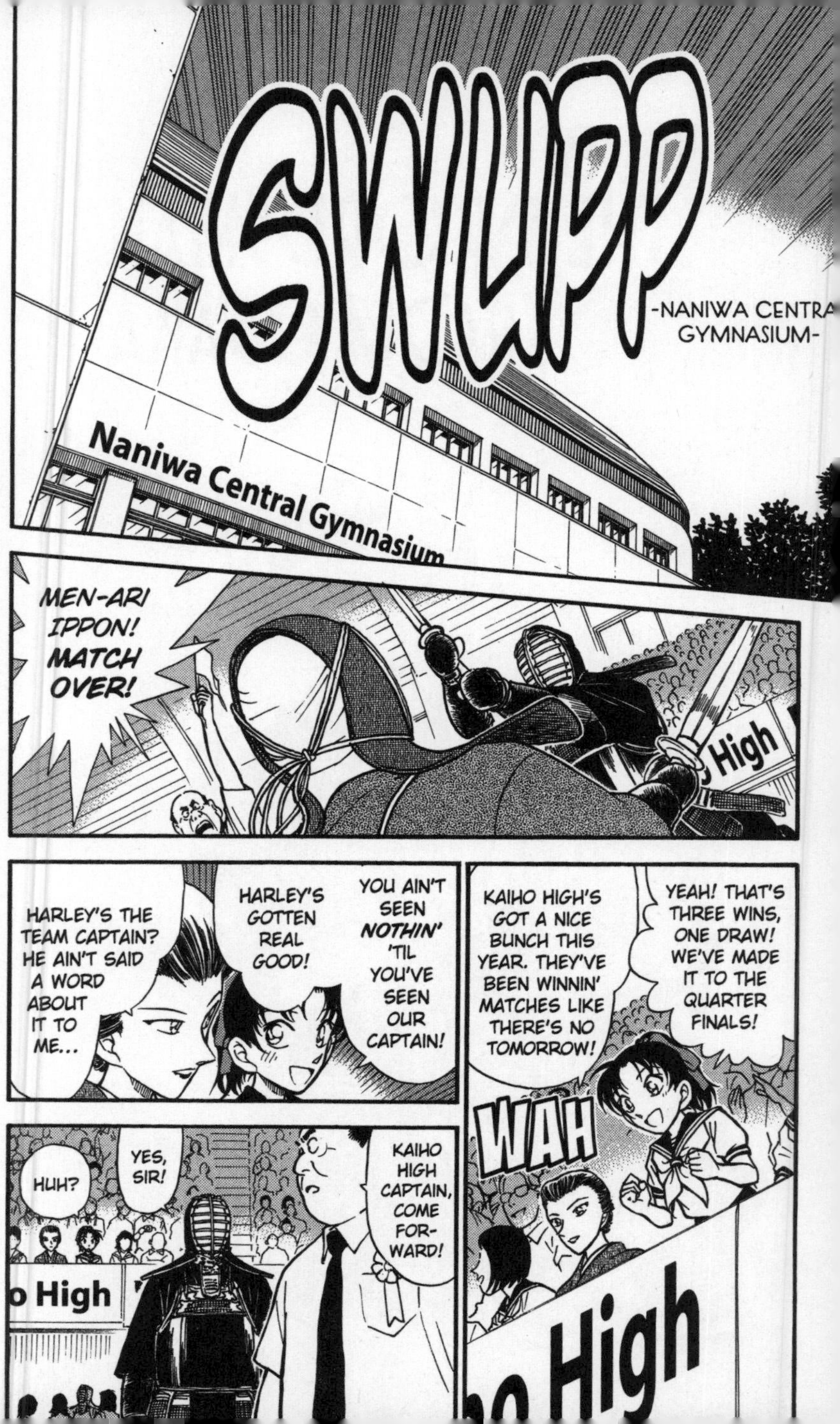
SWUPP
-NANIWA CENTRAL GYMNASIUM-
Naniwa Central Gymnasium
MEN-ARI IPPON! MATCH OVER!
High
YEAH! THAT'S THREE WINS, ONE DRAW! WE'VE MADE IT TO THE QUARTER FINALS!
KAIHO HIGH'S GOT A NICE BUNCH THIS YEAR. THEY'VE BEEN WINNIN' MATCHES LIKE THERE'S NO TOMORROW!
WAH
High
YOU AIN'T SEEN NOTHIN' 'TIL YOU'VE SEEN OUR CAPTAIN!
HARLEY'S GOTTEN REAL GOOD!
HARLEY'S THE TEAM CAPTAIN? HE AIN'T SAID A WORD ABOUT IT TO ME...
KAIHO HIGH CAPTAIN, COME FOR-WARD!
YES, SIR!
HUH?
High

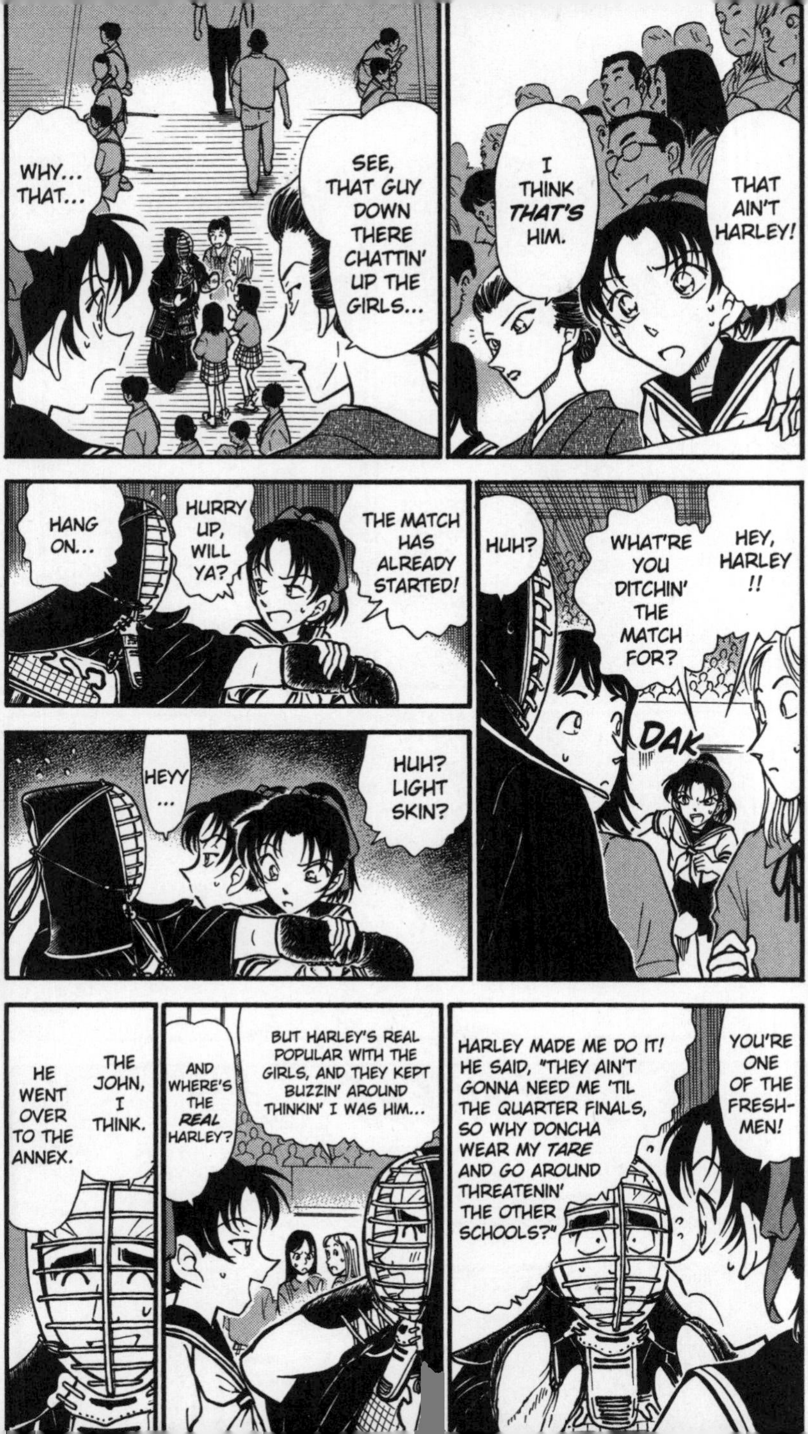
THAT AIN'T HARLEY!
I THINK *THAT'S* HIM.
SEE, THAT GUY DOWN THERE CHATTIN' UP THE GIRLS...
WHY... THAT...
HEY, HARLEY !!
WHAT'RE YOU DITCHIN' THE MATCH FOR?
DAK
HUH?
THE MATCH HAS ALREADY STARTED!
HURRY UP, WILL YA?
HANG ON...
HUH? LIGHT SKIN?
HEYY ...
YOU'RE ONE OF THE FRESH-MEN!
HARLEY MADE ME DO IT! HE SAID, "THEY AIN'T GONNA NEED ME 'TIL THE QUARTER FINALS, SO WHY DONCHA WEAR MY *TARE* AND GO AROUND THREATENIN' THE OTHER SCHOOLS?"
BUT HARLEY'S REAL POPULAR WITH THE GIRLS, AND THEY KEPT BUZZIN' AROUND THINKIN' I WAS HIM...
AND WHERE'S THE *REAL* HARLEY?
THE JOHN, I THINK.
HE WENT OVER TO THE ANNEX.

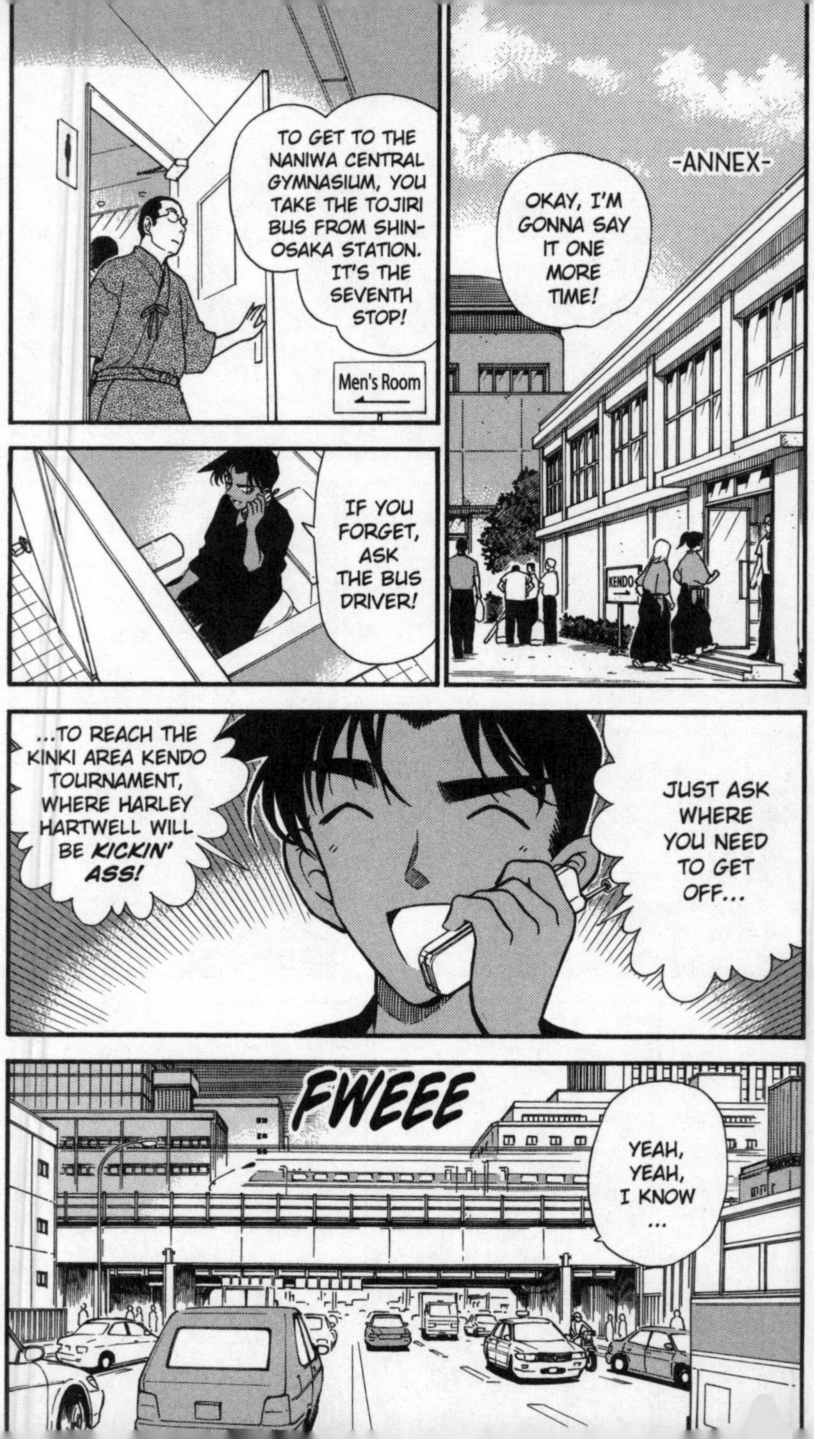
-ANNEX-
OKAY, I'M GONNA SAY IT ONE MORE TIME!
KENDO
TO GET TO THE NANIWA CENTRAL GYMNASIUM, YOU TAKE THE TOJIRI BUS FROM SHIN-OSAKA STATION. IT'S THE SEVENTH STOP!
Men's Room
IF YOU FORGET, ASK THE BUS DRIVER!
JUST ASK WHERE YOU NEED TO GET OFF...
...TO REACH THE KINKI AREA KENDO TOURNAMENT, WHERE HARLEY HARTWELL WILL BE *KICKIN' ASS!*
YEAH, YEAH, I KNOW ...
FWEEE

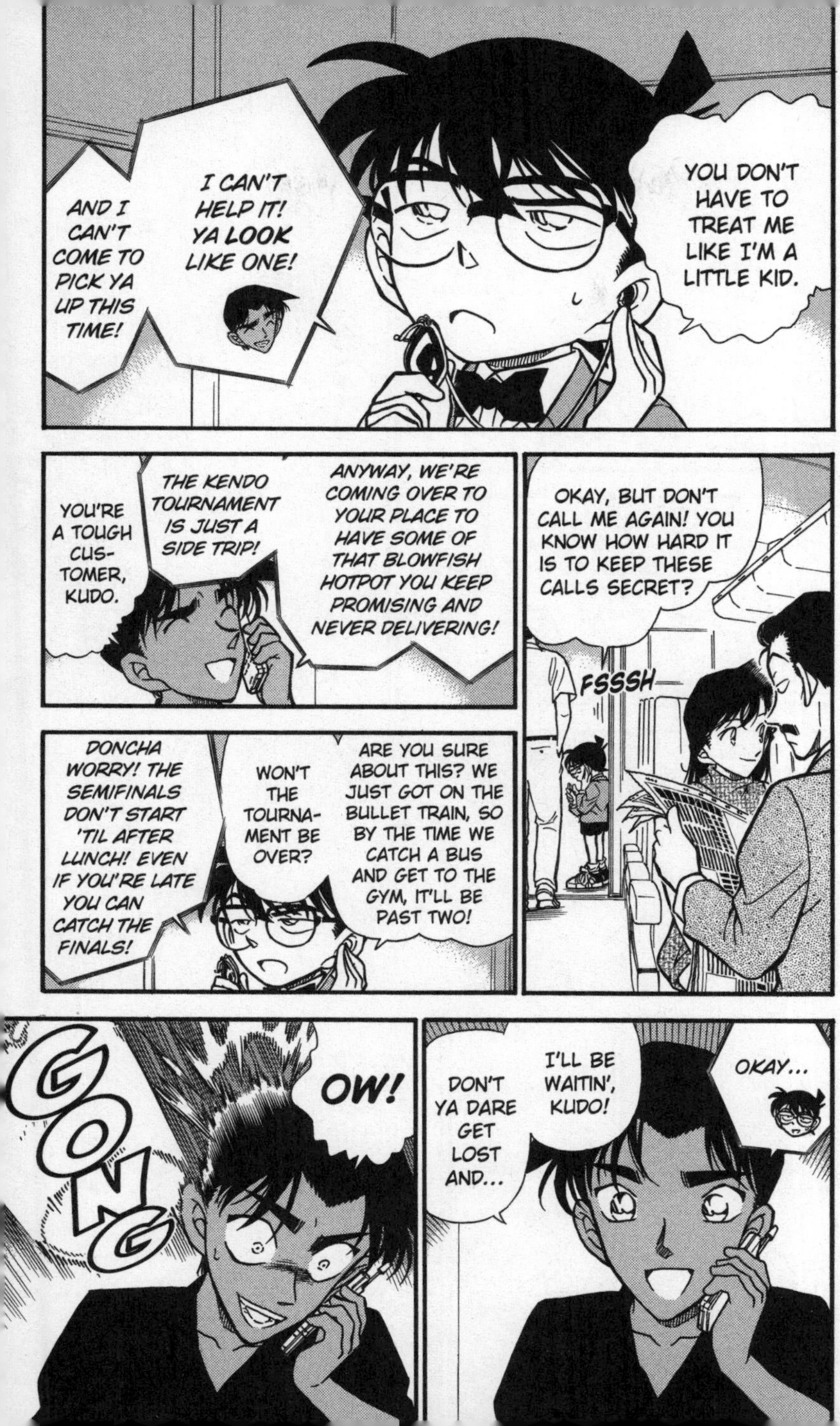
YOU DON'T HAVE TO TREAT ME LIKE I'M A LITTLE KID.
I CAN'T HELP IT! YA LOOK LIKE ONE!
AND I CAN'T COME TO PICK YA UP THIS TIME!
OKAY, BUT DON'T CALL ME AGAIN! YOU KNOW HOW HARD IT IS TO KEEP THESE CALLS SECRET?
FSSSH
ANYWAY, WE'RE COMING OVER TO YOUR PLACE TO HAVE SOME OF THAT BLOWFISH HOTPOT YOU KEEP PROMISING AND NEVER DELIVERING!
THE KENDO TOURNAMENT IS JUST A SIDE TRIP!
YOU'RE A TOUGH CUS-TOMER, KUDO.
ARE YOU SURE ABOUT THIS? WE JUST GOT ON THE BULLET TRAIN, SO BY THE TIME WE CATCH A BUS AND GET TO THE GYM, IT'LL BE PAST TWO!
WON'T THE TOURNA-MENT BE OVER?
DONCHA WORRY! THE SEMIFINALS DON'T START 'TIL AFTER LUNCH! EVEN IF YOU'RE LATE YOU CAN CATCH THE FINALS!
OKAY...
I'LL BE WAITIN', KUDO!
DON'T YA DARE GET LOST AND...
OW!
GONG

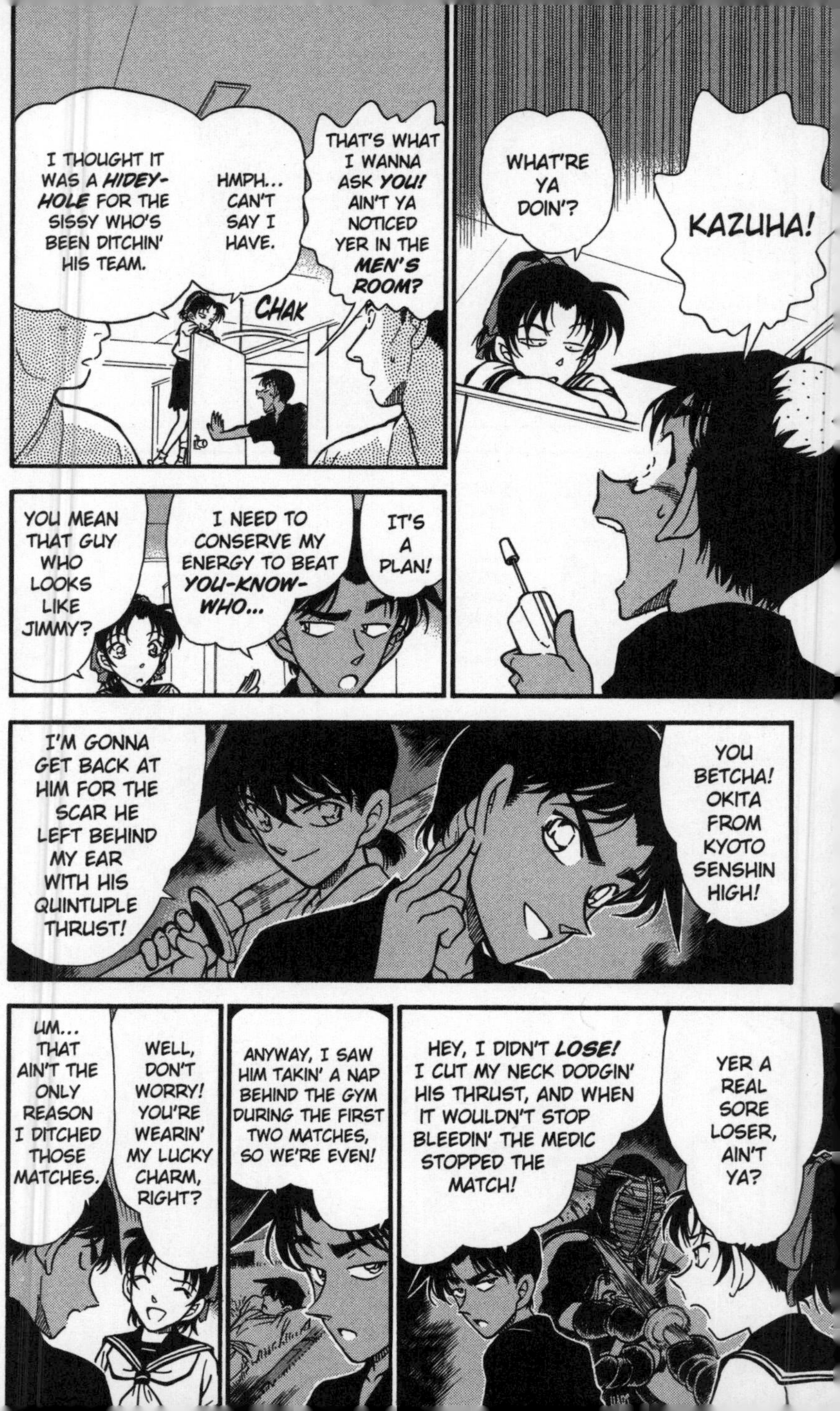
KAZUHA!
WHAT'RE YA DOIN'?
THAT'S WHAT I WANNA ASK YOU! AIN'T YA NOTICED YER IN THE MEN'S ROOM?
CHAK
HMPH... CAN'T SAY I HAVE.
I THOUGHT IT WAS A HIDEY-HOLE FOR THE SISSY WHO'S BEEN DITCHIN' HIS TEAM.
IT'S A PLAN!
I NEED TO CONSERVE MY ENERGY TO BEAT YOU-KNOW-WHO...
YOU MEAN THAT GUY WHO LOOKS LIKE JIMMY?
YOU BETCHA! OKITA FROM KYOTO SENSHIN HIGH!
I'M GONNA GET BACK AT HIM FOR THE SCAR HE LEFT BEHIND MY EAR WITH HIS QUINTUPLE THRUST!
YER A REAL SORE LOSER, AIN'T YA?
HEY, I DIDN'T LOSE! I CUT MY NECK DODGIN' HIS THRUST, AND WHEN IT WOULDN'T STOP BLEEDIN' THE MEDIC STOPPED THE MATCH!
ANYWAY, I SAW HIM TAKIN' A NAP BEHIND THE GYM DURING THE FIRST TWO MATCHES, SO WE'RE EVEN!
WELL, DON'T WORRY! YOU'RE WEARIN' MY LUCKY CHARM, RIGHT?
UM... THAT AIN'T THE ONLY REASON I DITCHED THOSE MATCHES.

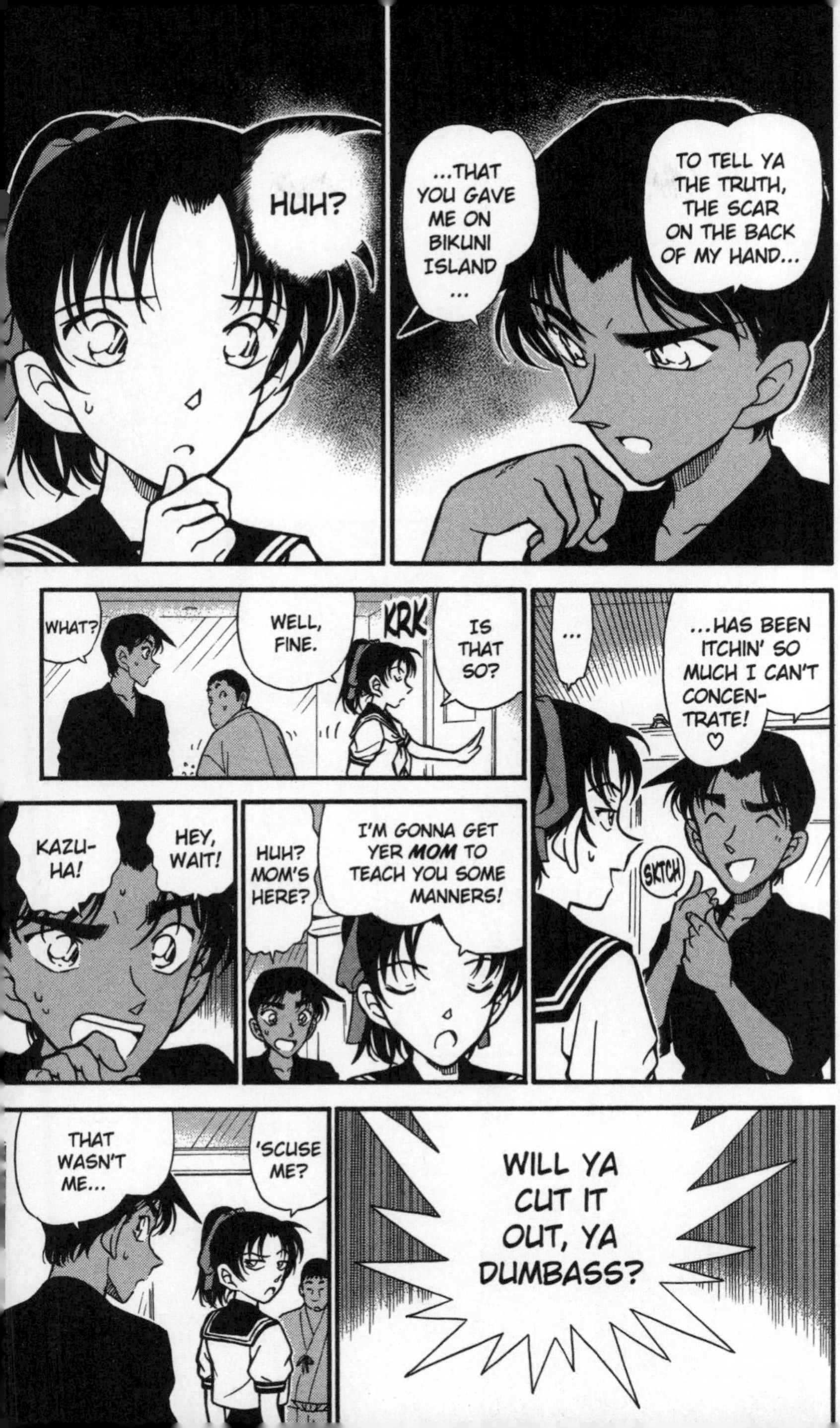
TO TELL YA THE TRUTH, THE SCAR ON THE BACK OF MY HAND...
...THAT YOU GAVE ME ON BIKUNI ISLAND ...
HUH?
...HAS BEEN ITCHIN' SO MUCH I CAN'T CONCEN-TRATE! ♡
...
SKTCH
IS THAT SO?
KRK
WELL, FINE.
WHAT?
I'M GONNA GET YER *MOM* TO TEACH YOU SOME MANNERS!
HUH? MOM'S HERE?
HEY, WAIT!
KAZU-HA!
WILL YA CUT IT OUT, YA DUMBASS?
'SCUSE ME?
THAT WASN'T ME...

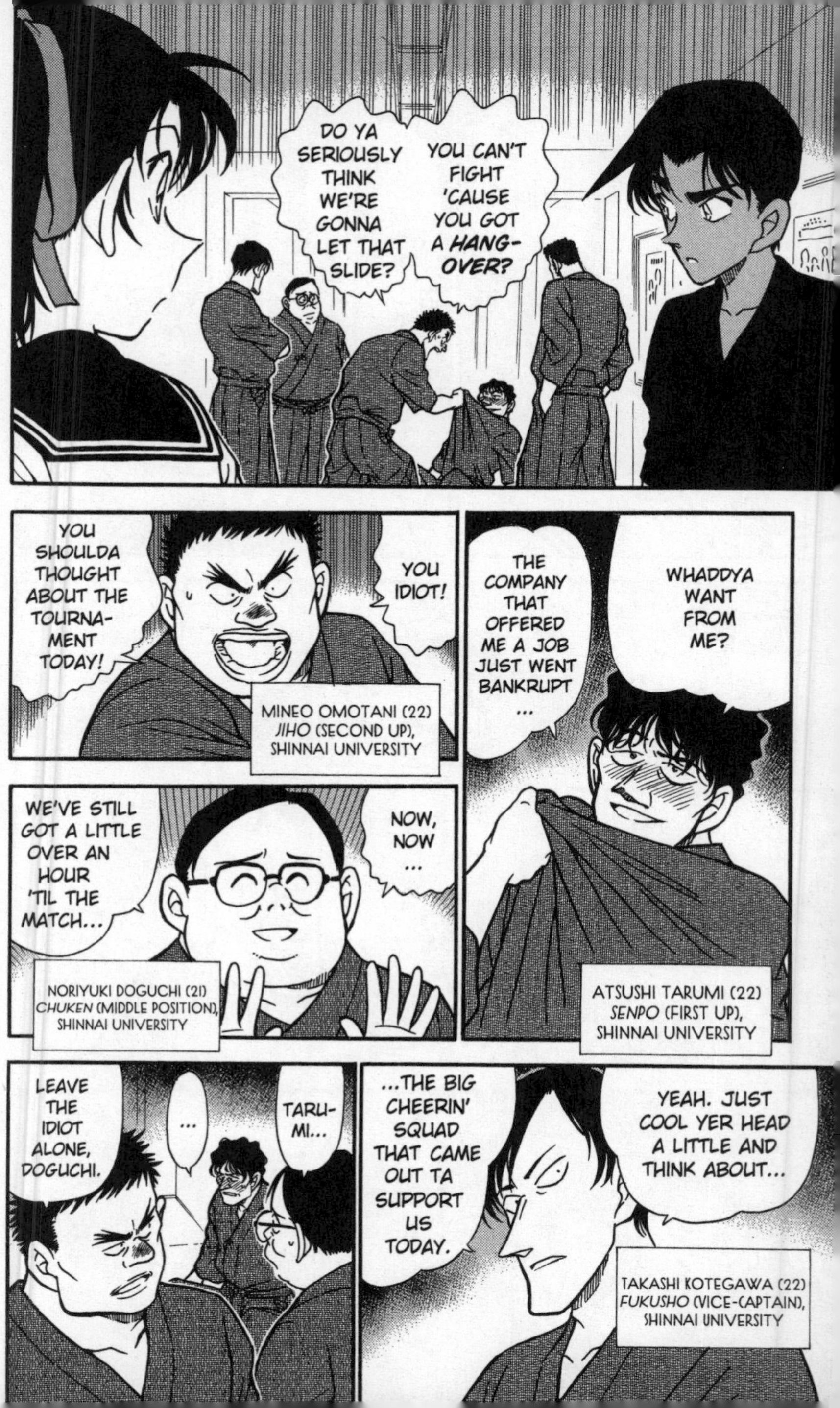
YOU CAN'T FIGHT 'CAUSE YOU GOT A *HANG-OVER?*
DO YA SERIOUSLY THINK WE'RE GONNA LET THAT SLIDE?
WHADDYA WANT FROM ME?
THE COMPANY THAT OFFERED ME A JOB JUST WENT BANKRUPT ...
ATSUSHI TARUMI (22) *SENPO* (FIRST UP), SHINNAI UNIVERSITY
YOU IDIOT!
YOU SHOULDA THOUGHT ABOUT THE TOURNA-MENT TODAY!
MINEO OMOTANI (22) *JIHO* (SECOND UP), SHINNAI UNIVERSITY
NOW, NOW ...
WE'VE STILL GOT A LITTLE OVER AN HOUR 'TIL THE MATCH...
NORIYUKI DOGUCHI (21) *CHUKEN* (MIDDLE POSITION), SHINNAI UNIVERSITY
YEAH. JUST COOL YER HEAD A LITTLE AND THINK ABOUT...
...THE BIG CHEERIN' SQUAD THAT CAME OUT TA SUPPORT US TODAY.
TAKASHI KOTEGAWA (22) *FUKUSHO* (VICE-CAPTAIN), SHINNAI UNIVERSITY
TARU-MI...
...
LEAVE THE IDIOT ALONE, DOGUCHI.

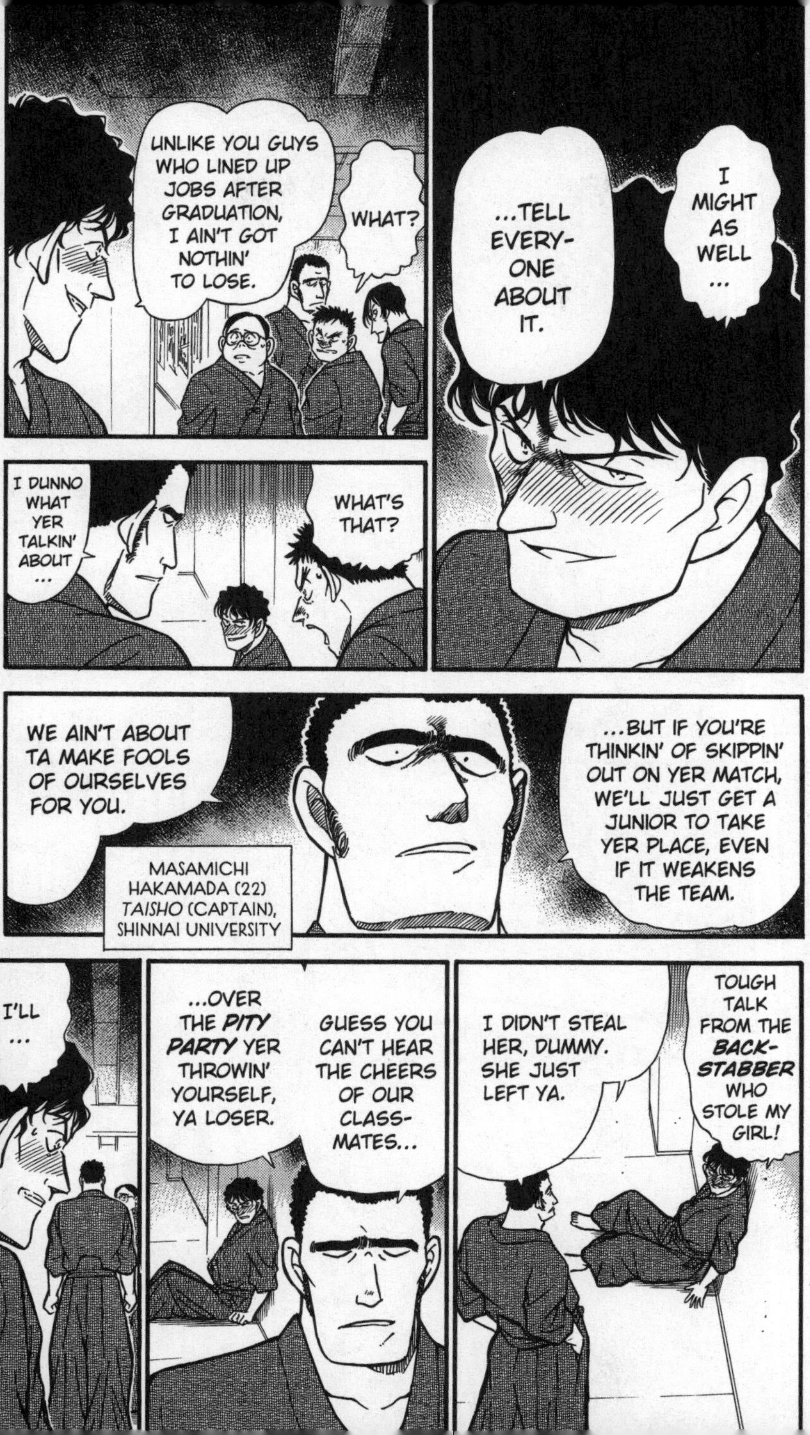
I MIGHT AS WELL ...
...TELL EVERY-ONE ABOUT IT.
WHAT?
UNLIKE YOU GUYS WHO LINED UP JOBS AFTER GRADUATION, I AIN'T GOT NOTHIN' TO LOSE.
WHAT'S THAT?
I DUNNO WHAT YER TALKIN' ABOUT ...
...BUT IF YOU'RE THINKIN' OF SKIPPIN' OUT ON YER MATCH, WE'LL JUST GET A JUNIOR TO TAKE YER PLACE, EVEN IF IT WEAKENS THE TEAM.
WE AIN'T ABOUT TA MAKE FOOLS OF OURSELVES FOR YOU.
MASAMICHI HAKAMADA (22) *TAISHO* (CAPTAIN), SHINNAI UNIVERSITY
TOUGH TALK FROM THE ***BACK-STABBER*** WHO STOLE MY GIRL!
I DIDN'T STEAL HER, DUMMY. SHE JUST LEFT YA.
GUESS YOU CAN'T HEAR THE CHEERS OF OUR CLASS-MATES...
...OVER THE ***PITY PARTY*** YER THROWIN' YOURSELF, YA LOSER.
I'LL ...

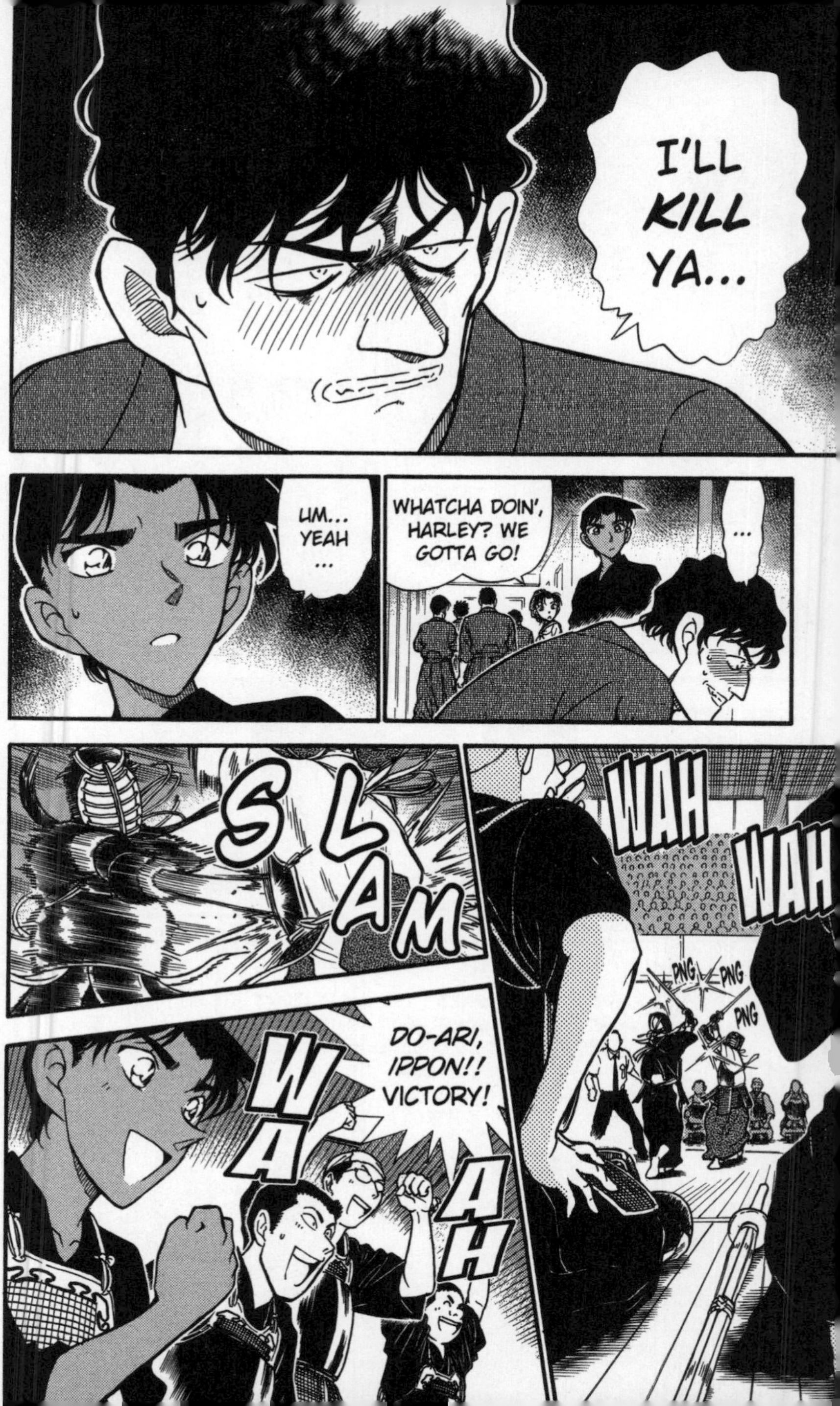
I'LL KILL YA...
...
WHATCHA DOIN', HARLEY? WE GOTTA GO!
UM... YEAH ...
WAH
WAH
PNG
PNG
PNG
SLAM
DO-ARI, IPPON!! VICTORY!
WAAAH

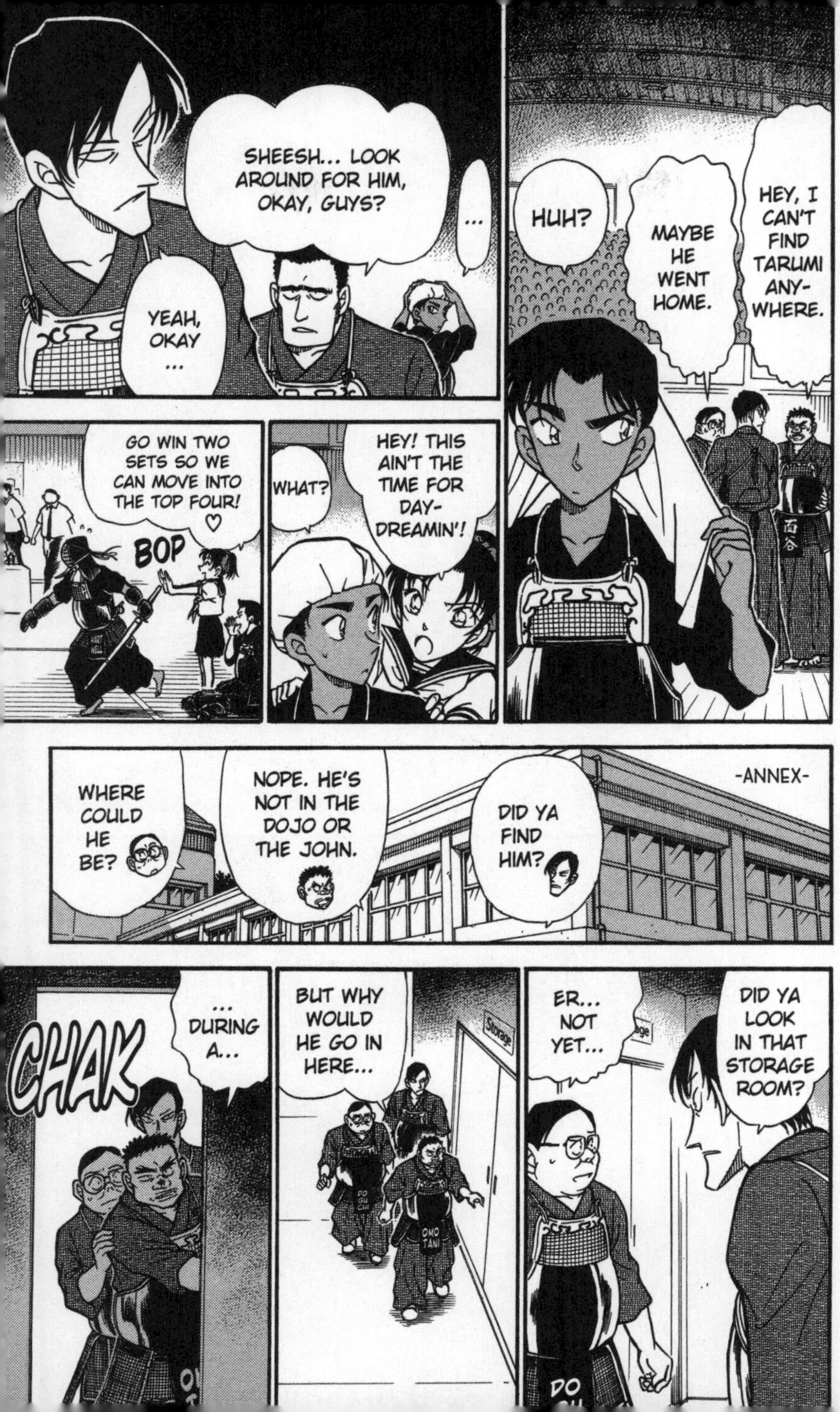
HEY, I CAN'T FIND TARUMI ANY-WHERE.
MAYBE HE WENT HOME.
HUH?
SHEESH... LOOK AROUND FOR HIM, OKAY, GUYS?
...
YEAH, OKAY ...
HEY! THIS AIN'T THE TIME FOR DAY-DREAMIN'!
WHAT?
GO WIN TWO SETS SO WE CAN MOVE INTO THE TOP FOUR! ♡
BOP
-ANNEX-
DID YA FIND HIM?
NOPE. HE'S NOT IN THE DOJO OR THE JOHN.
WHERE COULD HE BE?
DID YA LOOK IN THAT STORAGE ROOM?
ER... NOT YET...
BUT WHY WOULD HE GO IN HERE...
Storage
... DURING A...
CHAK

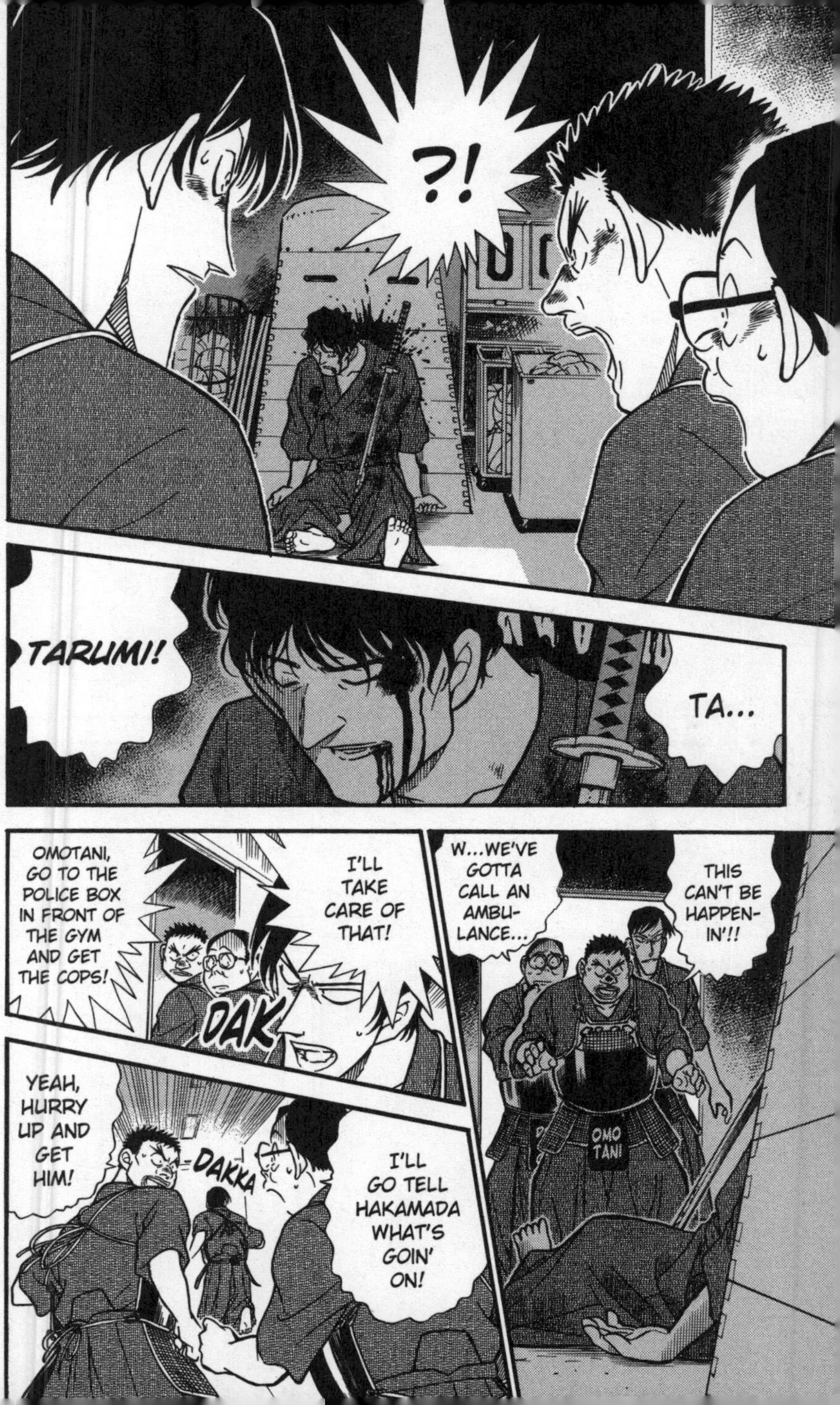
?!
TA...
TARUMI!
THIS CAN'T BE HAPPEN-IN'!!
W...WE'VE GOTTA CALL AN AMBULANCE...
OMO TANI
I'LL TAKE CARE OF THAT!
OMOTANI, GO TO THE POLICE BOX IN FRONT OF THE GYM AND GET THE COPS!
DAK
I'LL GO TELL HAKAMADA WHAT'S GOIN' ON!
DAKKA
YEAH, HURRY UP AND GET HIM!

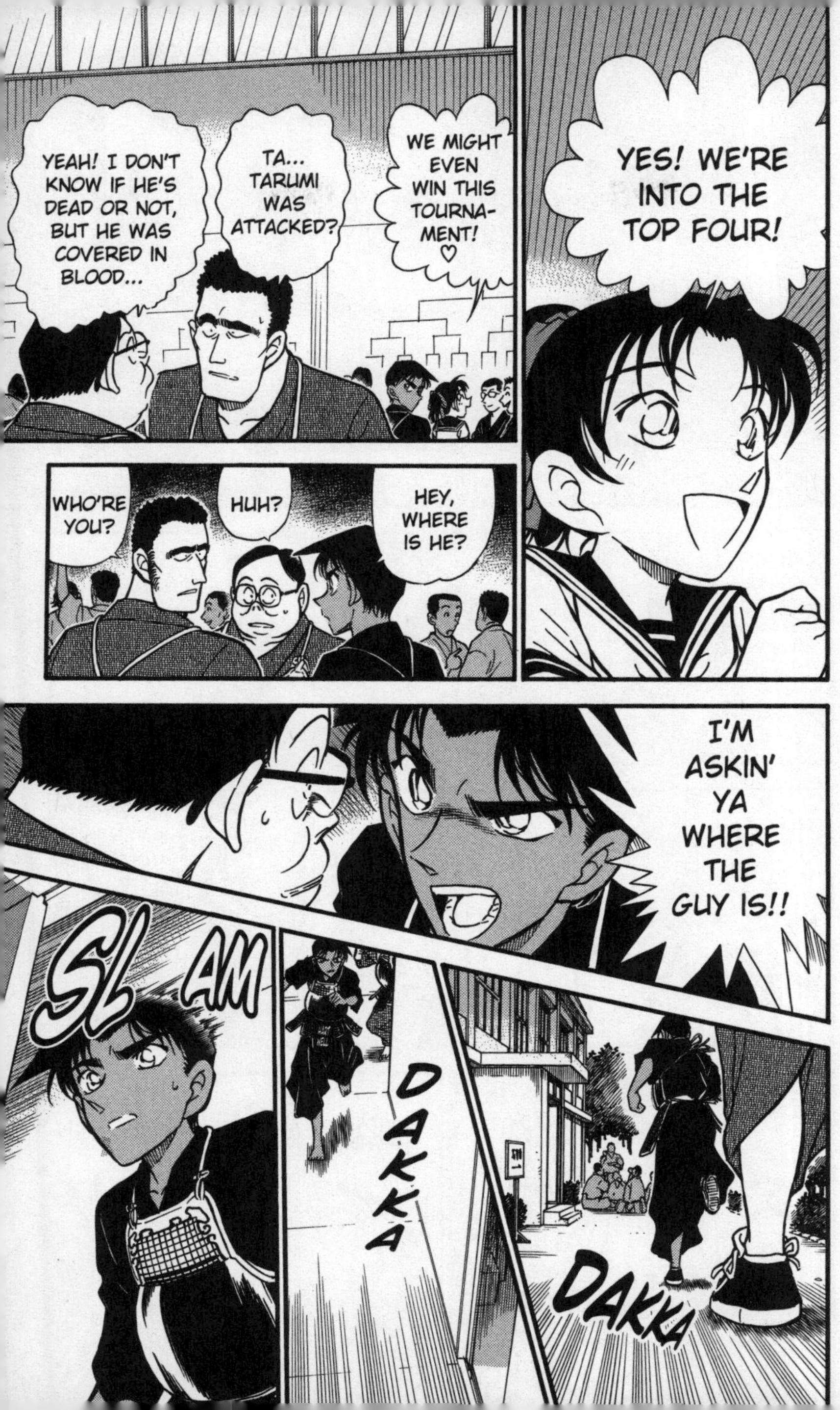
YES! WE'RE INTO THE TOP FOUR!
WE MIGHT EVEN WIN THIS TOURNA-MENT! ♡
TA... TARUMI WAS ATTACKED?
YEAH! I DON'T KNOW IF HE'S DEAD OR NOT, BUT HE WAS COVERED IN BLOOD...
HEY, WHERE IS HE?
HUH?
WHO'RE YOU?
I'M ASKIN' YA WHERE THE GUY IS!!
DAKKA
DAKKA
SL AM

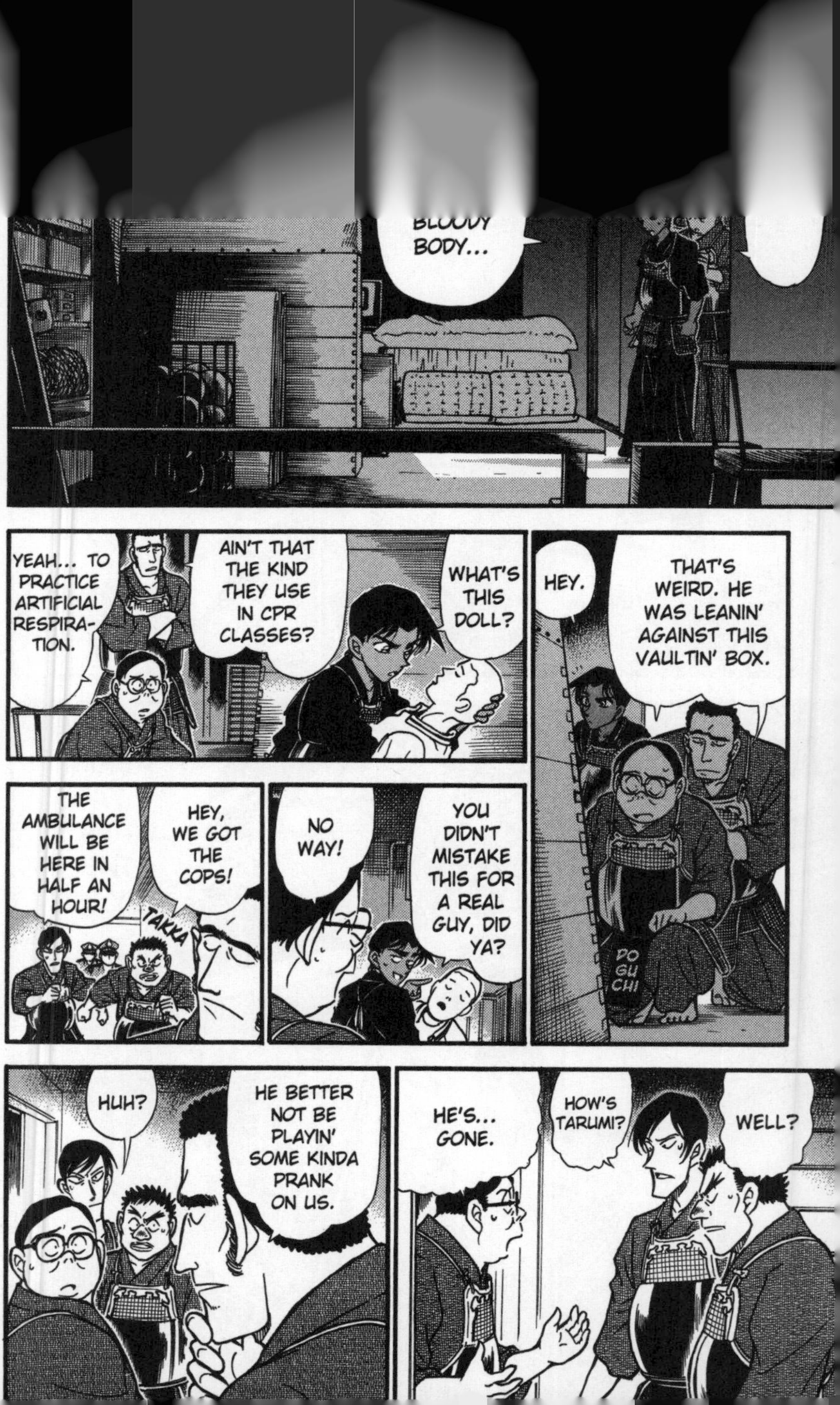
BLOODY BODY...
THAT'S WEIRD. HE WAS LEANIN' AGAINST THIS VAULTIN' BOX.
HEY.
DOGUCHI
WHAT'S THIS DOLL?
AIN'T THAT THE KIND THEY USE IN CPR CLASSES?
YEAH... TO PRACTICE ARTIFICIAL RESPIRA-TION.
YOU DIDN'T MISTAKE THIS FOR A REAL GUY, DID YA?
NO WAY!
HEY, WE GOT THE COPS!
THE AMBULANCE WILL BE HERE IN HALF AN HOUR!
TAKKA
WELL?
HOW'S TARUMI?
HE'S... GONE.
HE BETTER NOT BE PLAYIN' SOME KINDA PRANK ON US.
HUH?

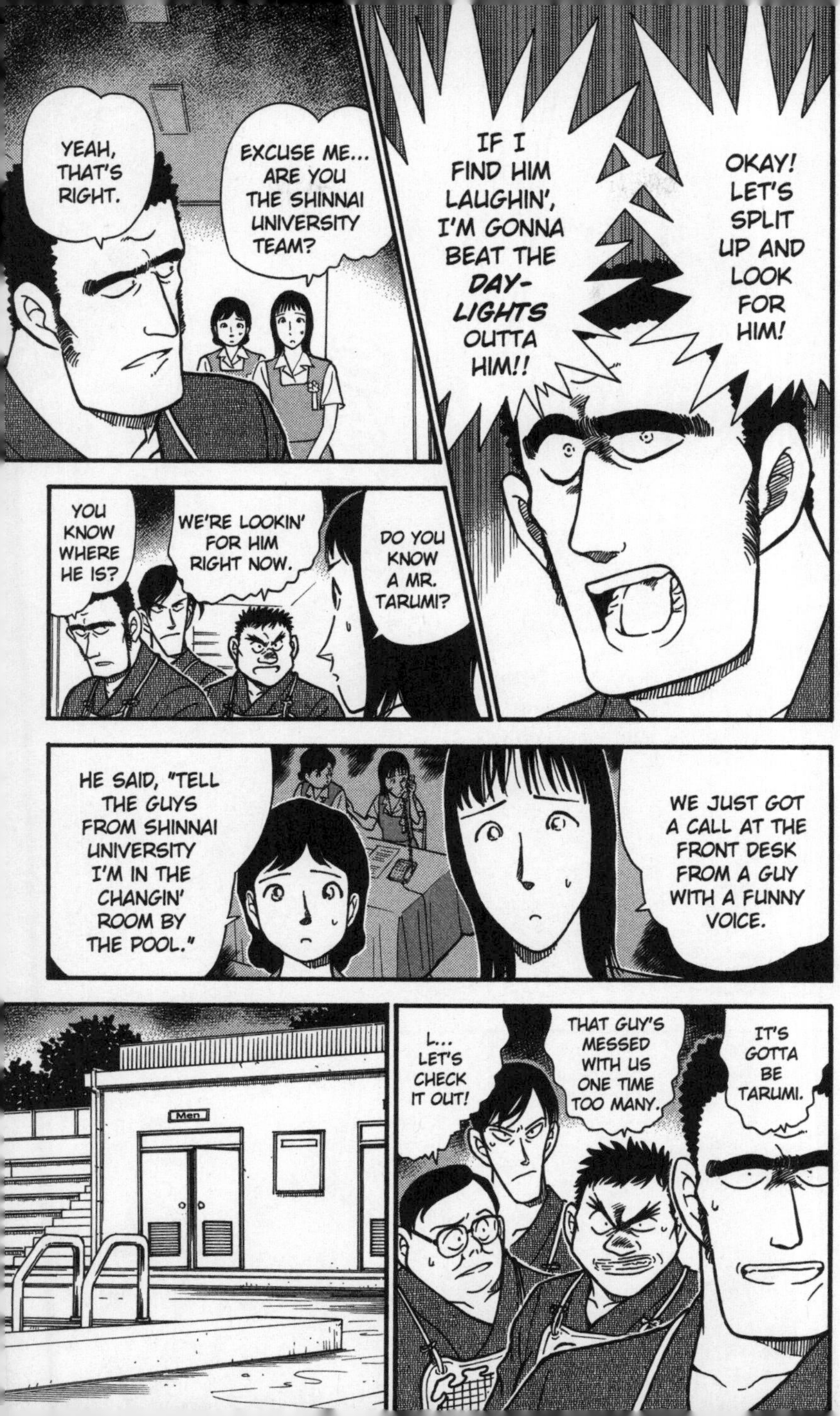

OKAY! LET'S SPLIT UP AND LOOK FOR HIM!
IF I FIND HIM LAUGHIN', I'M GONNA BEAT THE *DAY-LIGHTS* OUTTA HIM!!
EXCUSE ME... ARE YOU THE SHINNAI UNIVERSITY TEAM?
YEAH, THAT'S RIGHT.
DO YOU KNOW A MR. TARUMI?
WE'RE LOOKIN' FOR HIM RIGHT NOW.
YOU KNOW WHERE HE IS?
WE JUST GOT A CALL AT THE FRONT DESK FROM A GUY WITH A FUNNY VOICE.
HE SAID, "TELL THE GUYS FROM SHINNAI UNIVERSITY I'M IN THE CHANGIN' ROOM BY THE POOL."
IT'S GOTTA BE TARUMI.
THAT GUY'S MESSED WITH US ONE TIME TOO MANY.
L... LET'S CHECK IT OUT!
Men

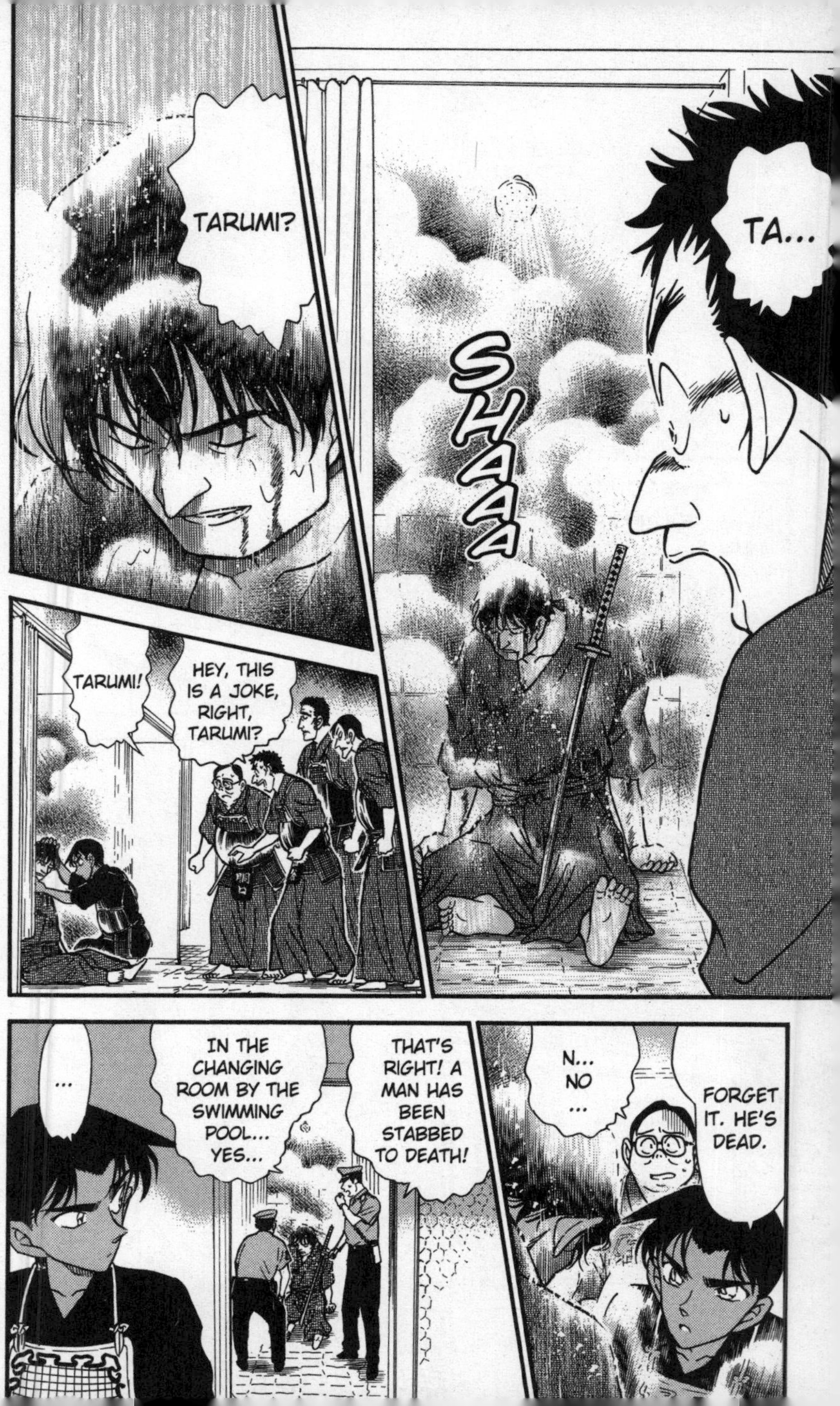
TA...
SHAAAA
TARUMI?
HEY, THIS IS A JOKE, RIGHT, TARUMI?
TARUMI!
N... NO ...
FORGET IT. HE'S DEAD.
THAT'S RIGHT! A MAN HAS BEEN STABBED TO DEATH!
IN THE CHANGING ROOM BY THE SWIMMING POOL... YES...
...

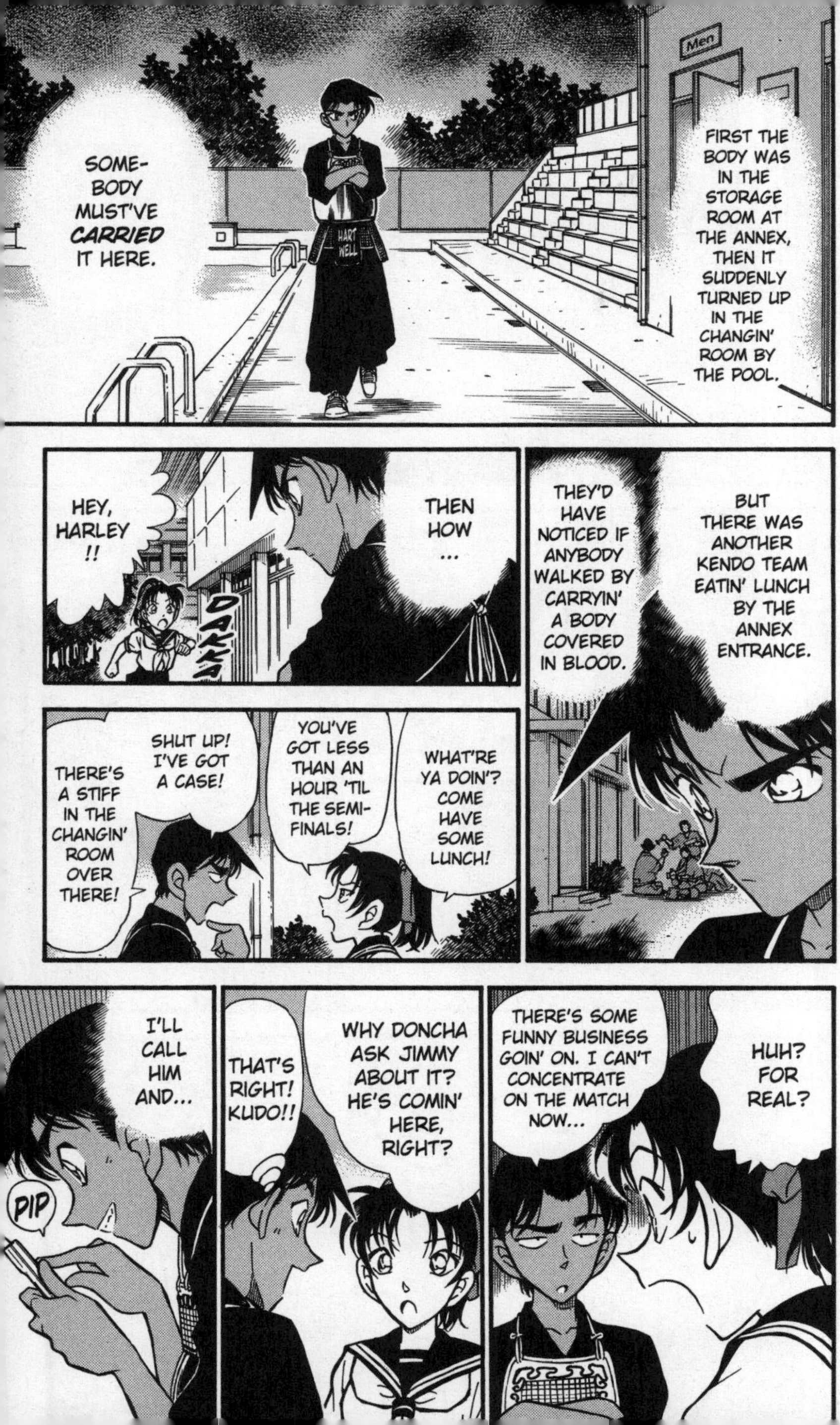
Men
FIRST THE BODY WAS IN THE STORAGE ROOM AT THE ANNEX, THEN IT SUDDENLY TURNED UP IN THE CHANGIN' ROOM BY THE POOL.
HART WELL
SOME-BODY MUST'VE CARRIED IT HERE.
BUT THERE WAS ANOTHER KENDO TEAM EATIN' LUNCH BY THE ANNEX ENTRANCE.
THEY'D HAVE NOTICED IF ANYBODY WALKED BY CARRYIN' A BODY COVERED IN BLOOD.
THEN HOW ...
HEY, HARLEY !!
DAKKA
WHAT'RE YA DOIN'? COME HAVE SOME LUNCH!
YOU'VE GOT LESS THAN AN HOUR 'TIL THE SEMI-FINALS!
SHUT UP! I'VE GOT A CASE!
THERE'S A STIFF IN THE CHANGIN' ROOM OVER THERE!
HUH? FOR REAL?
THERE'S SOME FUNNY BUSINESS GOIN' ON. I CAN'T CONCENTRATE ON THE MATCH NOW...
WHY DONCHA ASK JIMMY ABOUT IT? HE'S COMIN' HERE, RIGHT?
THAT'S RIGHT! KUDO!!
I'LL CALL HIM AND...
PIP

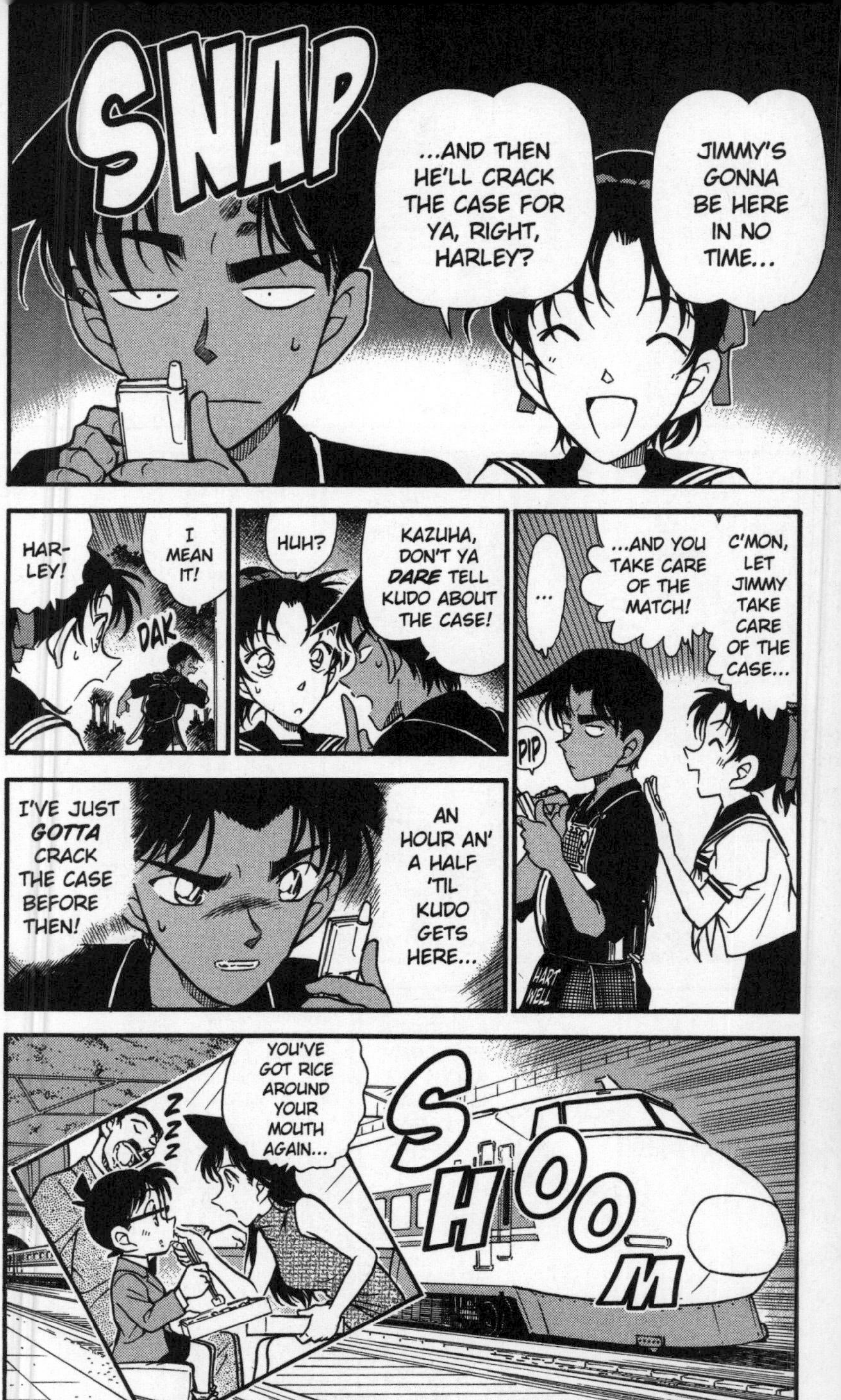
JIMMY'S GONNA BE HERE IN NO TIME...
...AND THEN HE'LL CRACK THE CASE FOR YA, RIGHT, HARLEY?
SNAP
C'MON, LET JIMMY TAKE CARE OF THE CASE...
...AND YOU TAKE CARE OF THE MATCH!
...
PIP
HART WELL
KAZUHA, DON'T YA *DARE* TELL KUDO ABOUT THE CASE!
HUH?
I MEAN IT!
HAR-LEY!
DAK
AN HOUR AN' A HALF 'TIL KUDO GETS HERE...
I'VE JUST *GOTTA* CRACK THE CASE BEFORE THEN!
SHOOOM
YOU'VE GOT RICE AROUND YOUR MOUTH AGAIN...
ZZZ

FILE 9: THE RESTLESS SWORDSMAN

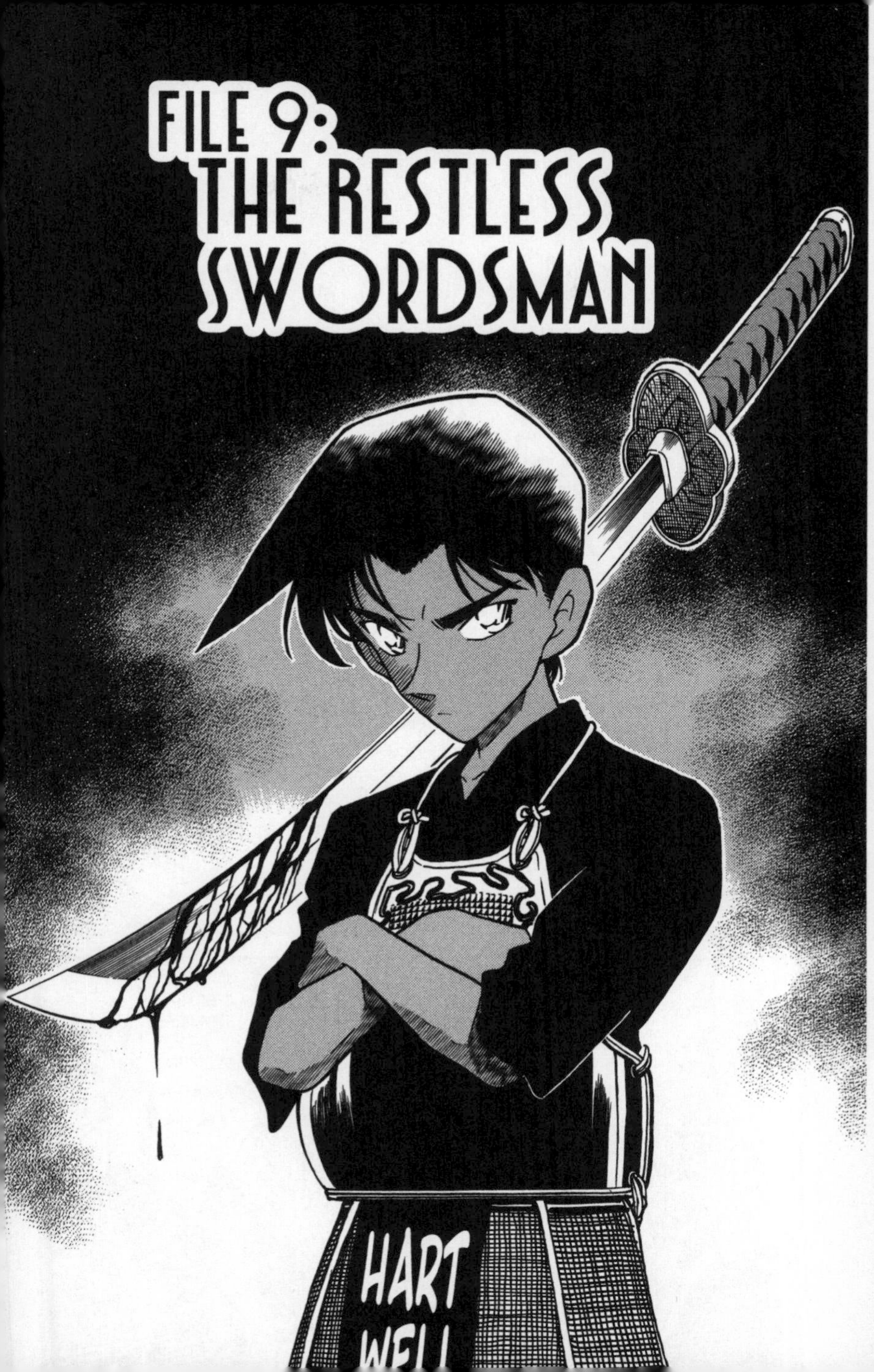
HART

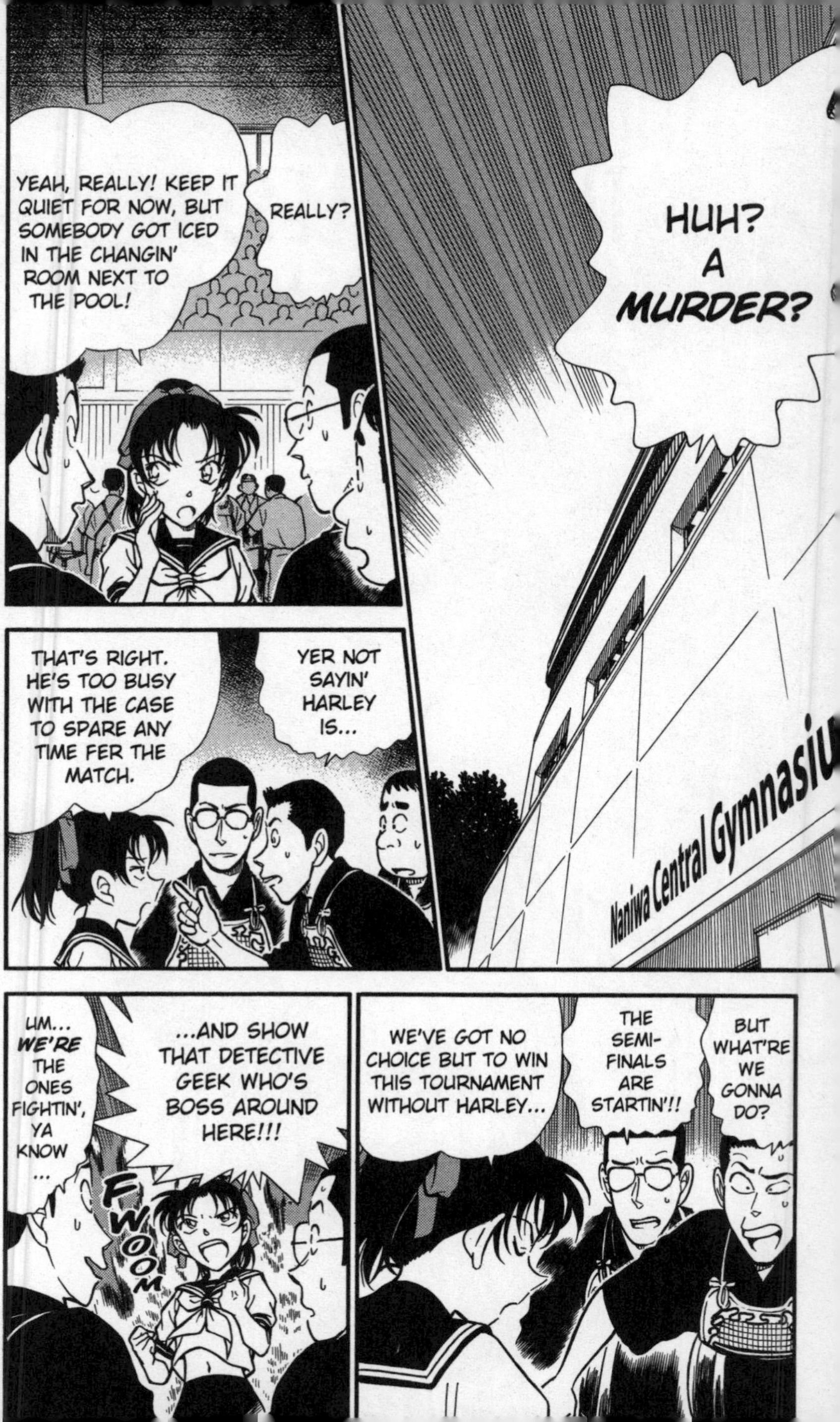
HUH? A MURDER?
Naniwa Central Gymnasiu
REALLY?
YEAH, REALLY! KEEP IT QUIET FOR NOW, BUT SOMEBODY GOT ICED IN THE CHANGIN' ROOM NEXT TO THE POOL!
YER NOT SAYIN' HARLEY IS...
THAT'S RIGHT. HE'S TOO BUSY WITH THE CASE TO SPARE ANY TIME FER THE MATCH.
BUT WHAT'RE WE GONNA DO?
THE SEMI-FINALS ARE STARTIN'!!
WE'VE GOT NO CHOICE BUT TO WIN THIS TOURNAMENT WITHOUT HARLEY...
...AND SHOW THAT DETECTIVE GEEK WHO'S BOSS AROUND HERE!!!
FWOOM
UM... WE'RE THE ONES FIGHTIN', YA KNOW...

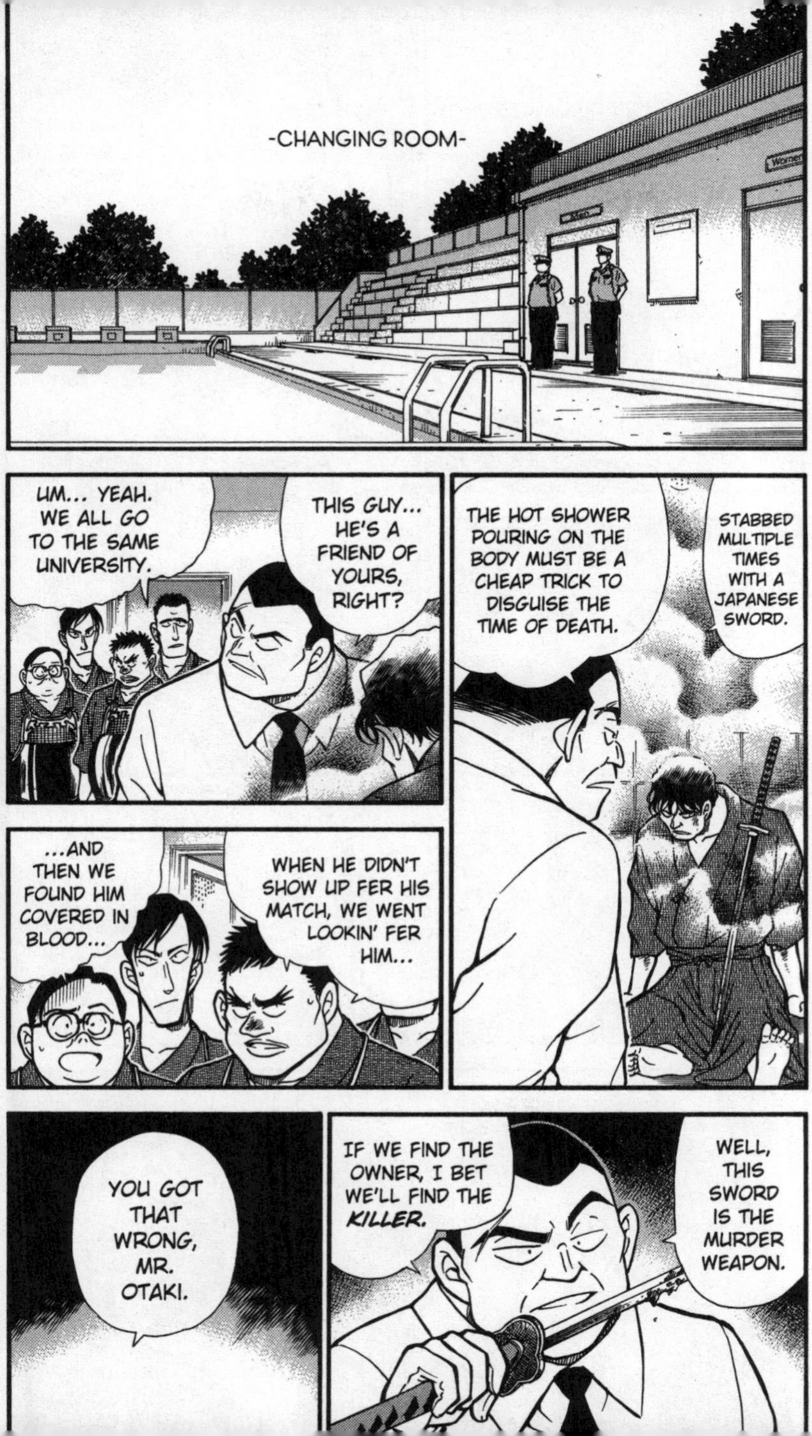
-CHANGING ROOM-
STABBED MULTIPLE TIMES WITH A JAPANESE SWORD.
THE HOT SHOWER POURING ON THE BODY MUST BE A CHEAP TRICK TO DISGUISE THE TIME OF DEATH.
THIS GUY... HE'S A FRIEND OF YOURS, RIGHT?
UM... YEAH. WE ALL GO TO THE SAME UNIVERSITY.
WHEN HE DIDN'T SHOW UP FER HIS MATCH, WE WENT LOOKIN' FER HIM...
...AND THEN WE FOUND HIM COVERED IN BLOOD...
WELL, THIS SWORD IS THE MURDER WEAPON.
IF WE FIND THE OWNER, I BET WE'LL FIND THE *KILLER.*
YOU GOT THAT WRONG, MR. OTAKI.

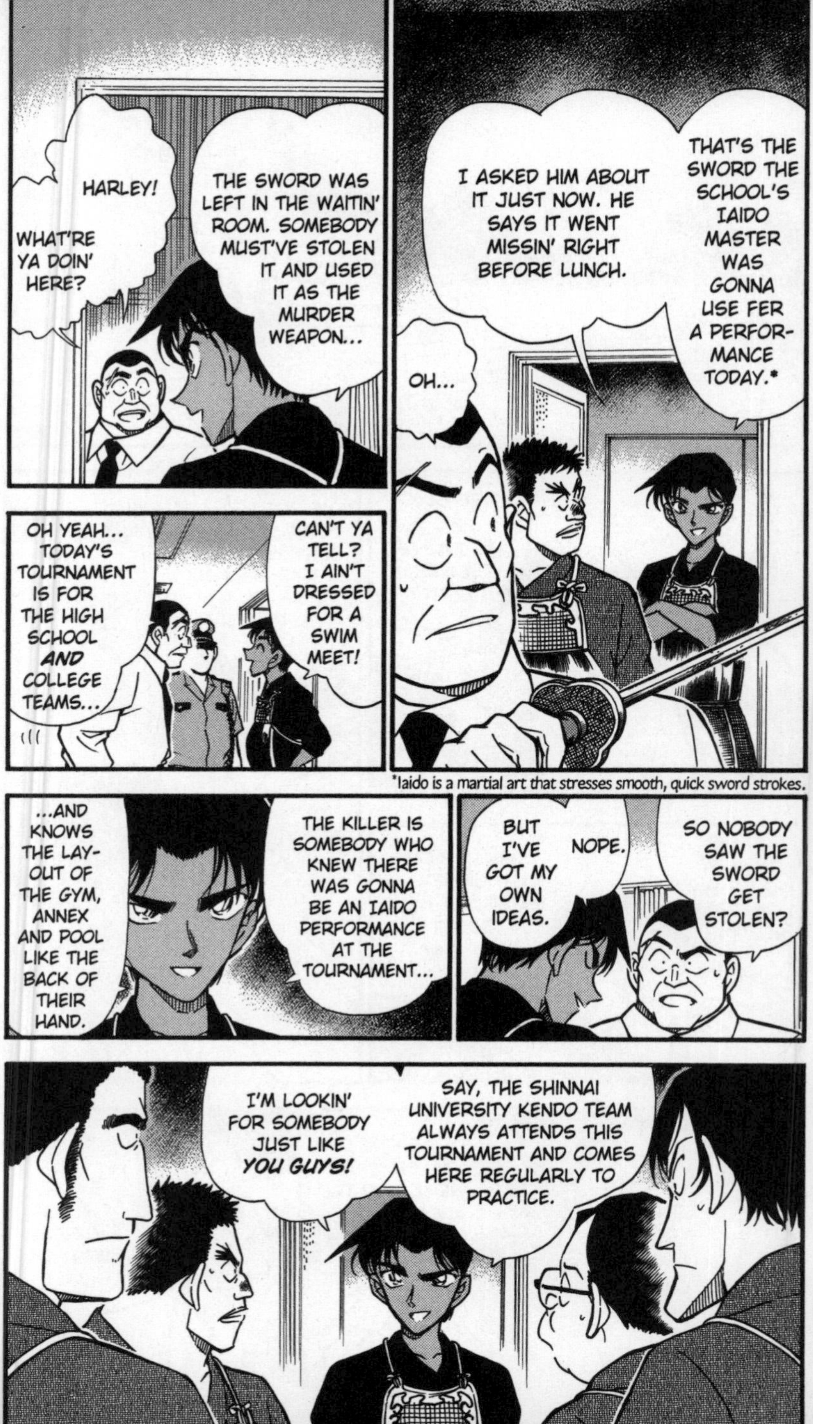
THAT'S THE SWORD THE SCHOOL'S IAIDO MASTER WAS GONNA USE FER A PERFORMANCE TODAY.*
I ASKED HIM ABOUT IT JUST NOW. HE SAYS IT WENT MISSIN' RIGHT BEFORE LUNCH.
OH...
THE SWORD WAS LEFT IN THE WAITIN' ROOM. SOMEBODY MUST'VE STOLEN IT AND USED IT AS THE MURDER WEAPON...
HARLEY!
WHAT'RE YA DOIN' HERE?
CAN'T YA TELL? I AIN'T DRESSED FOR A SWIM MEET!
OH YEAH... TODAY'S TOURNAMENT IS FOR THE HIGH SCHOOL AND COLLEGE TEAMS...
SO NOBODY SAW THE SWORD GET STOLEN?
NOPE.
BUT I'VE GOT MY OWN IDEAS.
THE KILLER IS SOMEBODY WHO KNEW THERE WAS GONNA BE AN IAIDO PERFORMANCE AT THE TOURNAMENT...
...AND KNOWS THE LAY-OUT OF THE GYM, ANNEX AND POOL LIKE THE BACK OF THEIR HAND.
SAY, THE SHINNAI UNIVERSITY KENDO TEAM ALWAYS ATTENDS THIS TOURNAMENT AND COMES HERE REGULARLY TO PRACTICE.
I'M LOOKIN' FOR SOMEBODY JUST LIKE YOU GUYS!

*Iaido is a martial art that stresses smooth, quick sword strokes.

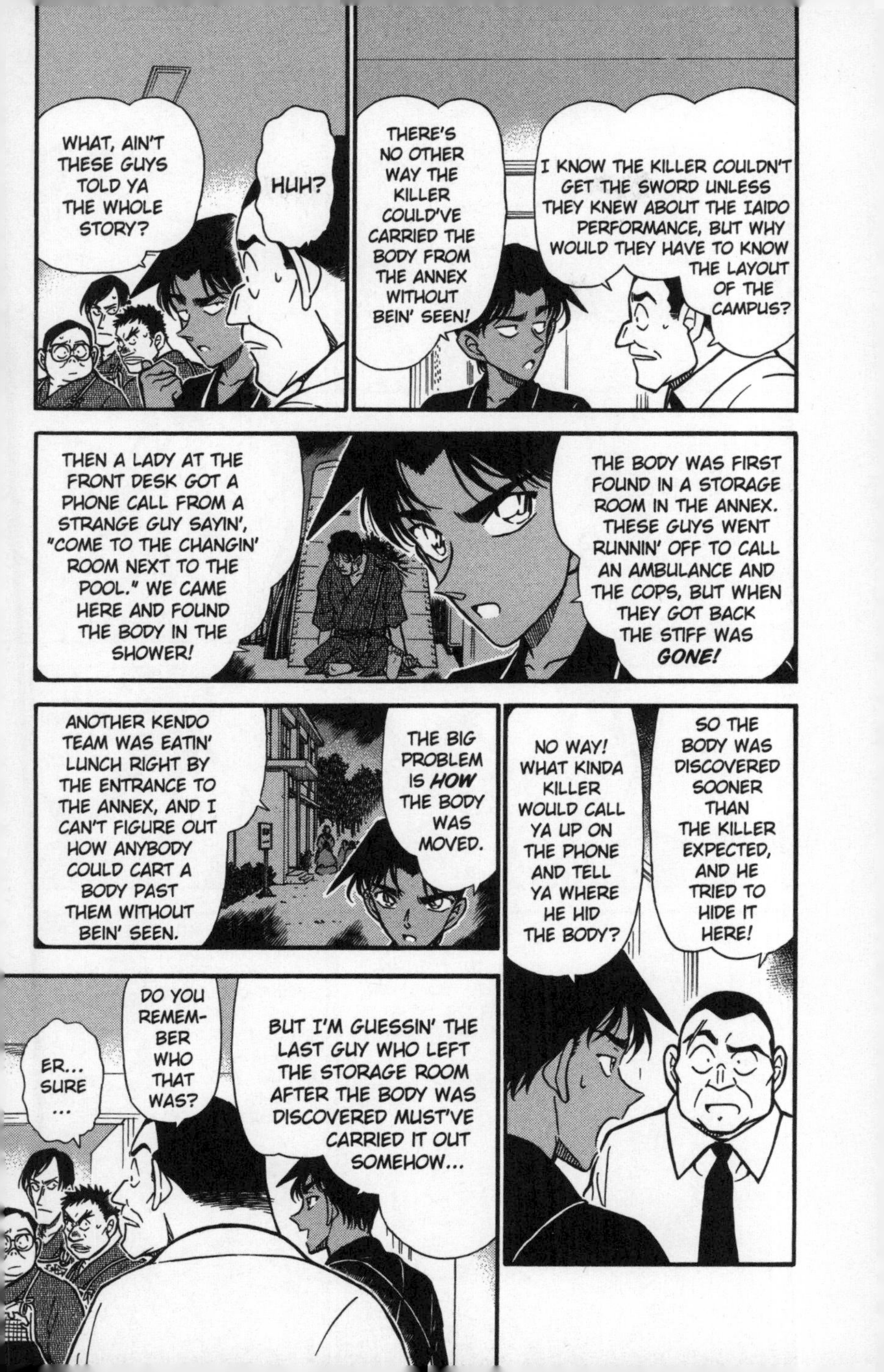
I KNOW THE KILLER COULDN'T GET THE SWORD UNLESS THEY KNEW ABOUT THE IAIDO PERFORMANCE, BUT WHY WOULD THEY HAVE TO KNOW THE LAYOUT OF THE CAMPUS?
THERE'S NO OTHER WAY THE KILLER COULD'VE CARRIED THE BODY FROM THE ANNEX WITHOUT BEIN' SEEN!
HUH?
WHAT, AIN'T THESE GUYS TOLD YA THE WHOLE STORY?
THE BODY WAS FIRST FOUND IN A STORAGE ROOM IN THE ANNEX. THESE GUYS WENT RUNNIN' OFF TO CALL AN AMBULANCE AND THE COPS, BUT WHEN THEY GOT BACK THE STIFF WAS ***GONE!***
THEN A LADY AT THE FRONT DESK GOT A PHONE CALL FROM A STRANGE GUY SAYIN', "COME TO THE CHANGIN' ROOM NEXT TO THE POOL." WE CAME HERE AND FOUND THE BODY IN THE SHOWER!
SO THE BODY WAS DISCOVERED SOONER THAN THE KILLER EXPECTED, AND HE TRIED TO HIDE IT HERE!
NO WAY! WHAT KINDA KILLER WOULD CALL YA UP ON THE PHONE AND TELL YA WHERE HE HID THE BODY?
THE BIG PROBLEM IS ***HOW*** THE BODY WAS MOVED.
ANOTHER KENDO TEAM WAS EATIN' LUNCH RIGHT BY THE ENTRANCE TO THE ANNEX, AND I CAN'T FIGURE OUT HOW ANYBODY COULD CART A BODY PAST THEM WITHOUT BEIN' SEEN.
BUT I'M GUESSIN' THE LAST GUY WHO LEFT THE STORAGE ROOM AFTER THE BODY WAS DISCOVERED MUST'VE CARRIED IT OUT SOMEHOW...
DO YOU REMEMBER WHO THAT WAS?
ER... SURE...

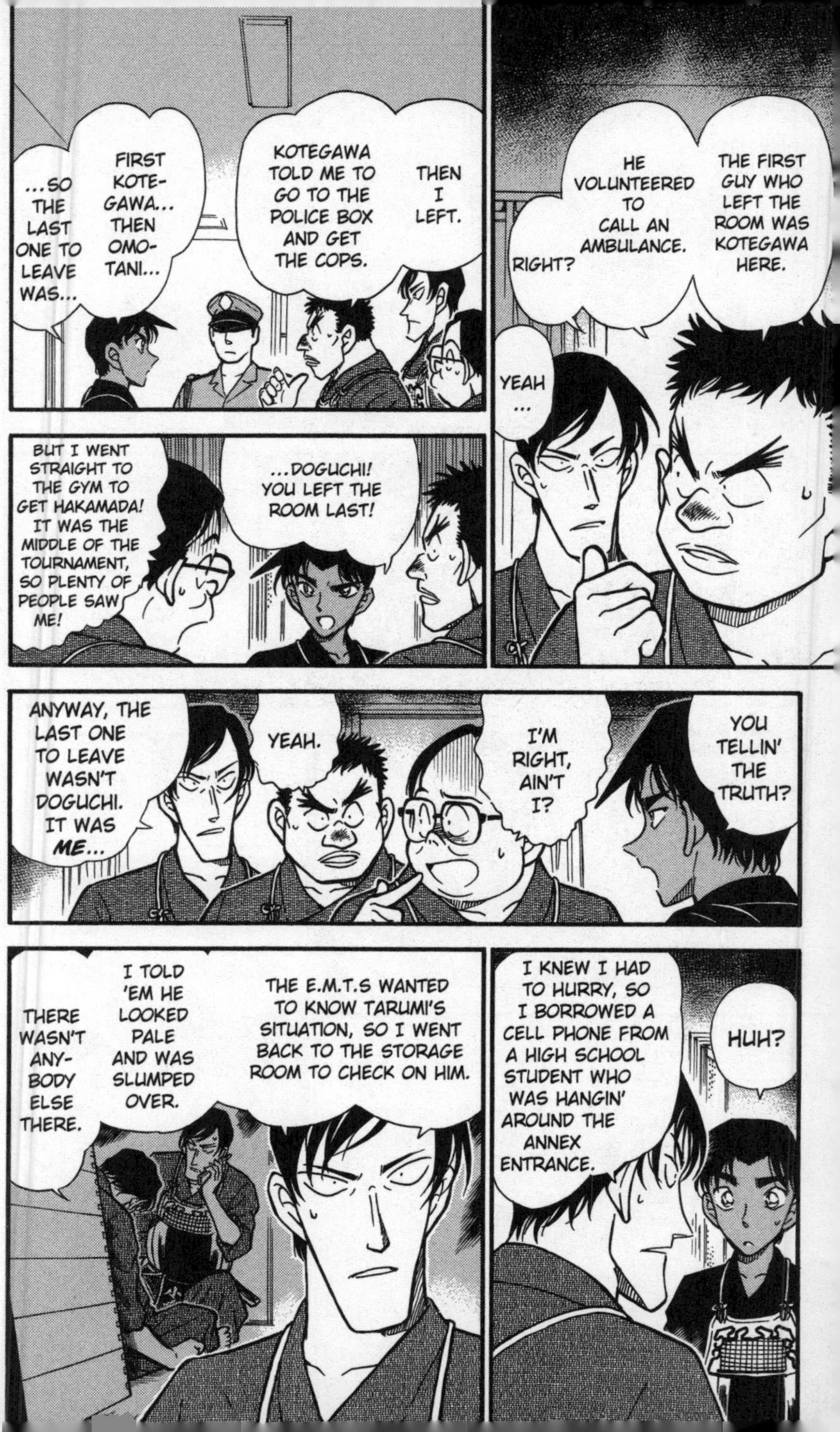
THE FIRST GUY WHO LEFT THE ROOM WAS KOTEGAWA HERE.
HE VOLUNTEERED TO CALL AN AMBULANCE. RIGHT?
YEAH ...
THEN I LEFT.
KOTEGAWA TOLD ME TO GO TO THE POLICE BOX AND GET THE COPS.
FIRST KOTE-GAWA... THEN OMO-TANI...
...SO THE LAST ONE TO LEAVE WAS...
...DOGUCHI! YOU LEFT THE ROOM LAST!
BUT I WENT STRAIGHT TO THE GYM TO GET HAKAMADA! IT WAS THE MIDDLE OF THE TOURNAMENT, SO PLENTY OF PEOPLE SAW ME!
YOU TELLIN' THE TRUTH?
I'M RIGHT, AIN'T I?
YEAH.
ANYWAY, THE LAST ONE TO LEAVE WASN'T DOGUCHI. IT WAS *ME*...
HUH?
I KNEW I HAD TO HURRY, SO I BORROWED A CELL PHONE FROM A HIGH SCHOOL STUDENT WHO WAS HANGIN' AROUND THE ANNEX ENTRANCE.
THE E.M.T.S WANTED TO KNOW TARUMI'S SITUATION, SO I WENT BACK TO THE STORAGE ROOM TO CHECK ON HIM.
I TOLD 'EM HE LOOKED PALE AND WAS SLUMPED OVER.
THERE WASN'T ANYBODY ELSE THERE.

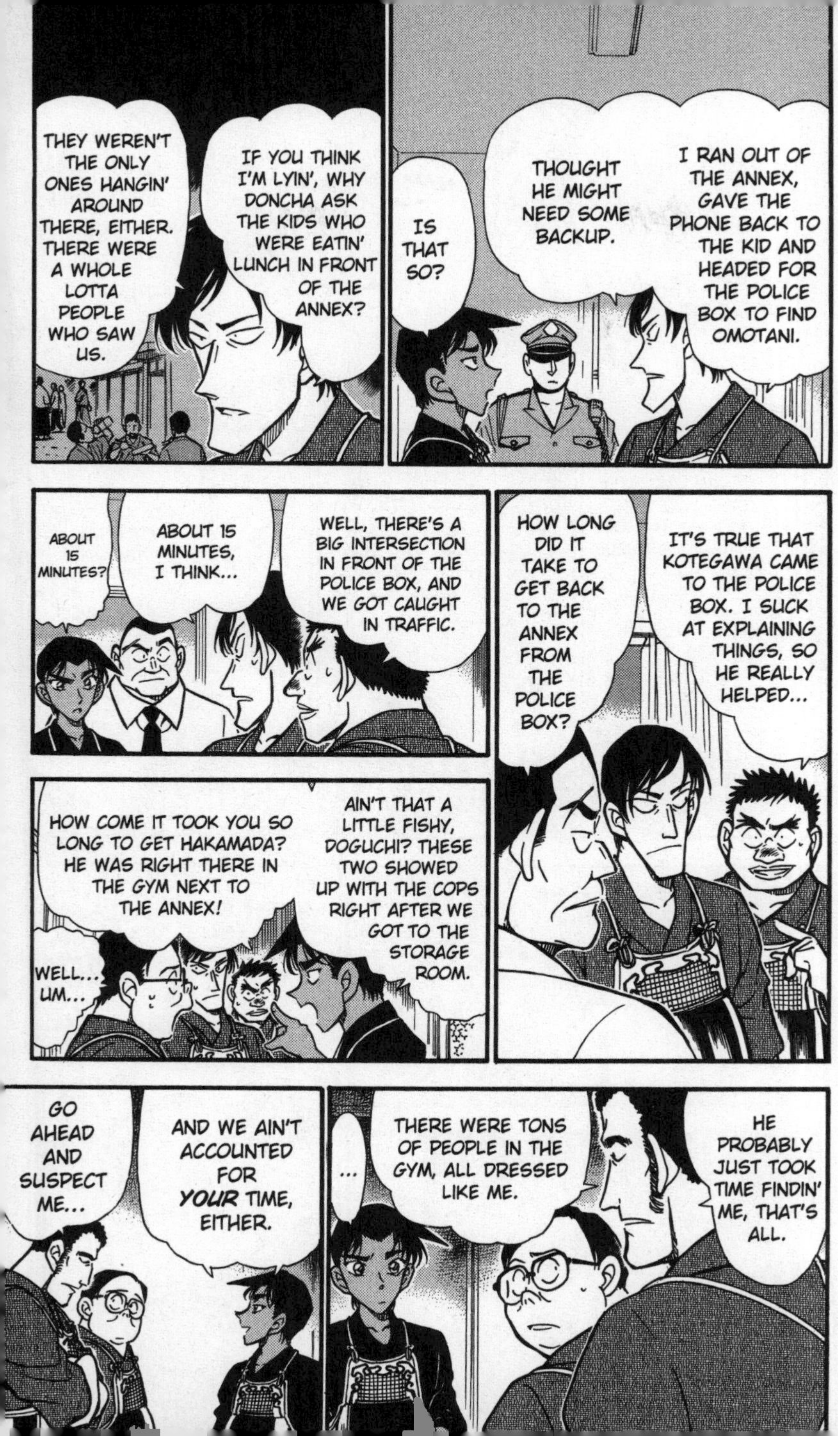
I RAN OUT OF THE ANNEX, GAVE THE PHONE BACK TO THE KID AND HEADED FOR THE POLICE BOX TO FIND OMOTANI.
THOUGHT HE MIGHT NEED SOME BACKUP.
IS THAT SO?
IF YOU THINK I'M LYIN', WHY DONCHA ASK THE KIDS WHO WERE EATIN' LUNCH IN FRONT OF THE ANNEX?
THEY WEREN'T THE ONLY ONES HANGIN' AROUND THERE, EITHER. THERE WERE A WHOLE LOTTA PEOPLE WHO SAW US.
IT'S TRUE THAT KOTEGAWA CAME TO THE POLICE BOX. I SUCK AT EXPLAINING THINGS, SO HE REALLY HELPED...
HOW LONG DID IT TAKE TO GET BACK TO THE ANNEX FROM THE POLICE BOX?
WELL, THERE'S A BIG INTERSECTION IN FRONT OF THE POLICE BOX, AND WE GOT CAUGHT IN TRAFFIC.
ABOUT 15 MINUTES, I THINK...
ABOUT 15 MINUTES?
AIN'T THAT A LITTLE FISHY, DOGUCHI? THESE TWO SHOWED UP WITH THE COPS RIGHT AFTER WE GOT TO THE STORAGE ROOM.
HOW COME IT TOOK YOU SO LONG TO GET HAKAMADA? HE WAS RIGHT THERE IN THE GYM NEXT TO THE ANNEX!
WELL... UM...
HE PROBABLY JUST TOOK TIME FINDIN' ME, THAT'S ALL.
THERE WERE TONS OF PEOPLE IN THE GYM, ALL DRESSED LIKE ME.
...
AND WE AIN'T ACCOUNTED FOR YOUR TIME, EITHER.
GO AHEAD AND SUSPECT ME...

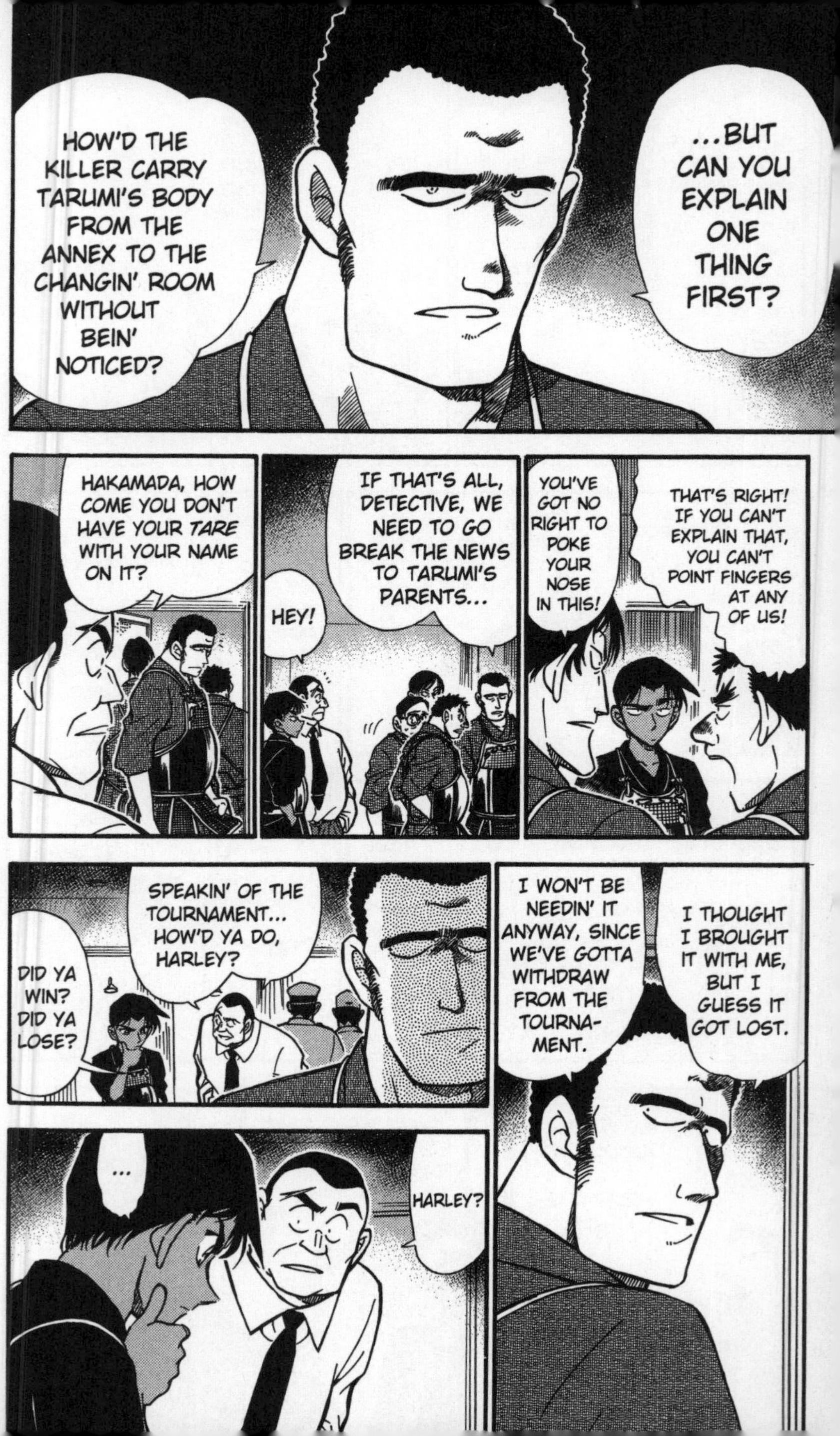
...BUT CAN YOU EXPLAIN ONE THING FIRST?
HOW'D THE KILLER CARRY TARUMI'S BODY FROM THE ANNEX TO THE CHANGIN' ROOM WITHOUT BEIN' NOTICED?
THAT'S RIGHT! IF YOU CAN'T EXPLAIN THAT, YOU CAN'T POINT FINGERS AT ANY OF US!
YOU'VE GOT NO RIGHT TO POKE YOUR NOSE IN THIS!
IF THAT'S ALL, DETECTIVE, WE NEED TO GO BREAK THE NEWS TO TARUMI'S PARENTS...
HEY!
HAKAMADA, HOW COME YOU DON'T HAVE YOUR *TARE* WITH YOUR NAME ON IT?
I THOUGHT I BROUGHT IT WITH ME, BUT I GUESS IT GOT LOST.
I WON'T BE NEEDIN' IT ANYWAY, SINCE WE'VE GOTTA WITHDRAW FROM THE TOURNA-MENT.
SPEAKIN' OF THE TOURNAMENT... HOW'D YA DO, HARLEY?
DID YA WIN? DID YA LOSE?
HARLEY?
...

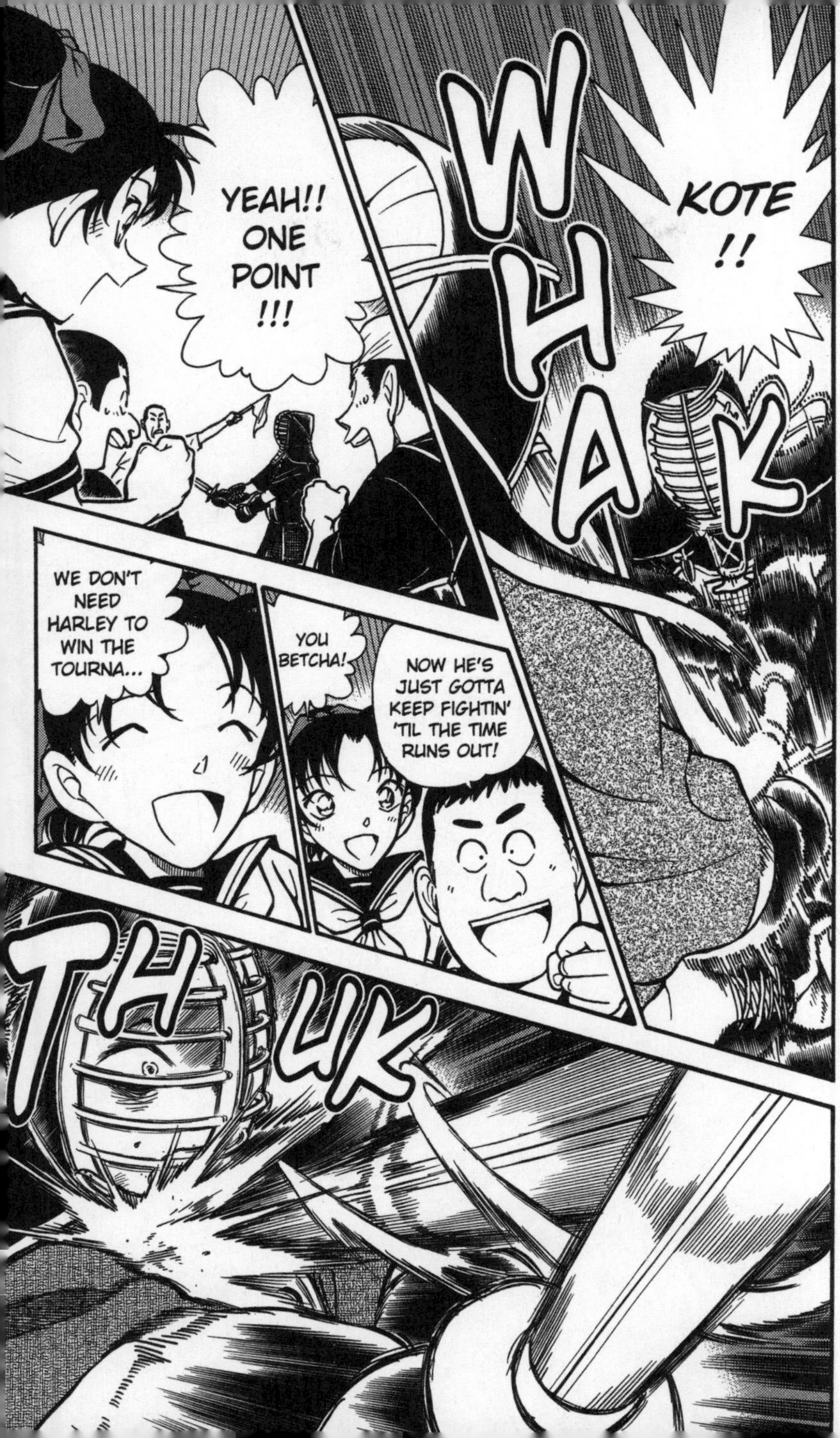
WHAK
KOTE !!
YEAH!! ONE POINT !!!
NOW HE'S JUST GOTTA KEEP FIGHTIN' 'TIL THE TIME RUNS OUT!
YOU BETCHA!
WE DON'T NEED HARLEY TO WIN THE TOURNA...
THUK

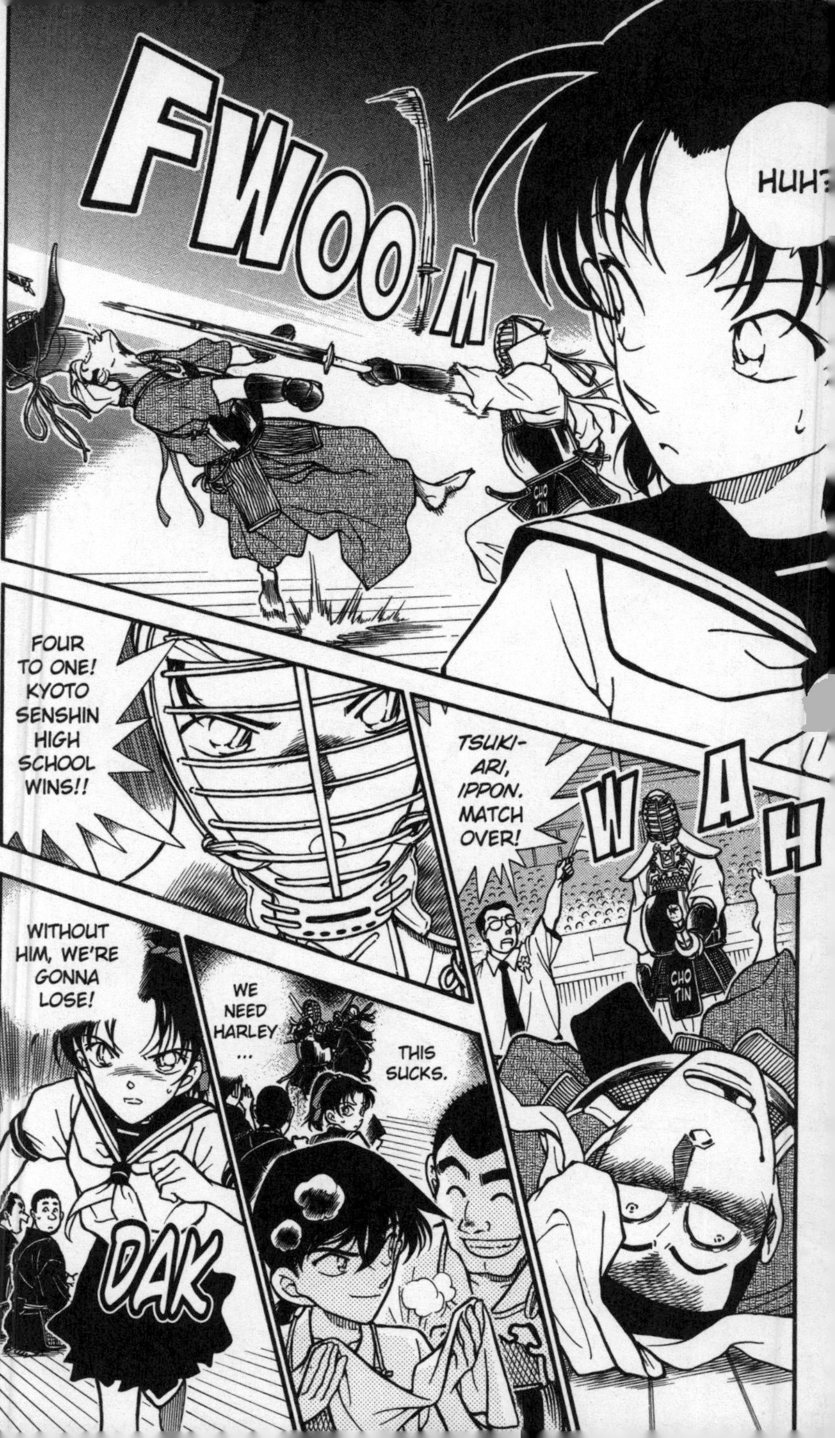
HUH?
FWOOM
CHO TIN
TSUKI-ARI, IPPON. MATCH OVER!
WAH
CHO TIN
FOUR TO ONE! KYOTO SENSHIN HIGH SCHOOL WINS!!
THIS SUCKS.
WE NEED HARLEY ...
WITHOUT HIM, WE'RE GONNA LOSE!
DAK

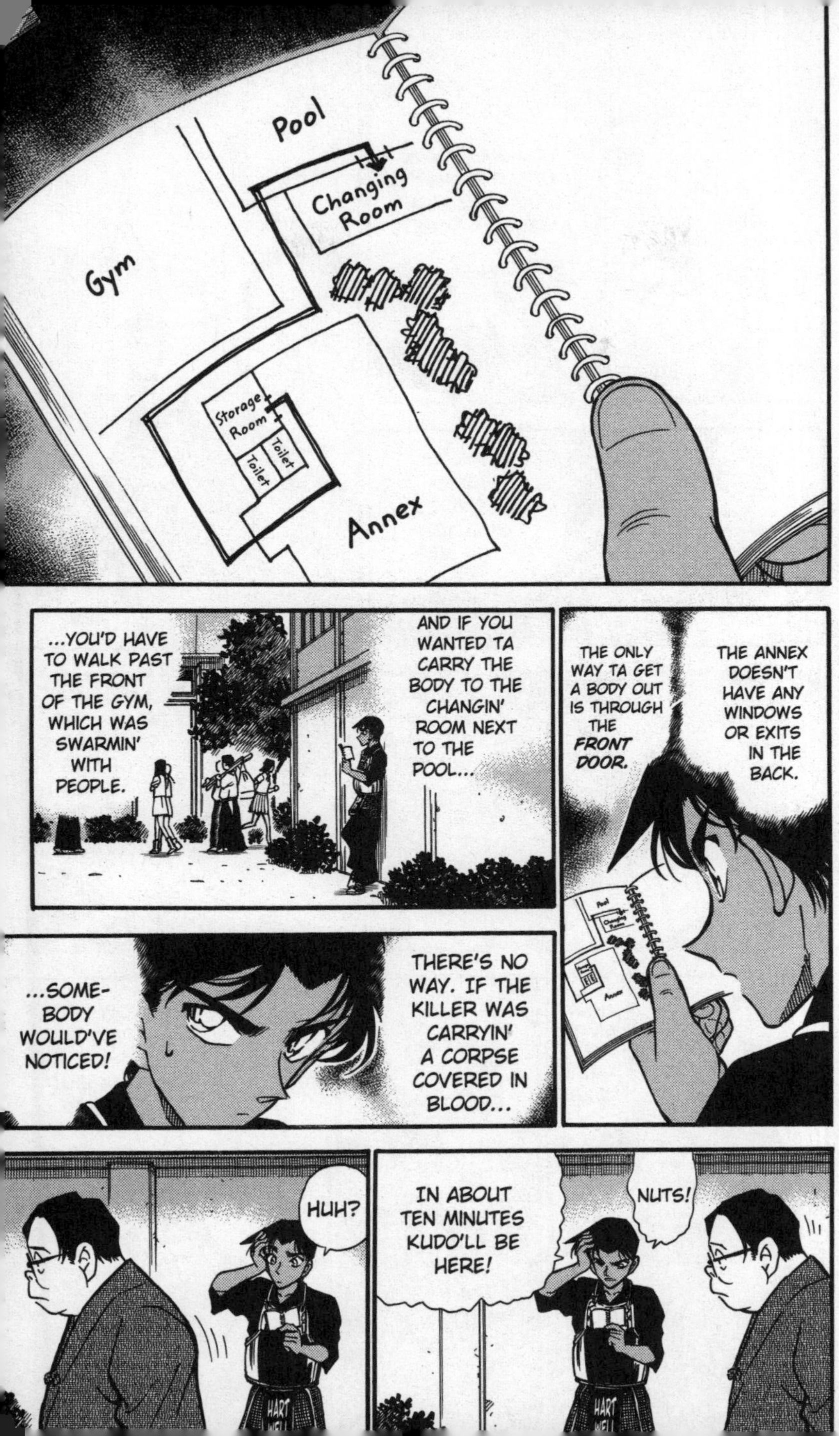
Pool
Changing Room
Gym
Storage Room
Toilet
Toilet
Annex
THE ANNEX DOESN'T HAVE ANY WINDOWS OR EXITS IN THE BACK.
THE ONLY WAY TA GET A BODY OUT IS THROUGH THE *FRONT DOOR.*
AND IF YOU WANTED TA CARRY THE BODY TO THE CHANGIN' ROOM NEXT TO THE POOL...
...YOU'D HAVE TO WALK PAST THE FRONT OF THE GYM, WHICH WAS SWARMIN' WITH PEOPLE.
THERE'S NO WAY. IF THE KILLER WAS CARRYIN' A CORPSE COVERED IN BLOOD...
...SOME-BODY WOULD'VE NOTICED!
NUTS!
IN ABOUT TEN MINUTES KUDO'LL BE HERE!
HUH?

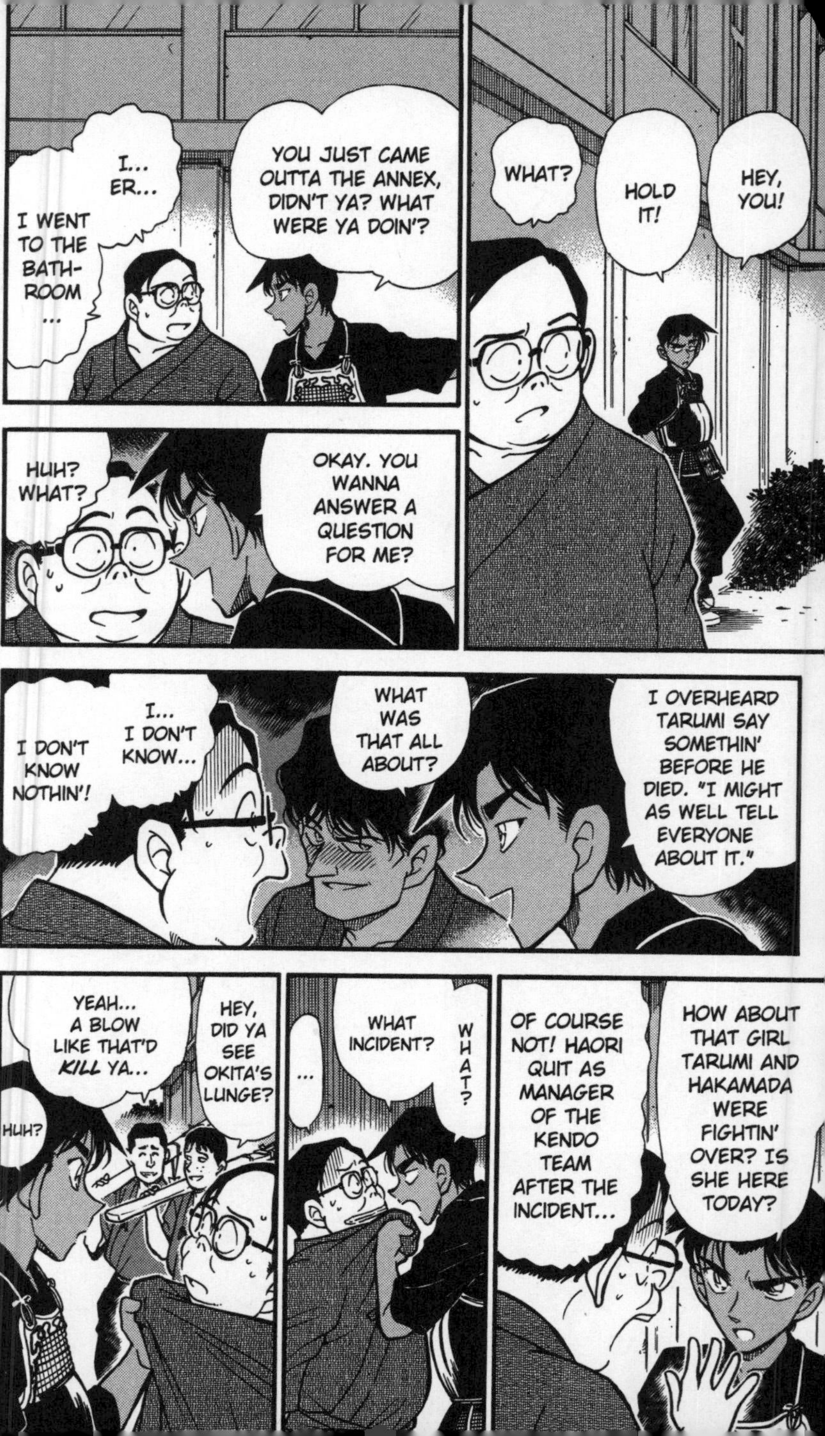
HEY, YOU!
HOLD IT!
WHAT?
YOU JUST CAME OUTTA THE ANNEX, DIDN'T YA? WHAT WERE YA DOIN'?
I... ER...
I WENT TO THE BATH-ROOM ...
OKAY. YOU WANNA ANSWER A QUESTION FOR ME?
HUH? WHAT?
I OVERHEARD TARUMI SAY SOMETHIN' BEFORE HE DIED. "I MIGHT AS WELL TELL EVERYONE ABOUT IT."
WHAT WAS THAT ALL ABOUT?
I... I DON'T KNOW...
I DON'T KNOW NOTHIN'!
HOW ABOUT THAT GIRL TARUMI AND HAKAMADA WERE FIGHTIN' OVER? IS SHE HERE TODAY?
OF COURSE NOT! HAORI QUIT AS MANAGER OF THE KENDO TEAM AFTER THE INCIDENT...
WHAT?
WHAT INCIDENT?
...
HEY, DID YA SEE OKITA'S LUNGE?
YEAH... A BLOW LIKE THAT'D *KILL* YA...
HUH?

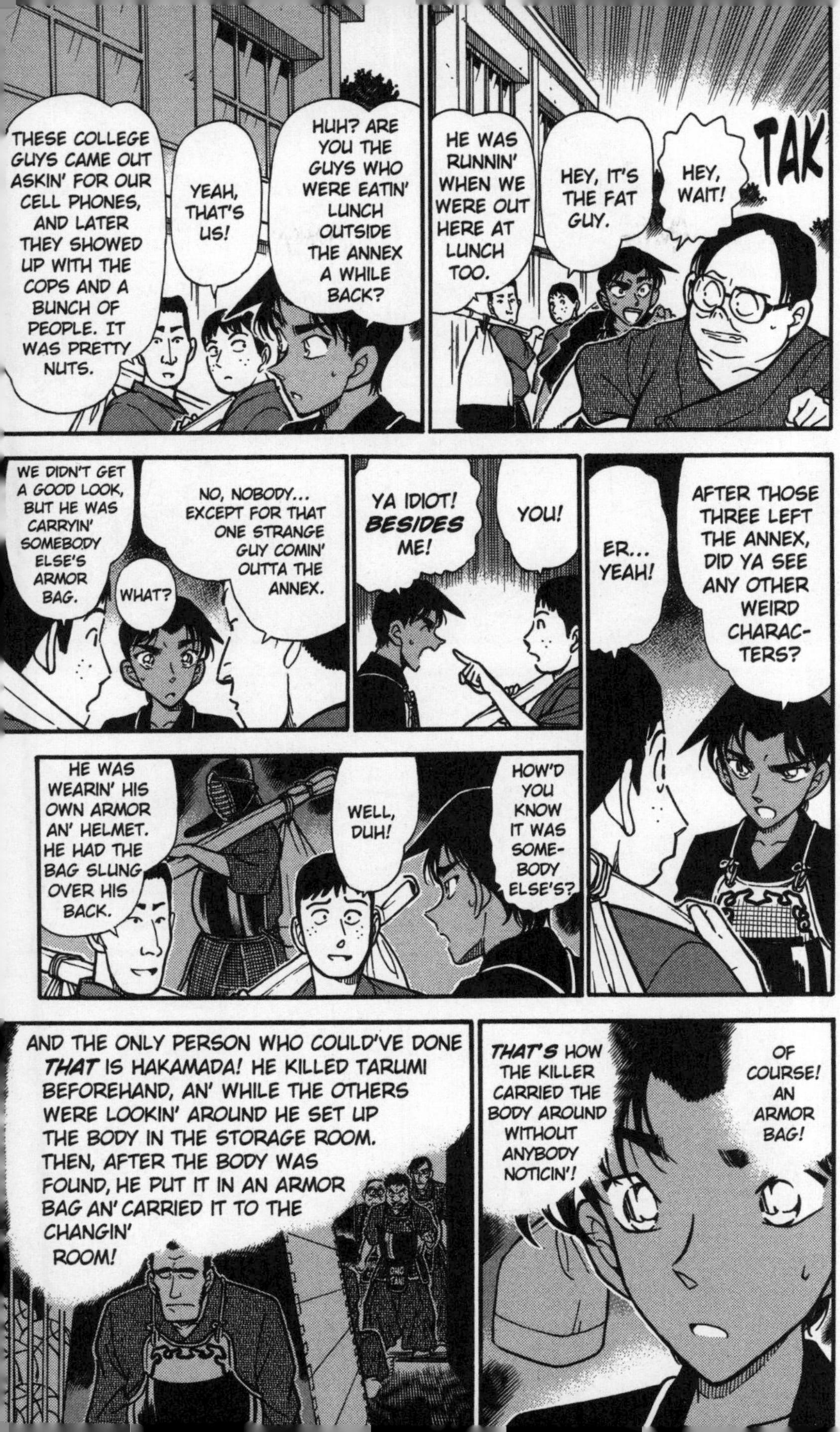
TAK
HEY, WAIT!
HEY, IT'S THE FAT GUY.
HE WAS RUNNIN' WHEN WE WERE OUT HERE AT LUNCH TOO.
HUH? ARE YOU THE GUYS WHO WERE EATIN' LUNCH OUTSIDE THE ANNEX A WHILE BACK?
YEAH, THAT'S US!
THESE COLLEGE GUYS CAME OUT ASKIN' FOR OUR CELL PHONES, AND LATER THEY SHOWED UP WITH THE COPS AND A BUNCH OF PEOPLE. IT WAS PRETTY NUTS.
AFTER THOSE THREE LEFT THE ANNEX, DID YA SEE ANY OTHER WEIRD CHARAC-TERS?
ER... YEAH!
YOU!
YA IDIOT! BESIDES ME!
NO, NOBODY... EXCEPT FOR THAT ONE STRANGE GUY COMIN' OUTTA THE ANNEX.
WHAT?
WE DIDN'T GET A GOOD LOOK, BUT HE WAS CARRYIN' SOMEBODY ELSE'S ARMOR BAG.
HOW'D YOU KNOW IT WAS SOME-BODY ELSE'S?
WELL, DUH!
HE WAS WEARIN' HIS OWN ARMOR AN' HELMET. HE HAD THE BAG SLUNG OVER HIS BACK.
OF COURSE! AN ARMOR BAG!
THAT'S HOW THE KILLER CARRIED THE BODY AROUND WITHOUT ANYBODY NOTICIN'!
AND THE ONLY PERSON WHO COULD'VE DONE THAT IS HAKAMADA! HE KILLED TARUMI BEFOREHAND, AN' WHILE THE OTHERS WERE LOOKIN' AROUND HE SET UP THE BODY IN THE STORAGE ROOM. THEN, AFTER THE BODY WAS FOUND, HE PUT IT IN AN ARMOR BAG AN' CARRIED IT TO THE CHANGIN' ROOM!

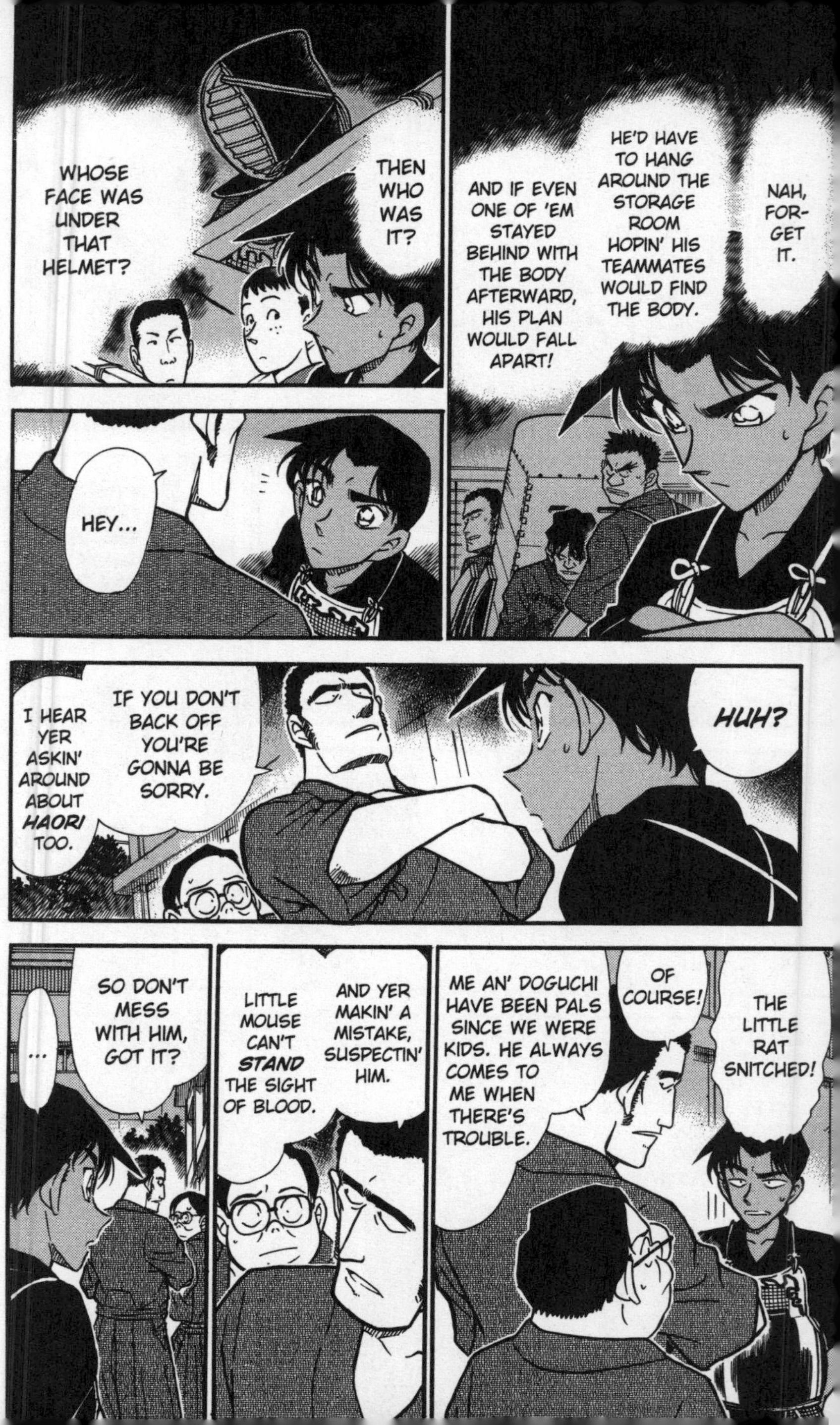
NAH, FORGET IT.
HE'D HAVE TO HANG AROUND THE STORAGE ROOM HOPIN' HIS TEAMMATES WOULD FIND THE BODY.
AND IF EVEN ONE OF 'EM STAYED BEHIND WITH THE BODY AFTERWARD, HIS PLAN WOULD FALL APART!
THEN WHO WAS IT?
WHOSE FACE WAS UNDER THAT HELMET?
HEY...
HUH?
IF YOU DON'T BACK OFF YOU'RE GONNA BE SORRY.
I HEAR YER ASKIN' AROUND ABOUT *HAORI* TOO.
THE LITTLE RAT SNITCHED!
OF COURSE!
ME AN' DOGUCHI HAVE BEEN PALS SINCE WE WERE KIDS. HE ALWAYS COMES TO ME WHEN THERE'S TROUBLE.
AND YER MAKIN' A MISTAKE, SUSPECTIN' HIM.
LITTLE MOUSE CAN'T *STAND* THE SIGHT OF BLOOD.
SO DON'T MESS WITH HIM, GOT IT?
...

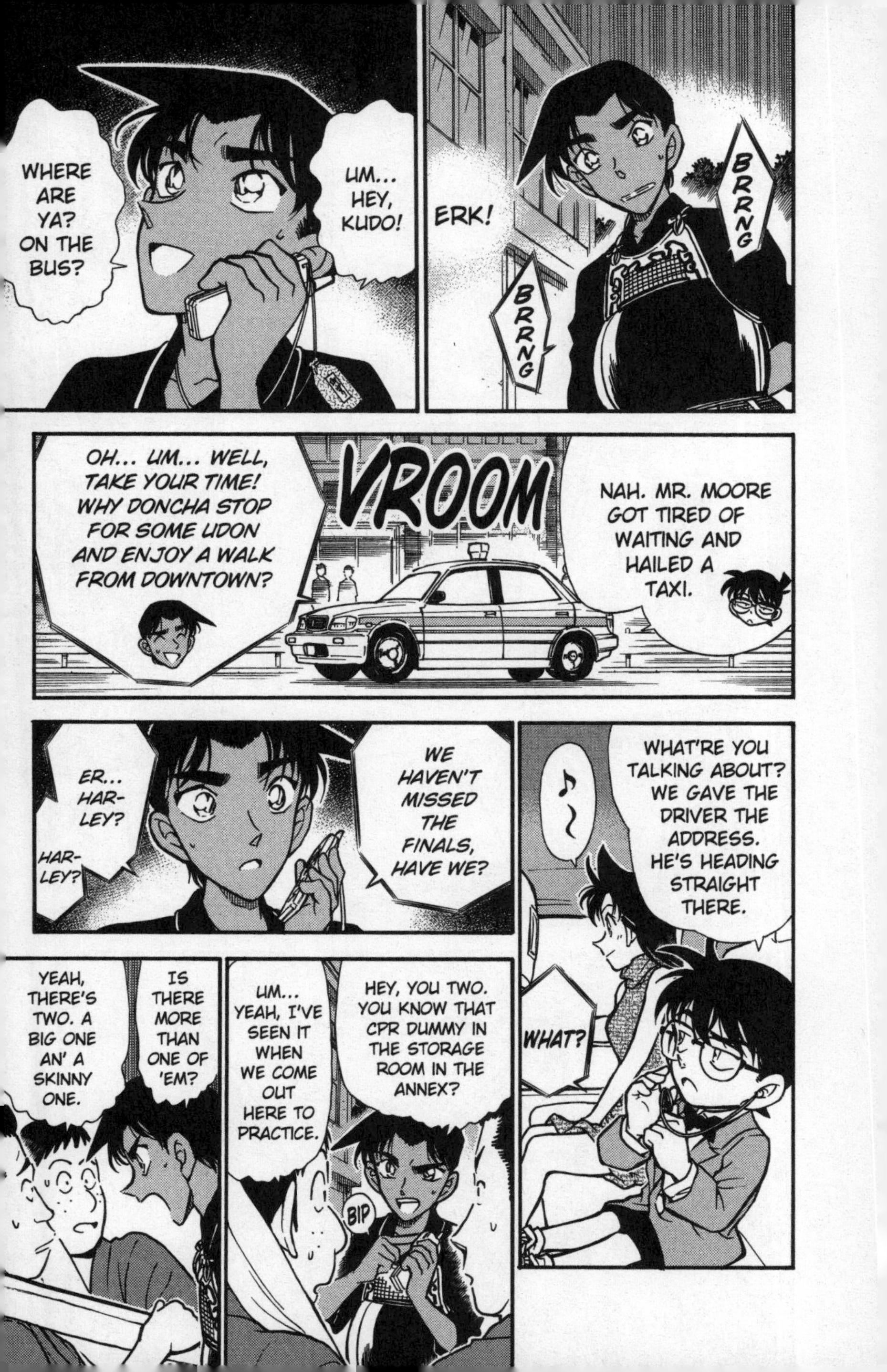
BRRNG
BRRNG
ERK!
UM... HEY, KUDO!
WHERE ARE YA? ON THE BUS?
NAH. MR. MOORE GOT TIRED OF WAITING AND HAILED A TAXI.
VROOM
OH... UM... WELL, TAKE YOUR TIME! WHY DONCHA STOP FOR SOME UDON AND ENJOY A WALK FROM DOWNTOWN?
WHAT'RE YOU TALKING ABOUT? WE GAVE THE DRIVER THE ADDRESS. HE'S HEADING STRAIGHT THERE.
♪~
WHAT?
WE HAVEN'T MISSED THE FINALS, HAVE WE?
ER... HARLEY?
HARLEY?
HEY, YOU TWO. YOU KNOW THAT CPR DUMMY IN THE STORAGE ROOM IN THE ANNEX?
UM... YEAH, I'VE SEEN IT WHEN WE COME OUT HERE TO PRACTICE.
BIP
IS THERE MORE THAN ONE OF 'EM?
YEAH, THERE'S TWO. A BIG ONE AN' A SKINNY ONE.

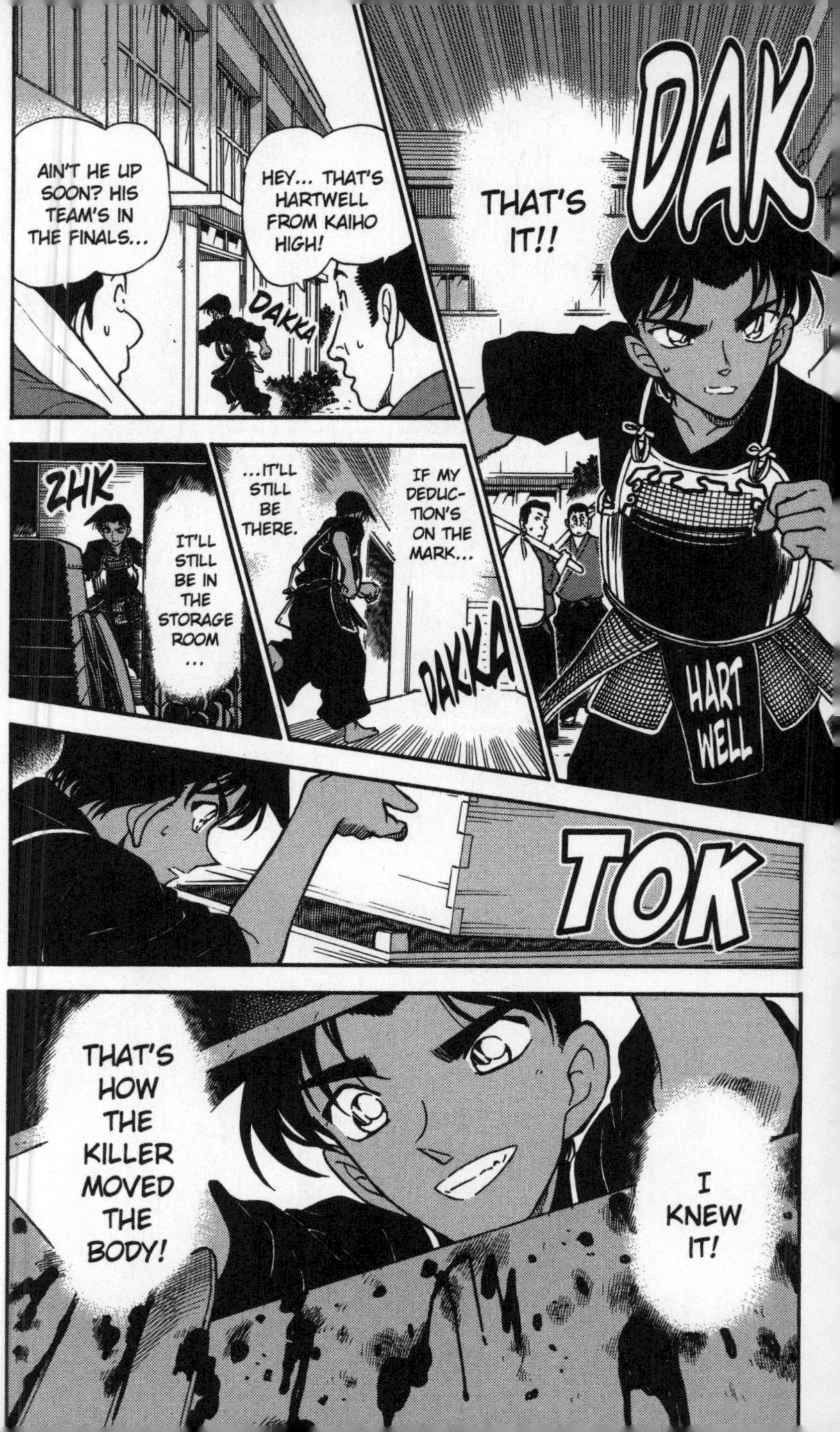
DAK
THAT'S IT!!
HART WELL
HEY... THAT'S HARTWELL FROM KAIHO HIGH!
AIN'T HE UP SOON? HIS TEAM'S IN THE FINALS...
DAKKA
IF MY DEDUCTION'S ON THE MARK...
...IT'LL STILL BE THERE.
DAKKA
ZHK
IT'LL STILL BE IN THE STORAGE ROOM ...
TOK
I KNEW IT!
THAT'S HOW THE KILLER MOVED THE BODY!

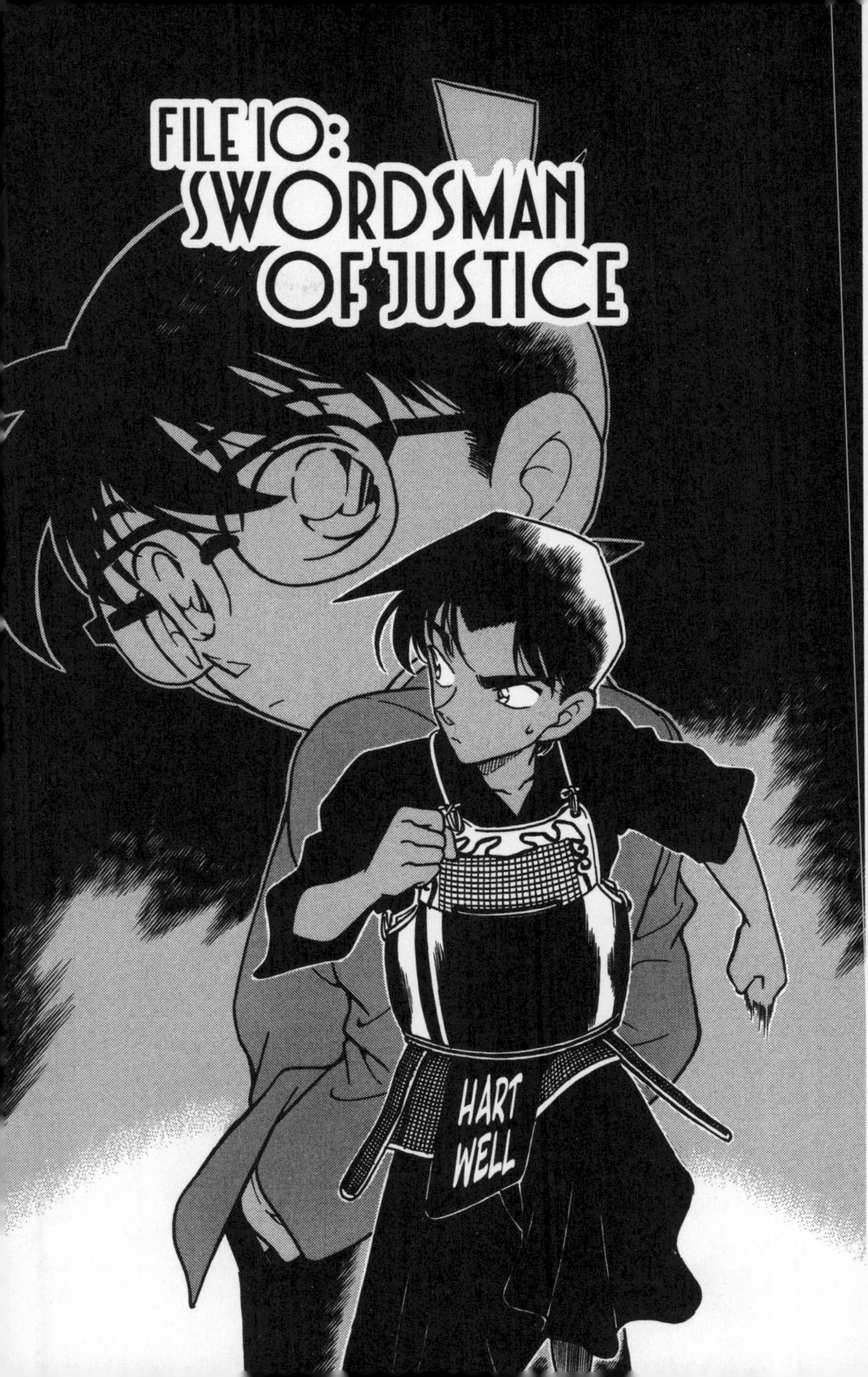
FILE 10:
SWORDSMAN OF JUSTICE
HART WELL

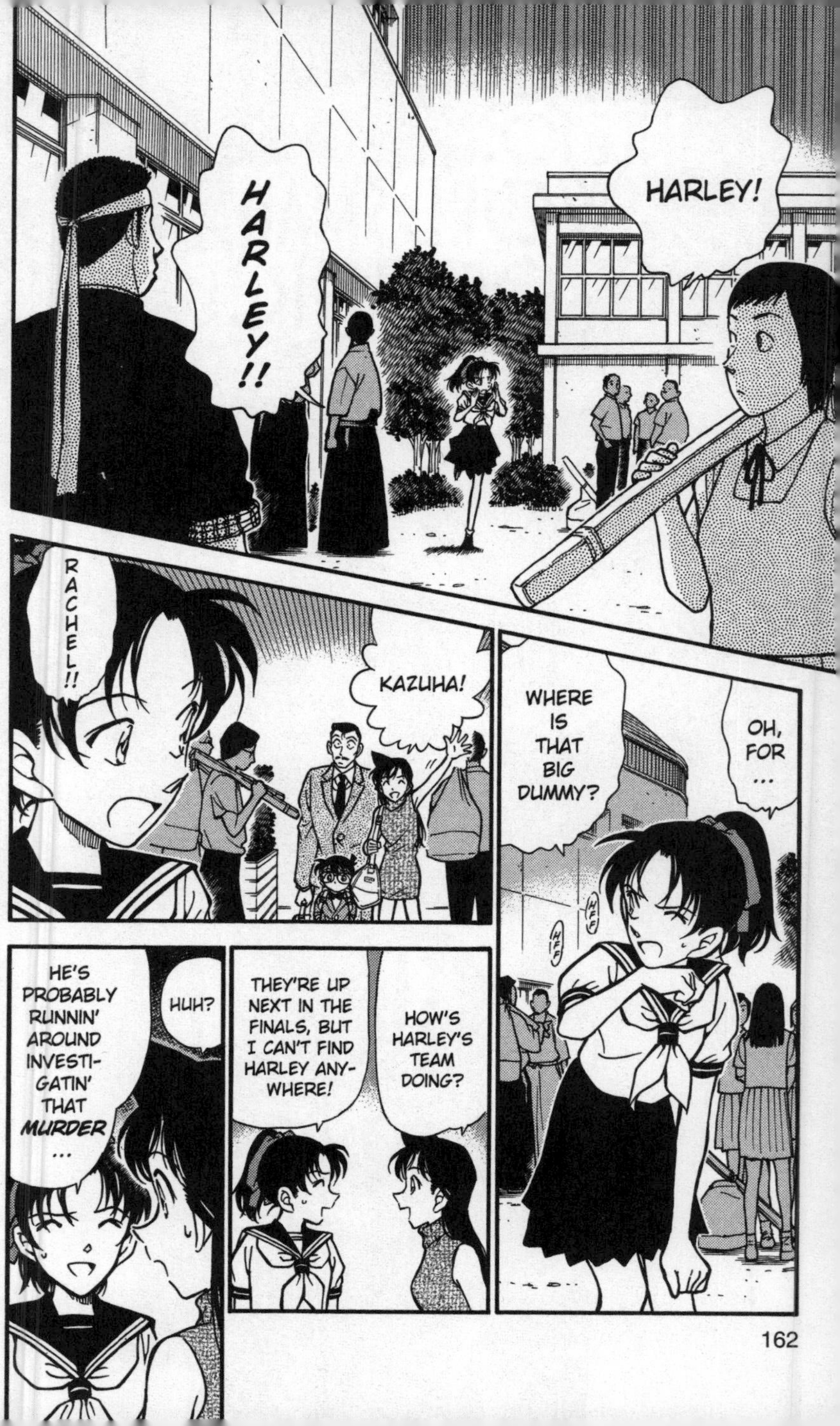
HARLEY!
HARLEY!!
OH, FOR ...
WHERE IS THAT BIG DUMMY?
HFF
HFF
KAZUHA!
RACHEL!!
HOW'S HARLEY'S TEAM DOING?
THEY'RE UP NEXT IN THE FINALS, BUT I CAN'T FIND HARLEY ANYWHERE!
HUH?
HE'S PROBABLY RUNNIN' AROUND INVESTIGATIN' THAT MURDER ...

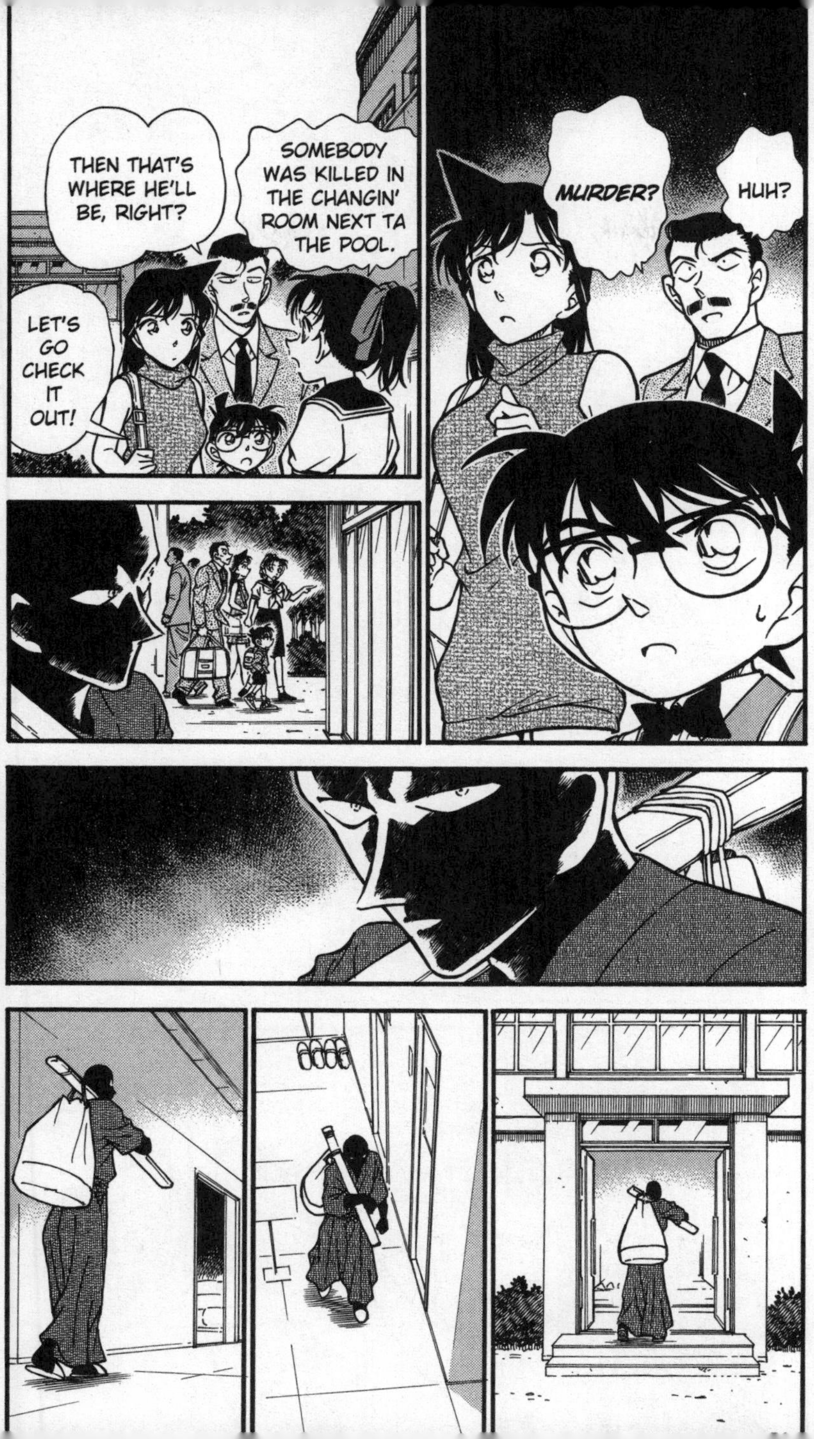
HUH?
MURDER?
SOMEBODY WAS KILLED IN THE CHANGIN' ROOM NEXT TA THE POOL.
THEN THAT'S WHERE HE'LL BE, RIGHT?
LET'S GO CHECK IT OUT!

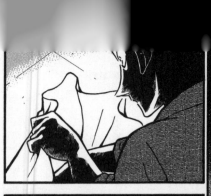

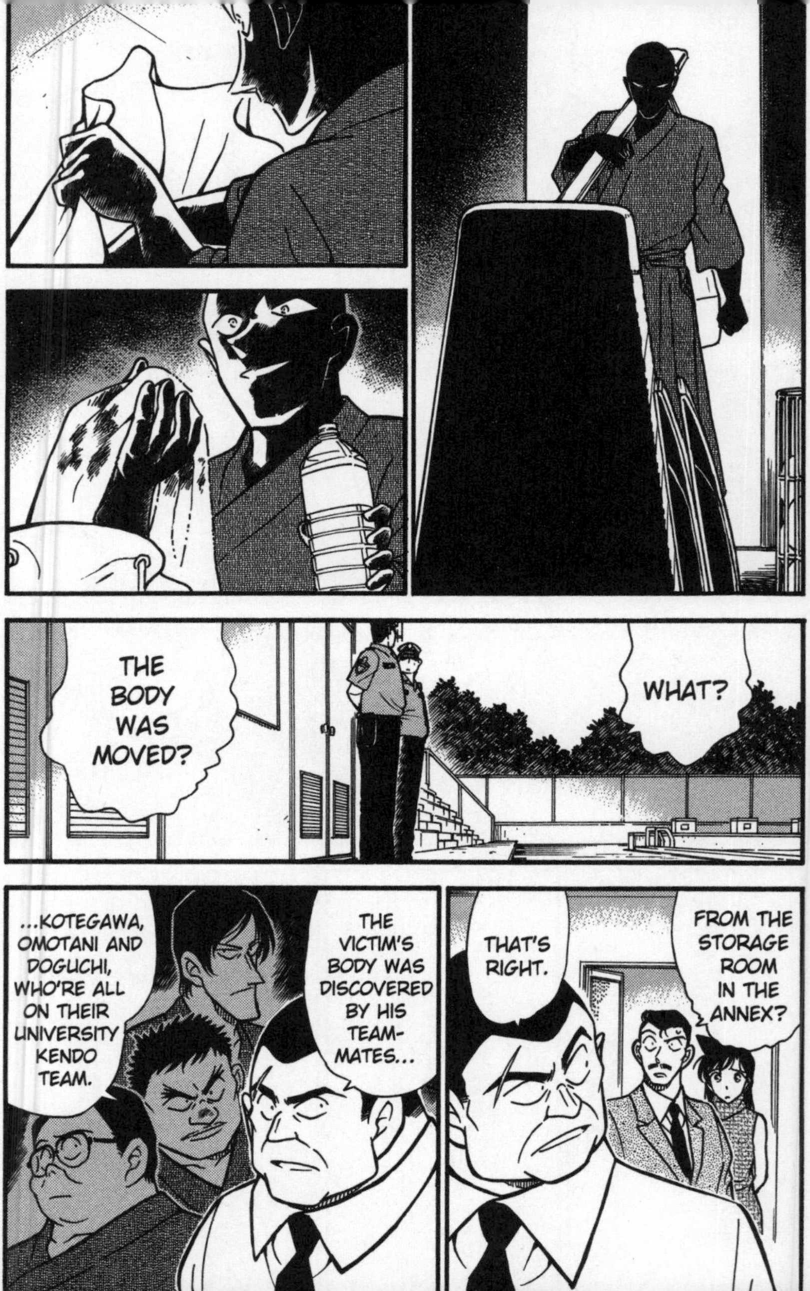
WHAT?
THE BODY WAS MOVED?
FROM THE STORAGE ROOM IN THE ANNEX?
THAT'S RIGHT.
THE VICTIM'S BODY WAS DISCOVERED BY HIS TEAM-MATES...
...KOTEGAWA, OMOTANI AND DOGUCHI, WHO'RE ALL ON THEIR UNIVERSITY KENDO TEAM.

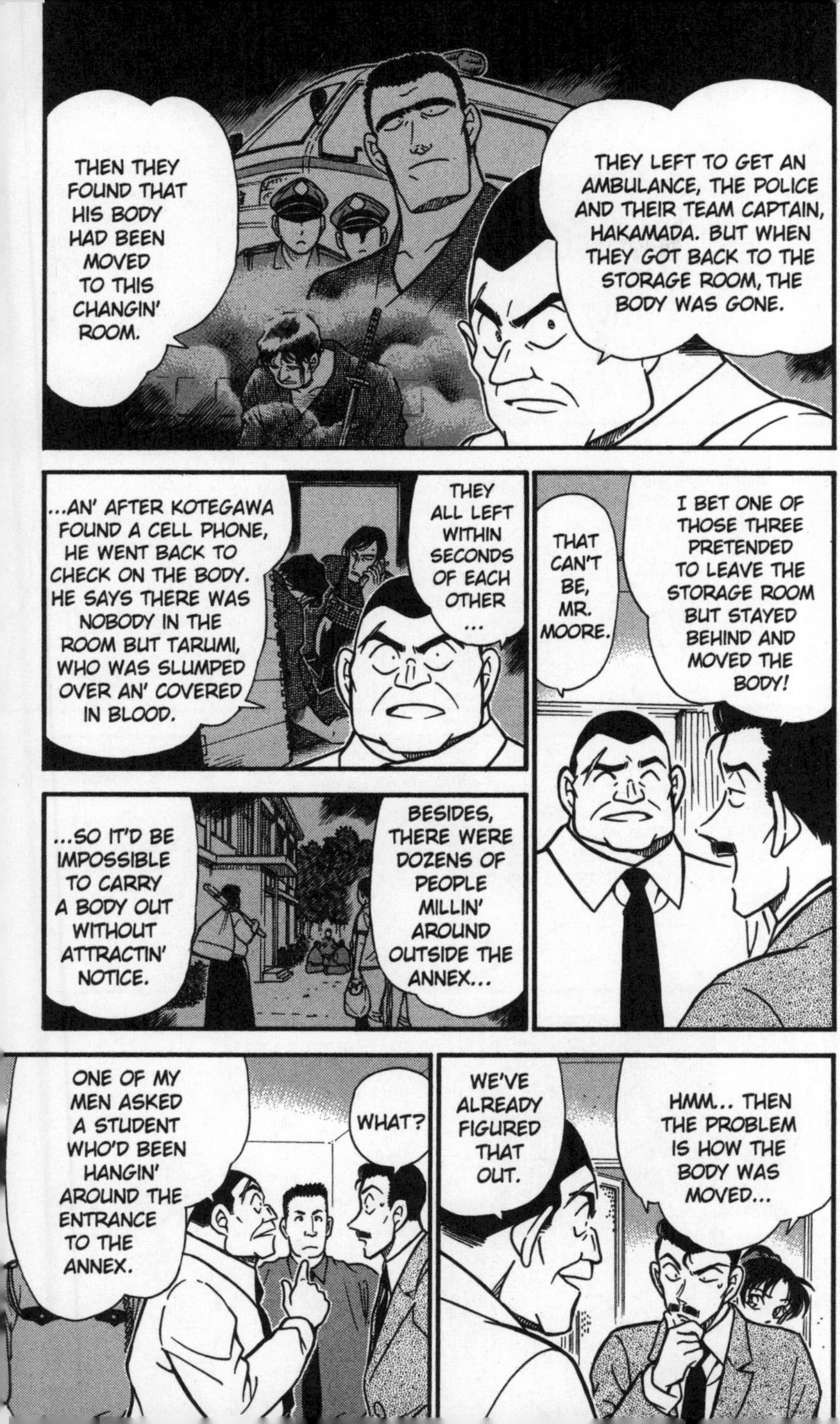
THEY LEFT TO GET AN AMBULANCE, THE POLICE AND THEIR TEAM CAPTAIN, HAKAMADA. BUT WHEN THEY GOT BACK TO THE STORAGE ROOM, THE BODY WAS GONE.
THEN THEY FOUND THAT HIS BODY HAD BEEN MOVED TO THIS CHANGIN' ROOM.
I BET ONE OF THOSE THREE PRETENDED TO LEAVE THE STORAGE ROOM BUT STAYED BEHIND AND MOVED THE BODY!
THAT CAN'T BE, MR. MOORE.
THEY ALL LEFT WITHIN SECONDS OF EACH OTHER...
...AN' AFTER KOTEGAWA FOUND A CELL PHONE, HE WENT BACK TO CHECK ON THE BODY. HE SAYS THERE WAS NOBODY IN THE ROOM BUT TARUMI, WHO WAS SLUMPED OVER AN' COVERED IN BLOOD.
BESIDES, THERE WERE DOZENS OF PEOPLE MILLIN' AROUND OUTSIDE THE ANNEX...
...SO IT'D BE IMPOSSIBLE TO CARRY A BODY OUT WITHOUT ATTRACTIN' NOTICE.
HMM... THEN THE PROBLEM IS HOW THE BODY WAS MOVED...
WE'VE ALREADY FIGURED THAT OUT.
WHAT?
ONE OF MY MEN ASKED A STUDENT WHO'D BEEN HANGIN' AROUND THE ENTRANCE TO THE ANNEX.

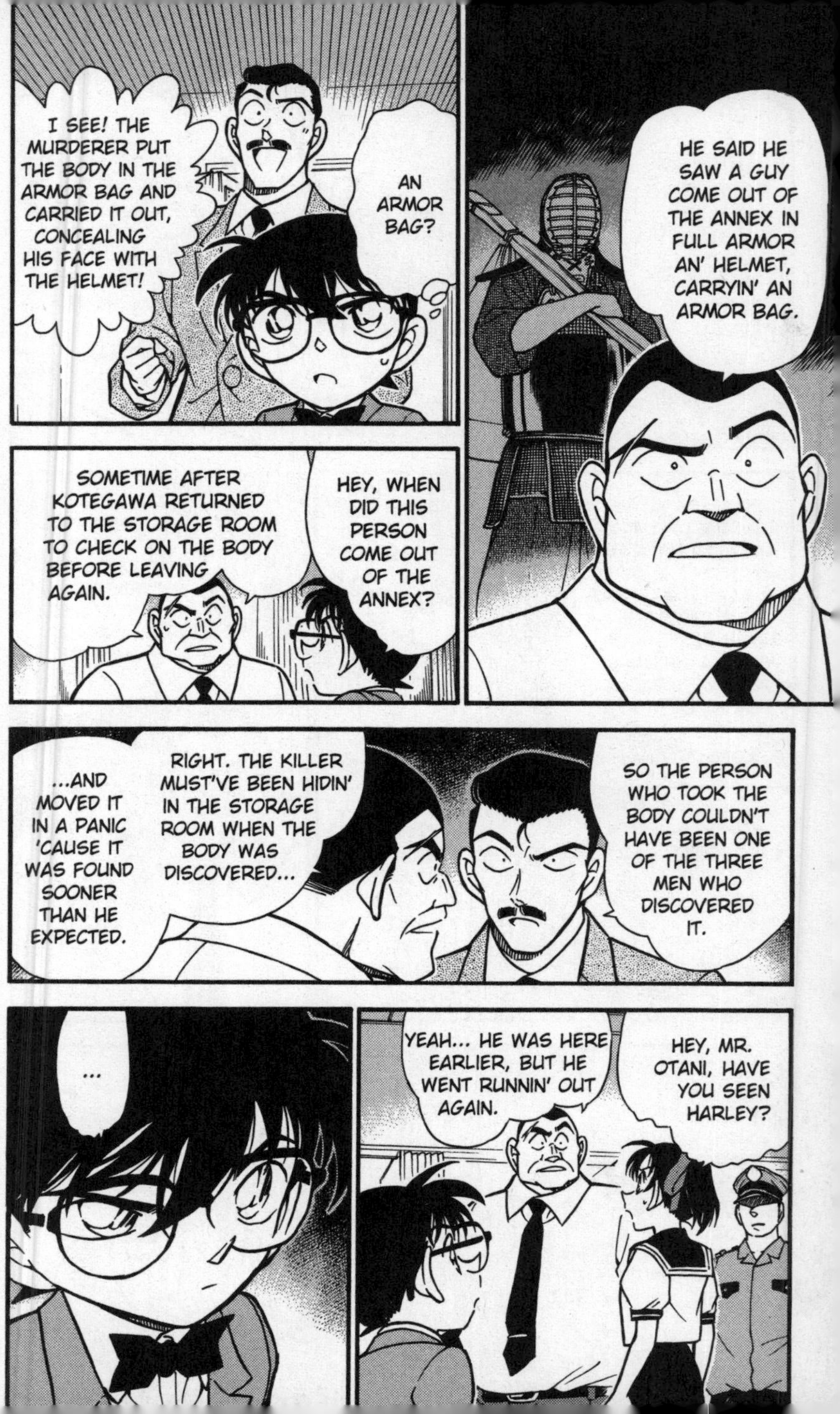
HE SAID HE SAW A GUY COME OUT OF THE ANNEX IN FULL ARMOR AN' HELMET, CARRYIN' AN ARMOR BAG.
AN ARMOR BAG?
I SEE! THE MURDERER PUT THE BODY IN THE ARMOR BAG AND CARRIED IT OUT, CONCEALING HIS FACE WITH THE HELMET!
HEY, WHEN DID THIS PERSON COME OUT OF THE ANNEX?
SOMETIME AFTER KOTEGAWA RETURNED TO THE STORAGE ROOM TO CHECK ON THE BODY BEFORE LEAVING AGAIN.
SO THE PERSON WHO TOOK THE BODY COULDN'T HAVE BEEN ONE OF THE THREE MEN WHO DISCOVERED IT.
RIGHT. THE KILLER MUST'VE BEEN HIDIN' IN THE STORAGE ROOM WHEN THE BODY WAS DISCOVERED...
...AND MOVED IT IN A PANIC 'CAUSE IT WAS FOUND SOONER THAN HE EXPECTED.
HEY, MR. OTANI, HAVE YOU SEEN HARLEY?
YEAH... HE WAS HERE EARLIER, BUT HE WENT RUNNIN' OUT AGAIN.
...

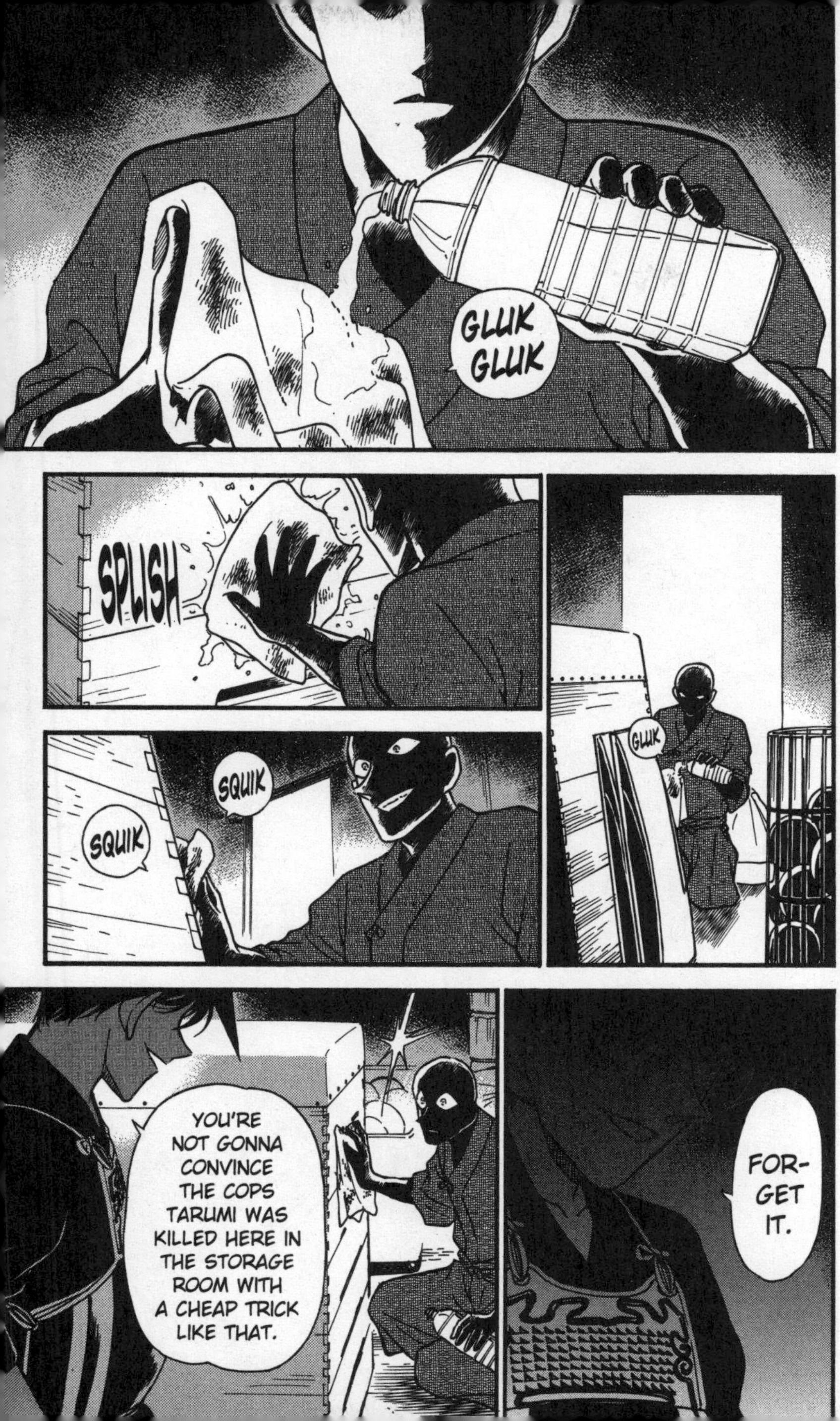
GLUK GLUK
GLUK
SPLISH
SQUIK
SQUIK
FOR-GET IT.
YOU'RE NOT GONNA CONVINCE THE COPS TARUMI WAS KILLED HERE IN THE STORAGE ROOM WITH A CHEAP TRICK LIKE THAT.

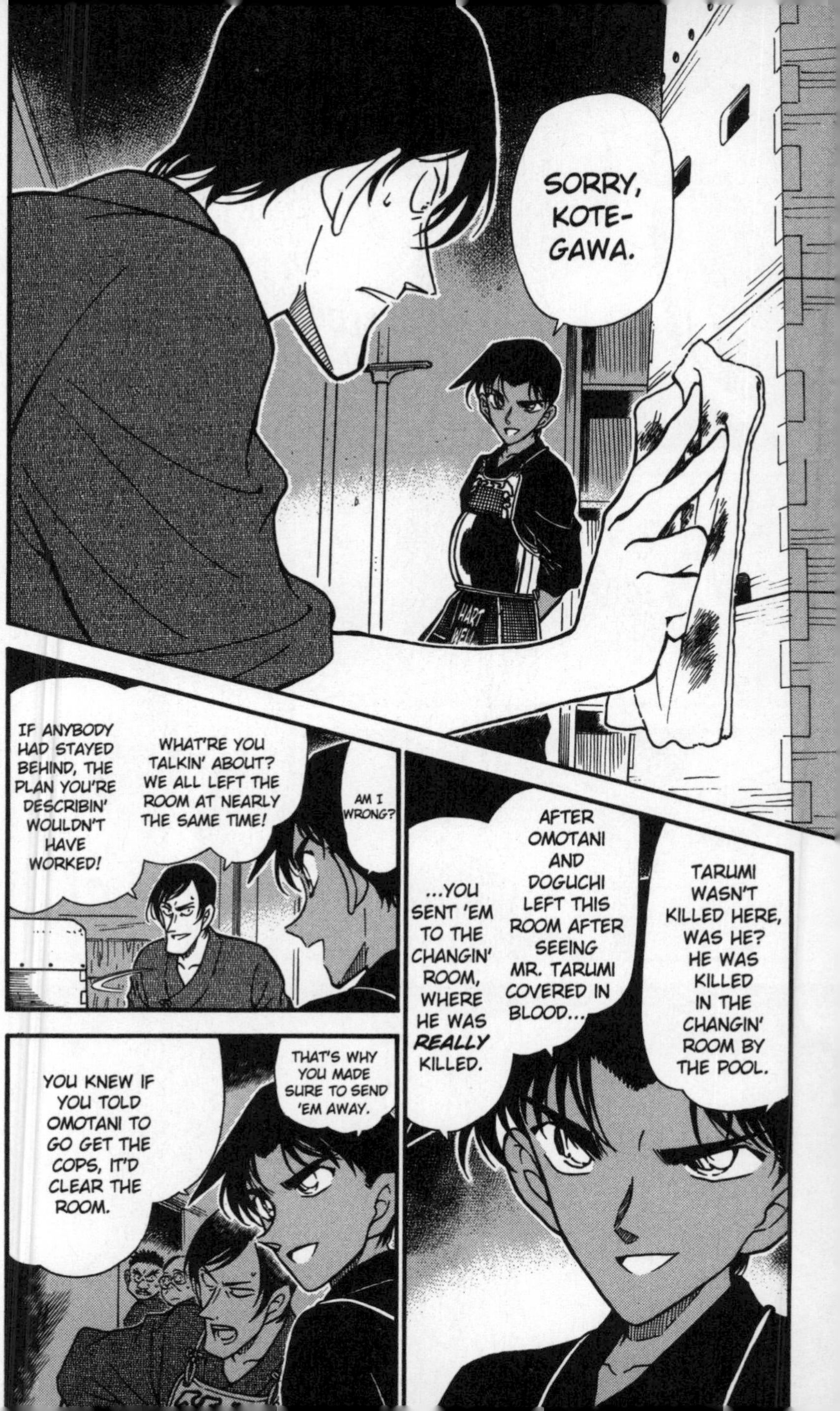
SORRY, KOTE-GAWA.
TARUMI WASN'T KILLED HERE, WAS HE? HE WAS KILLED IN THE CHANGIN' ROOM BY THE POOL.
AFTER OMOTANI AND DOGUCHI LEFT THIS ROOM AFTER SEEING MR. TARUMI COVERED IN BLOOD...
...YOU SENT 'EM TO THE CHANGIN' ROOM, WHERE HE WAS **REALLY** KILLED.
AM I WRONG?
WHAT'RE YOU TALKIN' ABOUT? WE ALL LEFT THE ROOM AT NEARLY THE SAME TIME!
IF ANYBODY HAD STAYED BEHIND, THE PLAN YOU'RE DESCRIBIN' WOULDN'T HAVE WORKED!
THAT'S WHY YOU MADE SURE TO SEND 'EM AWAY.
YOU KNEW IF YOU TOLD OMOTANI TO GO GET THE COPS, IT'D CLEAR THE ROOM.

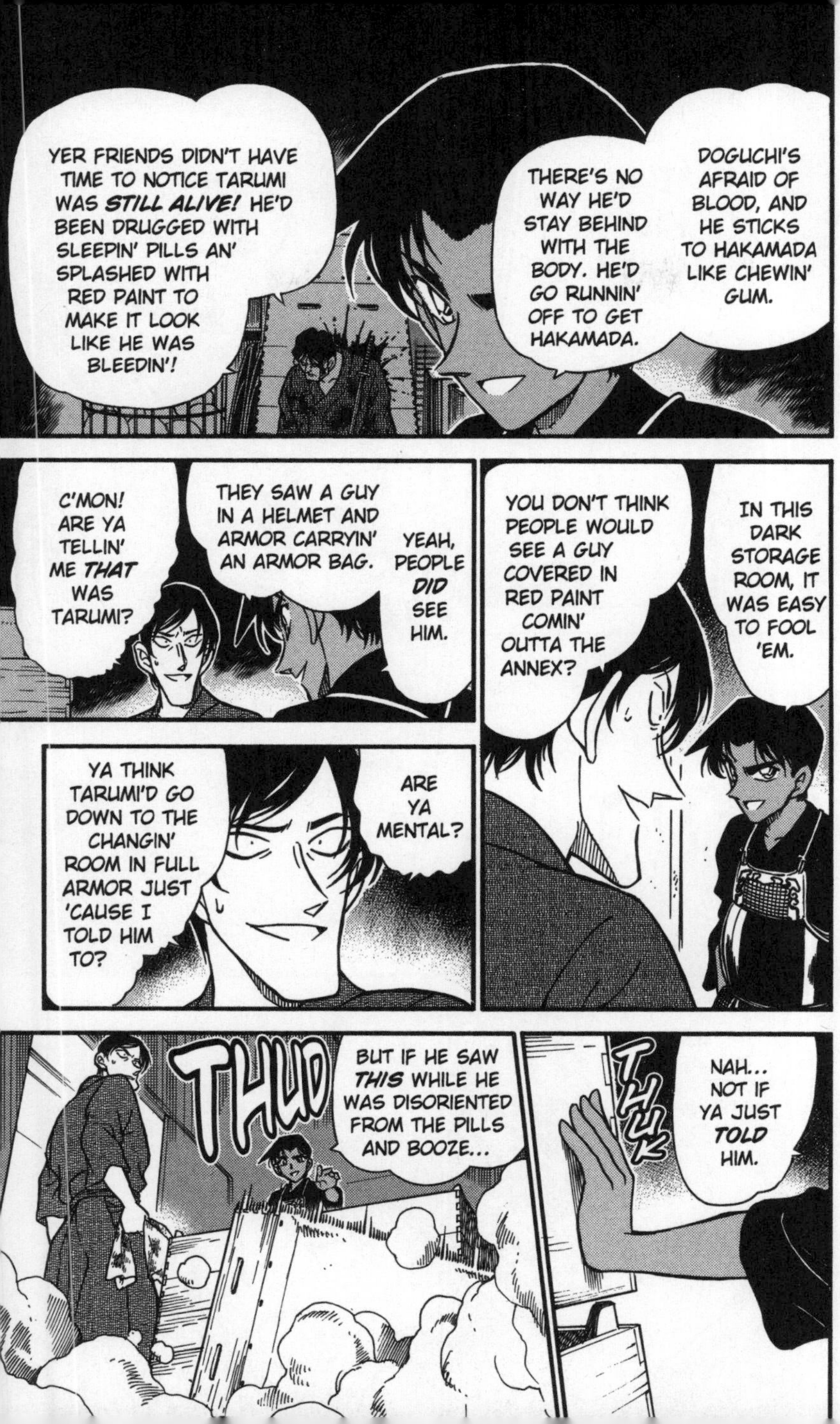
DOGUCHI'S AFRAID OF BLOOD, AND HE STICKS TO HAKAMADA LIKE CHEWIN' GUM.
THERE'S NO WAY HE'D STAY BEHIND WITH THE BODY. HE'D GO RUNNIN' OFF TO GET HAKAMADA.
YER FRIENDS DIDN'T HAVE TIME TO NOTICE TARUMI WAS *STILL ALIVE!* HE'D BEEN DRUGGED WITH SLEEPIN' PILLS AN' SPLASHED WITH RED PAINT TO MAKE IT LOOK LIKE HE WAS BLEEDIN'!
IN THIS DARK STORAGE ROOM, IT WAS EASY TO FOOL 'EM.
YOU DON'T THINK PEOPLE WOULD SEE A GUY COVERED IN RED PAINT COMIN' OUTTA THE ANNEX?
YEAH, PEOPLE *DID* SEE HIM.
THEY SAW A GUY IN A HELMET AND ARMOR CARRYIN' AN ARMOR BAG.
C'MON! ARE YA TELLIN' ME *THAT* WAS TARUMI?
ARE YA MENTAL?
YA THINK TARUMI'D GO DOWN TO THE CHANGIN' ROOM IN FULL ARMOR JUST 'CAUSE I TOLD HIM TO?
NAH... NOT IF YA JUST *TOLD* HIM.
THUK
BUT IF HE SAW *THIS* WHILE HE WAS DISORIENTED FROM THE PILLS AND BOOZE...
THUD

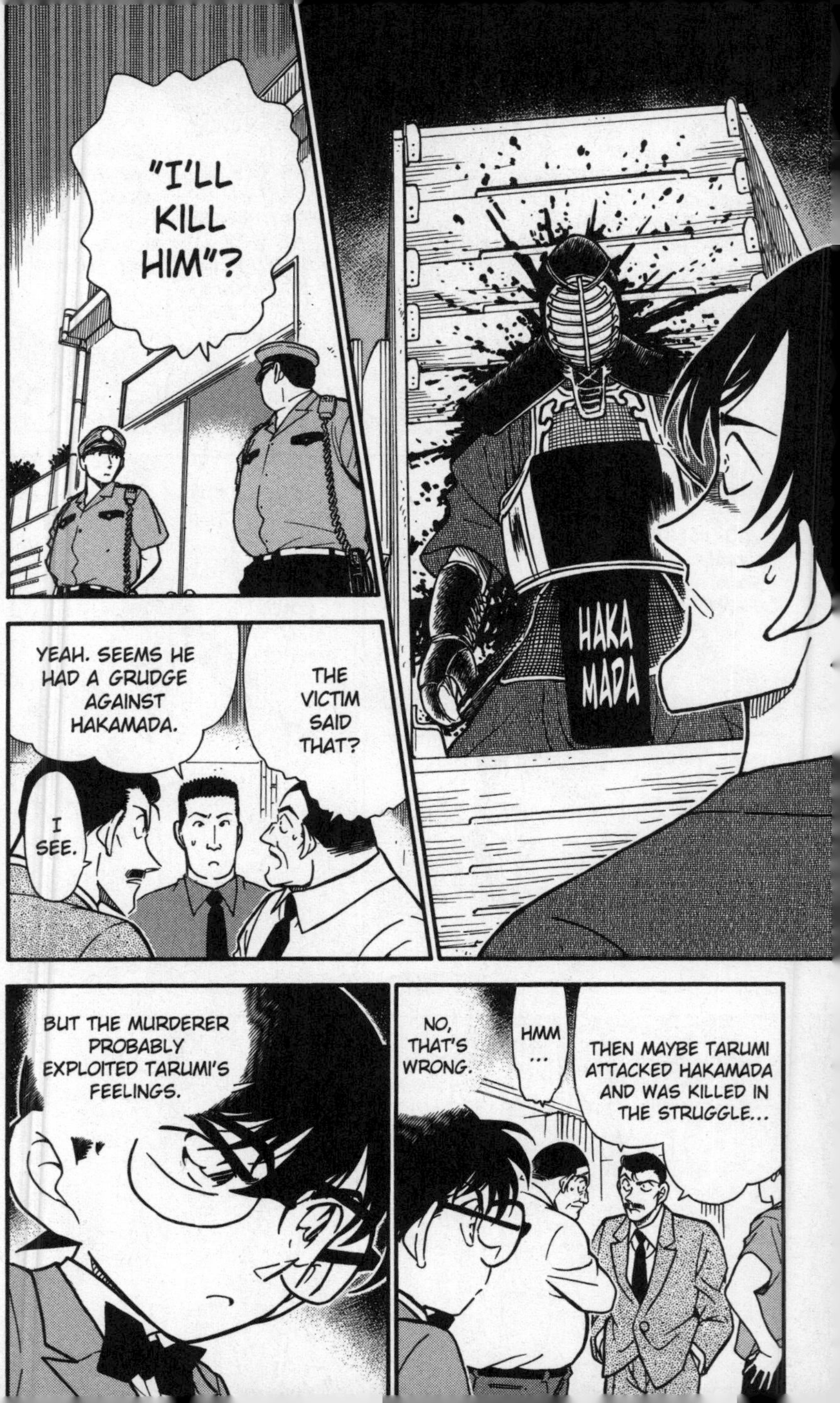
HAKA MADA
"I'LL KILL HIM"?
THE VICTIM SAID THAT?
YEAH. SEEMS HE HAD A GRUDGE AGAINST HAKAMADA.
I SEE.
THEN MAYBE TARUMI ATTACKED HAKAMADA AND WAS KILLED IN THE STRUGGLE...
HMM...
NO, THAT'S WRONG.
BUT THE MURDERER PROBABLY EXPLOITED TARUMI'S FEELINGS.

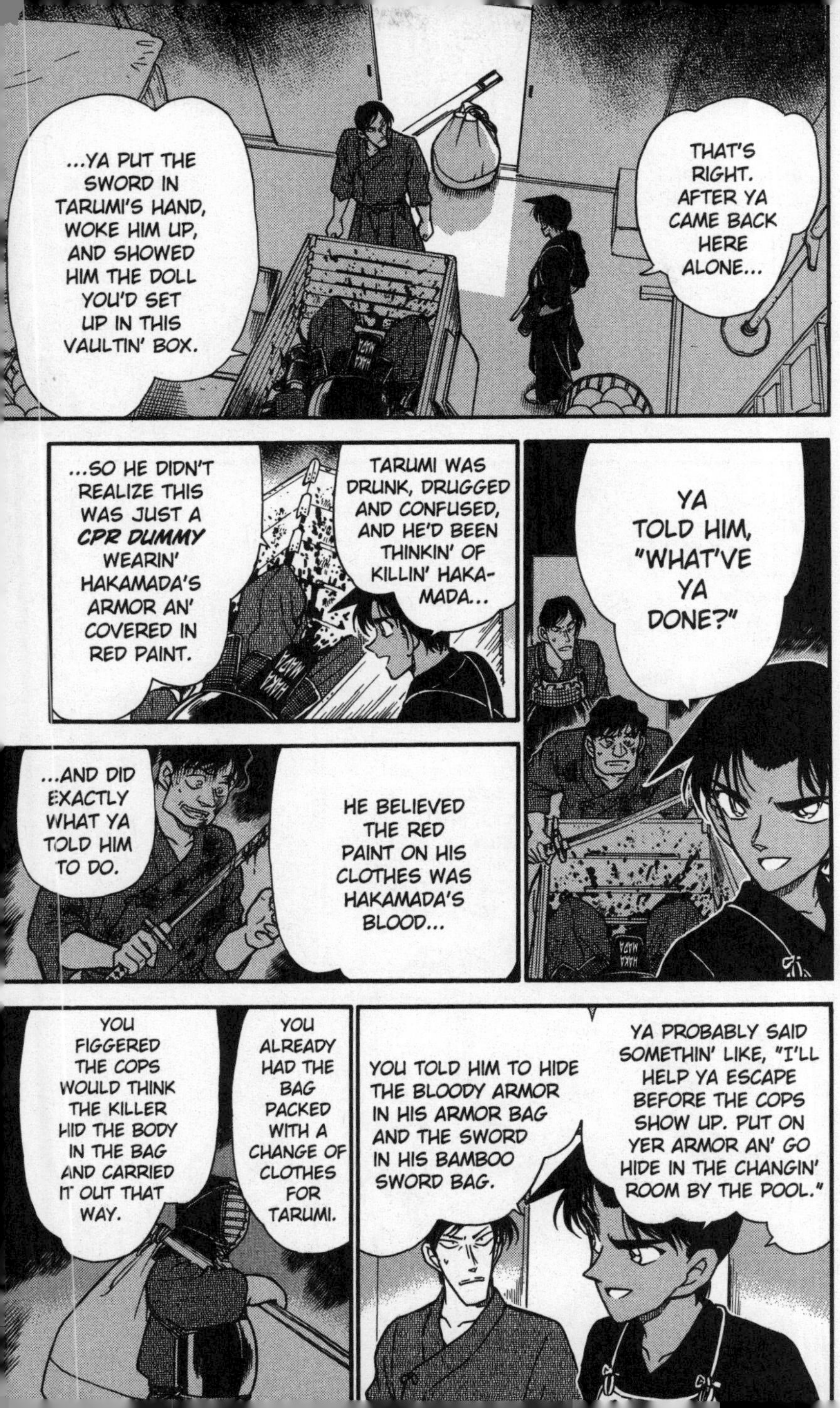
THAT'S RIGHT. AFTER YA CAME BACK HERE ALONE...
...YA PUT THE SWORD IN TARUMI'S HAND, WOKE HIM UP, AND SHOWED HIM THE DOLL YOU'D SET UP IN THIS VAULTIN' BOX.
YA TOLD HIM, "WHAT'VE YA DONE?"
TARUMI WAS DRUNK, DRUGGED AND CONFUSED, AND HE'D BEEN THINKIN' OF KILLIN' HAKA-MADA...
...SO HE DIDN'T REALIZE THIS WAS JUST A *CPR DUMMY* WEARIN' HAKAMADA'S ARMOR AN' COVERED IN RED PAINT.
HE BELIEVED THE RED PAINT ON HIS CLOTHES WAS HAKAMADA'S BLOOD...
...AND DID EXACTLY WHAT YA TOLD HIM TO DO.
YA PROBABLY SAID SOMETHIN' LIKE, "I'LL HELP YA ESCAPE BEFORE THE COPS SHOW UP. PUT ON YER ARMOR AN' GO HIDE IN THE CHANGIN' ROOM BY THE POOL."
YOU TOLD HIM TO HIDE THE BLOODY ARMOR IN HIS ARMOR BAG AND THE SWORD IN HIS BAMBOO SWORD BAG.
YOU ALREADY HAD THE BAG PACKED WITH A CHANGE OF CLOTHES FOR TARUMI.
YOU FIGGERED THE COPS WOULD THINK THE KILLER HID THE BODY IN THE BAG AND CARRIED IT OUT THAT WAY.

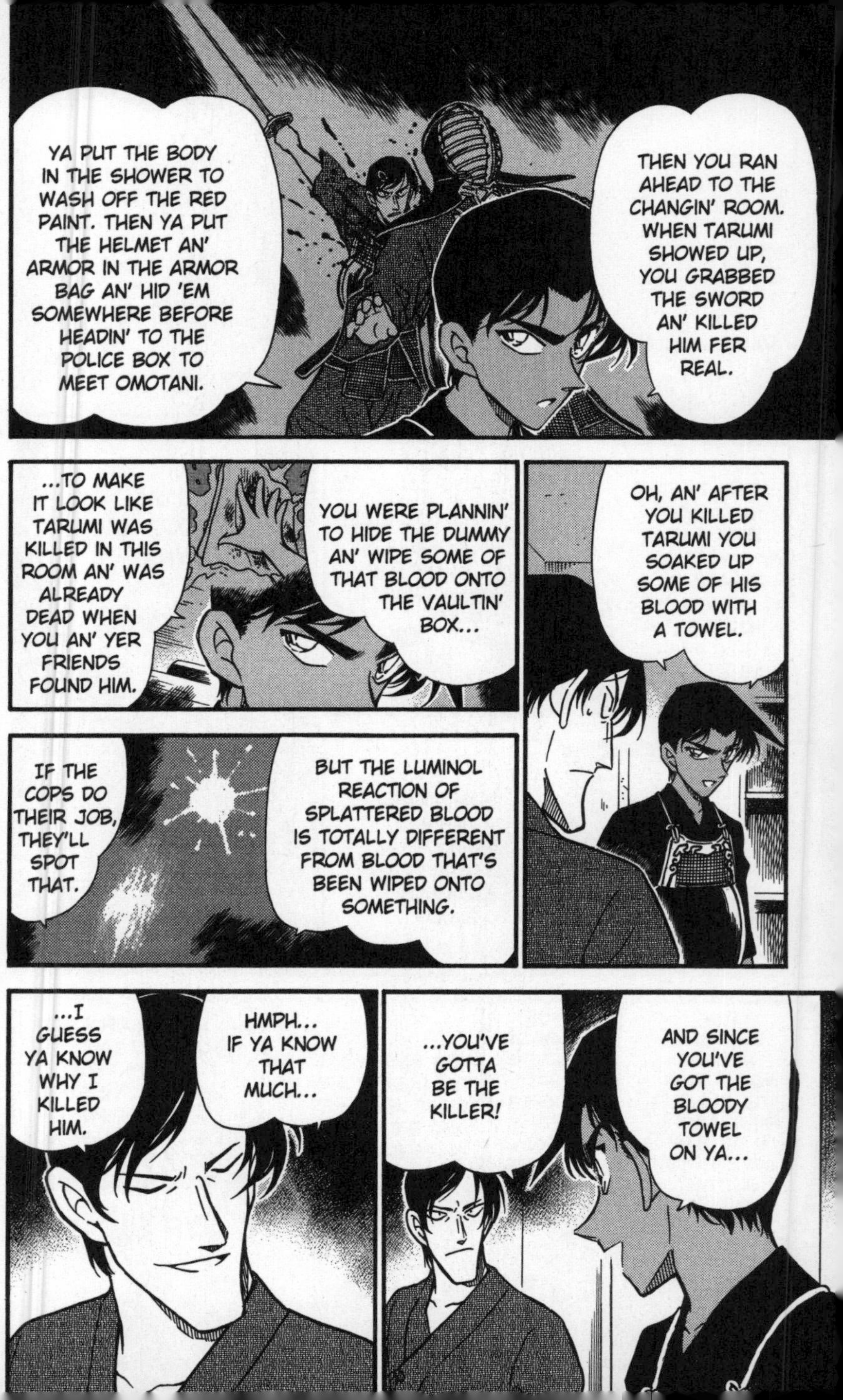
THEN YOU RAN AHEAD TO THE CHANGIN' ROOM. WHEN TARUMI SHOWED UP, YOU GRABBED THE SWORD AN' KILLED HIM FER REAL.
YA PUT THE BODY IN THE SHOWER TO WASH OFF THE RED PAINT. THEN YA PUT THE HELMET AN' ARMOR IN THE ARMOR BAG AN' HID 'EM SOMEWHERE BEFORE HEADIN' TO THE POLICE BOX TO MEET OMOTANI.
OH, AN' AFTER YOU KILLED TARUMI YOU SOAKED UP SOME OF HIS BLOOD WITH A TOWEL.
YOU WERE PLANNIN' TO HIDE THE DUMMY AN' WIPE SOME OF THAT BLOOD ONTO THE VAULTIN' BOX...
...TO MAKE IT LOOK LIKE TARUMI WAS KILLED IN THIS ROOM AN' WAS ALREADY DEAD WHEN YOU AN' YER FRIENDS FOUND HIM.
BUT THE LUMINOL REACTION OF SPLATTERED BLOOD IS TOTALLY DIFFERENT FROM BLOOD THAT'S BEEN WIPED ONTO SOMETHING.
IF THE COPS DO THEIR JOB, THEY'LL SPOT THAT.
AND SINCE YOU'VE GOT THE BLOODY TOWEL ON YA...
...YOU'VE GOTTA BE THE KILLER!
HMPH... IF YA KNOW THAT MUCH...
...I GUESS YA KNOW WHY I KILLED HIM.

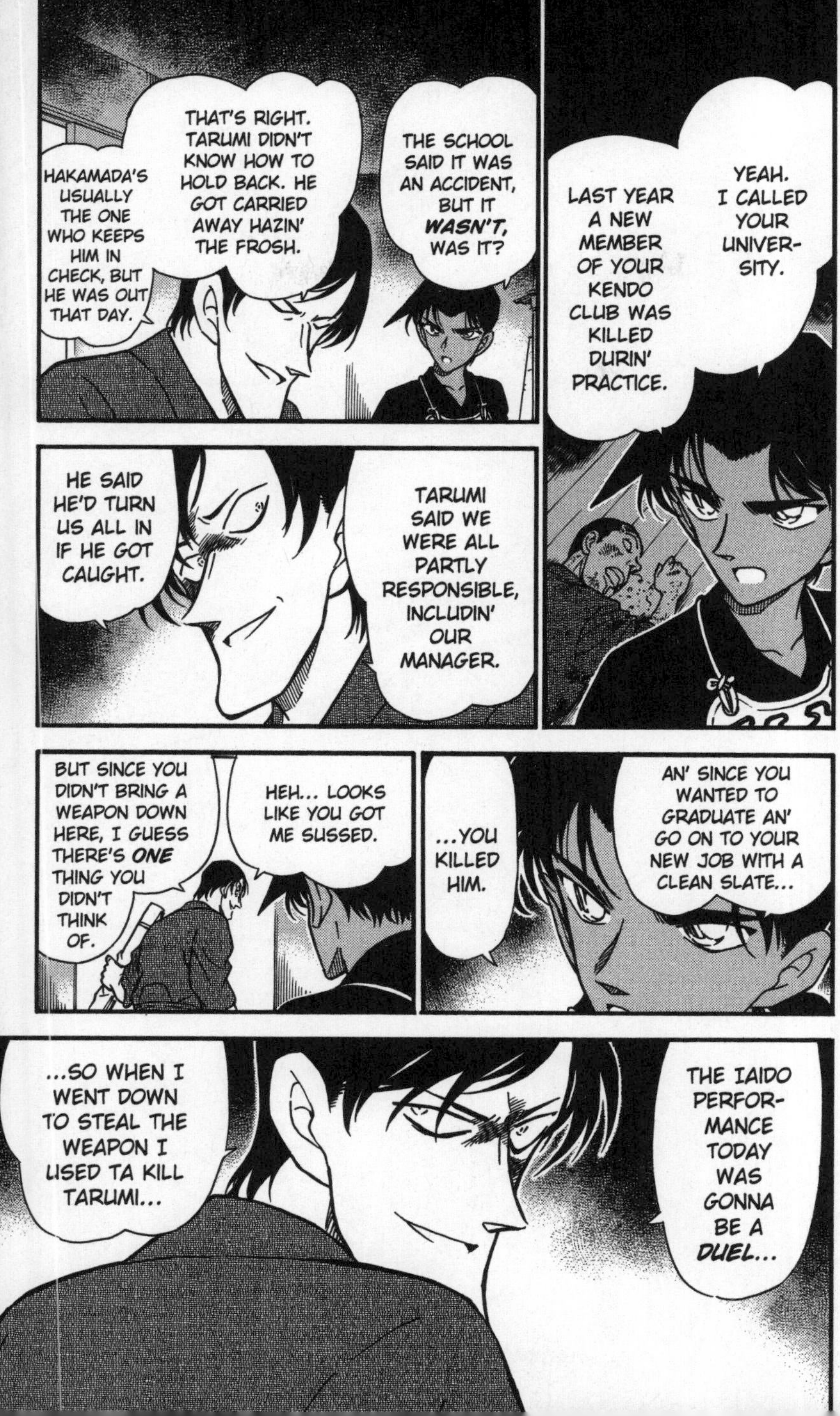
YEAH. I CALLED YOUR UNIVER-SITY.
LAST YEAR A NEW MEMBER OF YOUR KENDO CLUB WAS KILLED DURIN' PRACTICE.
THE SCHOOL SAID IT WAS AN ACCIDENT, BUT IT ***WASN'T,*** WAS IT?
THAT'S RIGHT. TARUMI DIDN'T KNOW HOW TO HOLD BACK. HE GOT CARRIED AWAY HAZIN' THE FROSH.
HAKAMADA'S USUALLY THE ONE WHO KEEPS HIM IN CHECK, BUT HE WAS OUT THAT DAY.
TARUMI SAID WE WERE ALL PARTLY RESPONSIBLE, INCLUDIN' OUR MANAGER.
HE SAID HE'D TURN US ALL IN IF HE GOT CAUGHT.
AN' SINCE YOU WANTED TO GRADUATE AN' GO ON TO YOUR NEW JOB WITH A CLEAN SLATE...
...YOU KILLED HIM.
HEH... LOOKS LIKE YOU GOT ME SUSSED.
BUT SINCE YOU DIDN'T BRING A WEAPON DOWN HERE, I GUESS THERE'S ***ONE*** THING YOU DIDN'T THINK OF.
THE IAIDO PERFOR-MANCE TODAY WAS GONNA BE A ***DUEL...***
...SO WHEN I WENT DOWN TO STEAL THE WEAPON I USED TA KILL TARUMI...

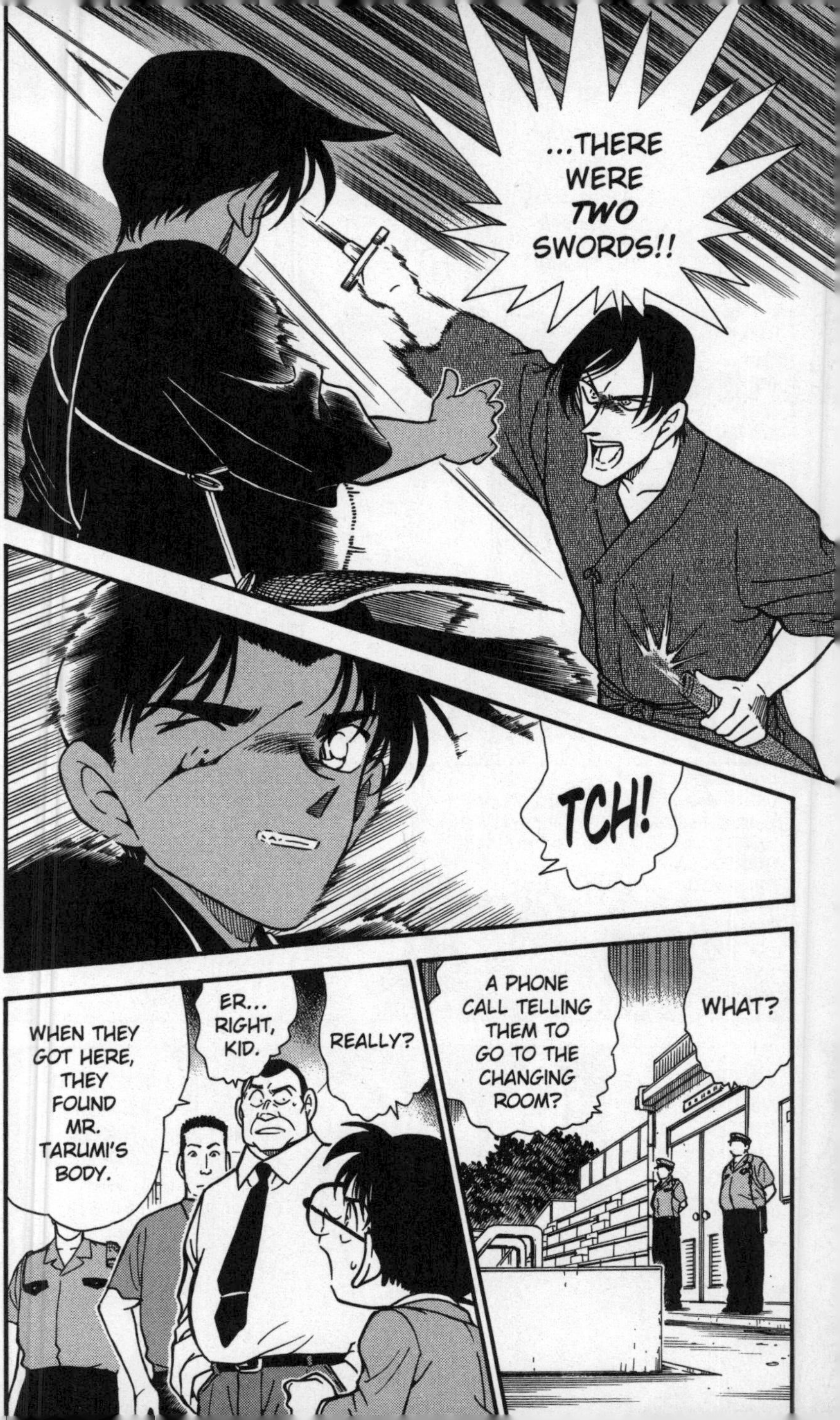
...THERE WERE *TWO* SWORDS!!
TCH!
WHAT?
A PHONE CALL TELLING THEM TO GO TO THE CHANGING ROOM?
REALLY?
ER... RIGHT, KID.
WHEN THEY GOT HERE, THEY FOUND MR. TARUMI'S BODY.

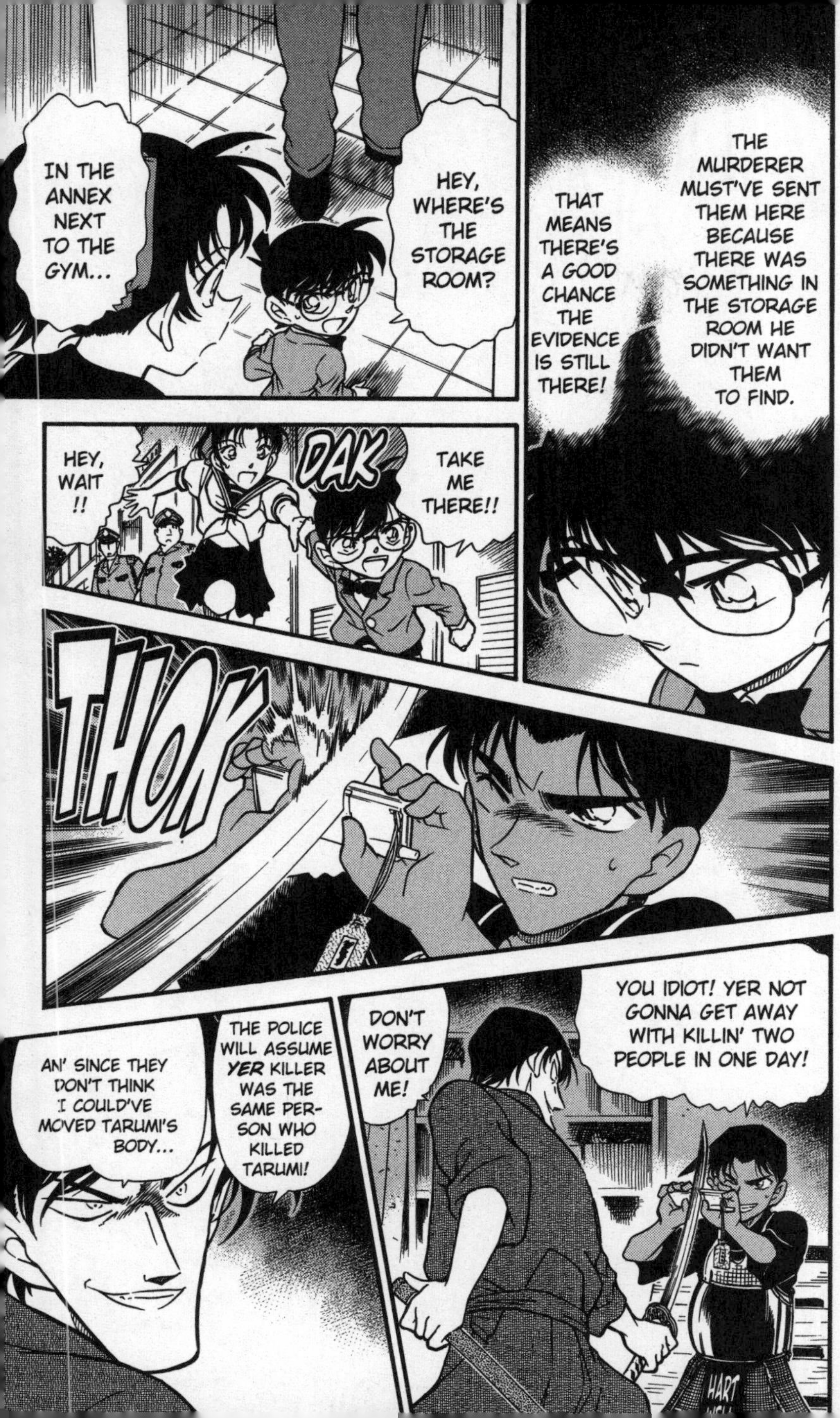

THE MURDERER MUST'VE SENT THEM HERE BECAUSE THERE WAS SOMETHING IN THE STORAGE ROOM HE DIDN'T WANT THEM TO FIND.
THAT MEANS THERE'S A GOOD CHANCE THE EVIDENCE IS STILL THERE!
HEY, WHERE'S THE STORAGE ROOM?
IN THE ANNEX NEXT TO THE GYM...
TAKE ME THERE!!
DAK
HEY, WAIT !!
THOK
YOU IDIOT! YER NOT GONNA GET AWAY WITH KILLIN' TWO PEOPLE IN ONE DAY!
DON'T WORRY ABOUT ME!
THE POLICE WILL ASSUME YER KILLER WAS THE SAME PER-SON WHO KILLED TARUMI!
AN' SINCE THEY DON'T THINK I COULD'VE MOVED TARUMI'S BODY...

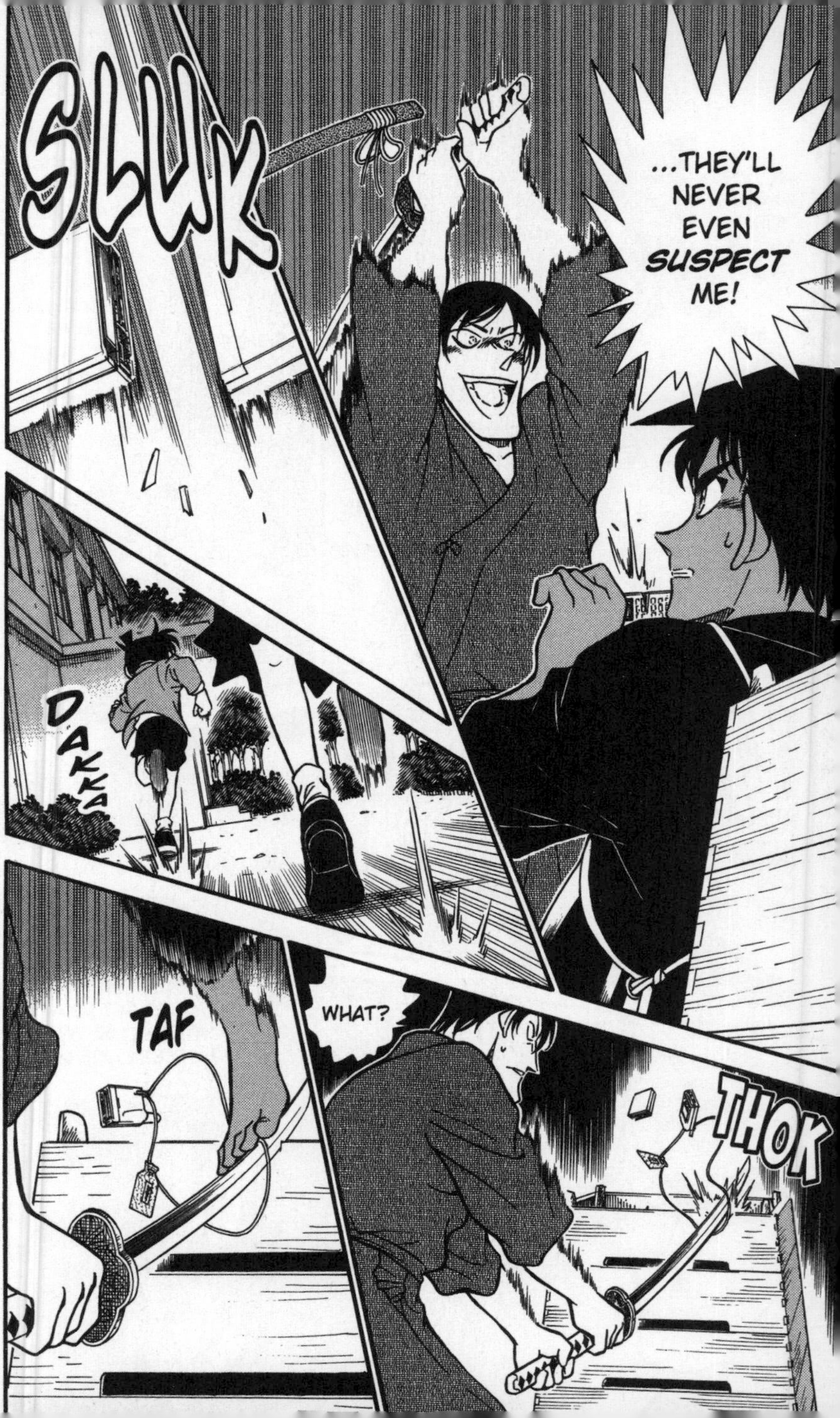
...THEY'LL NEVER EVEN SUSPECT ME!
SLUK
DAKKA
WHAT?
THOK
TAF

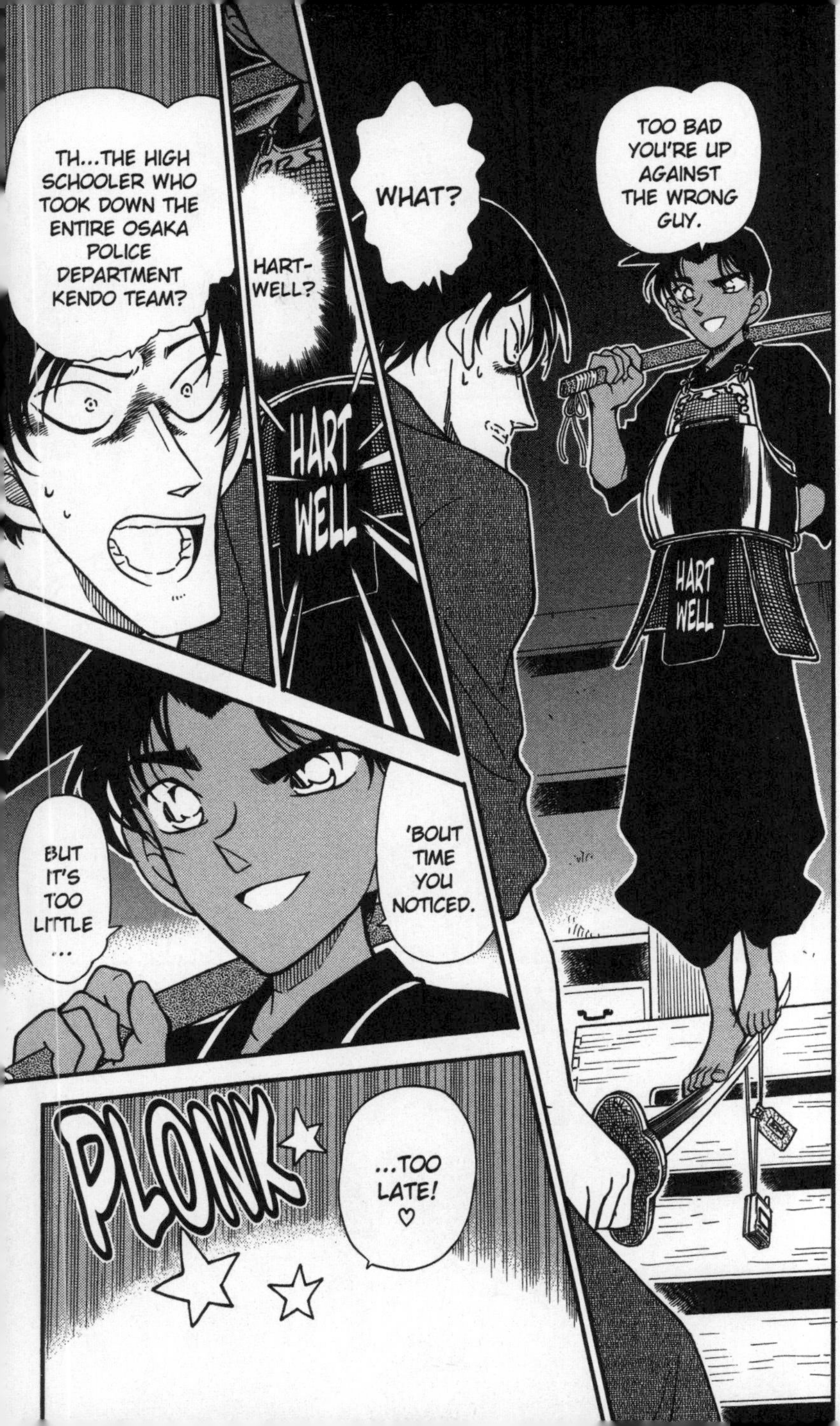
TOO BAD YOU'RE UP AGAINST THE WRONG GUY.
HART WELL
WHAT?
HART-WELL?
HART WELL
TH...THE HIGH SCHOOLER WHO TOOK DOWN THE ENTIRE OSAKA POLICE DEPARTMENT KENDO TEAM?
'BOUT TIME YOU NOTICED.
BUT IT'S TOO LITTLE...
...TOO LATE! ♡
PLONK

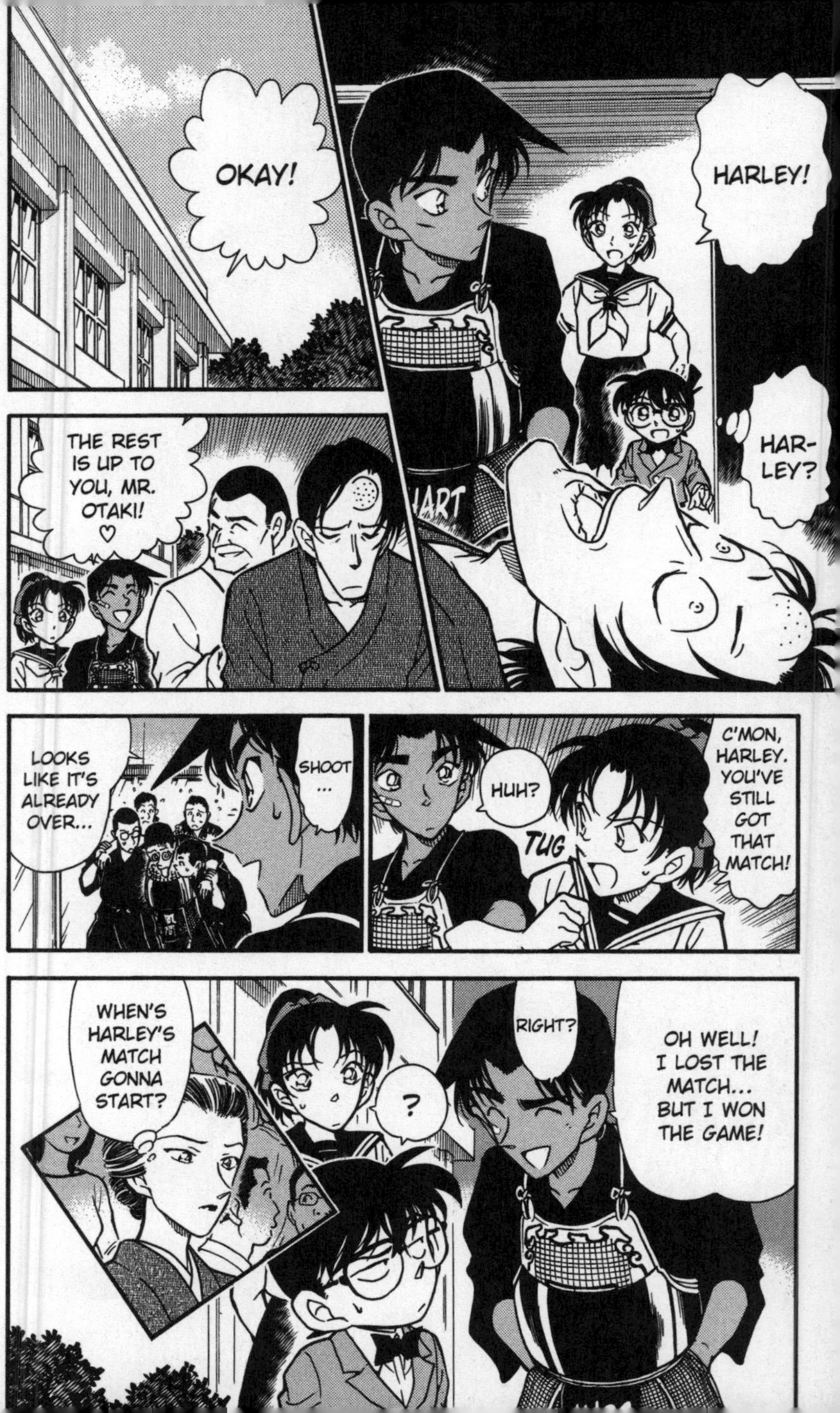
HARLEY!
HAR-LEY?
OKAY!
THE REST IS UP TO YOU, MR. OTAKI! ♡
C'MON, HARLEY. YOU'VE STILL GOT THAT MATCH!
HUH?
TUG
SHOOT...
LOOKS LIKE IT'S ALREADY OVER...
OH WELL! I LOST THE MATCH... BUT I WON THE GAME!
RIGHT?
?
WHEN'S HARLEY'S MATCH GONNA START?

FILE 11: THE CONQUEROR'S CASTLE

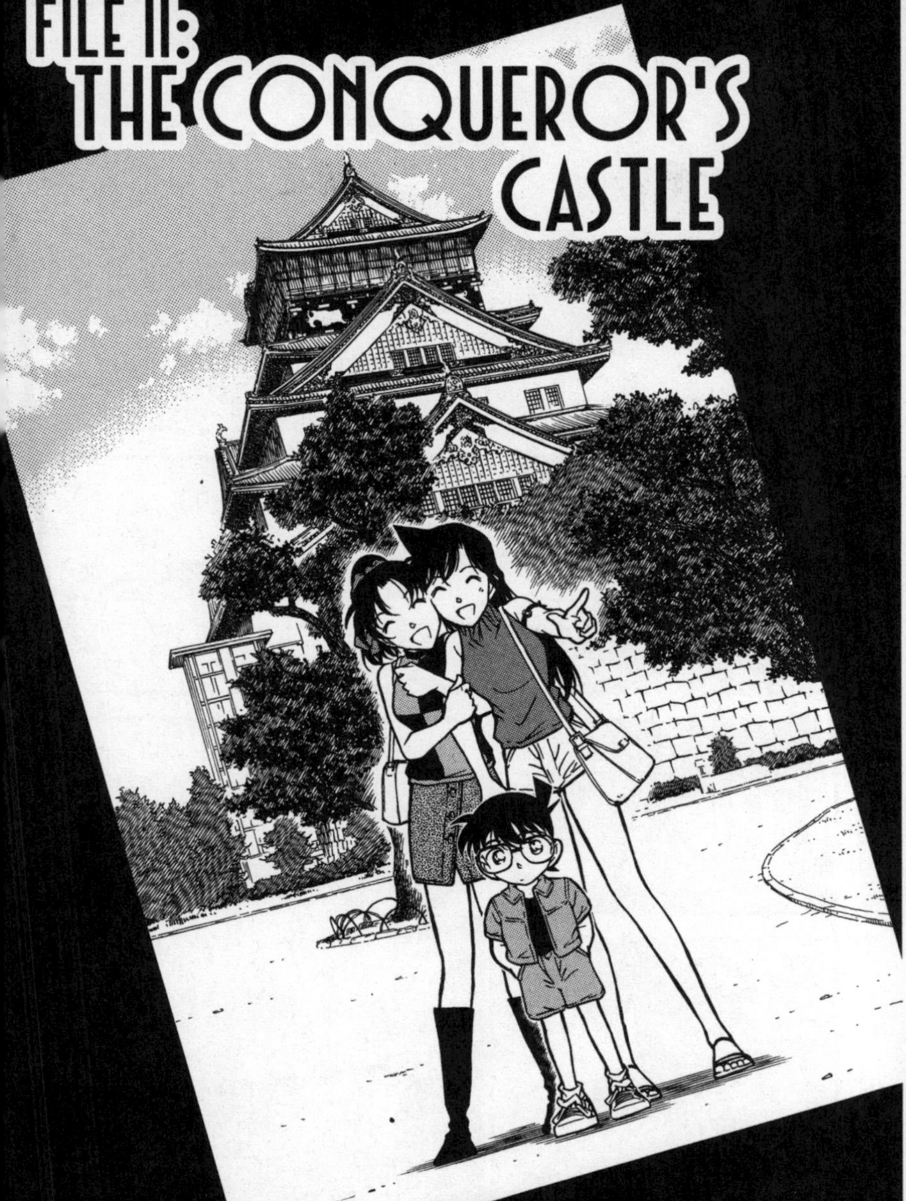

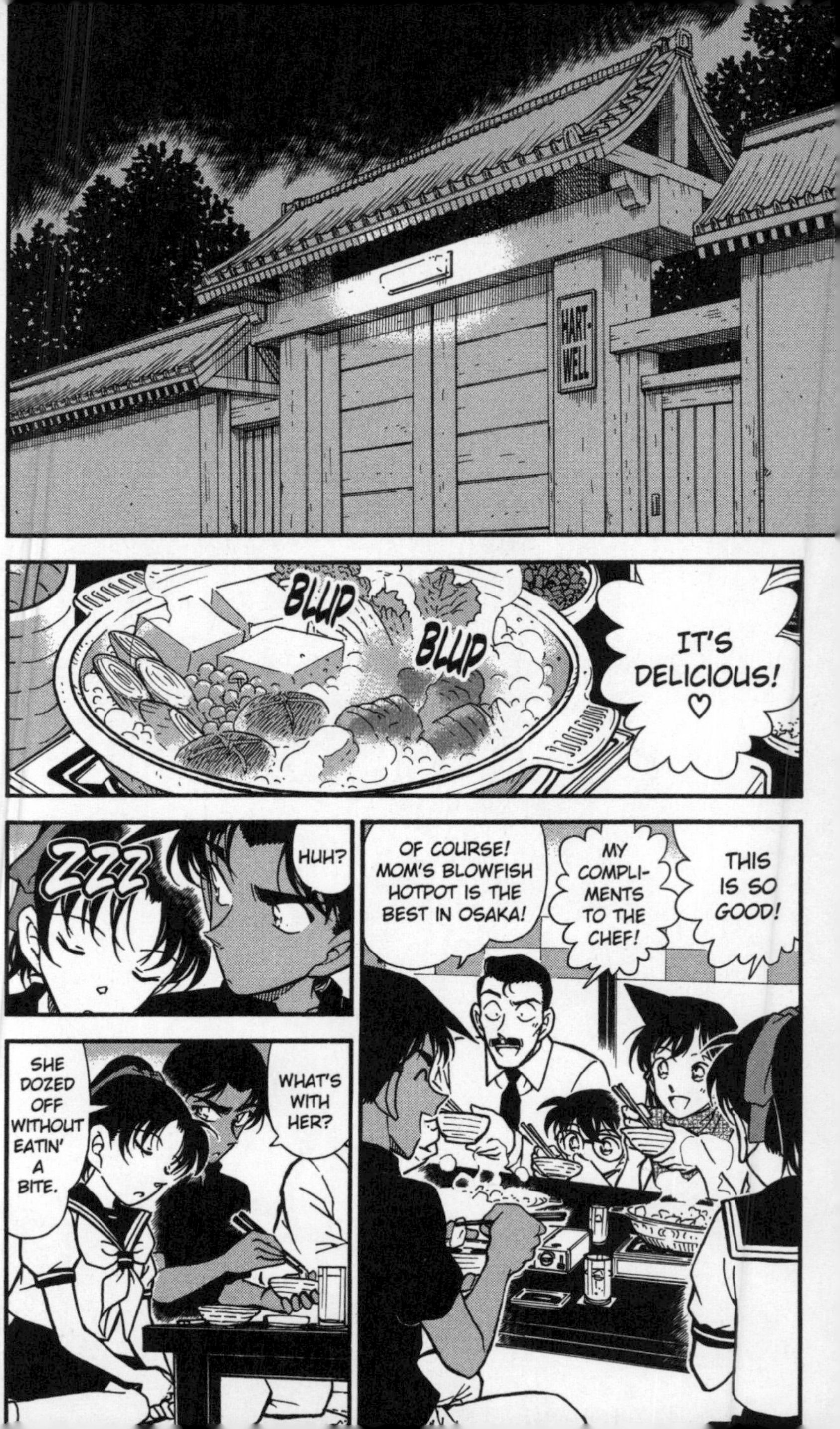
HART-WELL
IT'S DELICIOUS! ♡
BLUP
BLUP
THIS IS SO GOOD!
MY COMPLIMENTS TO THE CHEF!
OF COURSE! MOM'S BLOWFISH HOTPOT IS THE BEST IN OSAKA!
HUH?
ZZZ
WHAT'S WITH HER?
SHE DOZED OFF WITHOUT EATIN' A BITE.

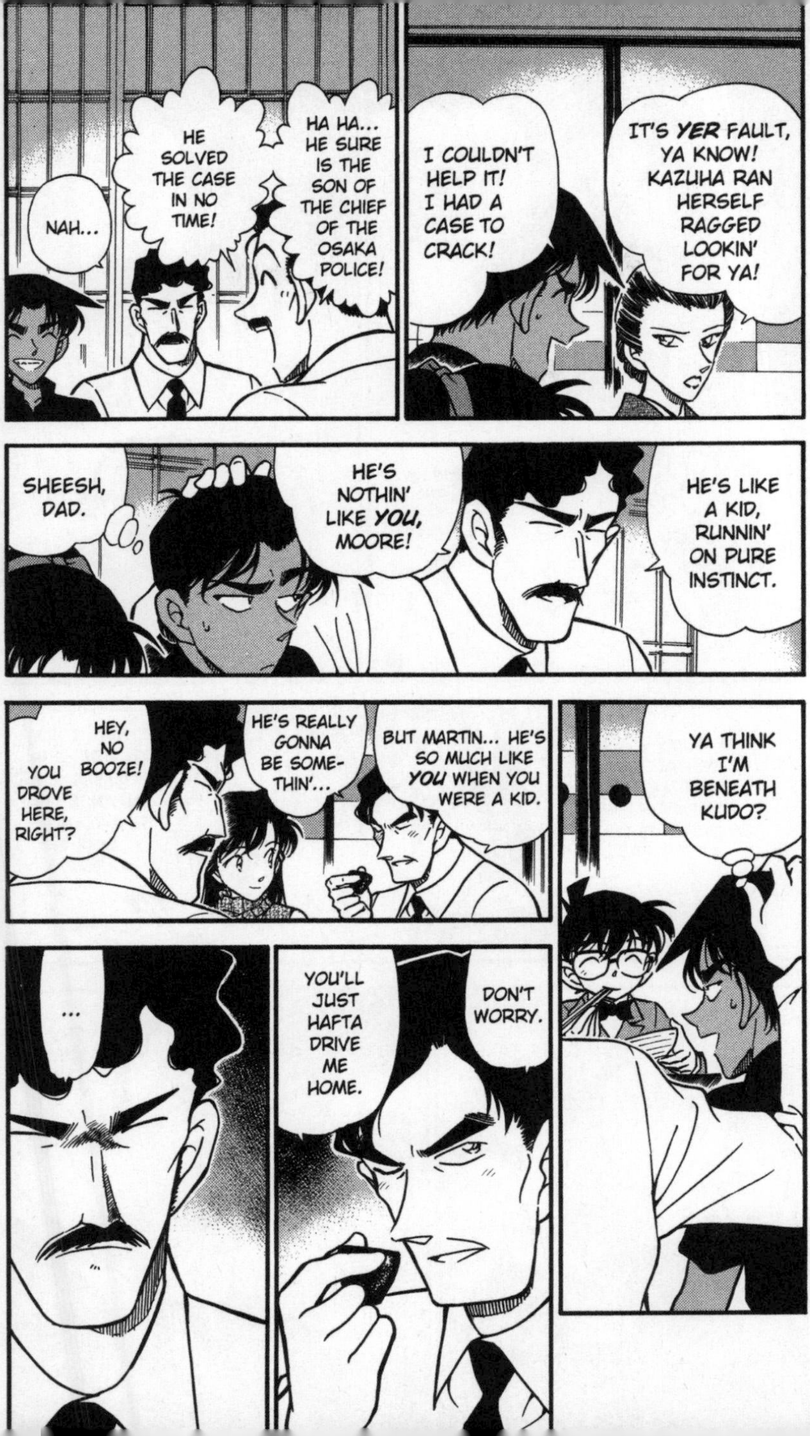
IT'S *YER* FAULT, YA KNOW! KAZUHA RAN HERSELF RAGGED LOOKIN' FOR YA!
I COULDN'T HELP IT! I HAD A CASE TO CRACK!
HA HA... HE SURE IS THE SON OF THE CHIEF OF THE OSAKA POLICE!
HE SOLVED THE CASE IN NO TIME!
NAH...
HE'S LIKE A KID, RUNNIN' ON PURE INSTINCT.
HE'S NOTHIN' LIKE *YOU*, MOORE!
SHEESH, DAD.
YA THINK I'M BENEATH KUDO?
BUT MARTIN... HE'S SO MUCH LIKE *YOU* WHEN YOU WERE A KID.
HE'S REALLY GONNA BE SOME-THIN'...
HEY, NO BOOZE!
YOU DROVE HERE, RIGHT?
DON'T WORRY.
YOU'LL JUST HAFTA DRIVE ME HOME.
...

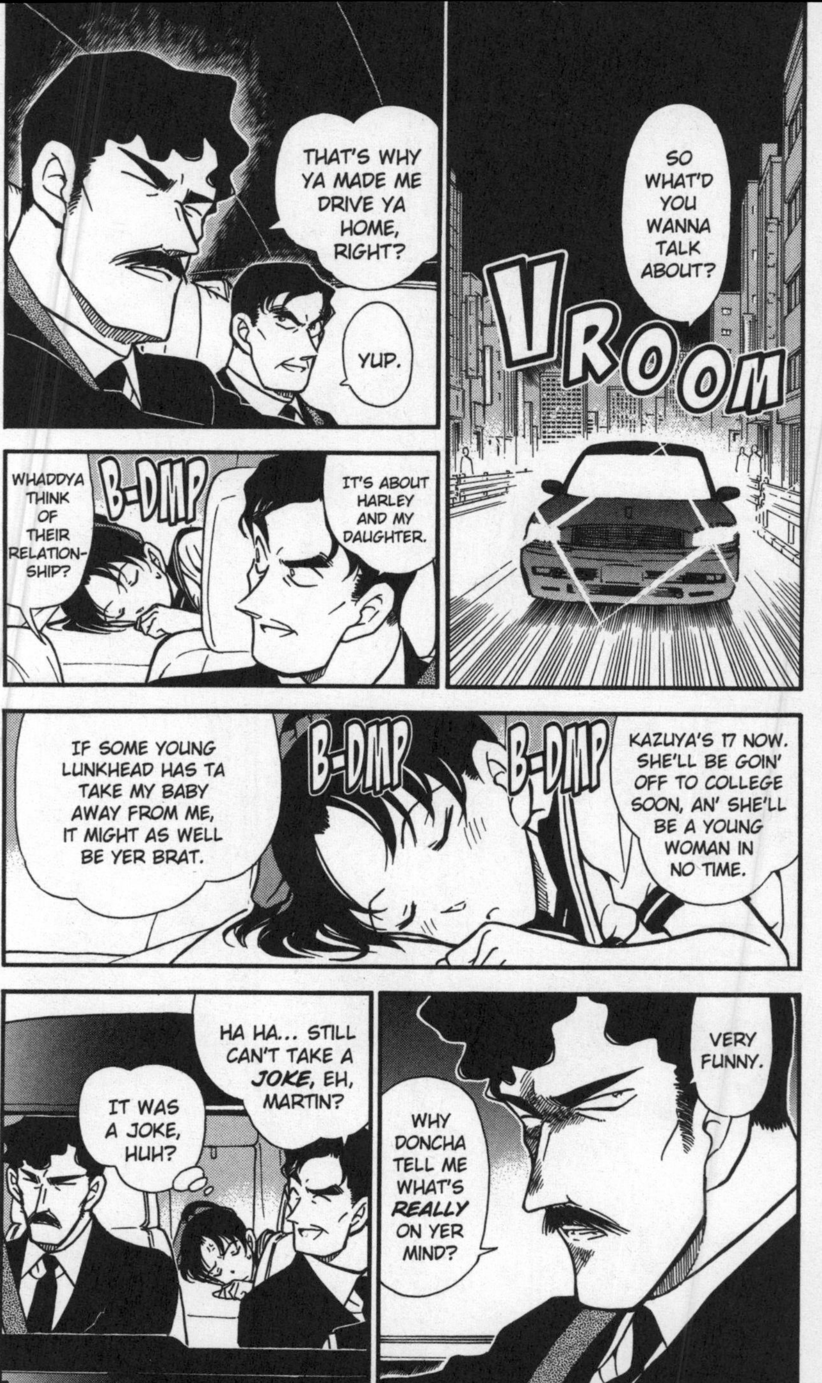
SO WHAT'D YOU WANNA TALK ABOUT?
VROOM
THAT'S WHY YA MADE ME DRIVE YA HOME, RIGHT?
YUP.
IT'S ABOUT HARLEY AND MY DAUGHTER.
B-DMP
WHADDYA THINK OF THEIR RELATION-SHIP?
KAZUYA'S 17 NOW. SHE'LL BE GOIN' OFF TO COLLEGE SOON, AN' SHE'LL BE A YOUNG WOMAN IN NO TIME.
B-DMP
B-DMP
IF SOME YOUNG LUNKHEAD HAS TA TAKE MY BABY AWAY FROM ME, IT MIGHT AS WELL BE YER BRAT.
VERY FUNNY.
WHY DONCHA TELL ME WHAT'S *REALLY* ON YER MIND?
HA HA... STILL CAN'T TAKE A *JOKE*, EH, MARTIN?
IT WAS A JOKE, HUH?

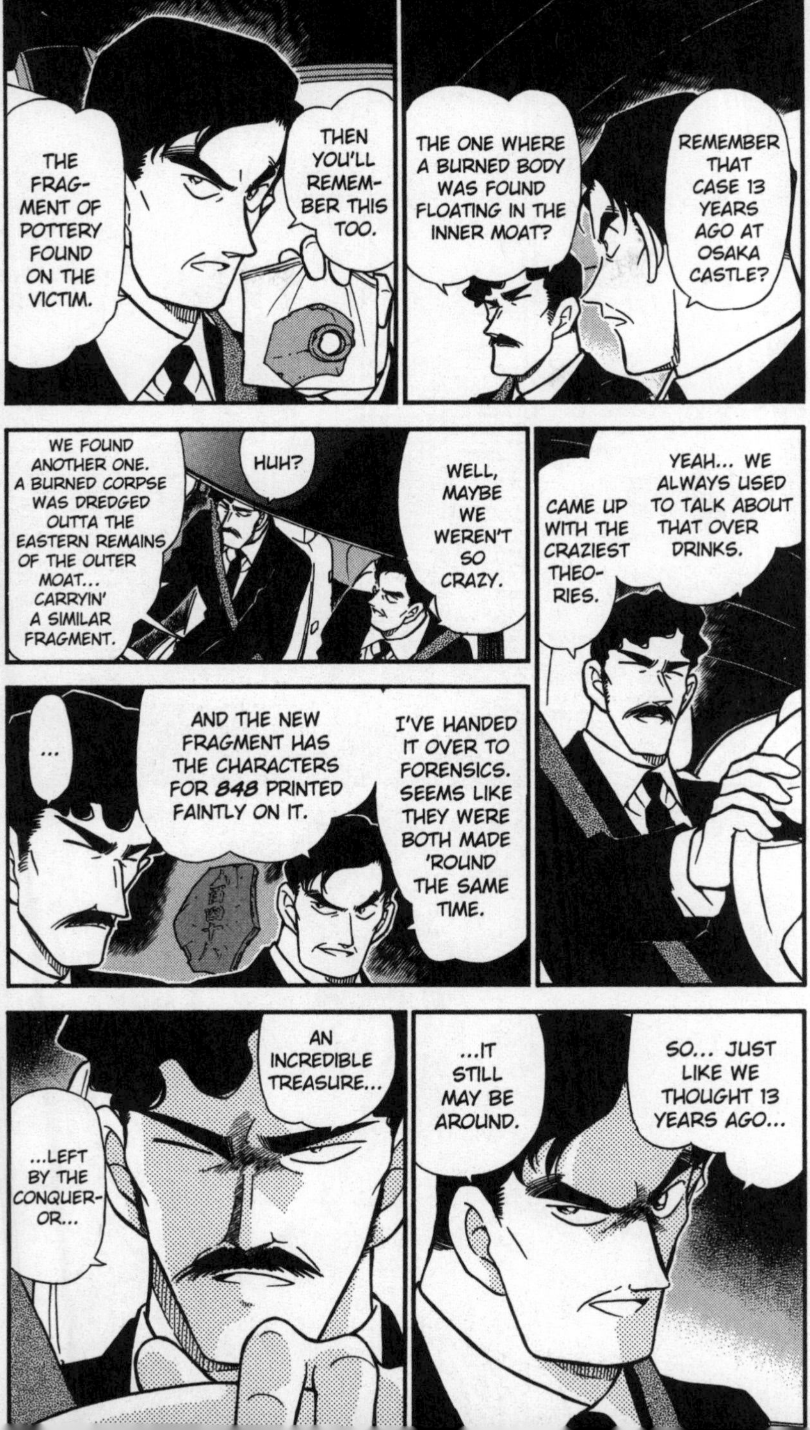
REMEMBER THAT CASE 13 YEARS AGO AT OSAKA CASTLE?
THE ONE WHERE A BURNED BODY WAS FOUND FLOATING IN THE INNER MOAT?
THEN YOU'LL REMEMBER THIS TOO.
THE FRAGMENT OF POTTERY FOUND ON THE VICTIM.
YEAH... WE ALWAYS USED TO TALK ABOUT THAT OVER DRINKS.
CAME UP WITH THE CRAZIEST THEORIES.
WELL, MAYBE WE WEREN'T SO CRAZY.
HUH?
WE FOUND ANOTHER ONE. A BURNED CORPSE WAS DREDGED OUTTA THE EASTERN REMAINS OF THE OUTER MOAT... CARRYIN' A SIMILAR FRAGMENT.
I'VE HANDED IT OVER TO FORENSICS. SEEMS LIKE THEY WERE BOTH MADE 'ROUND THE SAME TIME.
AND THE NEW FRAGMENT HAS THE CHARACTERS FOR 848 PRINTED FAINTLY ON IT.
...
SO... JUST LIKE WE THOUGHT 13 YEARS AGO...
...IT STILL MAY BE AROUND.
AN INCREDIBLE TREASURE...
...LEFT BY THE CONQUEROR...

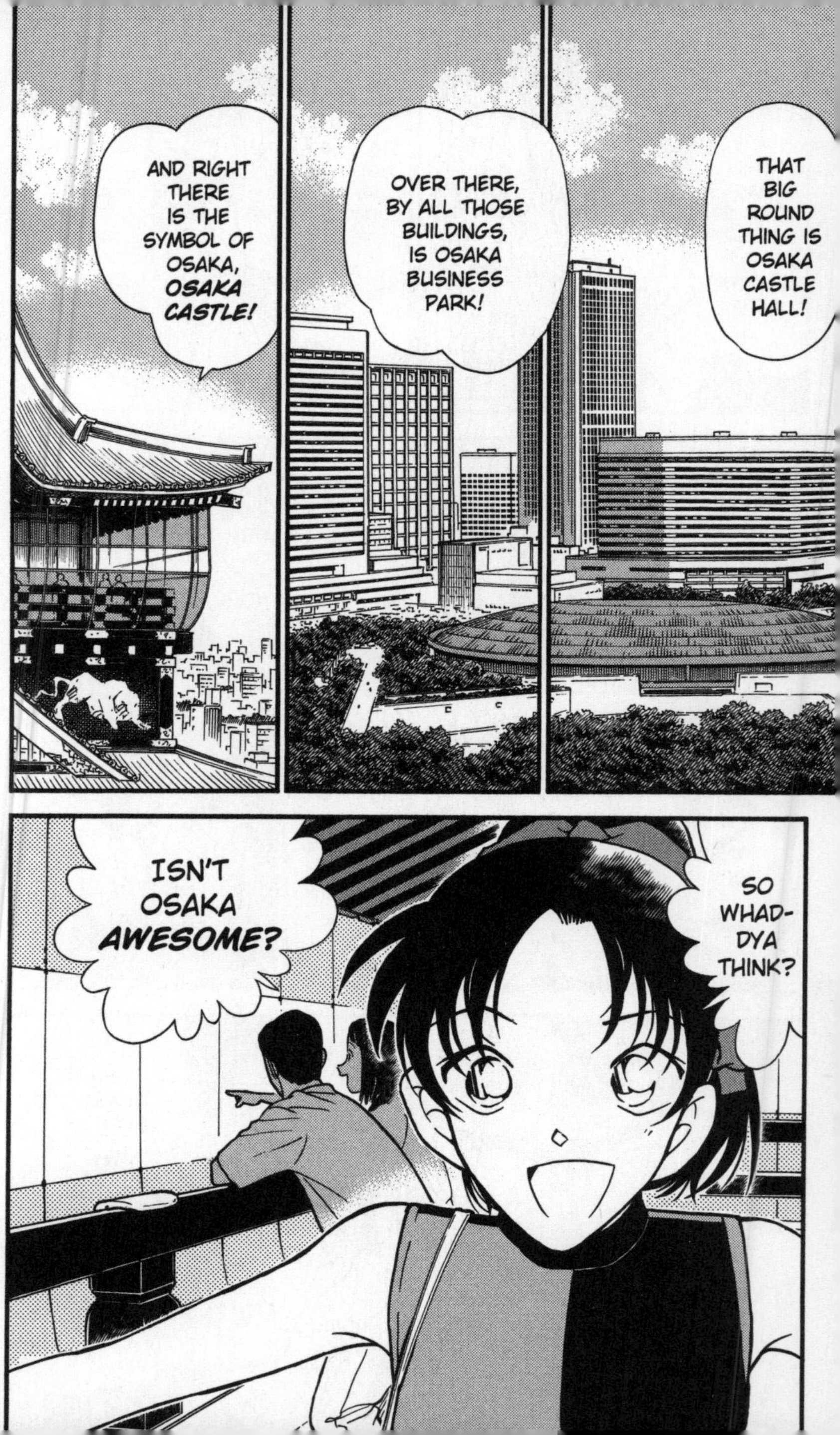
THAT BIG ROUND THING IS OSAKA CASTLE HALL!
OVER THERE, BY ALL THOSE BUILDINGS, IS OSAKA BUSINESS PARK!
AND RIGHT THERE IS THE SYMBOL OF OSAKA, OSAKA CASTLE!
SO WHAD-DYA THINK?
ISN'T OSAKA AWESOME?

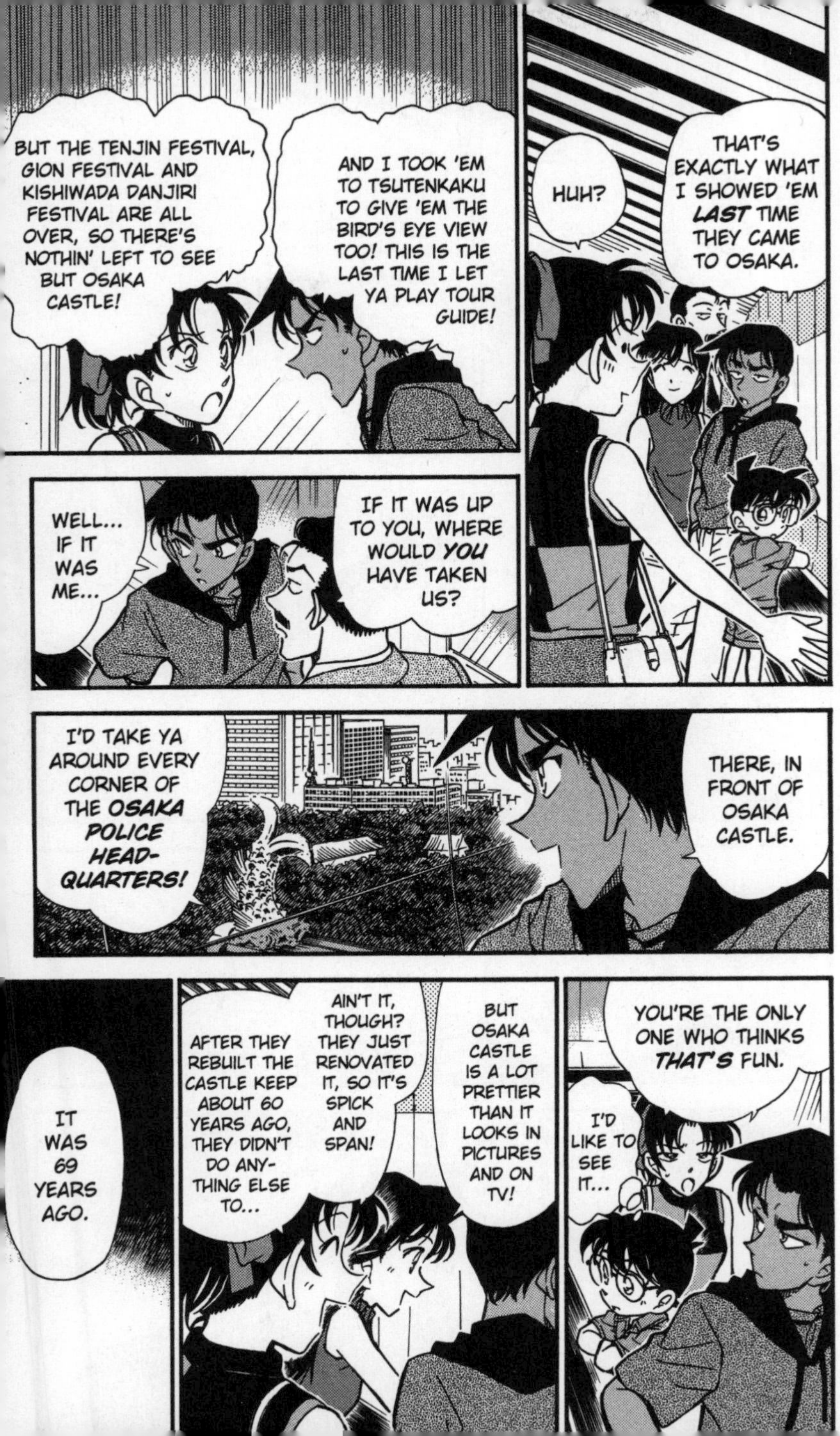
THAT'S EXACTLY WHAT I SHOWED 'EM *LAST* TIME THEY CAME TO OSAKA.
HUH?
AND I TOOK 'EM TO TSUTENKAKU TO GIVE 'EM THE BIRD'S EYE VIEW TOO! THIS IS THE LAST TIME I LET YA PLAY TOUR GUIDE!
BUT THE TENJIN FESTIVAL, GION FESTIVAL AND KISHIWADA DANJIRI FESTIVAL ARE ALL OVER, SO THERE'S NOTHIN' LEFT TO SEE BUT OSAKA CASTLE!
IF IT WAS UP TO YOU, WHERE WOULD *YOU* HAVE TAKEN US?
WELL... IF IT WAS ME...
THERE, IN FRONT OF OSAKA CASTLE.
I'D TAKE YA AROUND EVERY CORNER OF THE ***OSAKA POLICE HEAD-QUARTERS!***
YOU'RE THE ONLY ONE WHO THINKS ***THAT'S*** FUN.
I'D LIKE TO SEE IT...
BUT OSAKA CASTLE IS A LOT PRETTIER THAN IT LOOKS IN PICTURES AND ON TV!
AIN'T IT, THOUGH? THEY JUST RENOVATED IT, SO IT'S SPICK AND SPAN!
AFTER THEY REBUILT THE CASTLE KEEP ABOUT 60 YEARS AGO, THEY DIDN'T DO ANY-THING ELSE TO...
IT WAS 69 YEARS AGO.

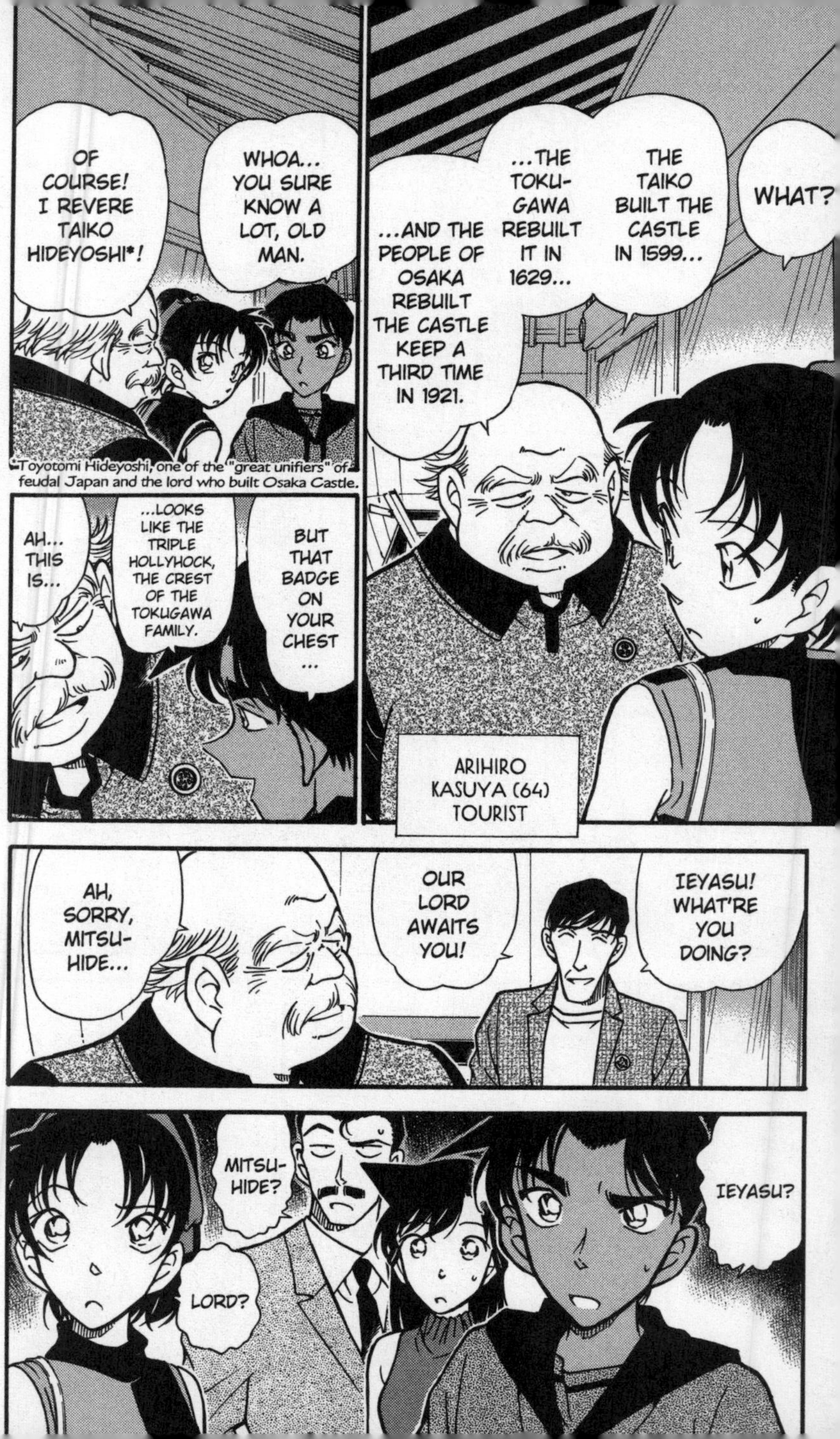
WHAT?
THE TAIKO BUILT THE CASTLE IN 1599...
...THE TOKUGAWA REBUILT IT IN 1629...
...AND THE PEOPLE OF OSAKA REBUILT THE CASTLE KEEP A THIRD TIME IN 1921.
ARIHIRO KASUYA (64) TOURIST
WHOA... YOU SURE KNOW A LOT, OLD MAN.
OF COURSE! I REVERE TAIKO HIDEYOSHI*!
BUT THAT BADGE ON YOUR CHEST...
...LOOKS LIKE THE TRIPLE HOLLYHOCK, THE CREST OF THE TOKUGAWA FAMILY.
AH... THIS IS...
IEYASU! WHAT'RE YOU DOING?
OUR LORD AWAITS YOU!
AH, SORRY, MITSUHIDE...
IEYASU?
MITSUHIDE?
LORD?
*Toyotomi Hideyoshi, one of the "great unifiers" of feudal Japan and the lord who built Osaka Castle.

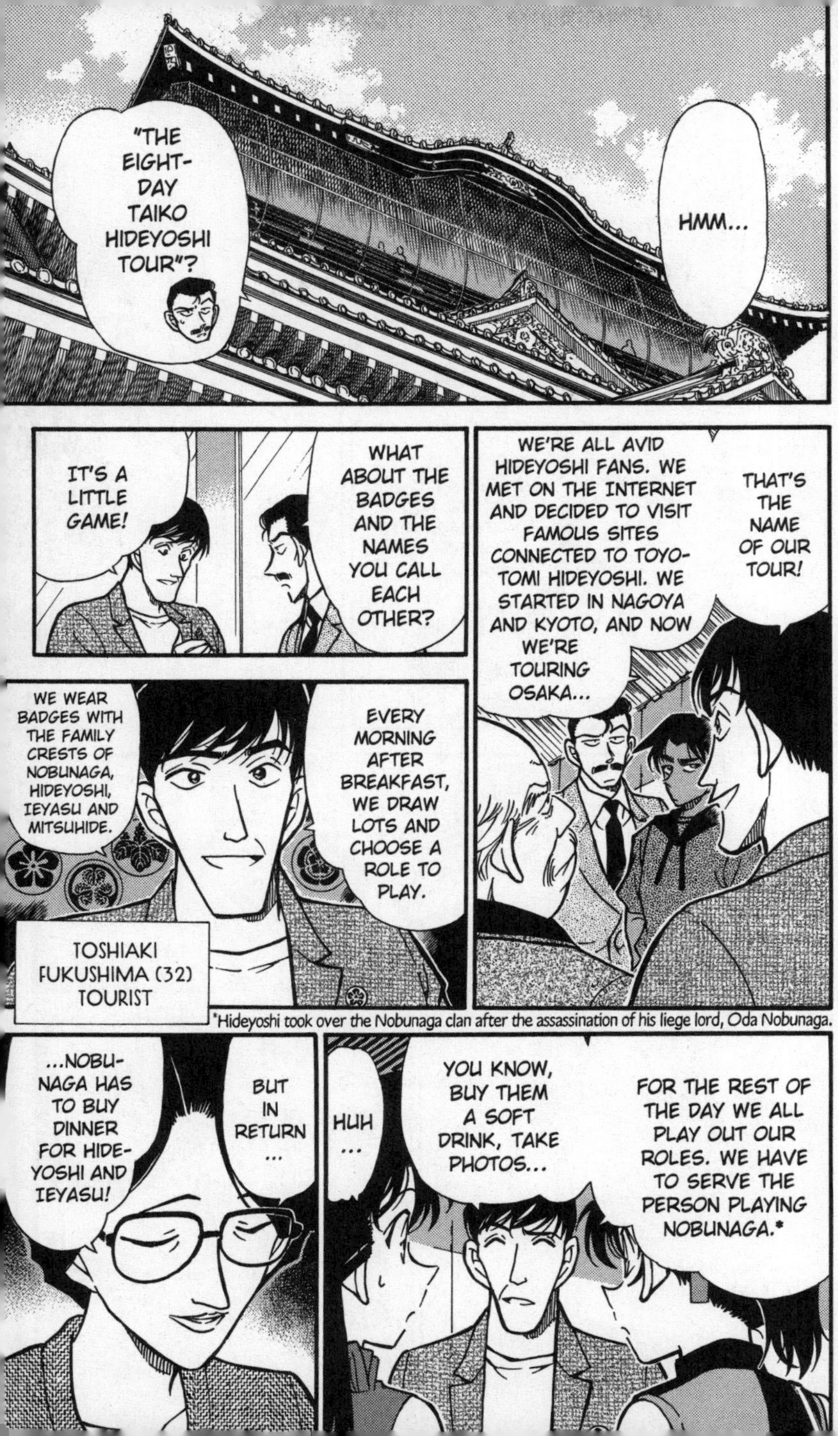
"THE EIGHT-DAY TAIKO HIDEYOSHI TOUR"?
HMM...
THAT'S THE NAME OF OUR TOUR!
WE'RE ALL AVID HIDEYOSHI FANS. WE MET ON THE INTERNET AND DECIDED TO VISIT FAMOUS SITES CONNECTED TO TOYOTOMI HIDEYOSHI. WE STARTED IN NAGOYA AND KYOTO, AND NOW WE'RE TOURING OSAKA...
WHAT ABOUT THE BADGES AND THE NAMES YOU CALL EACH OTHER?
IT'S A LITTLE GAME!
EVERY MORNING AFTER BREAKFAST, WE DRAW LOTS AND CHOOSE A ROLE TO PLAY.
WE WEAR BADGES WITH THE FAMILY CRESTS OF NOBUNAGA, HIDEYOSHI, IEYASU AND MITSUHIDE.
TOSHIAKI FUKUSHIMA (32) TOURIST
FOR THE REST OF THE DAY WE ALL PLAY OUT OUR ROLES. WE HAVE TO SERVE THE PERSON PLAYING NOBUNAGA.*
YOU KNOW, BUY THEM A SOFT DRINK, TAKE PHOTOS...
HUH...
BUT IN RETURN...
...NOBUNAGA HAS TO BUY DINNER FOR HIDEYOSHI AND IEYASU!

*Hideyoshi took over the Nobunaga clan after the assassination of his liege lord, Oda Nobunaga.

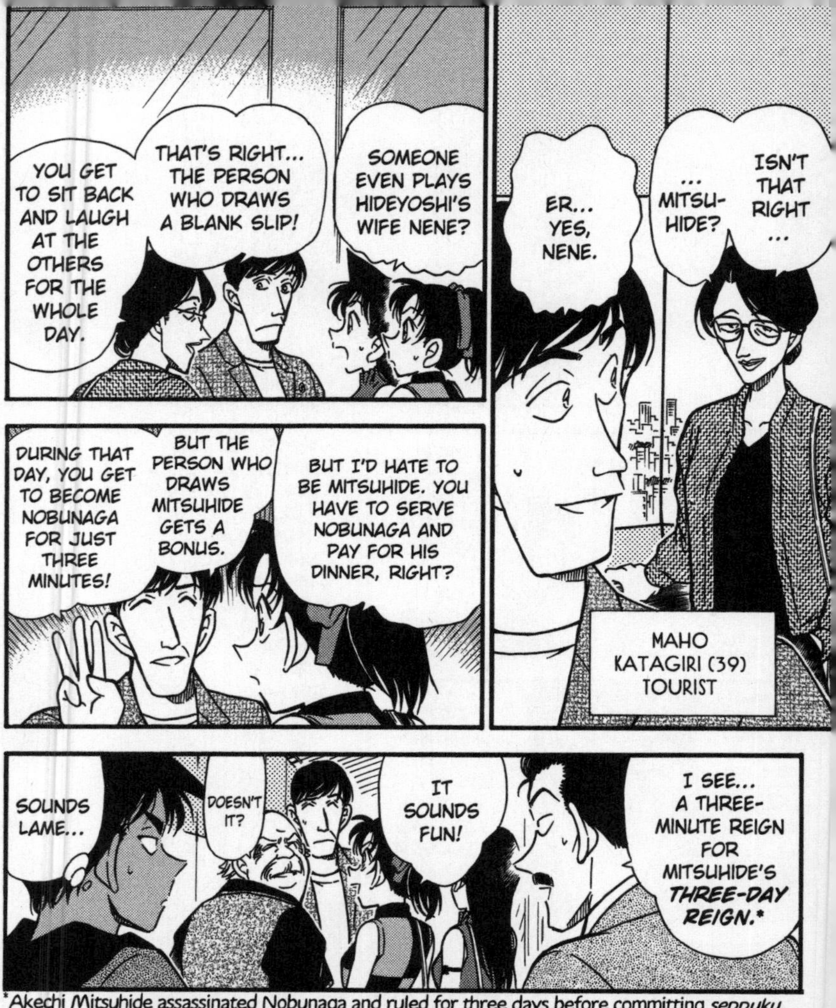
ISN'T THAT RIGHT ...
... MITSUHIDE?
ER... YES, NENE.
MAHO KATAGIRI (39) TOURIST
SOMEONE EVEN PLAYS HIDEYOSHI'S WIFE NENE?
THAT'S RIGHT... THE PERSON WHO DRAWS A BLANK SLIP!
YOU GET TO SIT BACK AND LAUGH AT THE OTHERS FOR THE WHOLE DAY.
BUT I'D HATE TO BE MITSUHIDE. YOU HAVE TO SERVE NOBUNAGA AND PAY FOR HIS DINNER, RIGHT?
BUT THE PERSON WHO DRAWS MITSUHIDE GETS A BONUS.
DURING THAT DAY, YOU GET TO BECOME NOBUNAGA FOR JUST THREE MINUTES!
I SEE... A THREE-MINUTE REIGN FOR MITSUHIDE'S *THREE-DAY REIGN.**
IT SOUNDS FUN!
DOESN'T IT?
SOUNDS LAME...

*Akechi Mitsuhide assassinated Nobunaga and ruled for three days before committing *seppuku*.

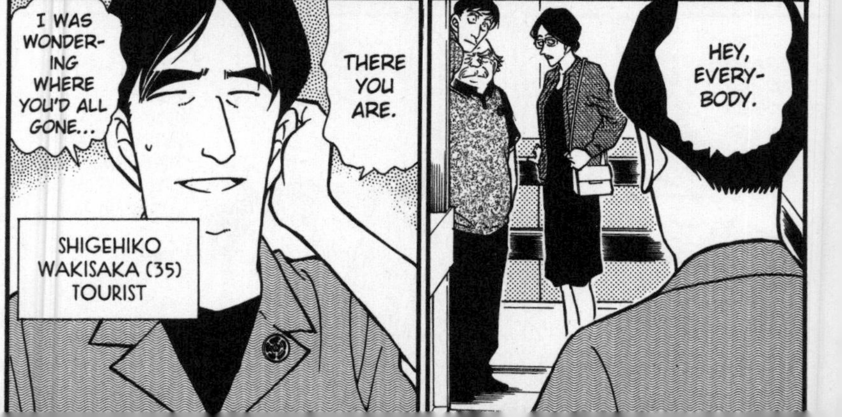
HEY, EVERYBODY.
THERE YOU ARE.
I WAS WONDERING WHERE YOU'D ALL GONE...
SHIGEHIKO WAKISAKA (35) TOURIST

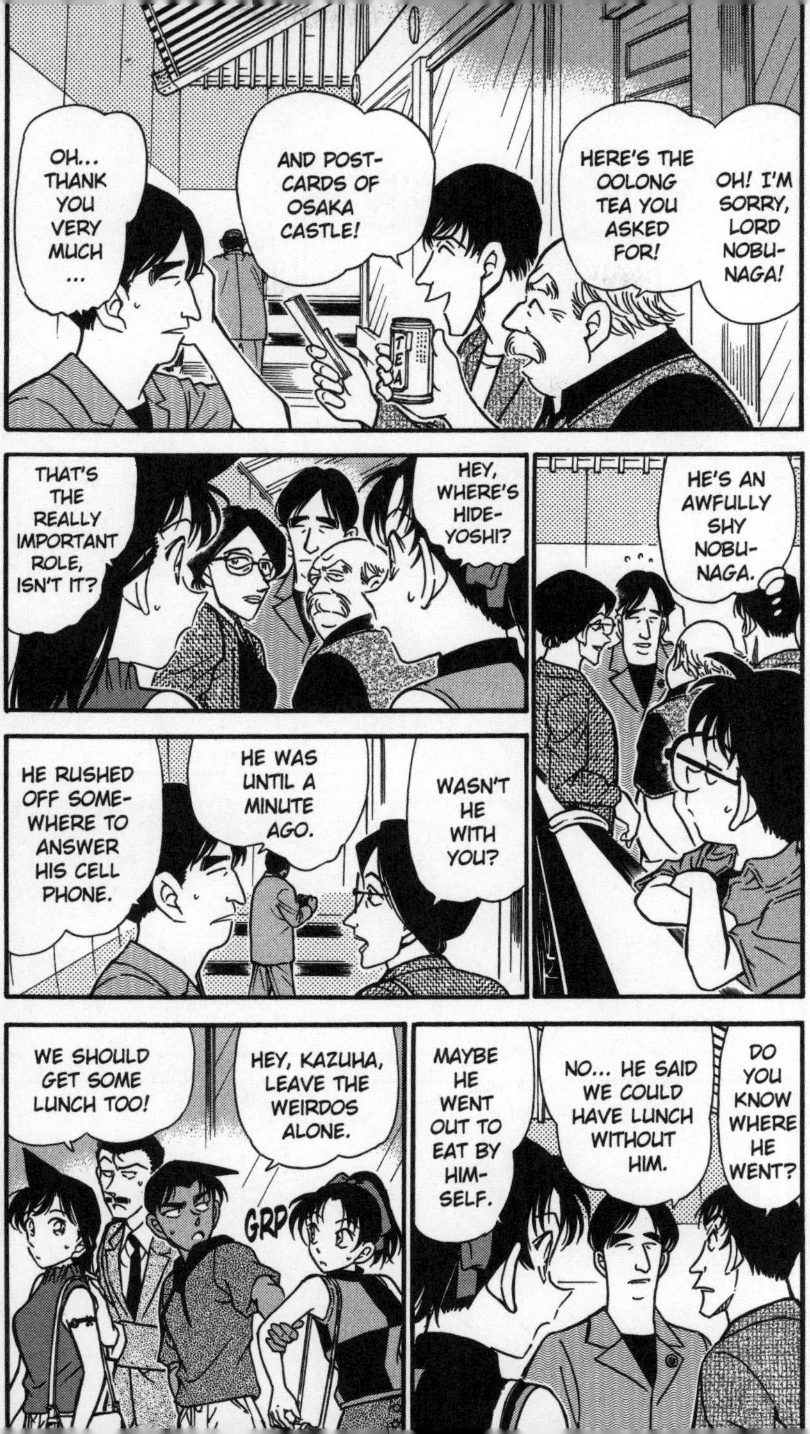
OH! I'M SORRY, LORD NOBUNAGA!
HERE'S THE OOLONG TEA YOU ASKED FOR!
AND POST-CARDS OF OSAKA CASTLE!
TEA
OH... THANK YOU VERY MUCH ...
HE'S AN AWFULLY SHY NOBU-NAGA.
HEY, WHERE'S HIDE-YOSHI?
THAT'S THE REALLY IMPORTANT ROLE, ISN'T IT?
WASN'T HE WITH YOU?
HE WAS UNTIL A MINUTE AGO.
HE RUSHED OFF SOME-WHERE TO ANSWER HIS CELL PHONE.
DO YOU KNOW WHERE HE WENT?
NO... HE SAID WE COULD HAVE LUNCH WITHOUT HIM.
MAYBE HE WENT OUT TO EAT BY HIM-SELF.
HEY, KAZUHA, LEAVE THE WEIRDOS ALONE.
GRP
WE SHOULD GET SOME LUNCH TOO!

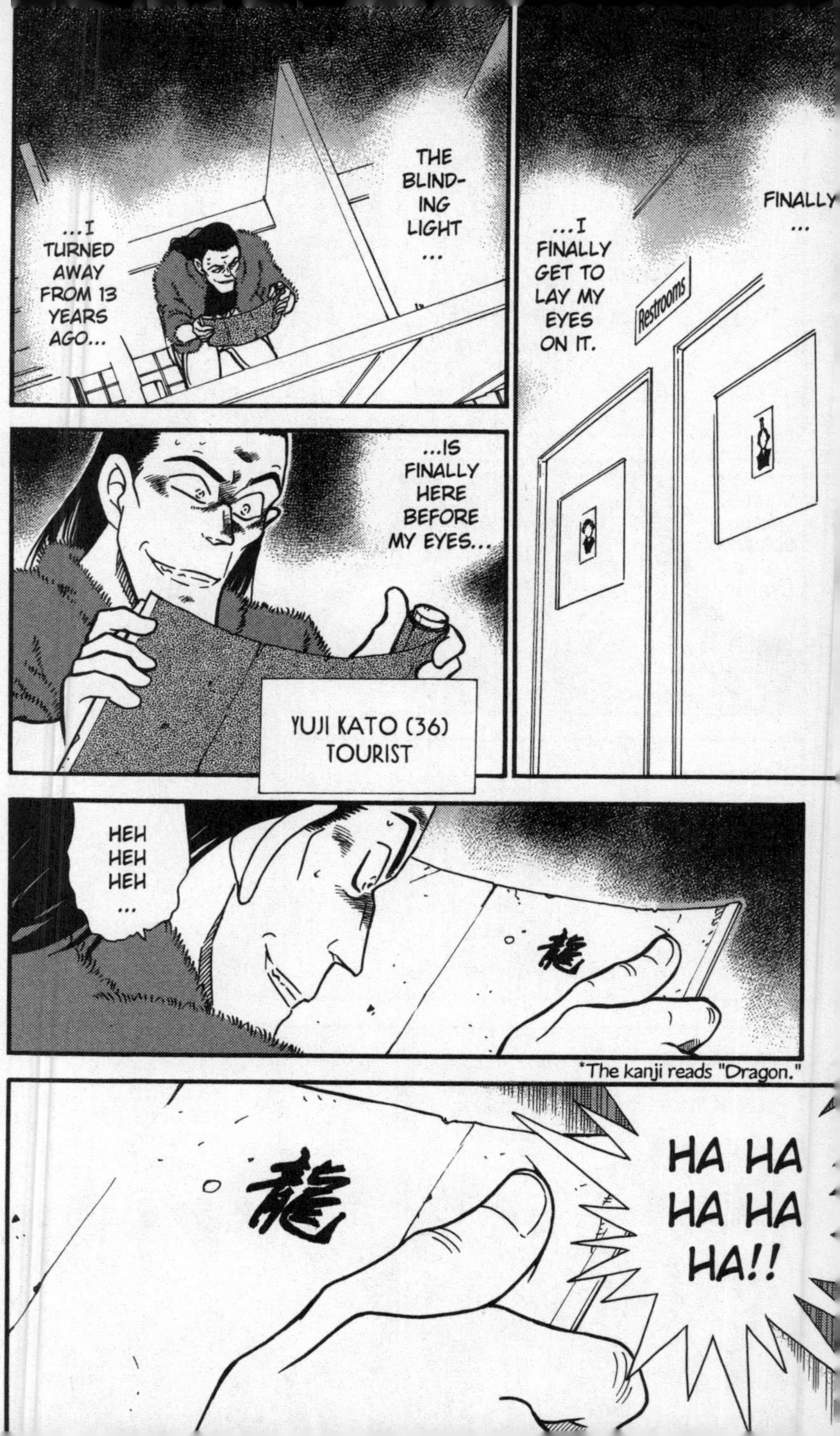

FINALLY...
...I FINALLY GET TO LAY MY EYES ON IT.
Restrooms
THE BLINDING LIGHT...
...I TURNED AWAY FROM 13 YEARS AGO...
...IS FINALLY HERE BEFORE MY EYES...
YUJI KATO (36) TOURIST
HEH HEH HEH ...
龍
*The kanji reads "Dragon."
龍
HA HA HA HA HA!!

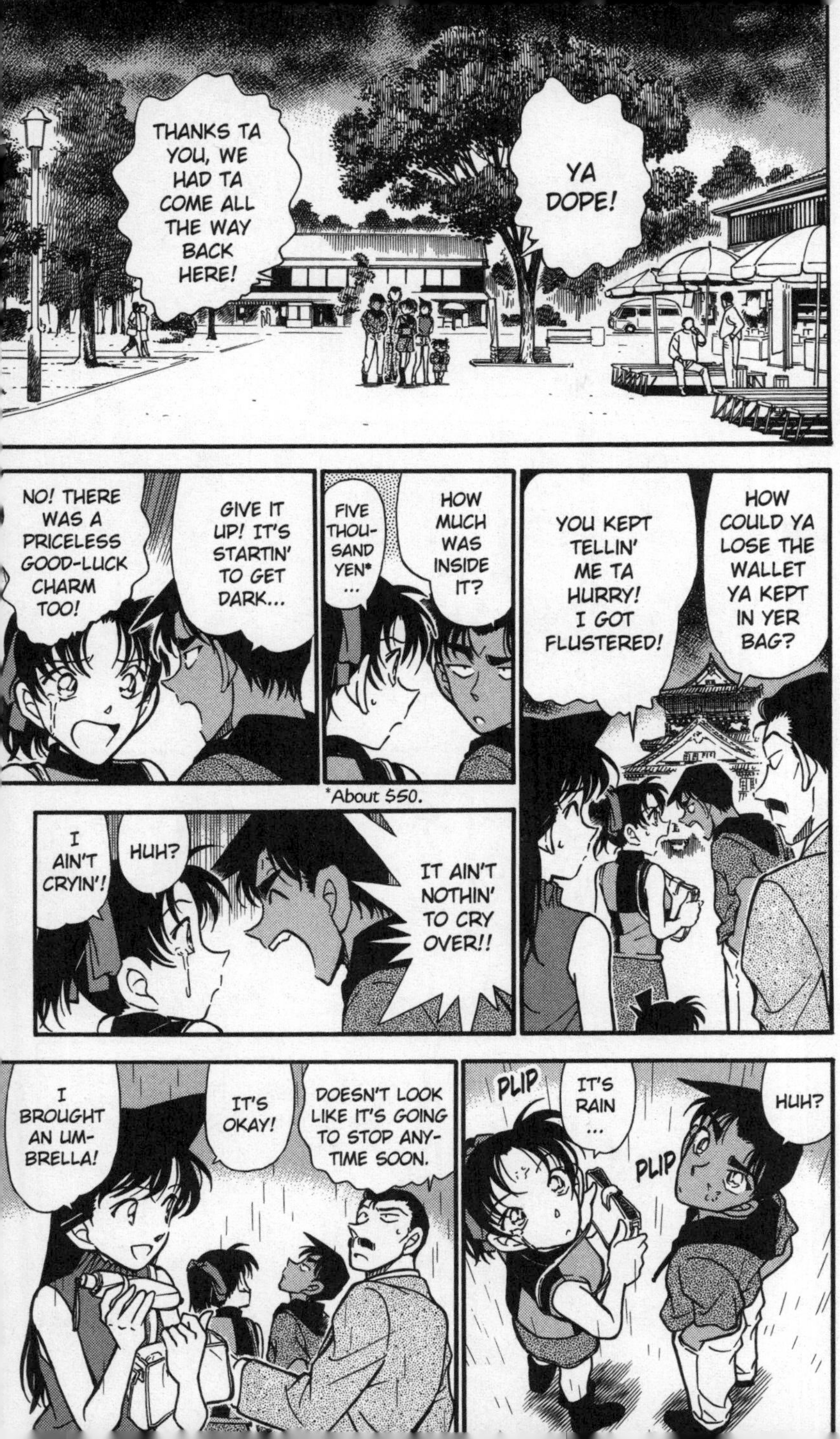
YA DOPE!
THANKS TA YOU, WE HAD TA COME ALL THE WAY BACK HERE!
HOW COULD YA LOSE THE WALLET YA KEPT IN YER BAG?
YOU KEPT TELLIN' ME TA HURRY! I GOT FLUSTERED!
HOW MUCH WAS INSIDE IT?
FIVE THOU-SAND YEN*...
GIVE IT UP! IT'S STARTIN' TO GET DARK...
NO! THERE WAS A PRICELESS GOOD-LUCK CHARM TOO!
*About $50.
IT AIN'T NOTHIN' TO CRY OVER!!
HUH?
I AIN'T CRYIN'!
HUH?
PLIP
IT'S RAIN ...
PLIP
DOESN'T LOOK LIKE IT'S GOING TO STOP ANY-TIME SOON.
IT'S OKAY!
I BROUGHT AN UM-BRELLA!

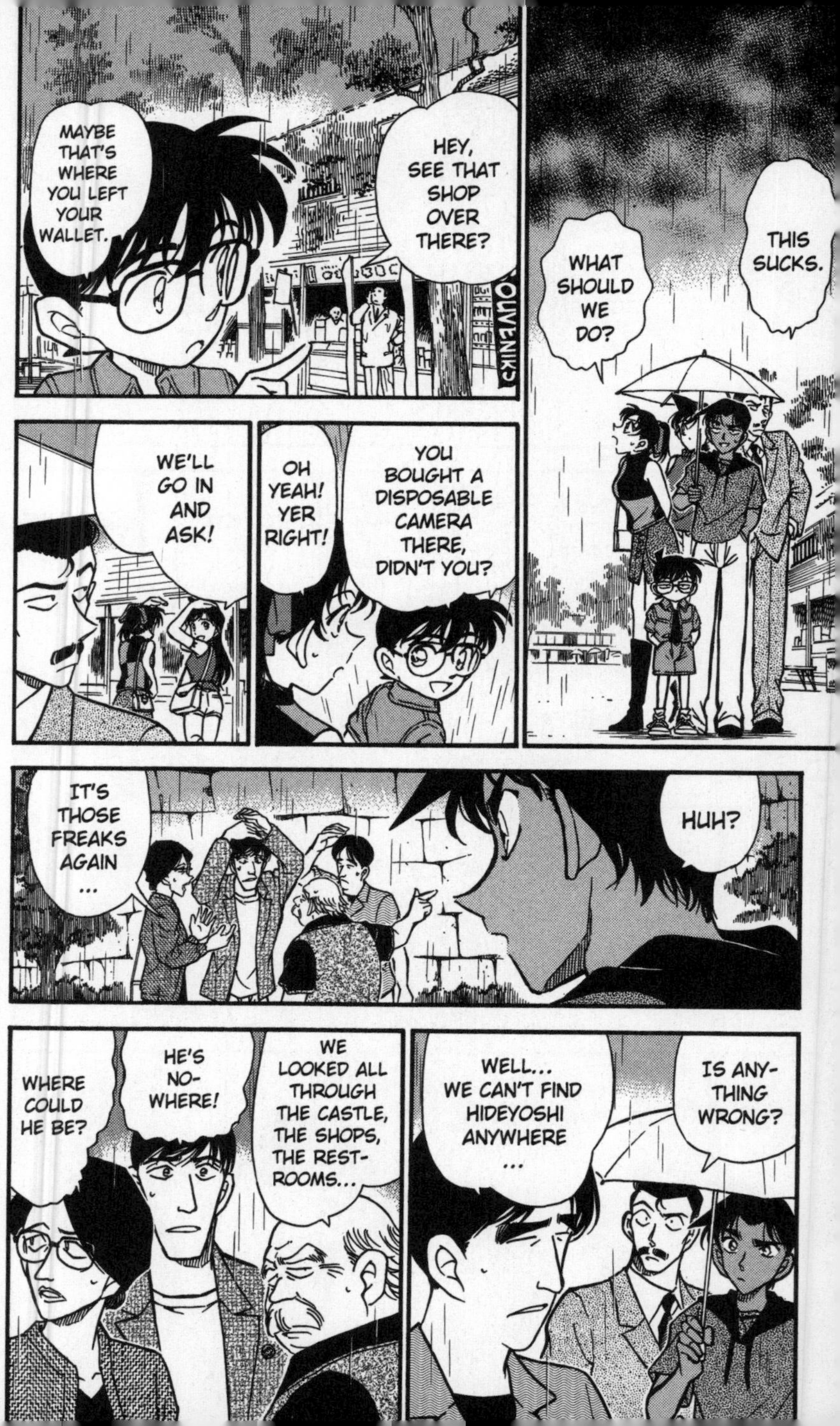
THIS SUCKS.
WHAT SHOULD WE DO?
HEY, SEE THAT SHOP OVER THERE?
MAYBE THAT'S WHERE YOU LEFT YOUR WALLET.
YOU BOUGHT A DISPOSABLE CAMERA THERE, DIDN'T YOU?
OH YEAH! YER RIGHT!
WE'LL GO IN AND ASK!
HUH?
IT'S THOSE FREAKS AGAIN...
IS ANY-THING WRONG?
WELL... WE CAN'T FIND HIDEYOSHI ANYWHERE...
WE LOOKED ALL THROUGH THE CASTLE, THE SHOPS, THE REST-ROOMS...
HE'S NO-WHERE!
WHERE COULD HE BE?

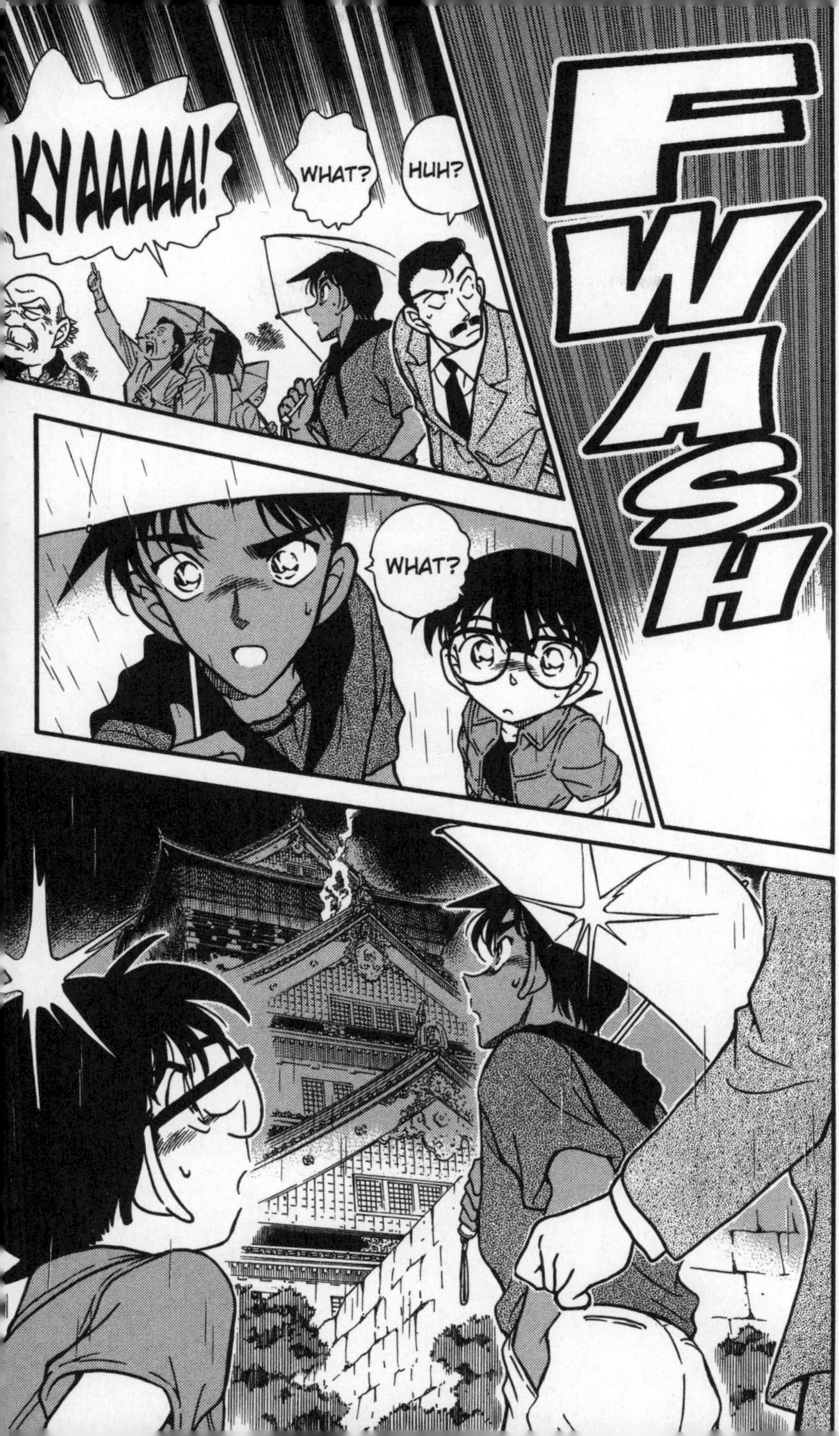
FWASH
HUH?
WHAT?
KYAAAAA!
WHAT?

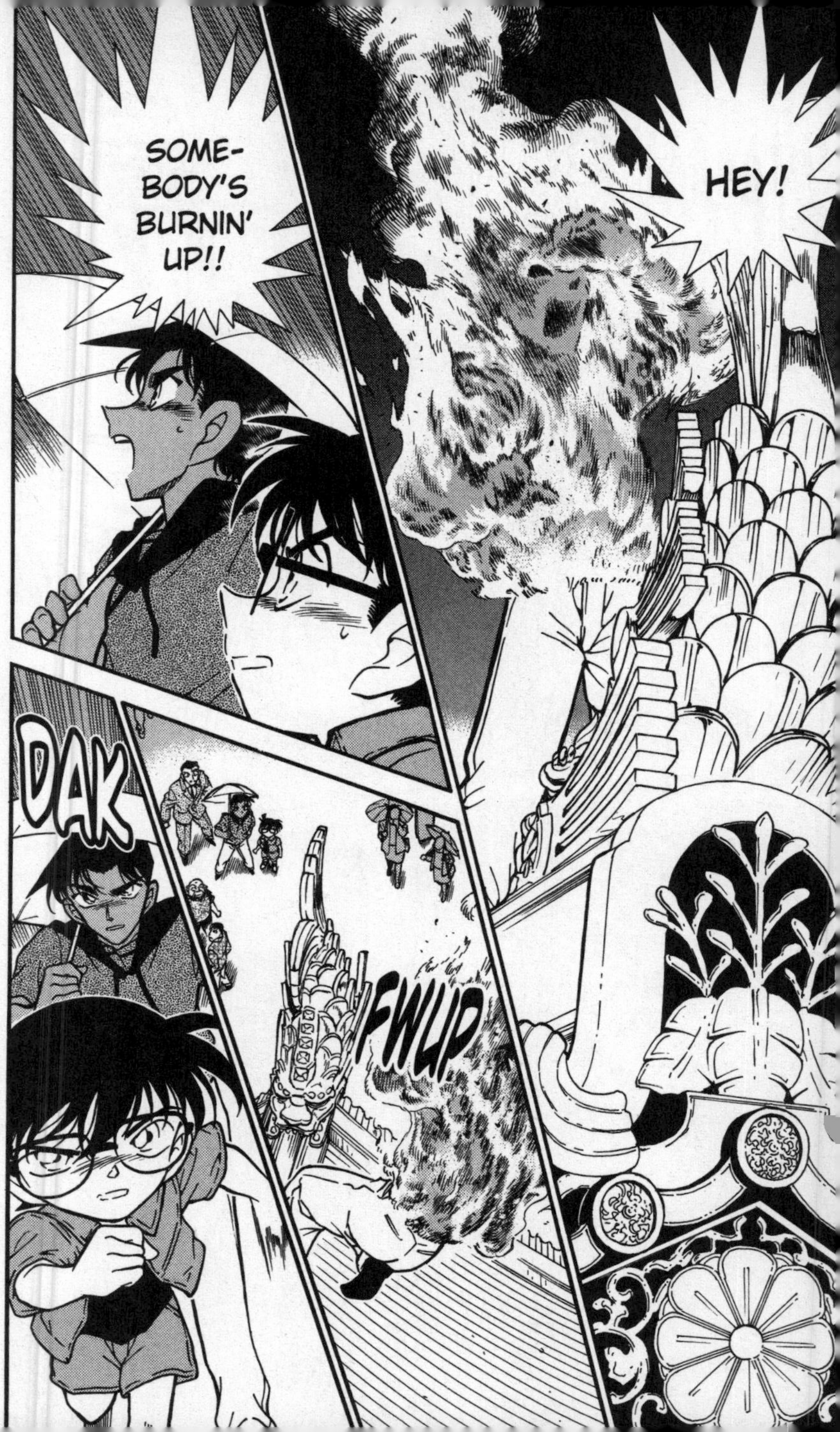

HEY!
SOME-BODY'S BURNIN' UP!!
FWUP
DAK

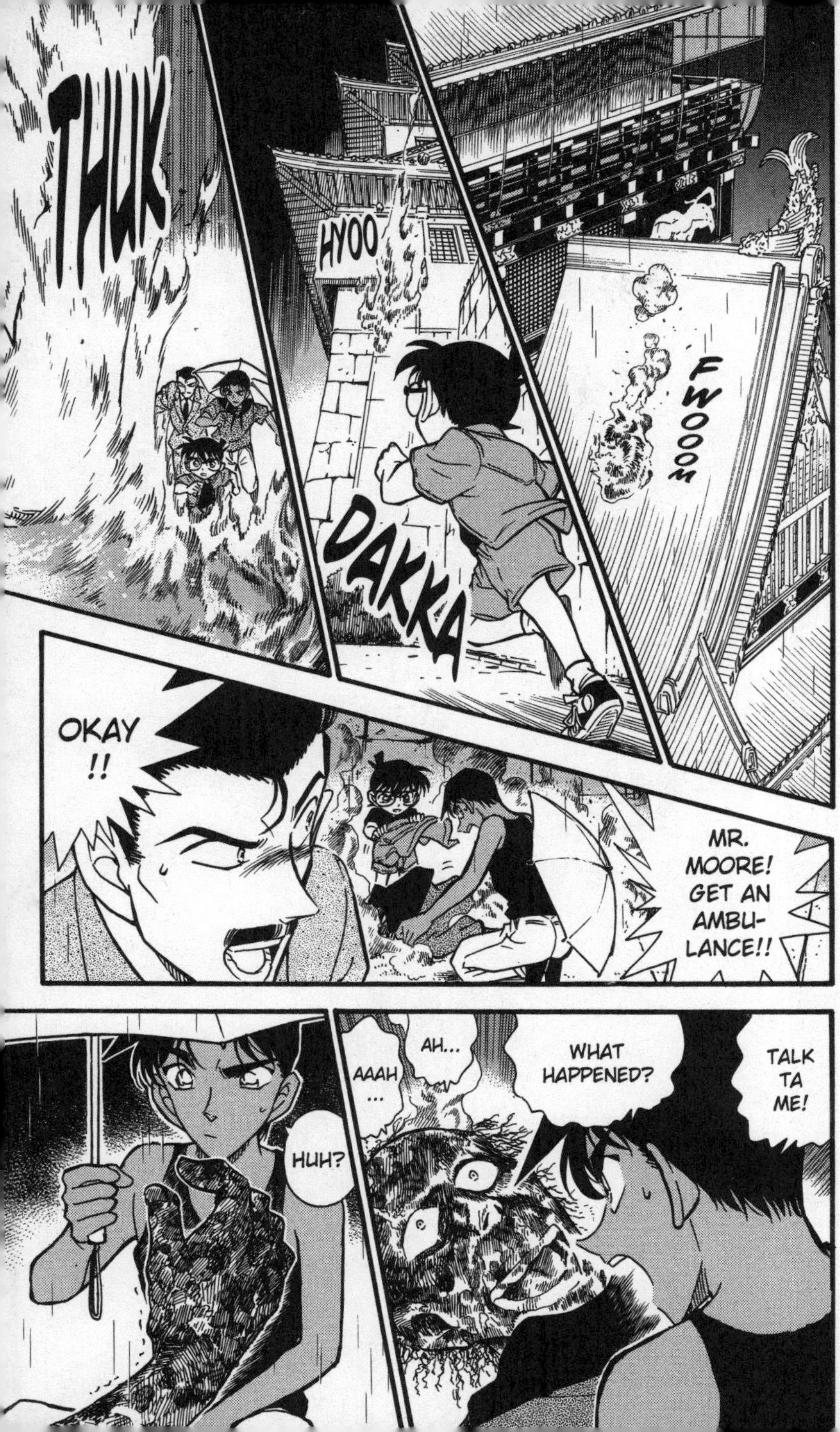
FWOOOM
HYOO
DAKKA
THUK
MR. MOORE! GET AN AMBULANCE!!
OKAY !!
TALK TA ME!
WHAT HAPPENED?
AH...
AAAH ...
HUH?

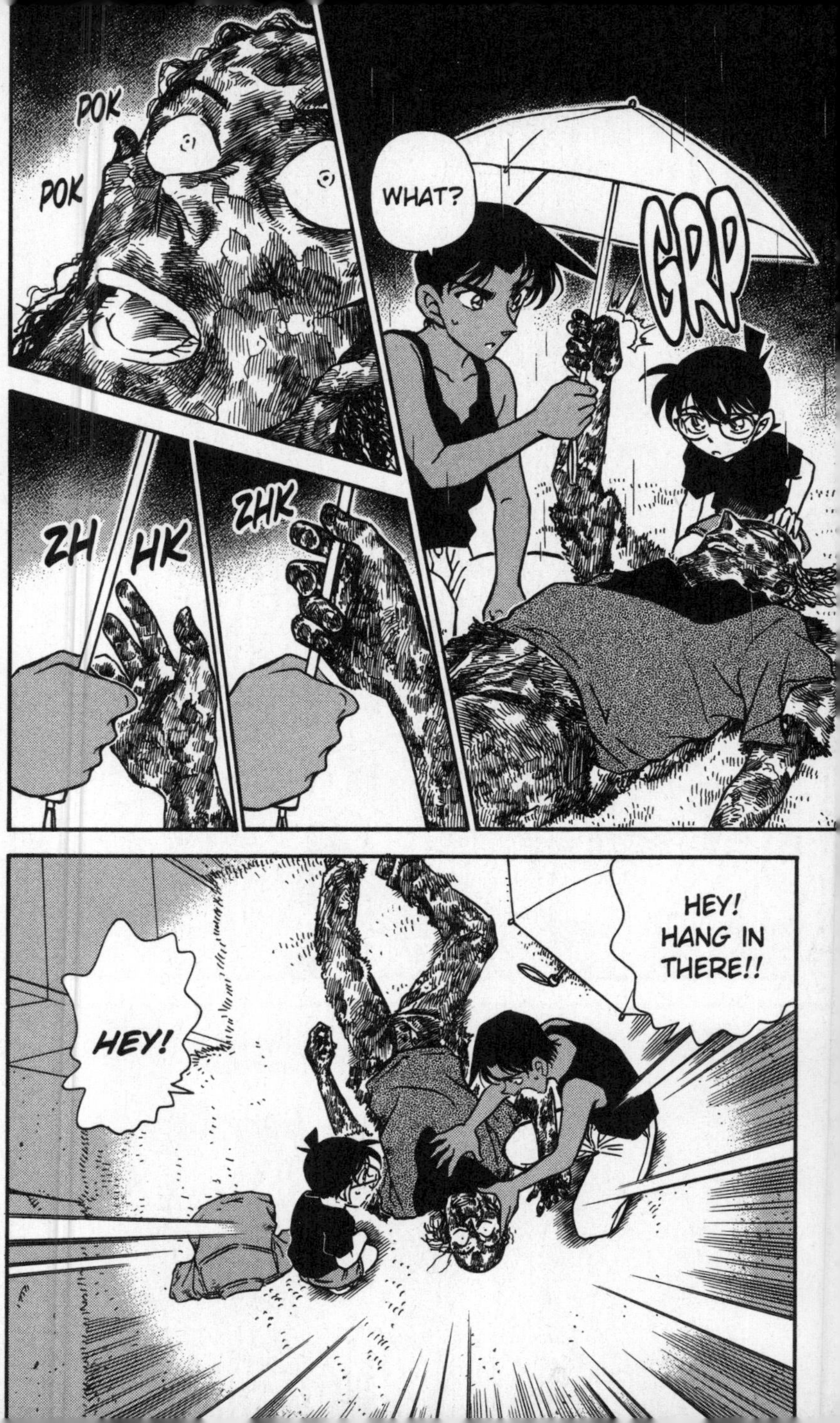
WHAT?
GRP
POK
POK
ZHK
ZH
HK
HEY! HANG IN THERE!!
HEY!

Hello, Aoyama here.

Thanks to the support of readers like you, *Case Closed* has won the Shogakukan Manga Award! Hooray!

The night the award was announced, Conan appeared to me in a dream. When I congratulated him, he just said, "You'd better come up with smarter cases," and I immediately woke up in bed. (True story!)

Gosho Aoyama's
Mystery Library

31

TOYAMA SAEMONNOJO KAGEMOTO

Undercover investigation is a common detective procedure. But there's even a head judge who hides his identity, cruising nightspots under the nickname "Pleasure-Seeker." He's the cool, witty Edo-period magistrate Toyama Saemonnojo Kagemoto, hero of the TV drama *Toyama no Kin-san*. Born to the honorable Toyama family, he led a life of debauchery, even getting a huge cherry-blossom tattoo. But after taking over as the head of the family, he turned his life around, becoming a magistrate known as "the best judge since Ooka Tadasuke."

As a judge, Toyama takes up his old identity as "Kinsho the Pleasure-Seeker" to gather information at seedy locales. When the criminals are brought before the magistrate, he bares his shoulder and intones, "Bet you recognize this blizzard of cherry blossoms!" The criminals have no choice but to confess! Incidentally, Toyama is based on a real magistrate from the Edo period, but whether he really was a tattooed playboy is unknown...

I recommend *Toyama no Kin-san Torimonocho* (Accounts of Toyama no Kin-san's Arrests).

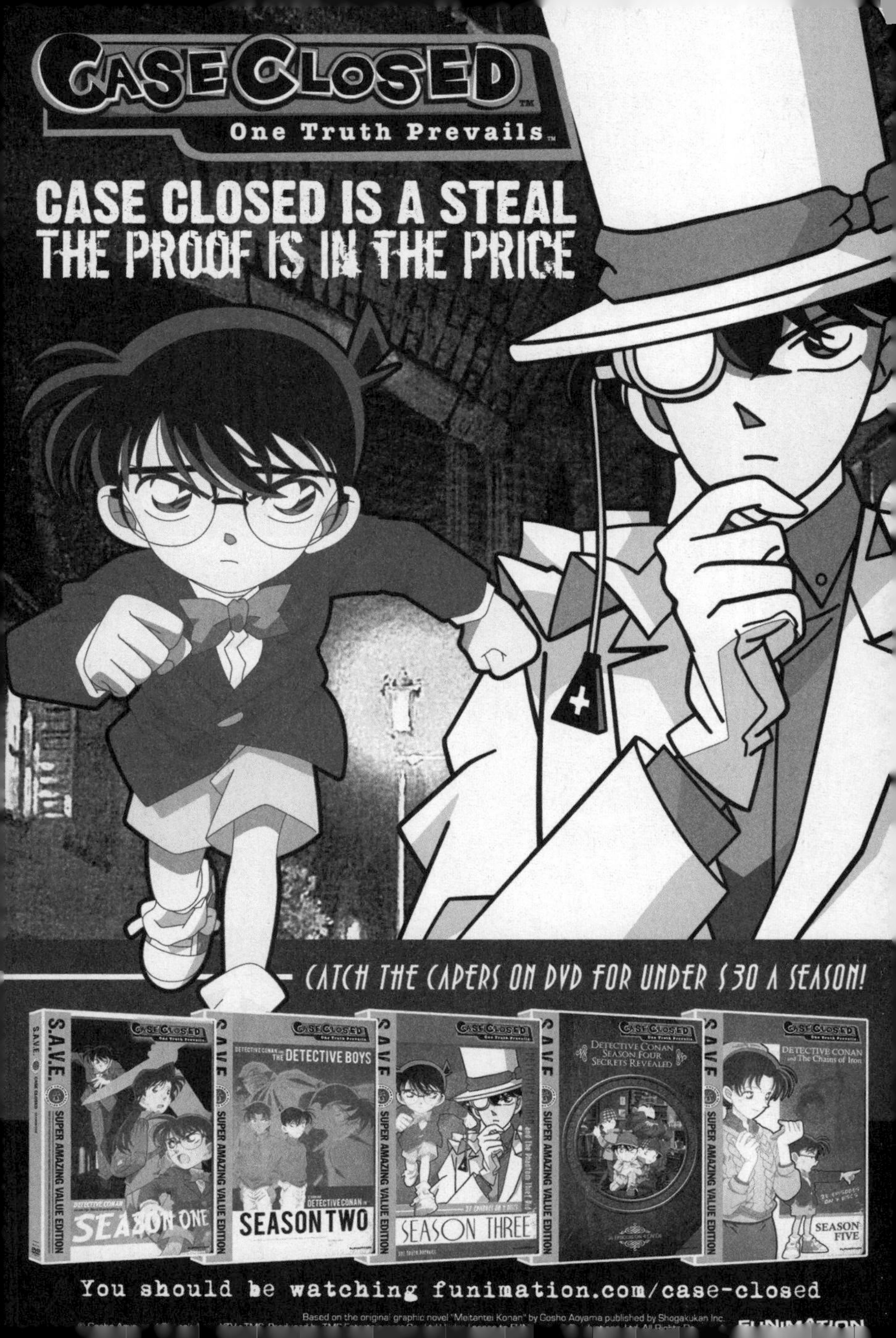

Hey! You're Reading in the Wrong Direction!

This is the *end* of this graphic novel!

To properly enjoy this VIZ graphic novel, please turn it around and begin reading from *right to left.* Unlike English, Japanese is read right to left, so Japanese comics are read in reverse order from the way English comics are typically read.

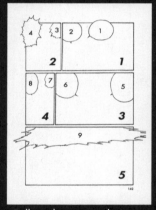

Follow the action this way

This book has been printed in the original Japanese format in order to preserve the orientation of the original artwork. Have fun with it!